French Politics, Society and Culture Series

General Editor: Robert Elgie, Paddy Moriarty Professor of Government and International Studies, Dublin City University

France has always fascinated outside observers. Now, the country is undergoing a period of profound transformation. France is faced with a rapidly changing international and European environment and it is having to rethink some of its most basic social, political and economic orthodoxies. As elsewhere, there is pressure to conform. And yet, while France is responding in ways that are no doubt familiar to people in other European countries, it is also managing to maintain elements of its long-standing distinctiveness. Overall, it remains a place that is not exactly *comme les autres*.

This new series examines all aspects of French politics, society and culture. In so doing it focuses on the changing nature of the French system as well as the established patterns of political, social and cultural life. Contributors to the series are encouraged to present new and innovative arguments so that the informed reader can learn and understand more about one of the most beguiling and compelling of all European countries.

Titles include:

Sylvain Brouard, Andrew M. Appleton, Amy G. Mazur *(editors)*
THE FRENCH FIFTH REPUBLIC AT FIFTY
Beyond Stereotypes

Jean K. Chalaby
THE DE GAULLE PRESIDENCY AND THE MEDIA
Statism and Public Communications

Pepper D. Culpepper, Bruno Palier and Peter A. Hall *(editors)*
CHANGING FRANCE
The Politics that Markets Make

Gordon D. Cumming
FRENCH NGOs IN THE GLOBAL ERA
France's International Development Role

David Drake
FRENCH INTELLECTUALS AND POLITICS FROM THE DREYFUS AFFAIR
TO THE OCCUPATION

David Drake
INTELLECTUALS AND POLITICS IN POST-WAR FRANCE

Graeme Hayes
ENVIRONMENTAL PROTEST AND THE STATE IN FRANCE

David J. Howarth
THE FRENCH ROAD TO EUROPEAN MONETARY UNION

Andrew Knapp
PARTIES AND THE PARTY SYSTEM IN FRANCE
A Disconnected Democracy?

Michael S. Lewis-Beck *(editor)*
THE FRENCH VOTER
Before and After the 2002 Elections

John Loughlin
SUBNATIONAL GOVERNMENT
The French Experience

French Politics, Society and Culture
Series Standing Order ISBN 0–333–80440–6 hardcover
Series Standing Order ISBN 0–333–80441–4 paperback
(outside North America only)

You can receive future titles in this series as they are published by placing a standing order.
Please contact your bookseller or, in case of difficulty, write to us at the address below with
your name and address, the title of the series and the ISBN quoted above.

Customer Services Department, Macmillan Distribution Ltd, Houndmills, Basingstoke,
Hampshire RG21 6XS, England

The French Fifth Republic at Fifty

Beyond Stereotypes

Edited by

Sylvain Brouard
Senior Research Fellow
Sciences Po-Bordeaux, France

Andrew M. Appleton
Associate Professor of Political Science
Washington State University, USA

and

Amy G. Mazur
Professor, Department of Political Science
Washington State University, USA

First published 2009 by
PALGRAVE MACMILLAN

Palgrave Macmillan in the UK is an imprint of Macmillan Publishers Limited,
registered in England, company number 785998, of Houndmills, Basingstoke,
Hampshire RG21 6XS.

Palgrave Macmillan in the US is a division of St Martin's Press LLC,
175 Fifth Avenue, New York, NY 10010.

Palgrave Macmillan is the global academic imprint of the above companies
and has companies and representatives throughout the world.

Palgrave® and Macmillan® are registered trademarks in the United States,
the United Kingdom, Europe and other countries

ISBN-13: 978–0–230–22124–6   hardback
ISBN-10: 0–230–22124–6   hardback

This book is printed on paper suitable for recycling and made from fully
managed and sustained forest sources. Logging, pulping and manufacturing
processes are expected to conform to the environmental regulations of the
country of origin.

A catalogue record for this book is available from the British Library.

Library of Congress Cataloging-in-Publication Data

The French Fifth Republic at fifty : beyond stereotypes / edited by
   Sylvain Brouard, Andrew M. Appleton, and Amy G. Mazur.
      p. cm. — (French politics, society, and culture series)
   Includes bibliographical references and index.
   ISBN 978–0–230–22124–6
   1. France—Politics and government—1958–   2. France—Social policy.
   I. Brouard, Sylvain.   II. Appleton, Andrew M.   III. Mazur, Amy.
   JN2594.2.F75 2009
   320.94409'045—dc22   2008030202

10   9   8   7   6   5   4   3   2   1
18   17   16   15   14   13   12   11   10   09

Printed and bound in Great Britain by
CPI Antony Rowe, Chippenham and Eastbourne

Contents

Part III   The Republican Universal Model as Institution

Tables and Figures

Tables

Figures

Notes on the Contributors

Andrew M. Appleton is Associate Professor of Political Science and Director of Global Studies at Washington State University. He is co-founder and co-editor, with Robert Elgie, of the journal *French Politics* (Palgrave Macmillan). His research interests include political parties, social movements, and political behavior.

Richard Balme is Professor at Sciences Po, Paris, where he teaches public policy analysis and comparative politics, and where he was director of the Graduate program for Public Policy and Political Sociology between 2000 and 2003. He was also Head of the Department of Government and International Studies at the Hong Kong Baptist University, 2003–2006. He is currently director of the program Governance and Globalization for Sciences Po in China. He teaches at Peking University, Tsinghua University and Fudan University. Among his recent publications are *European Governance and Democracy: Power and Protest in the European Union* (with D. Chabanet), and *Europe–Asia Relations: Building Multilateralisms* (with B. Bridges).

Frank R. Baumgartner is the Bruce R. Miller and Dean D. LaVigne Professor of Political Science at Penn State University and regular visiting professor at the Centre for Political Research (CEVIPOF) at Sciences Po Paris. His research has long focused on issues of agenda-setting and interest-group activities and he has written on these topics in relation to France and the United States. He is the author of seven books, including *The Politics of Attention* (with Bryan Jones) and, most recently, *The Decline of the Death Penalty and the Discovery of Innocence* (with Suzanna De Boef and Amber Boydstun). He is the co-director of the US-based Policy Agendas Project (www.policyagendas.org) and an active participant in the French agendas project as well.

Sylvain Brouard is Senior Research Fellow FNSP at SPIRIT, Institute of Political Studies Bordeaux. He studied at the Institute of Political Studies in Bordeaux where he received his PhD in political science in 1999. He studied at the Inter-University Consortium for Political Science Research and at the Oslo Summer School in Comparative Social Sciences. He has been a visiting scholar at the University of Oxford and University of Washington. His research focuses on comparative law-making, on European political behavior and minority politics. With Nicolas Sauger and Emiliano Grossman, he wrote a book dedicated to the French referendum on the ECT. He co-authored, with Vincent Tiberj, 'French as the other ones? Survey on the French citizens from Maghreb, Africa and Turkey'. He is an active participant in the

French and Comparative Agenda Project initiated by the seminal research of F. Baumgartner and B. Jones. He is also currently involved in a comparative research about the institutions of constitutional review.

Ariane Chebel d'Appolonia educated at Sciences Po (PhD, HDR), is co-director of the ISI Immigration Research Network. At Sciences Po she holds an appointment as an Associate Senior Researcher at the CEVIPOF (Center for Political Research). Professor Chebel d'Appolonia specializes in the politics of immigration and anti-discrimination in the United States and Europe, racism and xenophobia, extreme-right wing movements, immigrant integration, and urban racism. She has taught at undergraduate and postgraduate levels, both at universities in France (Paris III-Sorbonne, and the Columbia University and the University of Chicago Programs in Paris) and in the US (New York University, University of Pittsburgh). Professor Chebel d'Appollonia was selected as the Buffet Chair Professor at Northwestern University (2005) and a visiting fellow at the Ford Institute for Human Security (2004–6) and at the European Center of Excellence at the University of Pittsburgh. Furthermore, she was awarded the EU–US Fulbright scholar in 2006. In addition to three books (including one on the Far Right in France and another on Everyday Racism) and five edited volumes, Professor Chebel d'Appolonia recently co-edited, with Simon Reich, *Immigration, Integration and Security: America and Europe in Comparative Perspective*.

Ben Clift is Senior Lecturer in Political Economy in the Department of Politics and International Studies at the University of Warwick. He is author of *French Socialism in a Global Era: The Political Economy of the New Social Democracy in France* and co-editor of *Where Are National Capitalisms Now?* His research interests lie in comparative and international political economy, and he has written widely on French Socialism, the French model of capitalism, the political economy of social democracy, New Labour, global finance, and French party politics. He has published several book chapters, including in *The Handbook of International Political Economy* (edited by Mark Blyth) and *The Oxford Handbook of British Politics* (edited by Andrew Gamble, Colin Hay, Mike Kenny and Matthew Flinders). He has been a visiting fellow at CERI Sciences-Po, Paris. He is convener of the French Politics and Policy Group, and co-founder of the Political Economy Group of the PSA.

Robert Elgie is Paddy Moriarty Professor of Government and International Studies at Dublin City University. He is the Head of the School of Law and Government. His research interests include political leadership, public sector reform, particularly the delegation of responsibilities to independent organizations, and issues of institutional design more generally. His main area focus is European politics, particularly French politics. He is the co-editor (with Andrew Appleton at Washington State University) of the journal *French Politics*.

Abel François is an Associate Professor of Economics at Strasbourg University and associate researcher at Telecom ParisTech, Economics and Social Science department. He earned his PHD in Economics from the University of Paris Panthéon-Sorbonne. His current research deals with electoral campaign financing, electoral turnout and the budgeting processes. He is convenor of the *Groupe Argent et Politique* ('Money, Politics and Public Policy') of the French Political Science Association (AFSP). His research mainly proposes empirical perspectives on the interactions between the political dimension and the economic dimension within the political process and he has published in *Public Choice, Journal of European Public Policy, French Politics* and the *Revue Française de Science Politique*.

Martial Foucault is Assistant Professor at the University of Montreal, Political Science Department since 2006. He is currently associated research fellow at the Robert Schuman Centre for Advanced Studies at the European University Institute (Florence, Italy) and at the University of Paris I Panthéon-Sorbonne (Centre d'Economie de la Sorbonne) where he received his PhD in Economics in 2004. His research agenda concerns French and Canadian budgetary agendas, political economy of public spending, strategic interactions in fiscal choices, campaign spending, theory of public goods, and military spending in EU. His last research works have been published in *Public Choice, Journal of European Public Policy, Social Science Quarterly, French Politics, Revue Economique,* and*Revue d'Economie Politique*. A book in preparation titled *Political Economy of European Defense Expenditure* will be published in 2009.

Emiliano Grossman is a senior research fellow at CEVIPOF / Sciences Po and associate lecturer at the IEP Paris, where he is responsible for the post-graduate research program in European Studies. He has recently edited a special issue of the *Journal of European Public Policy* on 'France and the EU after the referendum' (October 2007). His research concentrates on economic interest groups, economic regulation and political institutions. His work has been published in the *Journal of Common Market Studies, French Politics* and the *Revue française de Science politique*.

Bastien Irondelle is senior research fellow at CERI / Sciences Po and Associate lecturer at Sciences Po Paris. He obtained his PhD in Political Science 'Governing Defence: A Decision-Making Approach of the Military Reform' in December 2003. He has been Lecturer at the IEP de Lille, Post-doctoral fellow at the Centre d'études européennes de Sciences Po and Associated Researcher at the IFRI (Institut Français des Relations Internationales). He now teaches at Sciences Po and serves on the editorial board of *Politique européenne, Critique Internationale* and *Cultures & Conflicts*. He has published articles about defense policy, military and security issues in *Journal of European Public Policy, Politique Européenne Security Studies, Journal of European Integration,* and *Revue Internationale de Politique Comparée*.

Eric Kerrouche is Senior Research Fellow CNRS at SPIRIT, Institute of Political Studies Bordeaux. His research focuses on comparative politics, parliament and subnational government. He has published and edited several books on both topics: *Qui sont les députés français? Enquête sur des élites inconnues* (with O. Costa); *Les Élus locaux en Europe: un statut en mutation* (with Élodie Guérin-Lavignotte); *Jeux d'échelle et changement politique. Le gouvernement des territoires au Québec et en France*, (co-edited with L. Behrer, J.P. Collin, J. Palard); and *Vers un renouveau du parlementarisme en Europe?* (co-edited with O. Costa and Paul Magnette).

Patrick Le Galès is a Research Director (CNRS) at the Centre for Political Research at Sciences Po (CEVIPOF) and Professor of politics and sociology at Sciences Po. His current research projects include comparative public policy in Europe through the analysis of policy instruments and the role of middle classes in European cities. He heads the public policy program within Sciences-Po PhD School and the LSE/Sciences Po urban policy master. A former editor of the *International Journal of Urban and Regional Research*, he now serves on the boards of the *British Journal of Political Science*, *Journal of Public Policy* and the *Socioeconomic Review*. He was a Stein Rokkan Prize winner for his book *European Cities, Social Conflicts and Governance* and received the Excellence prize for political science research in France (Association Française de Science Politique Mattei Dogan Foundation) in 2007. Recent books include *Changing Governance of Local Economies* (with Crouch, Trigilia Voelzkow), *Gouverner par les instruments* (with P. Lascoumes), *Tony Blair le bilan des réformes* (with F. Faucher-King) and *Developments in French Politics 4* (with A. Cole and J. Levy).

Eléonore Lépinard is Assistant Professor in Political Science at the Université de Montréal, Canada. Her research interests include feminist movements and theory, multiculturalism, equality policies and politics, and law. She has published on these themes in French as well as in English in journals such as *Signs, Social Politics* and *American Behavioral Scientist*. She is also the author of a book, *L'égalité introuvable. La parité, les féministes et la République* (*Elusive Equality. Parity, the Feminists and the Republic*).

Amy G. Mazur is Professor in the Department of Political Science at Washington State University. Her research and teaching interests focus on comparative feminist policy issues with a particular emphasis on France. She is co-editor of *Political Research Quarterly*. Her books include: *Comparative State Feminism* (editor, with Dorothy McBride Stetson); *Gender Bias and the State: Symbolic Reform at Work in Fifth Republic France*; *State Feminism, Women's Movement, and Job Training: Making Democracies Work in the Global Economy* (editor); *Theorizing Feminist Policy* and *Politics, Gender and Concepts* (editor with Gary

Goertz). She is co-convener of the Research Network on Gender Politics and the State and convener of the French Politics Group of the APSA.

Gilles Pinson is *Maître de Conférences* of Political Science at the Jean Monnet University in Saint-Étienne (France). He also teaches 'Urban policies and governance in European cities' at Sciences Po Paris. His research fields include urban politics and policies, urban planning and urbanization. He has published on sustainable development and social science epistemology and methodology. His forthcoming book is based on his PhD thesis on transformations of urban policies in Europe – *Gouverner par projet. Urbanisme, planification et gouvernance dans les villes européennes*. In 2002 he was awarded the Prize for Young Authors from the Foundation of Urban and Regional Studies for an article on strategic planning in Turin.

Nicolas Sauger is a Researcher at the Centre for Political Research at Sciences Po (CEVIPOF). Dr Sauger's current research focuses on transformations in the structures of political competition in France and Europe. He is convenor of the *Groupe d'analyse électorale* ('Electoral Analysis Group') of the French Political Science Association (AFSP) and plays an active role in the organization of the French module of the European Social Survey and of the Comparative Study of Electoral Systems. He was Vincent Wright Fellow at the Robert Schuman Centre of the European University Institute in Florence for the academic year 2005–6. He holds a PhD from Sciences Po, awarded in 2003, which deals with the break-up of the French right-wing UDF.

Mark I. Vail is Assistant Professor of Political Science at Tulane University. His research interests include comparative politics and political economy, social policy, industrial relations, and state–society relations in Western Europe. He is currently completing a book entitled *Recasting Welfare Capitalism: The Changing Dynamics of Economic Adjustment in Contemporary France and Germany*. He has also published work in the *European Journal of Political Research*, *West European Politics*, *French Politics*, and the *Journal of European Social Policy*.

Cornelia Woll is a Senior Research Fellow at the Centre d'Etudes et de Recherches Internationales (CERI) and lecturer at Sciences Po Paris and has previously worked at the Max Planck Institute for the Study of Societies in Cologne. She is the author of *Firm Interests: How Governments Shape Business Lobbying on Global Trade* and has published on lobbying, economic policy-making and French politics in journals such as the *Journal of Public Policy*, *Regulation and Governance*, the *Journal of European Public Policy* and the *Revue Française de Science Politique*.

Preface

The idea for this book was first proposed by Sylvain Brouard at the meeting of the French Politics Group (FPG) of the American Political Science Association in 2006 in Philadelphia. The following year, Sylvain organized a pre-conference short course at the APSA meetings in Chicago. The short course was sponsored by the FPG and provided an opportunity for an international team of scholars to present to and discuss with the wider political science community their on-going research on the institutions of the Fifth Republic in the context of the Republic's 50th anniversary. The French Politics Group has been the site of international collaboration, bringing together scholars from across the globe to discuss research and teaching issues related to French Politics and Political Science (http://www.wsu.edu/~frg/). A central part of the success of the group has been its work with other institutional partners in France (CEVIPOF, Sciences Po-Paris, Sciences Po-Bordeaux, and the Association Française de Science Politique), the USA (APSA, the French Embassy) and in the UK (the French Policy and Politics Group of the Political Studies Association). Thus, from beginning to end, this book has been an initiative inextricably linked to the FPG of APSA and its various partners; so much so that Sylvain invited the two present co-conveners of the group, Amy Mazur and Andrew Appleton, to co-edit the book with him.

As we discussed the project we developed a mutual conviction that several things should be accomplished. First, we are united in the conviction that, 50 years into the French Fifth Republic, the tired model of exceptionalism no longer has much analytical traction. To those who have followed the study of French politics in recent years, this will come as no surprise. Indeed, the cumulative impact of many studies of institutions, politics, and policies in France in recent years has been to demonstrate that cross-national and comparative analyses have brought a new set of theoretical and methodological tools to bear. France is a rich, unique, and compelling case; yet it lies no further outside the spectrum of advanced industrial democracies than any other.

Second, we all began to share the suspicion that the dragon of exceptionalism would not be completely slain until some alternative were proposed. We readily acknowledge it is possible, despite our aspirations that this volume may fall somewhat short of the ambition to do so. However, we would argue that the contributions below are united by a pair of common themes that deserve serious consideration. One of them is that the manner in which all the contributions address the chosen topics is threaded by institutionalism in its multitude of forms – a focus on classic political structures (i.e. the executive, political parties, or the constitutional council) – as well as a search for explaining how norms and rules structure political behavior (i.e. constitutions, electoral systems, or patriarchy). Perhaps a little unconventionally, perhaps not, we have chosen to present the original research of our authors framed in that way. The other is that we think all of the chapters bespeak to a process of concern to many, that of the consolidation of democracy in advanced industrial societies. We have, again, made a deliberate decision not to accept the question of democracy as a dichotomous variable, but to accept that it is a path-dependent process that has yet to run its course across all societies.

Thus the book is structured in three distinct parts. In the first of them, a series of contributions attack the problem of decision-making institutions under the Fifth Republic. We think that the reader will be struck by the consistency of the findings; once the mantle of exceptionalism is shed, we discover that the presidency transcends personality, that the office is part of a functional dual-executive to which power has accrued, but that the National Assembly has acquired a definable and consolidated role (maybe not power) comparable to other democratic societies with strong executives. We also find that this web of executive-legislative relations is buttressed by a consolidated party system; a strong party system may not be accurately stating the case, but it is a party system that has come to reflect (presidential) majoritarian politics. We treat the case of the military-industrial complex and also European integration and foreign policy as institutions, and the relevant chapters show to what extent France exists in a post-Gaullist, non-exceptional paradigm.

The second part of the book focuses upon institutions and state–society relations. We begin by examining changes in the French political economy, and in particular relations between the state and other economic actors. The move away from what was known as a classic French approach to economic management – *dirigisme* – and towards a more market liberal posture has had serious consequences. One of them is the changing face of public budgets; no longer does the central state reign with a tight fist over public finances, but there has been a movement towards regional and local autonomous action, a multiplication of actors, and a complex web of regulatory instruments. A second consequence that we address is that of increasing demands for labor market flexibility; however, we demolish the stereotype that the French state has been either protectionist or passive in this regard, and show that significant and consequential labor market reform has taken place. We also look at the decentralization of the state, and the concomitant rise of new local actors and a vitalization of civil society. What neo-corporatism might have characterized the French exception seems to have evolved into a pluralization of associational life – even if it falls yet short of the classic 'strong' pluaralist model.

In the third part of the volume we look at universalism and the republican tradition as essential highly codified norms, institutions which shape the conditions of inclusion, equality, and citizenship. We cannot yet conclude that the republican model is dead; however, the chapters show that it is under severe pressure from a series of forces, and that it almost certainly will not survive in its classic form. In the arena of women's rights policy, we find that the ability to enter and shape state institutions by the women's movement – 'femocracy' – has been a prime mover in what moves towards implementing gender equality policies have taken place. Looking at the question of race and citizenship, the incoherence and incapacity of the republican model is exposed.

These three distinct sections of the book are framed by an introductory chapter that places this study in the broader context of democratic development. As we will argue in Chapter 1, looking at the Fifth Republic in developmental terms provides a much more satisfying logic of analysis. Where there used to be little alternative to the paradigm of exceptionalism, our volume suggests that the study of France is ripe for comparative analysis, and may help enrich the process of theory building across nations. Just as the book is a product of an international partnership between institutional elements of the political science profession, so too do we aspire to forge partnerships with colleagues studying other cases, countries, and cross-national phenomena.

The way in which the book has grown out of this highly fruitful international partnership means that many individuals and institutions must be thanked. First and foremost, without Sylvain Brouard's vision and drive this project would never have seen the light of day. While the decision of Andrew and Amy to join the project as contributors and as co-editors was a crucial part of the realization of the book, it was Sylvain's hard work and ideas that made it all possible. Of course the strong scholarly records of the 16 other contributors and their consistent willingness to adhere to deadlines with high quality contributions was also a major factor in the book's publication. Together they proved that marshalling a team of academic researchers is not *always* like herding cats (and that the French are not so exceptional in this regard either!).

Special thanks go to the partner institutions of the FPG. Former FPG convener, Frank Baumgartner, and Bahram Rajaee and Michael Brintnall at APSA have also been important parts of the group's success. As administrative home to the group for the past several years, the Political Science Department at Washington State University must also be recognized with particular thanks going to Lisa Janowski. Aundrea Morrison in the International Programs office provided invaluable support for the preparation of the final manuscript, which was greatly appreciated. In addition, Sciences-Po-Paris and its Center for Political Research (CEVIPOF) welcomed several authors of the book and provided valuable intellectual and financial resources along with the Institute of Political Studies of Bordeaux. We are also grateful for the support that the French Embassy in the USA, through the good offices of François Rivasseau, has provided to the French Politics Group. Sylvain was lucky enough to be hosted by the University of Washington and Oxford University. Both gave him a highly supportive intellectual environment throughout the course of the project. A special thanks to Bryan Jones and Sophie Duchesne for their help. Robert Elgie, the series editor, played a crucial role in recommending this book to Palgrave Macmillan. We would like to thank Amy Lankester-Owen at Palgrave Macmillan for her foresight, advice and, most of all, patience, and to Sally Daniell for her prodigious copy-editing talents. Sylvain is pleased to thank Solveig, Christelle, Noah and Titouan for their (im)patience and love. Andrew is indebted to Ashley and Paige for their support, the staff of the Red Door restaurant for the unprintable humour (and Beau for trying!), and Amy thanks Geno and Minerva. Finally, we acknowledge that one tradition of the analysis of French politics lives on; it would be impossible to swear that no fine bottles of wine were unharmed in the making of this production.

SYLVAIN BROUARD
ANDREW M. APPLETON
AMY G. MAZUR

1
France the Unexceptional

Andrew M. Appleton

> 'Once upon a time, there was an old country, encased in tradition
> and caution... We must transform our old country of France into a
> new country, and it must marry its epoch' – Charles de Gaulle
> (quoted in Jackson 2003, p. 141).

1.1 Introduction

From the beginning, the Fifth Republic seemed to most observers to be a
political system unlike others. The story is familiar and has been told many
times; crafted in a moment of great crisis (the Algerian war), designed to
redress the institutional failures of the preceding regime, tailored to fit the
political (and moral) worldview of one man, and with the backdrop of a
political culture in which the legacy of the French Revolution still loomed
large, the new republican institutions appeared to be rather unique. A semi-
presidential executive, a prime minister responsible to both the president and
the legislature, a national Assembly devoid of legislative initiative, a judiciary
lacking in independence, the party weakening device of the popular referendum, and a defense policy placed by constitutional fiat in the presidential
domain – all of these elements added up to what became firmly entrenched
in political science as 'the French exceptionalism'.

This accorded exceptionalism had two important analytical consequences.
First, it seemed to overtly cast as irrelevant the models and theories of political institutions and action that were propelling the field of comparative
politics at the time. Exceptionalism seemed to suggest that France was not
just an outlier, but purely different. Generations of scholars were weaned
upon superb 'thick descriptive' works, such as Wylie's (1957) *Village in the
Vaucluse*. Textbook after textbook on French politics appeared, with almost
no reference to the systematic process of comparison. The standard refrain
became: 'to understand France, we must first understand French history
and culture, which is just profoundly different from anywhere else dating
back at least to the French Revolution'. The second consequence was that

1

the study of French politics was rarely incorporated into systematic cross-national research. While the lack of inclusion of France in such an early ground-breaking study as *The Civic Culture* (1963) has less to do with exceptionalism than the events themselves of 1958–59, it set a precedent that was barely troubled over subsequent decades. At an institutional level, it may have contributed to the lack of contact between French political science and the broader international community of scholars outside of the circle of French specialists. At an analytical level, it meant that the exclusion of France from cross-national comparison could not permit the French case to inform the models and theories themselves. Arguably, both our understanding of French politics and comparative politics itself suffered as a result.

As we look back at 50 years of constitutional experience under the Fifth Republic, it seems that the model of exceptionalism no longer accurately describes French politics. What was once considered a pedestal may well have become an intellectual ghetto. No matter how unique the institutions of the Fifth Republic may have appeared in 1958 when they were tailored, no matter how much policy practices seemed to be determined by the legacy of French political culture, five decades later they are the source for fruitful comparison with other advanced industrial societies. For example, as Elgie points out in the next chapter, the fact of semi-presidentialism – something that once seemed so, well, *French* – is one that characterizes dozens of political regimes around the world today. Merely by developing and including the analytical category into analyses of democratic institutions, institutional performance, and executive studies, our understanding of the universe of political regimes has improved. And on the other side of the coin, we may now apply the language of comparative politics to the study of the French executive and untangle the myth of the 'personal presidency'.

As we seek to evaluate the Fifth Republic at its mid-century point in this book, it will become apparent that a clear trend emerges from close scrutiny of each chapter. It is not just that the book documents the evolution of institutions, practices, and policies under the Fifth Republic (although it clearly does do this). It is that each author uses models and theories familiar to all political scientists – whether specialists of French politics or not – that inform and enrich the cases. And, conversely, we find that the situating of the French case within broader comparative models can inform and enrich those models. So this book is not just about continuity and change in French politics, nor simply an update on what has occurred since the last edited volume was produced. The ambition is broader; we argue, collectively, that the application of commonly-held theories from the arsenal of comparative politics makes sense at this developmental stage of the French polity – and we think that the results cannot be ignored by a universe of scholars whose proclivity in the past has been to relegate the study of France to its 'exceptional' place.

This chapter gives an overview of some of the major transformations that have taken place at both the institutional and policy levels in France, with a view to placing each subsequent chapter in the book in a broader context. The argument that will unfold, piece by piece, is that the sum total of the experience of the Fifth Republic is the consolidation of an unexceptional, if incomplete, European democracy. The personal presidency has given way to an effective executive authority, the National Assembly (all the while subordinated to the aforementioned executive) has developed a regulatory vocation, the Constitutional Council has emerged as a veto player, the military-industrial establishment has shed some of its Gaullist particularities, and France has become a 'Europeanized' country. Democratization, too, characterizes the transformation of civil society, and the successful decentralization of the *colbertiste* state.[1] Economic policy-making has moved away from the state-interventionist model that once seemed so peculiarly Gallic, and market liberalization and labor market flexibility are the order of the day. If we look at the experience of historically marginalized and under-represented groups, we can see the incompleteness of the democratic experience; yet here too, one might argue, there is little exceptional from a comparative vantage point. The triumph of the Fifth Republic is to have become a European regime comparable to any other – a far cry from *the coup d'état permanent*[2] that was derided by many at its genesis.

1.2 Decision-making institutions

Designing durable political institutions has been the Achilles' heel of politics in France dating back at least to the revolution. It may be easy to observe that the tradition of statism and centralized power is an old one, but the repartition of powers among institutions and actors has been more complicated. In the absence of effective and stable political institutions, the centrality of the bureaucratic administration was established and the myth of the neutral state was born. In tandem, another feature of French political life took root, the so-called *système notabiliare*; the solution to the ineffectiveness of political institutions and the hyper-centralization of the state was the emergence of a sophisticated set of clientalist networks based on personal power and authority.

The constitution of the Fifth Republic, to a certain extent imposed by de Gaulle as the price of his return to power, was designed to address these ills and to create a stable and effective form of executive authority. Elgie (2005) notes that the adoption of semi-presidentialism (or dual executive) was based on two old traditions of *personal leadership* and *parliamentarianism*. But in largely subjugating the power of the prime minister to that of the president, and particularly in diminishing the powers of the National Assembly, it is clear that for de Gaulle the former took precedence over the latter. And if his tenure in office was any guide, de Gaulle established the expectation that there should be a presidential style of politics.

As Elgie points out in Chapter 2 of this volume, the empiricist approach to the study of the French presidency has focused to a large extent upon the twin questions of leadership and style. Yet perhaps because of the unique character of the first of the Fifth Republic presidents, or perhaps because of the struggle to define the presidency (as an office) independent from Gaullism as an approach to wielding presidential power, the answers provided by political analysts over the years have tended towards explanations *sui generis*. The French presidency is unique because the constitution of the Fifth Republic is unique, and that is unique because France is unique – an infinitely recursive set of responses that ultimately yield little except the worn mantle of exceptionalism. But clearly things have changed; it is virtually unthinkable that a president today could make the (paraphrased) bold-faced claim, as did de Gaulle announcing his candidacy on 4 November 1965 that it was either 'me or chaos'.[3]

It is important to note that the constitution of the Fifth Republic actively tempers direct presidential leadership and despite warnings in the popular press about the presidentialization of French political life, the tendency has actually been in the other direction, at least until 2000 (Elgie 2005; Knapp 2005). Despite successive presidents attempting to emulate de Gaulle's style of politics, they have found themselves under increasing political constraints stemming for the most part from the lack of large, stable, and effective majorities in parliament. While the experience of cohabitation – a president and prime minister from opposing parties or coalitions – did not bring down the system, it was sufficiently traumatic to impel a constitutional change designed to reinforce the presidency (the reduction of the presidential term from seven to five years, making it concomitant with the life of parliament).

This reform (while not totally eliminating the possibility of cohabitation) makes it less likely that France will undergo the experience of a president and prime minister who have different policy agendas. In doing so, it makes it more likely that the dual executive will be able to function more in accordance with de Gaulle's expressed dictum that the president should be responsible for setting the broad lines of national policy – especially in the area of foreign and defense policy – while the prime minister would be responsible for the day-to-day running of the economy. This scenario seems to best describe the executive under the previous president since 2002, and many have assumed that it will become a more stable norm. Grossman demonstrates in Chapter 3 that this dynamic has particular consequences for executive-legislative; use of the (in)famous article 44.3 has subsided, and given way to article 38 of the constitution, which makes much more sense in an era of relatively stable partisan, presidential majorities.

Thus, it would be incorrect to suggest that there has been a fundamental change in the executive institutions of the Fifth Republic; with the exception of the length of the presidential mandate, the institutions remain on paper much as they were in 1958. But there has been a clear shift in the practice of power within those institutions; it may not be accurate to discuss the presidentialization of the French political system, but it may be more apposite to think in terms of (a) the institutionalization of the *presidency*, and (b) the consolidation of executive authority, even in the face of a more active national assembly. As we shall discuss below, these developments can only have taken place if they are inextricably linked to the emergence of presidential/executive majorities, which in turn rests upon a more robust party system that reflects the institutional dominance of the presidency.

Just as the Fifth Republic established an effective executive power, so too was the power of the National Assembly sharply reduced. The 'house without windows' of the Fourth Republic was replaced by the 'semi-sovereign' parliament (Williams 1969). The executive was given a formidable set of tools to intervene in the internal life of parliament, to control debate, and to shield legislation from over-scrutiny and modification (Huber 1996). While French parliamentarians may be among the highest paid in Europe, their political independence was among the lowest and their control over the legislative process the weakest.

However, there are some signs that this has changed in recent years. There has been a resurgence of both the oversight and the debating functions of the National Assembly, in part as a consequence of institutional reforms and in part due to emerging norms (Kerrouche 2006; Knapp 2005). Among the former is the ability to refer legislation to the Constitutional Council (the constitutional reform of 1974) and the ability to control at least some of the parliamentary agenda (1995). Among the latter is a new form of constituency work, informal relationships developed by members of the National Assembly and the government, and the crucial bridging role of political party organizations (Costa and Kerrouche 2007). The French parliament is constitutionally subordinated to the executive, and yet as Kerrouche shows in Chapter 4 there are indications that a new from of parliamentary action is emerging that enhances its role in the policy-making process.

The evidence that is presented in this volume tends to support the view that it is probably incorrect to analyse the National Assembly in terms of 'decline', 'strengthening', or any other unilinear dimensionality. The legislature in France has been transformed by the fact of presidential majorities within the body, and the reorganization of much of its work internally. Individual MPs still lack the ability to craft and introduce legislation, and the opposition lacks the institutional tools to challenge the government's agenda. However, the deliberative function of the legislature has been reinforced, and it is capable of independently scrutinizing both legislative proposals and government action. The mere fact that there are proposals to amend the constitution to enumerate the legislative powers of the National Assembly demonstrates the degree to which it has evolved. Parliament may not have accrued any additional powers, but the executive has become much more closely attuned to parliamentary majorities; perhaps we have witnessed the subtle transformation of the executive-legislative relationship from one of dominance to responsibility (in a 'lite' version).

The preceding discussion kept returning to the question of more stable, more readily identifiable governmental majorities. This brings us to the question of political parties and their ability to help throw up those majorities. It is fair to say that the French party system has always seemed atypical to those studying it from afar. In general, two words have consistently been applied as descriptors of party life in France: *instability* and *weakness*. Perhaps fitting for a country where the very concept of left and right was born, partisan identification has never been the psychological or sociological link between the individual and the organization. Indeed, Knapp (2004) refers to France as a 'disconnected democracy'. French analysts themselves developed the concept of *ideological families* to denote the stability in the electorate and electoral choices in the absence of stable and enduring party organizations. Finally, the historical ambivalence towards political parties that also dates back to the French Revolution (at least), and which is embedded in the political philosophy of Rousseau, was foremost in the minds of the creators of the constitution of the Fifth Republic in 1958.

Some analysts have portrayed the party system in the Fifth Republic as being inherently unstable (Machin 1990). A counter-perspective is that this period has been one of *consolidation*, propelled in the main by a (relatively) stable set of electoral institutions (Schlesinger and Schlesinger 1990). The two-ballot system (with single-member districts for the National Assembly) has produced an electoral dynamic whereby the first round equates to a primary on either left or right, and the second introduces competition between left and right. This model of the party system has been labeled the *quadrille bipolaire* (the bipolar quartet), and it has been fashionable to trace its roots in the recomposition of parties and party elites during the 1980s, the 1970s, the 1960s, or even beyond (e.g. Schlesinger and Schlesinger 1990).

Yet the consolidation argument faces some serious challenges, particularly when allied to the conceptual framework of the bipolar quartet. The 1980s saw the rise of the *Front National* (FN) as a major electoral competitor. Who could dismiss its showing in the presidential elections of 2002? By the same token, a host of new issue parties emerged in the 1990s, most notably the Greens. Haegel (2005) portrays the emergence of the FN and the new-issue based parties as spelling the demise of the bipolar quartet and ushering a period of intense party system fragmentation. The model of the bipolar quartet becomes even more difficult to sustain with the virtual extinction of the communist party (PCF) on the left and the fusion of the moderate right into the UMP.

These changes have some observers arguing that there has now been a recomposition of the party space in France into a bipolar system, minus the quartet (Haegel 2007; Grunberg 2006). The emergence of this system has been less determined by ideological factors than by institutional ones (election rules and public financing) and organizational ones (intra-party competition). In this adapted model, the first round no longer functions as a 'primary' between moderate and far competitors on each side of the ideological spectrum, but as a 'coalitional moment' where viable governing coalitions are formed and presented to electors in the second round.

The elections of 2007 seemed to both confirm and challenge this interpretation. On the one hand, the presidential election was reduced in the second round to a clear choice between a candidate of the left (Royal) and one of the right (Sarkozy). The subsequent legislative elections threw up a clear governing majority of the same political stripe as the new president. On the other, the brief but spectacular showing of the centrist candidate François Bayrou seems to suggest that there is a large portion of the electorate that remains firmly moderate and centrist in its orientation.

How much Bayrou's popularity was a product of political ideology and how much can be ascribed to antipathy towards either Sarkozy or Royal is still being analysed. However, it does seem clear that his ultimate failure to persuade voters to make the choice to vote for him is reminiscent of the fate of third-party candidates such as Perot and Anderson in the United States. Popularity in opinion surveys is hard to sustain at the polls when the institutional logic of the system points to a bipolar outcome. Perhaps it is apt to suggest that the institutional logic of the Fifth Republic has finally tamed the indiscipline and factionalism of French political parties.

We must not confuse these developments with party strengthening per se. Sauger's analysis below (Chapter 5) makes it clear that this is not the case; however, the institutional logic of the constitution, allied to the transformation of executive-legislative relationship discussed in the preceding section, has furnished the platform for a certain rigor and constraint to party competition. It would be incorrect to suggest that parties in France have become much stronger over the course of the Fifth Republic; it might be more accurate to suggest that the atypically weak French party system (as compared to, say, Britain, Germany, or Sweden in the early 1960s) has given way to one that is capable of providing stable governmental majorities – and in the interim, the party systems in those aforementioned countries have perhaps loosened somewhat. France's party system no longer looks so atypical.

To this must be added one more element. If the two-ballot system pushes towards a bipolar outcome, how is it that smaller parties and movements continue to emerge, survive, and even thrive? One tendency is to seek the answer to this question in terms of political culture and the historical experience of smaller parties in an often hyper-fragmented party system. But a more compelling explanation lies in the transformation of the political/electoral space in France since the 1970s, most notably with regional and European elections. Both sets of elections are fought using proportional representation, and both the regional assemblies and the European parliament are arenas where parties and movements can garner resources and participate in coalitions. The Greens and the FN have both proved adept at utilizing this new political space, and to a large extent their ability to maintain an electoral presence in national elections (especially legislative ones) is dependent on it. These elections allow them to contest for the popular vote in a comparatively unconstrained fashion and to demarcate themselves from other political movements without penalty.

At the inception of the Fifth Republic, the institution of the constitutional council was roundly criticized, especially on the left, as being weak, lacking in the power of judicial review, and overly tied to the prevailing executive power. Brouard's chapter on the Council in this volume (Chapter 6) shows to what extent exceptionalism in this arena too has given way to a set of practices comparable to other democratic societies. Indeed, his comparative analysis concludes that the only remaining vestiges of exceptionalism are to be found in the continued politicization of the Council; and here, as he writes, 'It is the pattern in which Council members are politicized which is specific, not the mere fact of the existence or indeed the level of politicization.' But if the Council is to be acknowledged as the veto-player in the political process that it has become, the careful analysis of its decision-making patterns adds value and power to our understanding of the way in which the regime functions in France today.

Switching directions a bit, if we are to examine the institutions of the Fifth Republic as articulated in its early years, nowhere do we find more self-consciously French ones than in the arena of foreign affairs and defense policy. De Gaulle's preoccupation with French grandeur and independence resulted in the arrogation of powers in these areas directly to the presidency. The historical legacies of the French revolution, its role as a colonial power (and post-decolonization relationships with the francophone world), its position as a permanent member of the United Nations security council, its status as a nuclear power, and its founding membership of the European Union combined to make foreign policy a self-reflexive practice in this France. While it might be an exaggeration to state that every act of foreign policy is a willful assertion of French national identity (as opposed to interest), there is no doubt that national identity enters into the foreign policy discourse more than in a country like Great Britain. The tension between interest and identity has produced a series of dualisms; independence versus cooperation in international institutions and regimes, sovereignty versus co-decision making through multilateral institutions, leadership versus domestic conflicts over policy orientations, etc.

The analysis of defense policy by Irondelle (Chapter 7) provides a neat framework within which to understand both these dualisms and the evolution of the approach to defense policy under the Fifth Republic. His analysis is categorical in stating that there was indeed a specific, Gaullist approach to this domain, and that it has left lasting traces in path-dependent fashion. That said, the chapter traces the conversion of this policy area from being in the 'reserved domain' of the presidency, to one that is firmly in control of the executive branch. This transformation is subtle, all the while allowing for a shift of power within the executive towards the presidency (see above). The importance of the argument is that it makes a compelling case to study defense establishment in France as an institution; and one that is firmly comparable to the defense apparatus in other European countries such as Britain and Germany. Irondelle charts a research agenda that is yielding fruitful information beyond the case-specific limitations of approaching it as merely the legacy of Gaullism. If we pose the question as, 'How much Gaullism is left in French defense policy?', we retain answers that have limited interest beyond the case. If we reframe it instead as, 'To what extent did Gaullism create path dependencies in French defense policy?', we have admitted both that the policy arena has substantially evolved since the departure of the General, and (even more importantly), that we can only fully address the question in a comparative framework.

It has been recently argued that the best way to view the evolution of foreign policy in Fifth Republic France is in three discrete stages (Balme 2007). The first period, from 1958–69, coincides with the presidency of Charles de Gaulle. Over the course of his tenure in office, there were several challenges that faced a modernizing France. First, what was to be the outcome of the demands of French colonies for independence? Second, in what guise could France maintain a nuclear deterrent under the conditions of the Cold War? And third, what role would France play in the new architecture of Europe? The outcome of these three processes is well-known and need not be recounted here; suffice to say that de Gaulle pinned the foreign policy identity of France on a course of mitigated independence: an independent (and expensive) nuclear deterrent, a qualified membership in NATO but with no military participation and coordination, and a leadership role – *primus inter pares* – in the European Union.

Grand though these ambitions were, all were inherently unsustainable in the long run. They have even been qualified as 'irrational' (Safran 2006). Over the course of the two decades following de Gaulle's departure from office, French foreign policy evolved to a more pragmatic engagement in Europe, a greater sympathy to the United States and the Atlantic alliance, and a more realistic view of Soviet ambition in Europe elsewhere. The commitment to *la francophonie* – predominantly France's former colonies – endured but some of de Gaulle's more grandiose ideas were quietly laid aside.

The third period of French foreign policy in the Fifth Republic emerged after the end of the Cold War. Three events converged to produce this shift; first, the collapse of the Soviet bloc and the reunification of Germany; second, the first war with Iraq; and third, the culmination of the single-market process in Europe in 1993. The juxtaposition of these events served to end any notions that France could continue to act as a big power on the world stage. Its role would be, at best, a 'small big power'. In particular, the war in Iraq served to expose many of the weaknesses of the French military; a lack of coordination with other NATO forces as a consequence of the long absence from NATO military institutions, poor equipment (since most of the defense budget had been consumed by the increasingly expensive *force de frappe*), and the personnel effects of a conscript force.

Given the abandonment of many of the cherished aims of de Gaulle during the periods following his presidency, what are the guiding rails of French foreign policy today? While there is disagreement on the degree to which traces of Gaullism are still to be found in it (see, for example, Keiger 2005 for a view counter to that expressed here), there is more agreement that a consistent replacement for Gaullism has yet to be found. With regards to Europe, France can no longer claim to be *primus inter pares*; both the evolution of the institutions of the EU (including joint foreign and defense policy mechanisms) and the expansion of its membership have inevitably diluted France's influence. Indeed, many have argued that a certain Euroskepticism has now crept into French foreign policy (Balme 2007). On the global stage, President Chirac attempted to sketch out a role for France as the leader of an alternative view of globalization, one that counters neoliberalism and economic globalization with an ideal of social responsibility, cultural respect, and human rights for all. There is little doubt that this idealized view runs counter to certain domestic economic policy practices (see above), and is far from reflected in actual policy outcomes. Perhaps the most apt summation of what French foreign policy is today is that it is defined mostly by what it is not (Keiger 2005).

1.3   Institutions and state–society relations

The French economic model is always prefaced by reference to *les trentes glorieuses*, the 30 years of sustained economic growth after World War II that transformed France from a semi-agricultural economy to a modern, industrialized country with large capitalist firms. During this period, the so-called *dirigisme* (direction) of the state was incontestable. Policy levers included the expansion of the nationalized sectors, constant intervention in the private sector, and an aggressive promotion of export markets. All of this was underpinned by the planning process, where the central planning agency (the CGP) served as a bridge between political and economic interests.

However, a fundamental turning point was reached in the early 1980s. Just as other European economies, that of France had been pressured by the 'oil shock' and the global economic downturn of the 1970s. In 1981 a Socialist government was elected, promising to reinforce and reinvigorate the *dirigiste* model (directly counter to what was taking place across the English Channel and across the Atlantic). Two years later, that same government was forced to make a choice: maintain its ideological commitment to state dominance in economic policy-making and abandon its European commitments, or tighten its monetary policy and defend the franc at the price of retreating from an expensive industrial policy.

In opting for the latter the austerity governments of 1983–84 and 1984–86 ended up enacting a series of reforms that set off a wholesale transformation of the French political economy. Levy (2005) points out that this was neither a case of the withering away of the state in the realm of economic policy-making nor a subtle form of business as usual. Rather, it was a radical overhaul of the primary objectives of the government in this domain (essentially substituting a strong fiscal and money policy for industrial policy), coupled with a reassessment of the main mechanisms of government intervention in the marketplace. Central planning was suspended and then abandoned entirely; nationalized firms were mandated to pursue profitability over job protection; and the state abandoned its long-cherished 'big projects' model (which had given the world such technological marvels – but market failures – as the Concorde).

Through the 1990s successive governments undertook large-scale privatizations of some of the most cherished firms. This process had already been foreshadowed in the mid-1980s when the right-wing government began to sell significant chunks of public firms to private investors, a practice that was continued by the left during its period in power from 1988–93 (Schmidt 1996). But from 1993 to 97 the pace and depth of privatization was accelerated, especially since the sales raised cash to pay for continued public expenditures on social programs. Perhaps the most telling sign that French economic and industrial policy had been changed was the fact that the Jospin government (socialist) which came to power in 1997 continued apace with privatizations, with barely a whimper from the left. Clift's contribution to this book (Chapter 9) summarizes these developments neatly, showing how the turn towards market liberalization proceeded apace through the last ten years or so. Nonetheless, it would be a mistake to say that *dirigisme* is dead; it lingers on both as a rhetorical device that frames calls to government action, and also as an enabling mechanism for limited intervention in specific cases. Whatever the actual extent of *dirigisme* today, political economic constraints have consigned its use to a marginal place in the panoply of macro-economic instruments at the disposal of the government.

The corollary to this scaled move away from the *dirigiste* model was an unemployment rate that climbed to 12 percent by 1986 as firms turned towards profitability by shedding jobs, and a rapid increase in social spending. The move away from state intervention in economic and industrial policy was accompanied by panoply of new labor market policies designed to ease the pain of liberalization on French workers and to provide short- and long-term retraining and reinsertion. Levy (2005) aptly labels this the 'social anesthesia state'; in essence, the individual-level effects of market liberalization and privatization of national champions were mollified by a generous – and expensive – set of programs that have cushioned the vicissitudes of the market. However, the macro effect of these policies is debatable; those in large industrial companies who have lost their jobs through restructuring may have received a comparatively generous range of benefits, but ultimately it has kept unemployment high and placed a fiscal burden upon the state.

All of this was accompanied by the so-called *réfondation sociale* (social refoundation) which was launched by the peak employers' association, the MEDEF, in 2000. Upset by what employers considered to be overly interventionist tactics by the socialist government of the day, most notably in imposing the very popular – on the left, at least – 35-hour working week, the social refoundation was aimed at getting employers and moderate trade unions to renegotiate some of the core aspects of the comprehensive system of social protection for workers. The *réfondation* was not uniformly successful, but it did produce some important agreements (Levy 2005). The return of a solid right-wing majority in 2002 then ushered in a government pledged to addressing some of the lingering ills of the 'social anesthesia' state. The Raffarin government was avowedly committed to introducing labor market flexibility, particularly for the young, reducing the burden of individual taxation, redressing the balance of France's costly pension schemes, and diminishing the cost to the state of health-care coverage.

Despite all of this recent reform activity, the most pressing issue for the French government remains a high level of public spending. In recent years France has failed to meet the targets set by the so-called stability pact that governs membership in the Euro and the European Monetary System, risking censure by its European partners. After the Commission launched an action against the Raffarin government in 2003, the government announced that it would sell off more state-held assets; in 2005 it succeeded in reducing the deficit to 2.5 percent, a rate which it maintained in 2006 (the Commission withdrew the action after these results were announced). Public debt has been held to 64.9 percent in 2007, in an election year when it was forecast that it would rise to 66.6 percent.

The analysis of public budgeting presented by Baumgartner, François, and Foucault in this book (Chapter 10) demonstrates the degree to which the central state has lost its budgetary autonomy. Again, one of the principal themes of the book finds its echo; this transformation has taken place not as a result of constitutional change or the redesign of state institutions, but as a result of a combination of factors. Importantly, each of the factors that they identify is common to other European countries – the rise of multi-level governance (which is discussed by Le Galès and Pinson in Chapter 12), Europeanization, and the maturation of the welfare state. Together, these represent a form of entropy, which they define as 'the idea that power will be spread increasingly among a greater range of relatively autonomous actors'.

The autonomy of the state may have declined, but so too has its capacity to control public spending in a direct fashion.

State-held assets are not infinite, and the stop-gap actions described above have not necessarily attacked the root of the problem, which remains an overly-rigid labor market and an overly-generous set of social policies. But it would be incorrect to perpetuate the stereotype of the French labor market as sclerotic, and those social policies as static and unsustainable. Vail's study of social protection in this book (Chapter 11) concludes that there is actually significant dynamism in labor market and social policy in contemporary France. Both the socialist government of Lionel Jospin from 1997 to 2002 and the right-wing majorities that have succeeded it have aspired to liberalize the labor market and to introduce flexibilities that did not exist before. Concomitantly, successive governments have experimented with a set of social policies aimed at maintaining the safety net for those caught in precarious situations as a consequence of this new approach to the labor market. The stereotypes of French politics often emphasize the resistance to these policies, especially from some of the unions; however, Vail shows that what has often been overlooked is the degree to which these policies have been successful in transforming the conditions of employment in France today.

Perhaps the biggest institutional transformation over the life of the Fifth Republic has been the decentralization of political powers to the regions and other territorial entities. Since 1986 regional governments are directly elected by proportional representations, have a combination of executive and legislative powers, and are endowed with the authority to directly tax. However, decentralization in France was not simply one event or one set of reforms; rather, it is best understood as an ongoing process, in which new administrative procedures and policy initiatives are introduced every few years. Collectively, these reforms add up to a massive transformation of the French state, both in style of governance and substantively in terms of the pattern of government expenditures (Le Galès 2005).

Elgie (2003) points out that the normative foundations of the centralized French state – national unity and equality of citizenship – have been translated into a centralization that was often more myth than reality. Many observers have pointed over the years to the functional networks, honeycombs of influence, which literally made things work at the local level in the face of these unyielding norms. So possibly one of the greatest impacts of the decentralization process has been to change views about the role of the state in the daily lives of ordinary French people. The republic described as 'one and indivisible' in the first constitution written after the revolution is now subject to an addendum: 'the organization of the republic is decentralized'.

The decentralization reforms have also altered the political space, as noted above. New political actors have emerged; for example, mayors of large cities have become, in many cases, powerful local executives with a range of policy instruments at hand to effectuate meaningful and visible change. Regional councils have undertaken initiatives in areas where it was not necessarily anticipated – transport policy, for example – and have been very successful. Often these kinds of initiatives have been undertaken in partnership with the European Union, allowing this new breed of local actor access to resources not forthcoming from the central state administration. All this has been accompanied by a transfer in public spending from the central state to local territorial entities, as Baumgartner, François, and Foucault persuasively document. Le Galès (2005) sums up the impact of decentralization in France by floating the notion that the country has moved from a centralized style of governance to a more regulatory one, where the state coordinates and regulates rather than imposes.

Pushing this further still, Le Galès and Pinson use their chapter in this book to show that the swollen expenditures of local government have caused a rethinking of the 'virtuous' role that was accorded to them in the golden era of decentralization. They suggest that this fact alone may be enough to precipitate a further transformation of center–periphery relations; it is possible that the regulatory relationship between central government and local authorities may be primarily conducted by means of macro-economic controls from the center. Such a solution would see a potential increase in the legal and normative powers of local authorities, but within a tighter set of fiscal and monetary constraints imposed from Paris. Neither federal nor centralized, the territorial organization of the French state is profoundly different today from 50 years ago. The political culture of territoriality persists, to be sure; but the dysfunctions and ad hoc remedies (the *système notabiliare* principle among them) have given way to a complex mosaic of regulatory controls and local action that would be familiar to students of local government in any modern democratic polity.

The Siamese twin of localism in France has been that associational life that is at the core of civil society. As the country that produced Alexis de Tocqueville, and one of the first to formally recognize the freedom of association, it may be considered paradoxical that France has historically witnessed somewhat low levels of participation in civic associations. Perhaps this is in part due to the tendency of the French to resort to contention and conflict (Tilly 1986), and in part reflective of low levels of social trust. Perhaps also it is a symptom of the lack of clear demarcation between state and civil society, where the state has had the upper hand in determining and regulating relations between it and voluntary associations (Levy 1999). There is little doubt that traditional economic associations have experienced a recent crisis of representation and have struggled to act as interlocutors with the state (Berger 2006).

That said, the emergence of new social movements (NSMs) has challenged this stereotype. In comparative terms, new social movement activity in France has been rather vigorous and sustained. Equally so, French NSMs have been much more oriented towards sub-group or individual interests than civic associations of the past, challenging the French republican ideal of equality (Appleton 2005; Duyvendak 1995). Much of the new issue agenda in France is colored by the experience of May 1968 and the generation that came of political age at that time. However, there is also much that has been shaped by the experience of other post-industrial societies in Europe and elsewhere.

The evolution of new social movements in Europe in the 1970s and early 1980s was largely driven by feminism, regionalism, ecology, and anti-nuclearism. For many reasons these issue agendas achieved less purchase in France than in countries like Britain, the Netherlands, and Germany. Furthermore, a primary limiting factor on NSM activity at this time was recomposition of the political left (Appleton 2000). This is not to suggest that these movements did not exist at all, but merely to point out that their influence on the political discourse and the policy agenda were rather limited (Tarrow 1994).

A critical turning point came with the emergence of the xenophobic FN in the mid-1980s. As it broke into the national spotlight following the municipal elections of 1983, a host of anti-racist groups emerged such as *SOS-Racisme*. In the late 1980s the focus on anti-racism gave way to a broader agenda that addressed the concerns of immigrants in all walks of society, and then further extended to address questions of poverty, unemployment and social precariousness. By the late 1990s this movement became known as the solidarity movement, encompassing a host of groups and organizations both engaging in advocacy and providing aid and assistance.

Concomitantly, there was a revitalization of the women's rights and environmental movements, both spurred by the decentralization reforms of the 1980s (see above) and the emergence of new political actors and spaces at the local levels. The women's rights movement broadened its agenda to call for a redefinition of democracy and citizenship (Baudino 2003), while the environmental movement achieved very public successes in halting large-scale projects through grassroots activism. Questions of food safety, such as the 'mad cow' scare in the United Kingdom or genetically modified foods, have provided causes around which local groups and activists can rally at the national level.

In this atmosphere ATTAC, one of the more influential new social movements in recent years, was born. This group, which brought together public intellectuals such as Alain Touraine and activists such as José Bové (most well known in the United States for leading the destruction of a McDonalds restaurant in southwest France),[4] has been at the core of the anti-globalization movement that burst into the public consciousness in the WTO riots in Seattle in 1999. While not large in terms of membership (it currently claims about 30 000 members), the group has had a disproportionate effect on the political agenda; successive governments of both the left and right sent official delegations to the World Social Forum, and the European Social Forum in Paris in 2003 was addressed by then-Prime Minister Raffarin.

The fate of the anti-globalization movement in France is of keen interest. At the United Nations in his millennium address of 2000, then-President Chirac suggested that French universalism, as it has been interpreted and refined since the revolution, should stand for a skepticism towards neoliberal variants of globalization. Indeed, he suggested that France's role in the world should be to give aid and protection to poorer countries exposed to the adverse effects of global market competition. Yet the new president, Nicholas Sarkozy, has seemingly abandoned this official embrace of some of the softer anti-market rhetoric of the anti-globalization movement.

So Woll's contribution to this volume (Chapter 13) concludes that the evidence shows overwhelmingly that there is a resurgence of associational life in France. Under these conditions, it is clear that whatever neo-corporatism existed in the early years of the Fifth Republic, it is under extraordinary pressure today. State–society relations have evolved. The state is keen to underwrite and support this growth in associational activity, but from the perspective of fostering and bolstering social capital. Once more, it seems, political practice in the mature years of the Fifth Republic has come to parallel that in other European countries – maybe with a 'French flair', maybe with a typically Gallic nod to the republican tradition, but certainly far from the stifling model described by Michel Crozier almost 40 years ago. It is not unrestrained pluralism, but it is a new dynamic that transcends the old academic debate opposing pluralism with neo-corporatism, and which seems to have much more to do with building and consolidating social capital.

1.4   The republican model

It is customary to conclude that the French state still largely controls and regulates access from civil society. Woll's analysis even indicates that the state may have gained a measure of autonomy that it did not previously possess. However, the obverse is apparent in the chapter by Lépinard and Mazur (Chapter 14) on the search for gender equality. Their rich analysis may be read, in part, as a case study of the power and limits of new social movements in modern France. Neither the republican tradition nor the institutions of the Fifth Republic could be said to be favorable, by vocation, to a comprehensive set of policies aimed at promoting gender equality. Yet the force of the women's movement was to gain an institutional foothold within the French state itself, through the creation of a succession of institutions devoted to just that. The case shows that the state itself may be reformed through the concerted action of associational organizations.

That said, their chapter also shows the limits to the process. There is little doubt that the vestiges of the republican model continue to circumscribe the pursuit for gender equity. Furthermore, they also highlight the fact that much of the impetus comes not from within the state itself, but from the European level. By the same token, we can also observe another truth about the Fifth

Republic at its half-century; much of the policy agenda – not just in the area of gender policies – is determined through complex external constraints. And if the commitment to implementing comprehensive gender equality policies falters at the European level, that might imperil the incremental advances that have been made in this domain. Objectively, the cause of gender equality still faces many obstacles; yet the activism of the women's movement and the concerted action of 'femocrats' both within the French state and at the European level have confronted many of the sacred tenets of the French republican tradition.

The other sustained challenge to the French republican model in recent years has come through immigration. The ideological core of French republicanism, dating back to the first days of the revolution, has been a commitment to equality of citizenship at all costs. As Duchesne (2005, p. 230) put it, 'The Republican political community is basically conceived as a neutral sphere, where all citizens are considered equal, regardless of any difference such as gender, religious affiliation, ethnic and/or geographic origins, cultural preferences'. In the abstract, this is a universal conception of citizenship which inextricably binds the citizen and the state through the nation. In practice, national identity and the precise meaning of the model have been the source of deep, bitter, and enduring conflicts in French history.[5]

If we leave aside the past and look at the way in which the French state is attempting to negotiate cultural policy today, we see enormous challenges that have been posed in recent years. The changing role of women in society, the transformed character of immigration, the increasing presence of non Judeo-Christian cultures, European integration, and the larger process of globalization have all taxed the ability to maintain even an idealized fiction of republican equality. It is not possible to give an exhaustive treatment of the heated debates over immigration and citizenship laws; however, it is important to note that these have been thrust to the forefront of the political agenda both by the social fact of immigration itself and by the political fact of a xenophobic, extreme right-wing party committed to reversing immigration, that had become an entrenched force by the late 1980s.

Across all these areas there is an uneasy tension between policies that have been enacted which seem to affirm the traditional model and others that seem to reflect an alternative vision of a positive anti-discrimination approach. The anti-veil law of September 2004 reflects the former approach. Following attempts by girls to wear Islamic veils in schools, the government passed a law (with little organized opposition) banning overt religious symbols in public schools. The latter approach is concretized in the so-called parity reforms of 2000, which instigated quotas for women seeking public office through political parties and elections. While the laws did not go as far as the government had hoped, the most significant outcome was a change to the constitution which repudiated the famous article 6 of the Declaration of the Rights of Man and the Citizen of 1789.

Thus it seems inevitable that policies aimed at maintaining a fictional version of French national identity are changing, whether through voluntarism or necessity. As much as anything else, one of the undeniable facts of the modern French state (as anywhere else in the advanced industrial world) is the nexus between immigration, marginalization, and poverty. It is perhaps as much a consequence of this reality, rather than because of any more lofty principles, that the French state is being forced to acknowledge what in the United States would be called the 'politics of difference'. There has been an increasing public discourse about one of the taboo subjects of immigration – racial discrimination – and there have been a number of policy proposals to address it. A ground-breaking survey in 2006 showed that over 50 percent of blacks in France said that they had been victims of harassment and discrimination.[6] In this context, it is almost inevitable that the adherence to a strict version of republicanism will be increasingly impossible.

Chebel d'Appolonia concludes, in the final chapter of this book, that the republican model is in an untenable position. Confidence in the model has waned, as it has manifestly failed to produce policies that will increase social cohesion and reduce marginalization based on race and ethnicity. Yet at the same time public officials use the language of race and ethnicity to describe policy approaches, the state does not even possess the data necessary to map the scale of the problem, let alone design adaptive solutions. French society suffers racism, racial tension, targeted poverty, and institutional barriers to people of color. It is, then, rather like most European, North American, and antipodal societies. In this, instead, the dogged adherence to the republican model retards the development of different policy solutions. How effective those solutions would prove to be anyway is cast into doubt by the observation above, namely that the problems surrounding race and immigration at a societal level seem to transcend political cultural barriers. It is hard to find successful examples of integration in Europe as a whole, and in this France may not be alone.

1.5   Conclusion

This chapter has staked out a clear line of argument. We do not intend to mitigate the conclusions that may be drawn from the original research presented in this volume, nor do we believe that there is much ambiguity about the demise of exceptionalism over the life-span of the Fifth Republic. Each of our team, either explicitly or implicitly, presents compelling evidence that the 'unexceptionalism' of France today places the analyst at a comparative advantage. Whether we use the language of path dependency, of 'new' or 'historical' institutionalism, of international political economy, of comparative public policy analysis, or any other of the approaches that are used in this book, it is clear that France is a case not unlike any other. As we argued above, we believe that the experience of the Fifth Republic is much better understood in terms of democratic consolidation; read in that vein, each of the chapters build the portrait of a regime and a society that may just be wedded to the epoch in which we all live.

Notes

1. For those readers who may not know what the term refers to, this serves as a perfect illustration of the tendency to analyse French politics and traditions *sui generis*! Jean-Baptiste Colbert (1619–83) is considered to be one of the three great architects of the centralized French state, and had a particular interest in the role of the state in fostering commerce and economic growth.
2. Again, for non-specialists of French politics, the reference is to a pamphlet authored by François Mitterrand in 1964, in which he denounced the Constitution of the Fifth Republic.
3. De Gaulle actually said, 'If there were to be a massive and direct demand from the citizens to get me to stay in power, then the future of the new Republic would surely be assured. If not, no-one can doubt that it will crumble straight away, and France will undergo an even more disastrous confusion within the state – this time, with no possible recourse' (translated from Giesbert 1977, p.217).
4. In the United States, the episode in question was portrayed as the sacking and destruction of the restaurant. French people are quick to point out that the restaurant was not destroyed but dismantled and the materials recycled as part of the political statement. Whatever the interpretation, the French continue to be among the highest consumers of hamburgers in Europe.
5. No wonder that in a poll taken in 1987 the top three elements of French national identity identified by respondents were its cuisine (63 percent), commitment to human rights (62 percent), and ideal of 'the French woman' (42 percent) (cited in Safran, 2003).
6. One of the problems in France is that official statistics and surveys of sub-populations are hard to come by. Inspired by the republican principles discussed above, survey takers are prohibited from asking any questions that would iden-tify the race or ethnicity of the respondent. The official census (and all statistics gathered by the Institut National de la Statistique et Etudes Economiques (INSEE)) conform to this stricture.

Bibliography

Andersen, R. and J. Evans (2003) 'Values, Cleavages, and Party Choice in France', 1988–95, *French Politics* 1:1.

Appleton, A. (2000) 'The New Social Movement Phenomenon', In: R. Elgie (ed.) *The Changing French Political System*, London: Frank Cass.

Appleton, A. (2005) 'Associational Life in Contemporary France', In: A. Cole, P. Le Galès, and J. Levy (eds) *Developments in French Politics 3*, New York: Palgrave Macmillan.

Balme, R. (2007) 'Diplomatic and Foreign Affairs: France, Europe, and the World', Paper prepared for presentation at the annual meetings of the American Political Science Association, Chicago, IL.

Baudino, C. (2003) 'Parity Reform in France: Promises and Pitfalls', *Review of Policy Research* 20:3.

Baumgartner, F., A. François, and M. Foucault (2007) 'Patterns of Public Budgeting in France: From Hierarchical Control to Multi-Level Governance', Paper prepared for presentation at the annual meetings of the American Political Science Association, Chicago, IL.

Bélanger, E., M. Lewis-Beck, J. Chiche, and V. Tiberj (2006) 'Party, Ideology, and Vote Intentions: Dynamics from the 2002 French Election Pane', *Political Research Quarterly* 59:3.

Berger, S. (2006) 'Representation in Trouble', In: P. Culpepper, P. Hall, and B. Palier (eds) *Changing France: The Politics that Markets Make*, Basingstoke: Palgrave Macmillan.

Boy, D. and N. Mayer (1997), *L'Electeur a ses raisons*, Paris: Presses de Sciences Po.

Boy, D. and N. Mayer (2000) 'Cleavage Voting and Issue Voting', In: M. Lewis-Beck, (ed.) *How France Votes*, New York: Seven Bridges Press.

Chiche, J. and V. Le Hay (2007) 'The Political Space of the French Electorate on the Eve of the Presidential Election of 2007', Paper prepared for presentation at the annual meetings of the American Political Science Association, Chicago, IL.

Costa, O. and E. Kerrouche (2007) *Qui sont les deputes? Enquête sur des élites inconnues*, Paris: Presses de Sciences Po.

Dahl, R. (ed.) (1966) *Political Oppositions in Western Democracies*, Yale: Yale University Press.

Dalton, R., S. Flanagan, and P. Beck (eds) (1984) *Electoral Change in Advanced Industrial Societies*, Princeton: Princeton University Press.

Duyvendak, J.-W. (1995) *The Power of Politics: New Social Movements in France*, Boulder: Westview Press.

Elgie, R. *Political Institutions in Contemporary France*, Oxford: Oxford University Press.

Elgie, R. (2005) 'The Political Executive', In: A. Cole, P. Le Galès, and J. Levy (eds) *Developments in French Politics 3*, New York: Palgrave Macmillan.

Elgie, R. (2007) 'Studying the French Presidency under the Fifth Republic: Past Approaches and Future Perspectives', Paper prepared for presentation at the annual meetings of the American Political Science Association, Chicago, IL.

Evans, J. and N. Mayer (2005) 'Electorates, New Cleavages, and Social Structures', In: A. Cole, P. Le Galès, and J. Levy, (eds) *Developments in French Politics 3*, New York: Palgrave Macmillan.

Grunberg, G. (2006) 'L'adaptation du système de partis : 1965–2006', In: P. Culpepper, P. Hall and B. Palier (eds) *La France en mutation: 1980–2005*, Paris: Presses de Sciences Po.

Grunberg, G. and Schweisguth, E. (1993) 'Social Libertarianism and Economic Liberalism', In: D. Boy and N. Mayer, *The French Voter Decides*, Ann Arbor: University of Michigan Press.

Grunberg, G. and Schweisguth, E. (1997) 'Vers une tripartition de l'éspace politique', In: D. Boy and N. Mayer, *L'Electeur a ses raisons*, Paris: Presses de Sciences Po.

Grunberg, G. and Schweisguth, E. (2003) 'Reply to Andersen and Evans, "Values, Cleavages, and Party Choice in France, 1988–95"', *French Politics* 1:1.

Haegel, F. (2005) 'Parties and Organizations', In: A. Cole, P. Le Galès, and J. Levy (eds) *Developments in French Politics 3*, New York: Palgrave Macmillan.

Haegel, F. (ed.) (2007) *Partis politiques et système partisan en France*, Paris: Presses de Sciences Po.

Huber, J. (1996) 'Rationalizing Parliament: Legislative Institutions and Party Politics in France', Cambridge: Cambridge University Press.

Inglehart, R. (1990) *Culture Shift in Advanced Industrial Society'*, Princeton: Princeton University Press.

Keiger, J. (2005) 'Foreign and Defence Policy: Constraints and Continuity', In: A. Cole, P. Le Galès, and J. Levy (eds) *Developments in French Politics 3*, New York: Palgrave Macmillan.

Kerrouche, E. (2006) 'The French National Assembly: The Case of a Weak Legislature', *Journal of Legislative Studies* 12:3/4.

Knapp, A. (2004) *Parties and the Party System in France: A Disconnected Democracy*, Basingstoke: Palgrave Macmillan.

Knapp, A. (2005) 'Prometheus (Re)Bound? The Fifth Republic and Checks on Executive Power', In: A. Cole, P. Le Galès, and J. Levy (eds) *Developments in French Politics 3*, New York: Palgrave Macmillan.

Le Galès, P. (2005) 'Reshaping the State: Administrative and Decentralization Reforms', In: A. Cole, P. Le Galès, and J. Levy, (eds) *Developments in French Politics 3*, New York: Palgrave Macmillan.

Levy, J. (1999) *Tocqueville's Revenge: State, Society, and Economy in Modern France*, Cambridge: Harvard University Press.

Levy, J. (2005) 'Economic Policy and Policy-Making', In: A. Cole, P. Le Galès, and J. Levy, (eds) *Developments in French Politics 3*, New York: Palgrave Macmillan.

Lewis-Beck, M. (2000) 'The Enduring French Voter', In: M. Lewis-Beck (ed.) *How France Votes*, New York: Seven Bridges Press.

Lipset, S. and S. Rokkan (1967) 'Cleavages and Cleavage Structures', In: S. Lipset and S. Rokkan (eds) *Party Systems and Voter Alignment: Cross-National Perspectives*, New York: Free Press.

Machin, H. (1990) 'Changing Patterns of Party Competition', In: P. Hall, J. Hayward, and H. Machin, (eds) *Developments in French Politics*, New York: St. Martin's Press.

Michelat, G. and M. Simon *Class, religion, et comportement politique*, Paris: Presses de la FNSP.

Safran, W. (2006) *Politics in France*, 6th edition, New York: Addison-Wesley.

Schlesinger, J. and M. Schlesinger (1990) 'The Reaffirmation of a Multi-Party System in France', *American Political Science Review* 84:4.

Schmidt, V. (1996) *From State to Market? The Transformation of French Business and Government*, New York: Cambridge University Press.

Tarrow, S. (1994) *Power in Movement: Social Movements and Contentious Politics*, Cambridge: Cambridge University Press.

Tiberj, V. 'Mobilization and Electorates in the 2007 Presidential Elections', Paper prepared for presentation at the annual meetings of the American Political Science Association, Chicago, IL.

Tilly, C. (1986) *The Contentious French: Four Centuries of Popular Struggle*, Cambridge: Belknapp.

Williams, P. (1969) *The French Parliament 1958–67*, London: George Allen and Unwin.

Part I
Decision-making Institutions

2
Studying the Presidency under the Fifth Republic: Past Approaches and Future Perspectives

Robert Elgie

The French Fourth Republic (1946–58) was characterized by extreme governmental instability. There were 25 governments during its brief history. The prime minister had to rely on often broad and unstable majorities in parliament and the government found that its bills were frequently amended and/or defeated there. The president of the republic was a figurehead who had little influence over events. The system was unable to deal with the problem of the Algerian war and the Republic collapsed in 1958. The Constitution of the Fifth Republic was designed to provide greater executive control. The power of parliament was reduced. The electoral system helped to create stable majorities. The constitutional authority of the government and, particularly, the president was increased. The first president, Charles de Gaulle, was a forceful, charismatic leader. He created the expectation of presidential leadership. The 1962 constitutional amendment that established the direct election of the president helped to institutionalize presidential leadership. From Charles de Gaulle through to the current incumbent, Nicolas Sarkozy, the president has been the focus of leadership in the system. The Fifth Republic is now associated with a presidentialized political system. This chapter briefly outlines the study of the presidency under the Fifth Republic. It examines the various ways in which scholars have tried to understand the presidentialization of the political system.

There is a vast amount of work dealing either directly or indirectly with the presidency. We examine only a small portion of that work. We do not examine the study of presidential elections; we do not focus on presidents and public policy; we pay no particular attention to the study of individual presidents or their terms in office, except when such studies reflect on or speak to the political process more generally; we concentrate only on the academic study of the presidency; we leave aside accounts by journalists, memoirs by former presidents, prime ministers and minister, insider accounts by advisers, as well as publications based on colloquia organized by institutions such as the Fondation Charles de Gaulle and the Institut François Mitterrand. Even restricting the literature review to such a small portion of presidential studies leaves us with a huge amount of work to review. To make sense of this work, we distinguish between three main approaches to the study of the presidency. So, in the following section, we outline the constitutional law approach, the institutionalist approach, and the empiricist approach. Having done so, we outline briefly some future perspectives for the study of the presidency. Overall, we argue that currently the study of the presidency is moribund. However, there is a variety of perspectives for the future study of the institution that could result in a much more vibrant debate and fresh insights into what is undoubtedly the key institution of the Fifth Republic.

2.1   The study of the presidency

There are three main approaches to the study of the presidency: the constitutional law approach, the institutionalist approach and the empiricist approach. The first two approaches have been dominated by French-language studies. The third approach has been present in both the French-language and English-language literature. The constitutional law approach is dominant within the scholarly community in France. The empiricist approach is dominant in Britain and the US. There are overlaps between all three approaches. However, it is useful to distinguish between them because each has a slightly different way of conceptualizing the presidency and accounting for the presidentialization of the Fifth Republic.

2.1.1   The constitutional law approach

There are many studies of the president from the perspective of constitutional law. The defining elements of the constitutional law approach are the focus on the president's formal powers with references to the use of such powers, and a description/narrative of political practice over time in relation to those powers. In the description of political practice and in the identification of France as a presidentialized regime type, these works have played a major role in underpinning the presidentialization thesis. In addition, as befits work from a legal perspective, these studies often have a normative element and sometimes aim to justify the use of presidential powers from a constitutional perspective.[1]

Work from a constitutional law perspective is often found in textbooks, the status of some of which is now verging on the venerable with books being regularly updated by authors and, sometimes necessarily, by co-authors and/or groups of authors because the original author has died or retired. Examples of such textbooks include Chantebout (2007 – 24th edn), Pactet and Mélin-Soucramanien (2006 – 25th edn), Ardant (2007 – 19th edn), Gicquel and Gicquel (2007 – 21st edn), Hamon and Troper (2007 – 30th edn), and Favoreu et al. (2007 – 10th edn). Textbook work that has more recent origins includes Cohendet (2006 – 3rd edn) and a clear example of a recent international journal article in the constitutional law tradition is Constantinesco and Pierré-Caps (2006). In addition, many of the contributions in journals such as *Revue française du droit constitutionnel* and *Revue du droit public et de la science politique en France et à l'étranger* also approach the presidency from this perspective. A number of publishing houses specialize in this form of work, including Dalloz, and the LGDJ (Librairie Générale de Droit et de Jurisprudence).

There are two main elements to the way in which the constitutional law approach addresses the study of the presidency. The first concerns the general classification of the regime. It might be noted that the word 'regime' in French is often used separately from the word 'system', meaning political system. The word 'regime' is used to describe the formal framework of laws within which political actors operate. In contrast the word 'system' tends to refer to the interactions, formal and informal, between political actors. The constitutional law approach is primarily concerned with specifying the Fifth Republic's regime. Again, in contrast, institutionalists and empiricists are more concerned with the working of the political system. So, a contribution of the textbook constitutional law literature has been the identification of the specific regime type of the Fifth Republic and its comparison with equivalent types in other countries. The standard argument by constitutionalists is that the Fifth Republic's regime is different from those in other countries. In particular, it has been argued that France has a 'presidentialist' regime (Gicquel and Gicquel 2007), as opposed to either a standard US-style presidential regime or a UK-style parliamentary regime. For example, whereas the US regime is characterized by a separation of institutional powers among the president, the Congress and the Supreme Court and the UK regime is characterized by mutually dependent institutions whereby the prime minister can dissolve parliament and parliament can dismiss the prime minister, the French 'presidentialist' regime is characterized by a concentration of authority in the presidency that is underpinned by multiple articles in the constitution. In other words, the constitutional and legal framework of the regime creates the necessary set of conditions for a presidentialized political system in which the president is the dominant actor in relation to all others.

An interesting example of work in the constitutional law tradition is by Jean-Louis Quermonne, the author of a long-standing textbook on France most recently in conjunction with Dominique Chagnollaud (Quermonne and Chagnollaud, 1991 – 4th edn). In his work Quermonne focuses on the constitutional powers of the president and discusses the nature of the political regime. Like other writers in the constitutional law tradition, he stresses the highly presidentialized nature of the Fifth Republic. However, in contrast to some of the writers associated with this approach, Quermonne draws upon another major figure in the constitutional law tradition Georges Burdeau (1984 – 20th edn) and provides an explicit theory of presidential power. He argues that presidential power is a manifestation of *le pouvoir d'État* (or 'State power'). In this interpretation, the president's power is guaranteed by a number of factors. Consistent with the constitutional law approach, the basic foundation of presidential power is the 1958 Constitution and, in particular, the way in which the Constitution provides the president with an authority that is independent of any other political actor. So, for example, Article 5 gives the president the right and the duty to intervene in the political process regardless of the composition of the parliamentary majority. The direct election of the president is fundamental in this regard as well. What sets the Quermonne thesis apart from much of the work in the constitutional law tradition is the attempt to identify broader foundations of presidential power as well. So, presidential power is considered to be a function of the president's relationship with the civil service, the judiciary, the military, and the media. In each case, with the possible exception of the media, there is a constitutional and/or legal foundation of presidential pre-eminence. As a result, the key point is that presidential power is structurally guaranteed under the Fifth Republic. The president's power is not dependent upon other factors such as the nature of the parliamentary majority. The attempt to provide a somewhat broader political explanation of presidential predominance means that Quermonne's approach differs from the standard constitutional law approach and that, in some regards, it is consistent with the logic of the institutionalist approach below. However, Quermonne's method is very different from the institutionalists and his essentially static understanding of presidential power is also at variance with the logic of the institutionalist approach.[2] Moreover, consistent with the constitutional law approach, the foundations of presidential power are almost always rooted in the constitution and/or law generally.

The second element to the way in which the constitutional law approach addresses the study of the presidency concerns the focus on specific constitutional articles. There are plenty of examples in journals such as *Revue française du droit constitutionnel* and *Revue du droit public et de la science politique en France et à l'étranger*. However, the texts by François Luchaire and Gérard Conac (1987 and 1989) are also good examples. They provide an in-depth analysis of each article of the 1958 Constitution, including those relating directly or indirectly to the president. The entries provide an analysis of the law relating to each of the articles of the Constitution as well as empirical examples relating to them. In this regard, the 1989 text dealing with constitutional law in the light of the 1986–88 period of cohabitation is particularly interesting. Even though this was a period where the president's decision-making powers in many areas were clearly curbed, the book as a whole gave the impression that the essential presidentialization of the regime was undiminished. In other words, while it clearly acknowledged the reductions in the president's powers, the foundations of the presidentialist regime were strong. As if to underline the continuing influence of the constitutional law approach, a new version of this book is being prepared in time for the 50th anniversary of the Fifth Republic's Constitution.

In France, the study of what the Anglo-Saxon academic tradition would call 'politics' long involved specialization in either philosophy, political sociology (e.g., elites, elections and voting, etc.), or constitutional law. Arguably, the first two areas either influenced the study of politics outside France and/or were themselves influenced by studies outside France. For example, work by French philosophers such as Michel Foucault has had an international impact; while work by US electoral studies experts has had a great influence on studies of elections in France. By contrast, debates in the constitutional law approach have remained resolutely Franco-French. They have neither borrowed from the work of political scientists outside France nor have they been influenced by them in any way.[3] That said, within France the long-term dominance of the constitutional law approach can hardly be underestimated both in terms of the undergraduate teaching of the presidency and the academic study of the presidency. Overall, it is hardly controversial to say that the study of the presidency in France from what US scholars would understand as a political science perspective is underdeveloped because of the long-term dominance of the constitutional law approach.

2.1.2 The institutionalist approach

The institutionalist literature has its origins in the constitutional law approach. For example, institutionalist writers such as Maurice Duverger were long associated with work in the French constitutional law tradition (e.g., Duverger 2004 – 14th edn). However, what sets the institutionalist approach apart is the attempt over the last 30 years to provide a systematic explanation of the operation of the Fifth Republic including the presidency, an explanation that is not necessarily rooted in the constitution or law generally. According to the institutionalist approach, presidential power is understood either as the dependent variable with the electoral system and political parties as the standard explanatory variables (Duhamel 1995), or, more usually, as one explanatory variable among others that have an impact on the wider political system. It should be noted, though, that the positivist language of explanatory variables and dependent variables is rarely used explicitly in the institutionalist literature. Moreover, it should also be noted that while institutionalists often include the president and/or presidential powers as a variable in their work, by the very nature of this work they almost always interact this variable with other institutional variables. So, it is slightly misleading to consider institutionalists as being students of the French presidency. Nonetheless, institutionalists are defined by a general approach that invariably includes the study of the presidency.

Textbook examples of the institutionalist approach are Duverger (1996 – 21st edn) and Olivier Duhamel (2003). Duverger focuses on the interaction of political institutions and the party system. This interaction causes variations in the power of the president and, thus, clearly explains why presidents are sometimes dominant, why cohabitation nonetheless occurs, why sometimes the president has a majority but still faces difficulties exercising leadership and so on. (See, for example, Duverger 1978, p. 122; 1980, p. 186; 1982, p. 230). In other work, Duhamel (1985, pp. 17–18) has identified ten institutional factors that have combined to cause the presidentialization of the system. Using a similar institutionalist method, he has combined variables to identify ten different types of presidential power under the Fifth Republic (Duhamel 1995). In these examples of the institutionalist approach, presidential power is the dependent variable. Also, and crucially so, in two of the examples above presidential power is shown to vary over time. This variation in presidential power is one aspect of the institutionalist approach that sets it apart from the constitutional law approach. In the latter, presidential power is essentially static, unless the constitution is amended and/or the legal position of the president changes. So, for example, constitutional lawyers were very exercised by the constitutional and legal debate during the Chirac presidency as to whether a president could be held responsible during his/her term of office for any criminal acts. (See, for example, Badinter 2000.) If so, then the constitutional/legal position of the presidency would be permanently weakened and the presidentialization of the regime would be reduced. For institutionalists, though, such an issue may have been politically tantalizing, but it was largely irrelevant to their explanation of presidential power and its variations over time. For institutionalists, presidential power is dependent upon a number of variables that combine to produce ongoing variations in presidential power within the same constitutional and legal framework. Thus, as noted above, constitutionalists focus on the political regime of the Fifth Republic, whereas institutionalists focus on the political system.

For his part, Jean-Luc Parodi has taken the institutionalist approach further than anyone else, combining/interacting the effects of multiple institutions with the aim of both explaining why particular political outcomes have occurred and predicting what scenarios are possible given other combinations of variables in the future. (See, for example, Parodi 1985, 1997, 2002). Parodi has labeled this approach the 'strategic analysis of institutions'. This approach has a predictive element that sets it apart from the constitutional law approach. A good example of this predictive capacity was Parodi's (1981) identification of a 35-year electoral cycle prior to the 2000 constitutional reform that introduced a five-year presidential term. Prior to that time the president served for a seven-year term, whereas National Assembly elections were held every five years. Assuming the two elections were held simultaneously in year 0, then all else being equal there would be either a presidential or a parliamentary election in year 5, 7, 10, 14, 15, 20, 21, 25, 28, 30 before, eventually, in year 35 they would be held simultaneously again and the cycle would recommence. This uneven electoral rhythm created regular opportunities for periods of presidential majorities to be succeeded by periods of cohabitation and, therefore, for presidential power to vary accordingly. The shift to a five-year presidential term and synchronized elections in year 2002 has greatly reduced the likelihood of such variations as a function of the electoral cycle. Moreover, given this change was brought about by a constitutional amendment, it illustrates that those working in the institutionalist tradition include constitutional variables in their analysis. However, what is key is that institutionalists include many other variables too. For example, Duhamel (1992, pp. 333–4) has argued that a change in presidential power has been wholly or partly brought about not just by the results of presidential and/or parliamentary elections, but also by referendums (1962 and 1972), European elections (1984) and local elections (1992). It should be noted that the method used by institutionalists never involves the testing of hypotheses using quantitative methods, such as regression analysis. Instead, the predictions are always tested using narratives and/or indicative examples.

The institutionalist approach has considerable affinity with the neo-institutionalist revival that has dominated Anglo-Saxon political science since the mid-1980s (Peters 1999) and particularly with rational choice institutionalism of the 'soft' variety and/or with what Peters calls the 'empirical institutional' tradition. Indeed, this label indicates that there is an overlap between the institutionalist approach to the study of the presidency and the empiricist approach outlined below. That said, even though there is this affinity between the institutionalist approach and the broader neo-institutionalist literature, the French institutionalist literature and its study of the presidency has had absolutely no impact on presidential studies outside France or indeed on more general studies of institutions. Moreover, the French literature on institutionalism has not incorporated comparative work on presidencies or, indeed, work on institutions generally that has been conducted outside France. So, like the constitutional law approach, to date the institutionalist approach to the study of the French president has remained largely a Franco-French affair. The only exception to this statement is Maurice Duverger's work on semi-presidentialism (Duverger, especially 1978 and 1980). Duverger identified semi-presidentialism as a regime type that was separate from presidentialism and parliamentarism and classified France as an example of semi-presidential regime. In so doing Duverger was working within the constitutional law tradition. However, as noted above, he differed from it in that he then explicitly and systematically interacted institutional and political variables to explain variations in presidential power within this framework. The irony is that, for whatever intellectual or personal reason, French constitutional lawyers have almost unanimously rejected Duverger's schema and prefer to classify France as a presidentalist regime or as some other regime type as described above. Outside France, though, the study of semi-presidentialism is booming as a way of understanding the impact of variation in institutional arrangements on political outcomes. Therefore, Duverger is unique in that his work on the French presidency has had a considerable impact on the international scholarly community. However, those in the international scholarly community who have been influenced by Duverger's work have had no reciprocal impact on those working in the institutionalist tradition in France. In the main, the institutional approach to the study of the French presidency has remained a very insular approach.

2.1.3 The empiricist approach

The empiricist approach is defined by a desire to explain political outcomes and to do so using evidence based on thick (or fairly thick) description. In this sense, it is closer to the institutionalist approach than the constitutional law approach. For the most part, though, it does not use any sort of positivist (or even quasi-positivist) terminology or methodology associated with the institutionalist approach.

The empiricist tradition is theory-light and empirically incrementalist. Work in the this tradition provides an analysis of the political system as a whole, including the president's important position within it, as well as explanations of particular events relating to the presidency, but hypotheses are never explicitly tested. There is little or no talk of variables, never mind their strategic interaction. This is the sense in which the empiricist tradition is theory-light. Moreover, this work reacts to events. In other words, it provides explanations of what has happened. It does not aim to predict future events. This is the sense in which the empiricist tradition is empirically incrementalist. For example, by the mid-1970s the theme of presidentialization had become common to work in this tradition and the explanations for it include the by now standard reasons such as the direct election of the president, the electoral system, party system, and personal factors, particularly the impact of de Gaulle's presidency. With Mitterrand's election the focus shifted to the impact of Europeanization. The onset of cohabitation in 1986 sparked a further flurry of work. The post-Mitterrand era has been marked by an emphasis on the impact of the changing party system on presidential power and so on.

There is an empiricist tradition among academics in France. We find it particularly in a revue like *Pouvoirs*, which has had special issues on cohabitation (1999 – no. 91), and the president (1987 – no. 41), as well as issues with articles on the presidency (e.g., Ponthoreau, 2001 – no. 99; Colliard, 1994 – no. 68). We also find examples of this work in political histories of the Fifth Republic (e.g., Chevallier et al., 2004). The best collection in the empiricist tradition specifically on the presidency is Wahl and Quermonne (1995). We might also include work that has a stronger constitutional law focus than other examples in this tradition, but which also includes a greater sensitivity to political explanation than work in the standard constitutional law tradition. Examples might include Massot (1986, 1987, 1993) and Morabito

(1995). Overall, in France the empiricist approach is often a home for people associated with both the constitutional law and institutionalist approaches when they write outside their standard domain.

In addition to work in France, there is a very strong and long-standing Anglo-American empiricist tradition of studying the French presidency. Those associated with this tradition include Hoffman (1967), Williams and Harrison (1971), Wright (1974), Andrews and Hoffman (1980), Suleiman (1980), Hayward (1983 – 2nd edn), Wright (1989 – 3rd edn), Keeler (1993). More recent textbook work includes Cole (2004), Elgie (2003), Safran (2008), Stevens (2003), and Wright and Knapp (2006). Rather like the work in the institutionalist tradition, this work usually takes the form of a general analysis of the French political system, rather than a specific study of the presidency itself. This general work often provides an explicit thesis about French politics. For example, Hayward adopts a state-centered analysis of French politics that acknowledges the important role of state actors, but that also notes the limitations to the state's power to shape political outcomes. Within this general analysis the presidency is a key actor with considerable political influence. However, the power of the presidency is also subject to the same limitations as the state-centered system in general. So, Hayward's argument is that the presidentialization of the system is extensive but nonetheless restricted. While much of the Anglo-American empiricist work treats the presidency as part of a broader study in this way, there is also a literature on the presidency specifically, most notably Hayward (1993). There are also plenty of articles on the presidency in general journals, such as *Parliamentary Affairs*, *Political Studies*, and *West European Politics*, as well as in more specialized journals, such as *French Politics and Society*, and *Modern and Contemporary France*.

The Anglo-American work has had some impact on the academic work conducted in France. For example, Vincent Wright's work was well known in France and, arguably, influenced scholars such as Yves Mény. Also, people such as Stanley Hoffman (1994) and Jack Hayward (1997) have published in *Pouvoirs*, though not directly on the president. In addition, work in France has strongly affected the thinking of people in the Anglo-American empiricist tradition. Their analysis of the French political system is shaped by their time in France and by their contacts there. Paradoxically, though, there is a sense in which work in the empiricist tradition is almost as insular as the work associated with the constitutional law and institutionalist approaches. Arguably, its almost exclusive focus on events in France meant that it neither shaped political science outside those working on France nor did it try to test general theories on the French case with the aim of adding value to them. Overall, work in the empiricist tradition has provided often profound insights into the operation of the French political system and how it has developed over time, but it has had little to offer a wider political science audience.

2.2   Perspectives for the future study of the presidency

There is a sense in which the study of the French presidency is alive and well. The need for constitutional law textbooks is strong and these books invariably include long sections on the political regime of the Fifth Republic in which the presidency is an important part. Moreover, each new edition includes up-to-date examples to illustrate its points. In addition, the empiricist tradition is also strong. Recent Anglo-American contributions include those by Bell (2000), Hayward and Wright (2002), and Clift (2005) and no doubt the Sarkozy presidency will generate a new set of studies from the empiricist perspective. For its part, the impact of the institutionalist approach has diminished somewhat with the retirement of Duverger, but, as noted above, there are still contributions from Parodi.

There is another sense, though, in which the study of the French presidency is, currently, almost utterly moribund. For example, the Association française de science politique has neither a working group on the presidency nor a group that focuses on a set of institutions explicitly including the presidency. The last article on the presidency to appear in the *Revue française de science politique* was Parodi's (2002) article on the legislative elections of that year and cohabitation. The review *French Politics* has yet to publish an article on the presidency in five volumes. More generally, the study of the presidency has stagnated. The main themes in all of the three main approaches identified above are now very familiar. True, each new presidential incumbent provides fresh examples to illustrate the arguments being made, but these arguments are now well-rehearsed and very familiar. There is little sense that we are living through a period of vibrant and exciting debate about the presidency and even less sense in which we are on the verge of a paradigm shift in the study of the presidency.

Assuming there is a malaise in the study of the presidency, it is for at least two specific reasons. First, as suggested above, much of the debate on the French presidency has been very insular. There has been little attempt to incorporate insights from comparative politics. Thus, the debates in each school tend to turn 'in on themselves' and are not reinvigorated by new ideas and approaches. Secondly, and partly in defense of French insularity, the study of executives generally has been fairly moribund. In the US presidential scholars are often considered second-class academic citizens when compared, for example, with 'Congress jocks' who study the intricacies of congressional committee assignments and the like on the basis of more or less advanced statistical techniques. In the UK Dunleavy and Rhodes (1990, p. 4) argued that prime ministerial studies had long been dominated by a meager and largely anecdotal debate about whether there was prime ministerial or cabinet government. In short, comparative work on executives has itself produced very few new ideas and approaches that might have reinvigorated French debates on the topic.

In this context, what are the perspectives for the future study of the French presidency? There are three points. First, and most generally, the study of the presidency has the potential to become more exciting and, certainly, less insular if works in this area were to be based on much more rigorous and explicit methodological foundations. It is less important whether those foundations are resolutely positivist and involve hypothesis testing and statistical analysis, or whether they are anti-foundationalist and adopt relativist and constructivist approaches. It is more important that the methodological foundations are clearly specified so that the work has the potential to speak to a wider political science community. To date there is very limited literature on the French presidency that explicitly uses a post-modern and/or discourse approach (Lacroix and Lagroye 1992; also the review *Mots*; and Drake and Gaffney 1996). There is virtually no literature that adopts an American-style positivist approach. The work by Huber (1992, 1996) on the National Assembly showed that US-style techniques could be applied to French institutions and that the resulting work could reach a wide audience. The challenge for students of the presidency is to do the same.

One of the key problems with adopting a more positivist approach to the study of the presidency is the operationalization of 'presidential power' as a dependent variable. It is unclear how such a concept can be measured in a way that would invite statistical analysis. However, O'Malley (2007) has shown that it is possible to use expert surveys to capture cross-national variations in prime ministerial influence. It should be possible to undertake a similar survey to capture across-time variations in presidential power in France. In addition, the academic community needs to be more creative in coming up with proxies for presidential power. For example, the number of interministerial councils chaired by the president may be one such, perhaps allied with the number of presidential speeches on a topic per year and/or the number of presidential decrees or appointments in a given area. None of these measures of presidential power is perfect in itself, but together they may have some potential for advancing the study of the presidency. Another very specific way in which rigorous methodological principles might be applied to the French case is in the application of methods from political psychology to the study of the presidency. The sub-discipline of political psychology has developed a rigorous research method that has been applied to the study of all types of political leaders including presidents. (For example, see the articles in the journal *Political Psychology*.) The application of these methods to the French case may have much to offer the study of the presidency both in terms of the development of new ideas within the community of people who work on France and also in the way in which their work is received internationally.

Secondly, there is a broader political science literature that might be applied very productively to the French case. In this regard, the work on veto players by George Tsebelis (2002) is an obvious example,[4] as is the work on agenda setting by Baumgartner and Jones (1993). This work is not intrinsically focused on the presidency, but it can be applied to presidential politics and, if so, the resulting work is likely to be of interest to scholars internationally. There is also work that is more explicitly focused on study of executive politics and that might usefully be applied to the French presidency. For example, the UK-based core executive research agenda provides a ready-made template that could be applied to France. (See an overview of this research agenda by Rhodes, 2000.) This work uses primarily historical and interpretive methods and would ask questions of the presidency in a way that might generate new insights. This work is premised on the idea that the role of the chief executive – the prime minister in the British system – can only be understood in the context of the broader core executive. Thus, the study of the chief executive needs to be conducted in the context of a study of networks of political actors who interact and who are mutually dependent. This focus on policy networks has great potential to be applied to the study of the French presidency. This approach also has the potential to reconcile those who work in the French tradition of political sociology and their emphasis on the background of elites with institutionalists and empiricists who are more concerned with the outcomes of interactions between political actors.

Finally, even within the three existing approaches to the study of the presidency, there is some potential for the constitutional law and institutionalist perspectives to be combined. In this regard the work of Cohendet is perhaps most interesting. She writes in the constitutional law tradition, but she is clearly very influenced by the institutionalist approach. So, for example, Cohendet (2006, p. 402) insists on the standard distinction between the regime and the system. The regime is the collection of rules and norms in the constitution. The system is the actual manifestation of political life. She then interacts the two in a manner that would be familiar to the institutionalist students of Duverger. On this basis, she even sets out an equation:

$$SP = RP \; R \; SVD$$

where SP = political system; RP = political regime; R = Reacts with; and SVD = System of Determining Variables (e.g., presidential legitimacy, political crisis, etc.). The value of this approach lies less in the equation *per se* and in the starkly underspecified and under-theorized notion of the System of Determining Variables,[5] but more in the very attempt to break out of the usual confines of the constitutional law approach and in the argument that a political regime can operate in various ways as a function of systemic variables. This logic takes forward the constitutional law approach and offers room for the systematic study of the interaction of constitutional rules and, for example, party system variables within this approach. It does seem to be the case that this is exactly the sort of approach that Duverger was pioneering 30 years ago. Nonetheless, it still offers the opportunity for advancing the study of the presidency and even, perhaps, for altering the fixed perspectives of the still dominant constitutional law approach to the study of the presidency in France.

2.3 Conclusion

The French presidency has been the subject of considerable academic attention. There have been three main approaches to the study of the presidency. These approaches have tended to generate long-standing but now somewhat moribund debates that speak almost exclusively to scholars of French politics rather than scholars of presidencies and executives more broadly. There is the potential for these approaches to be combined in ways that would allow new insights to be gained. There are also plenty of ways in which the work of comparativists could enrich the study of the French presidency. There are also ways in which such studies may also enrich the work of comparativists. Both of these developments would be welcome.

Notes

1. Arguably, the approach is sometimes party political with, for example, gaullist constitutionalists seeming to justify the General's actions from a legal perspective.
2. Elsewhere I have reviewed the difference between Duverger's approach and Quermonne's approach is some detail (Elgie, 1996).
3. There were influenced by constitutional law work outside France, notably the work of jurists like Hans Kelsen. Thus, there is often positivism in the work of constitutionalists, but it is a legal positivism, rather than positivism as it is understood in political science.
4. Tsebelis, of course, has often used examples from the French case in his work on veto players.
5. Cohendet's (1993) more substantive work fails to clarify the variables with any significantly greater degree of rigour (ibid., p. 72).

Bibliography

Andrews, W. and S. Hoffman (eds) (1980) *The Impact of the Fifth Republic on France* (Albany: State University of New York Press).

Ardant, P. (2007) *Institutions politiques et droit constitutionnel*, 19th edn (Paris: LGDJ).

Badinter, R. (2000) 'La responsabilité pénale du président de la République sous la Ve République', in *Mélanges Patrice Gélard. Droit constitutionnel* (Paris: Monchrestien), pp. 151–9.

Baumgartner, F.R. and B.D. Jones (1993) *Agendas and Instability in American Politics* (Chicago: University of Chicago Press).

Bell, D.S. (2000) *Presidential Power in Fifth Republic France* (London: Berg).

Burdeau, G. (1984) *Manuel de Droit constitutionnel et institutions politiques*, 20th edn (Paris: LGDJ).

Chantebout, B. (2007) *Droit constitutionnel et science politique*, 24th edn (Paris: Sirey).

Chevallier, J.-J., G. Carcassonne, and O. Duhamel (2004) *La Ve République 1958–2004: Histoire des institutions et des régimes politiques de la France*, 11th edn (Paris: Armand Colin).

Clift, B. (2005) 'Dyarchic presidentialization in a presidentialized polity: The Fifth French Republic', in T. Poguntke and P. Webb (eds) *The Presidentialization of Politics. A Comparative Study of Modern Democracies* (Oxford: Oxford University Press), pp. 221–45.

Cohendet, M.-A. (1993) *La cohabitation. Leçons d'une expérience* (Paris: Presses Universitaires de France).

Cohendet, M.-A. (1993) *Droit constitutionnel* (Paris: Montchrestien).

Cole, A. (2004) *Introduction to French Politics and Society*, 2nd edn (London: Longman).

Colliard, J.-C. (1994) 'Que peut le president?', *Pouvoirs*, 68, 15–29.

Constantinesco, V. and S. Pierré-Caps (2006) 'France: The Quest for Political Responsibility of the President of the Fifth Republic', *European Constitutional Law Review*, 2, 341–57.

Drake, H. and J. Gaffney (eds) (1996) *The Language of Leadership in Contemporary France* (Aldershot: Dartmouth).

Duhamel, O. (1985) 'Les logiques cachées de la Constitution de la Cinquième République', in O. Duhamel and J.-L. Parodi (eds) *La Constitution de la Cinquième République* (Paris: Presses de la FNSP), pp. 11–23.

Duhamel, O. (1992) 'Et après? Sur les conséquences politiques nationales des élections de mars 1992', in P. Habert, P. Perrineau and C. Ysmal (eds) *Le vote éclaté, les élections régionales et cantonales des 22 et 29 mars 1992* (Paris: Département d'Etudes politiques du Figaro et Presses de la FNSP), pp. 327–42.

Duhamel, O. (1995) 'Président, premier ministre, gouvernement. Les différents cas de figure', in N. Wahl and J.-L. Quermonne (eds) *La France présidentielle. L'influence du suffrage universel sur la vie politique* (Paris: Presses de Sciences Po), pp. 121–37.

Duhamel, O. (2003) *Les démocraties. Régimes, histoire, exigences* (Paris: Seuil).

Dunleavy, P. and R.A.W. Rhodes (1990) 'Core executive studies in Britain', *Public Administration*, 68, 3–28.

Duverger, M. (1978) *Echec au roi* (Paris: Albin Michel).

Duverger, M. (1980) 'A new political system model: semi-presidential government', in *European Journal of Political Research*, 8, 165–87.

Duverger, M. (1982) *La République des citoyens* (Paris: Ramsay).

Duverger, M. (1996) *Le système politique français*, 21st edn (Paris: Presses Universitaires de France).

Duverger, M. (2004) *Les constitutions de la France*, 14th edn (Paris: Presses Universitaires de France).

Elgie, R. (1996) 'The French Presidency – Conceptualizing Presidential Power in the Fifth Republic', *Public Administration*, 74: 2, 275–91.

Elgie, R. (2003) *Political Institutions in Contemporary France* (Oxford: Oxford University Press).

Favoreu, L. et al. (2007) *Droit constitutionnel*, 10th edn (Paris: Dalloz).

Gicquel, J. and J.-E. Gicquel (2007) *Droit constitutionnel et institutions politiques*, 21st edn (Paris: Montchrestien).

Hamon, F. and M. Troper (2007) *Droit constitutionnel*, 30th edn (Paris: LGDJ).

Hayward, J. (ed.) (1993) *De Gaulle to Mitterrand, Presidential Power in France* (London: Hurst).

Hayward, J. (1997) 'Un premier ministre, pour quoi faire?', *Pouvoirs*, 83, 5–20.

Hayward, J.E.S. (1983) *Governing France: The One and Indivisible Republic*, 2nd edn (London: Weidenfeld and Nicolson).

Hayward, J. and V. Wright (2002) *Governing from the Centre. Core Executive Coordination in France* (Oxford: Oxford University Press).

Hoffman, S. (1967) 'Heroic Leadership: The Case of Modern France', in L.J. Edinger (ed.) *Political Leadership in Industrialized Societies* (New York: John Wylie and Sons, Inc.), pp. 108–54.

Hoffman, S. (1994) 'Les Français sont-ils gouvernables?', *Pouvoirs*, 68, 7–14.

Huber, J.D. (1992) 'Restrictive legislative procedures in France and the United States', *American Political Science Review*, 86, 675–87.

Huber, J.D. (1996) *Rationalizing Parliament. Legislative Institutions and Party Politics in France* (Cambridge, Cambridge University Press).

Keeler, J.T.S. (1993) 'Executive Power and Policy-Making Patterns in France: Gauging the Impact of the Fifth Republic Institutions', *West European Politics*, 16, 518–44.

Lacroix, B. and J. Lagroye (eds) (1992) *Le Président de la République. Usage et genèses d'une institution* (Paris, Presses de la FNSP).

Luchaire, François, and Gérard Conac (1987) *La constitution de la république française*, 2nd edn, (Paris: Economica).

Luchaire, F. and G. Conac (1989) *Le droit constitutionnel de la cohabitation* (Paris: Economica).

Massot, J. (1986) *La Présidence de la République en France* (Paris, La Documentation française).

Massot, J. (1987) *L'arbitre et le capitaine. Essai sur la responsabilité présidentielle* (Paris: Flammarion).

Massot, J. (1993) *Chef de l'Etat et chef du Gouvernement. Dyarchie et hiérarchie* (Paris: La Documentation française).

Morabito, M. (1995) *Le chef de l'État en France* (Paris: Montchrestien).

O'Malley, E. (2007) 'The power of prime ministers: results of an expert survey', *International Political Science Review*, 28, 7–27.

Pactet, P. and F. Mélin-Soucramanien (2006) *Droit constitutionnel*, 25th edn (Paris: Dalloz-Sirey).

Parodi, J.-L. (1981) 'Sur quelques enseignements institutionnels de l'alternance à la française', *Revue politique et parlementaire*, 892, May–Jun, 42–9.

Parodi, J.-L. (1985) 'Imprévisible ou inéluctable, l'évolution de la Cinquième République?', in O. Duhamel and J.-L. Parodi (eds) *La Constitution de la Cinquième République* (Paris: Presses de la FNSP), pp. 24–43.

Parodi, J.-L. (1997) 'Proportionnalisation périodique, cohabitation, atomisation partisane: un triple défi pour le régime semi-présidentiel de la Cinquième République', *Revue Française de Science Politique*, 47, 297–312.

Parodi, J.-L. (2002) 'L'énigme de la cohabitation, ou les effets pervers d'une présélection annoncée', *Revue Française de Science Politique*, 52: 5–6, 485–504.

Peters, B.G. (1999) *Institutional Theory in Political Science. The 'New Institutionalism'* (London: Cassells).

Ponthoreau, M.-C. (2001) 'Le Président de la République. Une fonction à la croisée des chemins', *Pouvoirs*, 99, 33–44.

Quermonne, J.-L. and D. Chagnollaud (1991) *Le gouvernement de la France sous la Ve République*, 4th edn (Paris: Dalloz).

Rhodes, R.A.W. (2000) 'A Guide to the ESRC's Whitehall Programme, 1994–2000', *Public Administration*, 78, 251–82.

Safran, W. (2008) *The French Polity*, 7th edn (London: Longman).

Stevens, A. (2003) *Government and Politics of France*, 3rd edn (Basingstoke: Palgrave Macmillan).

Suleiman, E.N. (1980) 'Presidential Government in France', in E.N. Suleiman and R. Rose (eds) *Presidents and Prime Ministers* (Washington DC: American Enterprise Institute), pp. 94–138.

Tsebelis, G. (2002) *Veto Players. How Political Institutions Work* (Princeton NJ: Princeton University Press).

Wahl, N. and J.-L. Quermonne (eds) (1995) *La France présidentielle. L'influence du suffrage universel sur la vie politique* (Paris: Presses de Sciences Po).

Williams, P.M. and M. Harrison (1971) *Politics and Society in de Gaulle's Republic* (London: Longman).

Wright, V. (1974) 'Politics and Administration under the French Fifth Republic', in *Political Studies*, 22, 44–65.

Wright, V. (1989) *The Government and Politics of France*, 3rd edn (London: Unwin Hyman).

Wright, V. and A. Knapp (2006) *The Government and Politics of France*, 5th edn (London: Routledge).

3
Governments under the Fifth Republic: The Changing Instruments/Weapons of Executive Control

Emiliano Grossman

According to the eminent jurist and government adviser, Guy Carcassonne, divided government 'à la française' – or *cohabition* – does not affect what government *does* (Carcassone 1994). This is certainly true, as governments' everyday work is mainly concerned with coordinating departments and taking decisions. Whatever the political colour of president and parliament, this is not likely to change. Hence it is important to understand the essential characteristics of this everyday work.

In this chapter, we focus only on executive politics, concentrating more particularly on the role of the government in the Fifth Republic. The government in a truly semi-presidential system is said to be subject to 'dual responsibility', i.e. it has to be supported or accepted by parliament, as in parliamentary systems, but also by the president. In France, this constellation emerged in 1962, when the introduction of the direct election of the president made the latter the most important and legitimate representative in the eyes of French voters. Yet, those institutions have evolved over time. There are some institutional changes, the most significant of which is the 2000 constitutional amendment that reduced the presidential mandate from seven to five years (in the constitutional amendment of 2008, a two-term limit on presidential mandates was introduced). But there have also been changing perceptions and practices of the Fifth Republic's institutions.

The French Fifth Republic raises a fascinating question: what happens when an increasingly presidentialist political system meets the contemporary challenges to politics such as the politics of blame avoidance (Weaver 1986) and the constriction of policy competition associated with the rise of cartel parties (Blyth and Katz 2005)? Both these theses have hardly ever been tested systematically for French politics.[1] Within the limits of this chapter it will be difficult to develop a strong thesis to be tested by empirical data. We therefore proceed in a more exploratory manner in order, first, to account for change in the practice of the Fifth Republic and, second, to provide potential explanations for this change based on the existing literature. This exploratory analysis is based on original data.

The major argument made in this contribution is that the role of government in the institutional architecture of the Fifth Republic has somewhat declined over time. This decline, however, concerns the position of the government in relation to the office of president. This can be explained essentially by political reasons, reinforced by the constitutional amendment of 2000. The parliament has not benefited from this decline. While the instruments of executive authority have declined over time, this has not been matched by any significant increase of parliamentary power.

The first section discusses the role of government in the architecture of the Fifth Republic and its evolution over time. Later sections look at the practice of executive politics and the way in which governments have used the powers at their disposal over time.

3.1   The government and the institutional architecture of the Fifth Republic

The Fifth Republic aimed at re-establishing executive authority as a means of improving cabinet stability and legislative capacity. This was ensured through a variety of institutional means. Yet, governments are in a somewhat awkward position in the institutional architecture of the Fifth Republic. While they are clearly very powerful, they also have a particularly ambiguous standing, being responsible both to the *Assemblée nationale* and to the 'irresponsible' president. This, we argue, has clear consequences for government and ministerial stability. Moreover, this institutionally-induced ambiguity has been reinforced by the evolution of politics and party competition.

3.1.1   Semi-presidentialism and the dual responsibility of governments

As is shown elsewhere in this volume (cf. chapters by Elgie and Kerrouche), one of the Fifth Republic's major objectives was to strengthen the executive with regard to Parliament. Weak government and too strong a parliament were blamed for the excessive government instability of the Fourth Republic. The constitution of 4 October 1958 explicitly set out to remedy this, as government instability was made responsible for having brought France to the brink of civil war.

The centre-piece of this constitution was the strengthening of the role of the president. Yet, many consider that the actual major change took place not in 1958, but in 1962, when General de Gaulle – in a highly controversial move – introduced the direct election of the president (e.g. Conley 2007). For the first elections he had been elected through a special Electoral College made up of local elected representatives, similar to the Electoral College that elects the French Senate. It is true, though, that there was a

'Gaullist' interpretation of the Constitution, which granted pre-eminence to the president. Yet it is uncertain whether this interpretation would have prevailed once de Gaulle stepped down without the constitutional amendment of 1962.

There is some debate as to whether the political system created by the 1958 Constitution can be called semi-presidential. Originally coined by Maurice Duverger, the concept of 'semi-presidential government' has been contested by French legal scholars like Georges Vedel (Vedel 1997) or Olivier Duhamel (Duhamel 2003). These scholars argue that the French political system is 'ultra-presidentialist', when presidential and legislative majority coincide under cohabitation. Moreover, recent scholarship has focused on the great variety of semi-presidential regimes and the conditions of 'success' (Shugart 2005; Skach 2007). Others have called it a 'dualist presidential' system (Chagnollaud 2005: 108).

It is not our aim here to resolve these ongoing controversies. Rather, we would like to focus on the point of view of government. Provided that France is regularly acknowledged to be 'tough' or a 'real' semi-presidentialist regime (Elgie 1999; Shugart 2005), the role of the government is somewhat awkward. Probably because of existing research agendas in comparative politics, the problem of divided government, called *cohabitation* in the French case, has received much more than its fair share of attention. Looking back at 50 years of history, one can hardly argue that cohabitation has been the rule, rather than the exception. Nine years out of 50 – or 18 per cent – should have made observers more concerned with the 'normal' situation, i.e. the one that has prevailed for 41 out of 50 years.

French constitutional lawyers have of course studied this situation of *fait majoritaire*, i.e. of coincidence between presidential and parliamentary majorities. The major issue here is the nature of 'intra-executive' relations, i.e. of relations between president and government and, more specifically, the prime minister. While under cohabitation the president is forced to pick the designated leader of the majority, he has much more freedom under *fait majoritaire*. Looking at the practice of the presidents of the Fifth Republic, it is difficult to find a clear pattern. Presidents may feel forced to chose major party leaders or coalition partners, as was the case for Mitterrand with Rocard or Giscard d'Estaing with Chirac. In both these cases, relations between the two leaders were far from good and often turned into open rivalry. In some cases the president may pick a junior leader of the majority in order to enhance his status as a potential successor. While rather more difficult to find, this certainly occurred recently with the nomination of Dominique de Villepin by Jacques Chirac and also may have occurred in other circumstances.

Yet the most common configuration is where the President picks a rather secondary player in the majority party. This may be motivated by the fact that a proactive president does not want a rival working at Matignon. The autonomy of the government with regard to the presidency varies over time and many of the subtleties can hardly be accounted for other than through the personality of the incumbent president. To a lesser extent, as we will see further on, the practice of executive politics may be influenced through the presence of more or less reliable majorities.

As a consequence of this dependency, the resignations of governments have followed either a lost parliamentary election or the president's demand to do so. Since 1962, no government has been forced to step down after a successful 'motion de censure', as laid out by art. 49.2 of the Constitution. In fact, eight of the 18 prime ministers of the Fifth Republic have stepped down without having lost the majority in parliament.[2]

Under these circumstances the prime minister is in a particularly awkward position. If s/he has some leadership potential, s/he must aspire to be a credible presidential candidate. This is particularly so as the end of the presidential term approaches and re-election is unlikely – for whatever reason. This has indeed been the case for the great majority of prime ministers under the Fifth Republic. Then the prime minister has to demonstrate autonomy and leadership qualities that his/her institutional position hardly allows for. Whenever there is some political contention or simply that the popularity figures of either head of government or the head of state are going down, changing the prime minister is a useful and expedient option for the president.

Put differently, the cabinet is clearly subordinate to the president under 'normal' conditions. This often reduces it to a 'presidential lightning rod' (Ellis 1994): whenever voters – through polls, demonstrations or any other public display – show signs of discontent, changing the lightning rod may help. This may not solve the problem, but it may allow for public opinion to change its focus or to reconsider given problems in light of promises made by the newly named minister or prime minister. This also applies to major ministries: e.g. the powerful minister of economy and finance has changed ten times in the last ten years. Here, this logic is not reduced to 'normal' time, as a prime minister under cohabitation may adopt the same strategy. This evolution appears to be fuelled by the centrality of the head of state in French politics, as well as by the increasing personalization of French politics due to media coverage (Clift 2005).

Jean-Louis Quermonne summarizes the role of the government as follows:

> Unlike the President (. . .) the government is maintained in a situation of dependency, where it had already been (under the Fourth Republic). Formerly the executive of Parliament, it has now become the 'bras séculier' of the President. And even if it is the place of administrative decision-making (. . .), it is no more than before the place of autonomous political power. (Quermonne 1987: 211)

This has significant consequences for the careers of ministers and prime ministers. As political observers have often noticed, no outgoing prime minister has ever won a presidential election. It is true that only three outgoing prime ministers – Chirac in 1988, Balladur in 1993 and Jospin in 2002 – have actually attempted this. But even for ordinary ministers having participated in an outgoing government, the experience has usually not been conclusive (Nicolas Sarkozy is of course the major exception here). All other successful candidates have chosen to leave the national arena for some while, usually retaining a deputy seat and maybe a regional or departmental presidency.

From an institutional point of view, this creates – surprisingly enough – a strong bias *in favour* of cabinet instability. This is, of course, in harsh contradiction to the stated goals of the Fifth Republic (see above). Given the extent of power of the president, however, changing individual ministers or simply organizing a reshuffle within the cabinet are other available options. Figure 3.1 confirms this comparatively high volatility of ministers, compared to governments that last close to two years.[3] This volatility is rather stable over time. Yet, there are other changes which maybe cannot be explained through the institutional features of the Fifth Republic.

3.2 The changing politics of semi-presidentialism?

Any analysis that takes as long a period as the one we are focusing on, aims of course at identifying and explaining changes. Yet, looking at the institutional context of governments under the Fifth Republic, few significant changes have taken place. The single most important reform took place in 2000, bringing in line presidential and parliamentary mandates. Apart from this, as the bulk of the literature suggests, cohabitation may account for variation over time. A different source of change may be due to the evolution of politics in the Fifth Republic.

In terms of the evolution of institutions there is little to say since the introduction of the direct election of the president in 1962. Of course, institutions change not just through clearly stated reforms, but also through practice. Yet while, as we will see later in this chapter, some of the major competences have been employed differently over time, there is nothing that amounts to actual significant change. The major constitutional amendments of course had an effect on the government. For instance, the revision of 24 October 1974, which simplified the triggering of constitutional control, opening it to 60 parliamentarians, turned the original intention of constitutional control upside down. If it had been thought of as a way to better control parliament, judicial review increasingly became the privileged, if not the only significant weapon at the disposal of parliamentary opposition (see Chapter 6 by Brouard). Yet, this has not fundamentally altered the underlying logic of the Fifth Republic or of executive politics as described above.

The other major reform was the introduction in 2000 of the five-year presidential term. If anything the shorter term is likely to reinforce the existing dependency of the government on the president.[4] While it is not impossible, of course, that voters choose a different majority at two elections held within five or six weeks, this is highly unlikely, at least for the time being. In this sense, constitutional lawyers have done a great job in pointing to the incoherence of the situation of 'cohabitation'. In the early 1990s two different committees were charged by President François Mitterrand to think about necessary amendments to the 1958 Constitution. The major conclusion of one of the main figures had been to bring the two mandates in line, in order to limit the danger of cohabitation (Vedel 1997). While other semi-presidential systems can live with two different majorities, it is certain that most French politicians consider this to be an anomaly in the French case. French voters appear to agree with them, since 73 per cent voted in favour of the five-year mandate at the referendum of 24 September 2000.[5]

However, the five-year term could be the consequence, rather than the cause. Change may also stem from a changing political context. In particular, the party system has changed significantly since the beginning of the Fifth Republic. The French party system was very unstable under the Fourth Republic. Yet the only successful censure was adopted against the second government of the Fifth Republic (Pompidou 1) in October 1962. Since then parties have come to dominate politics in France. They negotiate coalitions but, even before that, they nominated candidates for local constituencies. This is, at least partially, a delayed effect of the so-called 'third Duverger Law' (e.g. Duverger 1992), which predicts the emergence of two dominating 'camps', rather than parties, as a consequence of two-round plurality ballot systems.

While this is certainly true to some extent, there may be something else. As Grunberg and Haegel (2007) recently stated, within those camps, the major parties have become increasingly dominant. This has been the result of a clearly stated 'imperialist' strategy in the case of the right-wing UMP (Sauger 2007b). This process started in the early 1970s for the Socialist Party (cf. Bergounioux and Grunberg 2005). As a result, there are now really *two* leading parties that actually compete for presidential and parliamentary majorities, even though there were 12 candidates participating in the last presidential elections, each supported by his or her political party or grouping. This tendency is far from confirmed, for the time being, as most indicators, such as 'effective number of parties' rather invalidate this statement. We will nevertheless look further into this argument.

A related argument concerns the increasing personalization of politics that has most of the time been analysed under the heading of 'presidentialization' of the Fifth Republic. The reasons for personalization are various, the main one of course being the development of mass media,[6] but there is also the larger context of the 'constriction of the policy space' (Blyth and Katz 2005): there is fiercer competition over fewer things, as policy prerogatives are increasingly delegated to other actors (Grossman and Saurugger 2006). As delegation and personalization increase, we argue, executives under

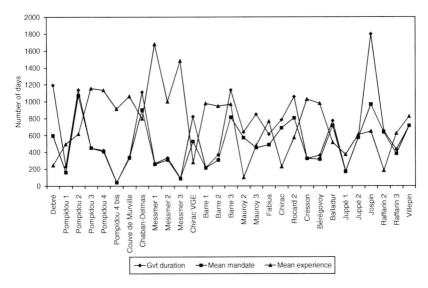

Figure 3.1   Government duration, ministerial mandates and experience under the Fifth Republic

political pressure tend to have fewer 'weapons' at their disposal. Under these circumstances, changing cabinet members becomes a privileged tool of answering to public opinion discontent.

Figure 3.1 summarizes the above mentioned problems rather well.[7] There is some kind of 'natural' turnover for cabinets and ministers in a strongly semi-presidential regime. The mean cabinet mandate length as well as government duration show that there is some variance, but that this variance is more or less stable over time. It is, of course, higher if one includes the double/triple and quadruple governments (Pompidou, Messmer, Mauroy, Juppé and Raffarin). Maybe the most interesting observation here is that in the early periods ministerial mandates and government duration coincided, but this is increasingly less true over time. This may be explained by the fact that the first president of the Fifth Republic, General de Gaulle, built the government around a core group of political allies that he decided to stick with as long as they were not too powerful (Chevallier et al. 2004: 52–3). In later periods, as the party system stabilized and the political personnel became more experienced, changing individual ministers, rather than the entire government, became more common.

Yet, these 'slight' changes are a gradation of the lightning-rod function of government that we discussed in the last section. Announcing a government reshuffling, however profound, allows for a discourse on general politics, some new heads and faces that may curb the president's and the government's popularity, even if the prime minister stays in place.

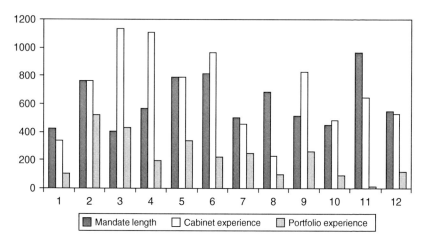

Figure 3.2   Mandates and experience under the Fifth Republic (by legislature)

Therefore, we add a third measure here that is more interesting: mean experience. Mean experience is a measure of the legacy of previous cabinets. Here the tendency is very clear and partly contradictory with an argument based on institutional incentives only. In fact this shows that there is a degree of continuity in ministerial mandates, indicated by an increase in cabinet experience in the early years of the Fifth Republic. This confirms a recent study that shows that the new regime clearly succeeded, at least at first, in stabilizing governments and also, which was maybe less expected, in increasing both ministerial and portfolio stability (Huber and Martinez-Gallardo 2004). It also shows, however, that this greater experience has been diminishing strongly over time.[8]

Looking at the Fifth Republic, this effect is undeniable for the first decade and a half or so. The first real break is the first government of Jacques Chirac from 1974 to 1976. This government brought a host of new people into government, many of whom were imposed by the newly elected president Valéry Giscard d'Estaing. The situation was rather complex at the time, considering that Giscard owed his election to the support of the much larger Gaullist party.[9] Yet he was not willing to let Chirac rule alone and, eventually, Chirac stepped down complaining about his lack of autonomy.

The turnover of ministers on critical portfolios is another indicator of this evolution. The 'hottest' seat by far has been the Economics and Finance portfolio with an extremely high turnover – more than ten in ten years. This mirrors the more general evolution of both cabinet and portfolio experience. Figure 3.2 presents the figures by legislature. The general tendency is the same: after a period of rather high cabinet experience, this comes to a 'natural' halt with the Socialists' victory in 1981. The overall tendency remains similar, as experience has stabilized at an average below mandate length.

Figure 3.2 adds another measure: portfolio experience. This indicator in this case measures the previous experience in the same portfolio. Here, too, there is a clear decline over time. Moreover, the fact that this is much lower than cabinet experience is an indicator of the importance of 'musical chairs' games, i.e. the switching between ministries of cabinet members. While the relation between the two has varied widely over time, it has been particularly low in recent legislatures.

Summing up, one can say that there is an institutional bias in the Fifth Republic in favour of a certain degree of government and ministerial turnover due to a French-style 'presidential lightning-rod'. In fact the analysis shows that average government turnover is quite stable, even slightly increasing over time, mainly due to the five-year term of the Jospin government (1997–2002), provided that government change is not an option under cohabitation. At the same time, however, cabinet experience and, to a lesser extent, portfolio experiences have been diminishing. We argue here that the institutional setting can hardly be held accountable for this. Rather, this should be explained through changes in French politics and the practice of French presidents over time. While we cannot provide a theoretically-informed explanation in this contribution, we have sketched out several potential reasons for those changes. We believe that they are mainly related to changes in the nature of the political competition in France. The next section will further investigate this broad theory by looking at the practice of executive authority.

3.3 The changing tools of executive authority

Executive authority has been clearly enhanced by the institutional setting of the Fifth Republic. In order to fulfil the promise of stable government, the 1958 Constitution gave substantial powers to the executive. Most of these powers aim at limiting the competences of the *Assemblée nationale*, the lower chamber of Parliament. Yet, the instruments of executive authority have evolved over time. In particular, this section will try to suggest potential relations between the evolution described earlier and the relative importance of different instruments of executive power over time that we are turning to now.

Article 16 of the 1958 Constitution created a comparatively liberal exceptional-powers regime that is subject to few effective checks and balances (Huber 1998); however, the constitutional amendment of 2008 granted the Constitutional Council the authority to control the use of Article 16 after 30 days. This power, however, belongs to the president rather than to the government, and even though it was the main target of the early critiques of the Fifth Republic it has hardly played any role in French

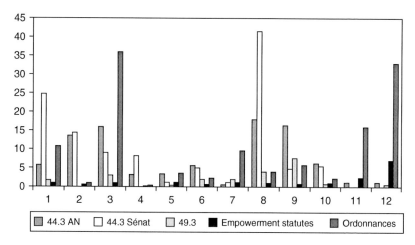

Figure 3.3   Different instruments of executive power and their use over time (yearly average)
Sources: Sénat (2007), Boyer-Mérentier (1996) and author's data.

politics since its only use in 1961.[10] However, the French Constitution provides a host of other 'instruments' to governments that want to impose their will to uncooperative majorities or to filibustering minorities. We discuss the four most significant provisions in turn: (1) the package vote, (2) the confidence vote procedure, (3) the distinction between law and regulation, and (4) empowerment statutes.

3.3.1   Article 44.3: the declining importance of package votes?

Article 44.3 or the 'vote bloqué' (package vote) creates a powerful tool to control parliamentary activity, similar to the British 'Kangaroo' procedure:

> If the Government so requests, the assembly having the bill before it shall decide by a single vote on all or part of the text under discussion, on the sole basis of the amendments proposed or accepted by the Government.

The explanations of the use of this procedure vary. The most comprehensive analysis has been presented by John Huber (1996). He shows that this procedure is particularly useful in preserving extra-parliamentary or coalition bargains during the readings. His exhaustive study shows that the likeliness of package votes increases with issue complexity, thin majorities and on distributive issues.

In recent years the use of the package vote has substantially declined as Figure 3.3 shows. In fact, this is mainly due to the evolution of French politics, we argue. The package vote preserves coalition agreements and, thus, is particularly used in the context of coalitions with one or more pivotal players and in the context of thin majorities or minority government.

Unsurprisingly, its use has been strongest when the government majority was particularly divided on certain issues or on the question of leadership, such as under the Barre governments and, even more, during the 9th legislature (1988–93) when a minority socialist-led government had to deal with often hostile communists and other smaller parties. While Figure 3.3 shows a somewhat cyclical pattern for the use of article 44.3, it is also clear that it has never been as weak as in the last two legislatures. Yet, there are highly contextual effects, too. While there is a generally declining tendency there is some kind of revival of the 44.3 under the first cohabitation (1986–88; 8th legislature), in response to massive 'filibustering' (see below) by Socialist senators. This does not offset, however, the overall decline of package votes.

We believe that this evolution can be tied back to the more general changes presented in the previous section. Since 1993, majorities have been very clear, on average. Moreover, the vote share of the leading party within each camp has steadily increased, favoured by specific 'imperialistic' strategies such as in the case of the centre-right UMP party since 2002 (Grunberg and Haegel 2007) or the erosion of the communist electorate on the Left. This evolution may explain the sharply declining use of article 44.3 after the end of the 9th legislature.

A further explanatory element may be the development of 'fake amendments' as a filibustering technique. On particularly controversial bills the statutorily weak opposition may draft several thousands of computer-generated amendments in order to slow down the procedure, as happened in 2004 on the bill concerning the regional elections law. Under these circumstances article 44.3 loses some of its efficiency. This kind of filibustering is also a way of pushing the government to resorting to the much more controversial article 49.3.

3.3.2   Article 49.3: the institutionalization of government by decree

Much of what has been said about article 44.3 can be applied to the confidence vote procedure. The procedure of article 49.3 is considered to be one of the most powerful instruments at the disposal of contemporary democratic governments.[11] In the French context its use is extremely controversial and usually highly publicized, as most of time it is used on extremely salient issues only. Here again, the two most common uses tend either to ensure the coherence of an either fragile or divided majority, or to put an end to filibustering through opposition MPs.

The procedure is very different from the one outlined in article 44.3. While the latter forces MPs to vote on entire sections or on an entire text, taking into account only those amendments that suit the government, this procedure does not limit debate. In fact, speech time is not at all affected. Hence if this allows for shortening the procedure especially under conditions where opposition MPs produce thousands of 'fake' amendments, these will still have to be debated. Under article 49.3, once the government invokes its responsibility, all debate ends. If the opposition wishes to debate some part of the bill con-cerned, it has no choice but to file a motion of censure, which is of course much larger in scope than the bill itself. Moreover, those motions have – at best – a signalling effect for the opposition's voters. Huber rightly asserts that there is an 'electoral politics' dimension to this procedure that is lacking in the case of 44.3.

And it clearly is not as light-handed as has long been the case for the article 44.3. Even though, again, no motion of censure has succeeded since 1962, this clearly is a very significant measure and no prime minister appears to have been sufficiently confident in his own electoral success and/or the sup-port of 'his' MPs as to abuse the procedure. The only significant exception to this has been the 9th legislature, characterized by a minority Socialist gov-ernment. In particular, during his two-year term as prime minister, Michel Rocard accounted for 27 uses of article 49.3. This equates to roughly a third of the uses during the entire Fifth Republic.

Apart from the 9th legislature, there has been little variation. The main reason is that the procedure is highly contested not only by opposition MPs, but also by fellow MPs, who consider it disrespectful of Parliament. Hence, the use has become very rare in recent times, as the Figure 3.3 shows. But unlike for article 44.3, the movement is hardly significant enough to say anything meaningful concerning its variation over time. Finally, it should be noted that the recent constitutional amendment of 2008 has limited the use of 49.3 to one bill per session, and only to financial and social security bills.

3.3.3   Defining the law: articles 34 and 37

One of the most spectacular changes introduced by the Constitution of 1958 was a substantive definition of law and regulation. It opposes a purely for-mal definition of law, according to which laws are simply acts adopted by Parliament. It was meant to fight observed abuses of Parliament impinging on regulatory politics and thereby limiting executive competences under the Fourth Republic. In fact, both articles represent catalogues that list the areas subject to either law (art. 34) or regulation (art. 37). Contemporary observers and legal scholars believed this to be a major revolution.[12]

Yet, in fact, starting in the late 1970s, the Constitutional Council relaxed the distinction between law and regulation, favouring a more formal defini-tion of law. In different early rulings it made clear that article 34 could at best be complementary with more formal definitions of law, but by no means an exhaustive definition of law. This was most clearly put in the 1982 ruling *Blocage des prix et des revenues*. The conservative opposition had attacked a law on price control on the grounds that legislators had gone beyond the definition of article 34 and intruded into the area of regulation, reserved to the executive (Drago 2006: 47–8).

Hence, the Constitutional Council ruled that the distinctions and def-initions of articles 34 and 37 could not be considered mandatory. Put differently, the Council strengthened Parliament by adopting an essentially formal definition of law and by refusing to 'protect' the executive against potential intrusions by the legislator. The legal revolution that some observers expected in 1958 did simply not take place. Yet, as we will see, the use of empowerment statutes under article 38 may cause new problems in this area.

3.3.4 Article 38: the recent explosion of empowering statutes

Article 38 provides for the possibility of delegated legislative authority. It was originally thought of as a way of limiting the abuses of empowerment statutes that were commonplace under the Fourth Republic. Indeed, the authors of the Constitution granted constitutional status to the empowerment statute and hoped thereby to limit its use.[13] In fact, in his review of French politics, Huber concluded that 'decisions to delegate occur less than once a year, and generally – but not always – on issues that are not of widespread concern' (1998: 247). Things have changed since, however. There have been more empowerment statutes adopted in Parliament since 2000, than between 1958 and 2000. This also applies for the ordinances, i.e. individual acts, taken under each statute, and the so-called 'ratification acts' (not shown in Figure 3.3).

Legal scholars in France are very critical of this evolution. For instance, Gaudemet criticizes the disempowerment (*désinvestiture*) of the legislative (Gaudemet 2006: 65; also cf. Portelli 2007). Drago opposes the formal definition of law adopted by the Constitutional Council in its rulings on articles 34 and 37 to the relative indifference in the control of statutes adopted under article 38. It is true that the rulings of the Council on article 38 have been much less regarding of parliamentary sovereignty than those (quoted above) on the surveillance of articles 34 and 37. Drago goes as far as accusing the governments – for he refrains from blaming the Council – of being responsible for an increasing 'normative disorder' in the French legal system (Drago 2006: 53–5). The Senate itself has published a highly critical report (Sénat 2007). It is true, though, that some observers are less critical. For instance, Delvolvé argues that 'ordinances do not appear as measures that replace law, but as measures that complete the law, executive regulations rather than substitution laws' (2005: 913). The main justifications put forth in the concerned statutes are of administrative and legislative efficiency, but are also related to the increasingly specialized character of many areas of legislative action and, finally, to the transposition of EU law.

Yet, this evolution demands some further explanation. It is true that most of the empowerment statutes have dealt with rather technical matters. In particular, since the early 1980s two-thirds of those statutes have dealt with the transposition of French law to the 'Dom-Toms', i.e. the overseas territories, especially in the Caribbean. In fact this has become the normal procedure. As, for a variety of reasons, 'metropolitan' bills require to be adapted to local contexts, it has become commonplace to resort to enabling statutes.

On two occasions in the past five years, the government resorted to empowering statutes according to article 38 of the Constitution for European matters. The main justification was the consistently below-average implementation record of France. Hence in 2001, the government of Lionel Jospin requested an empowering statute from Parliament to reduce the French implementation gap. Three years later the government of Jean-Pierre Raffarin was granted the same rights. They adopted respectively 19 and 15 ordinances.[14]

In principle, the early rulings of the Constitutional Council forced the government to give a precise content to enabling statutes.[15] However, in later decisions, the Council has somewhat watered down the obligations of governments towards Parliament on enabling statutes (Verpeaux 2005: 4–5). In fact, several recent tendencies are rather interesting. First, the statutes are now often included in larger laws rather than specific enabling statutes. It is often just one article of a given bill that opens this possibility. Second, the periods covered by the statutes are increasing, now often reaching 18 and up to 24 months. The above mentioned Senate report (2007) complains about the lengthening of the periods covered. Third, under these conditions, it is more and more common that ordinances are adopted under statutes that were granted to previous governments. This has happened, for example, in the 'summer of ordinances' in 2005, when the Villepin government adopted a host of ordinances, many under enabling statutes adopted under the previous Raffarin government (Delvolvé, 2005: 917). Fourth, many recent bills are less and less precise in their wording, opening almost infinite possibilities for the ground covered by ordinances. Drago (2006: 51) underlines the significance of recent bills on 'legal simplification' (2 July 2003 and 9 December 2004) that fix very general limits to governmental action. In July 2005 a new statute was adopted enabling the government to take 'urgent measures with regard to employment'. Under these circumstances, the government obtains more or less a wild card on legislation with little or no input by MPs. Finally, this last element is even reinforced by the practice of ratifying ordinances – i.e. turning them into permanent laws – through different kinds of 'package bills'. Put differently, many recent ordinances have been ratified through amendments to otherwise unrelated bills, such as finance bills.

The actual function of article 38 has not been analysed in any detail, so far. We argue that article 38 is becoming a functional equivalent and even substitute for the procedures of article 44.3 and, to a lesser extent, 49.3. The usual justifications are certainly important: European integration and the need to adapt legislation for the overseas departments are clearly important explanations for the increase in empowerment statutes. Yet this is certainly not the whole story. Looking again at Figure 3.3, we notice that the use of article 44.3 has diminished. We have argued earlier that this may be due to the development of effective filibustering. Yet it may also be due to the overall evolution of semi-presidential government in France. As we have shown earlier, as governments have become less large and diverse, they have been more dependent on the president, leading to higher ministerial volatility and inexperience in the main portfolios.

The counterpart of this effect on the instruments of executive power may result in increase of the use of article 38. If we accept Huber's thesis, that article 44.3 serves primarily to preserve extra-parliamentary bargains (1996), this explanation appears to be straightforward. As the two-camp party system slowly transforms into a two-party system, preserving extra-parliamentary bargains becomes increasingly superfluous or secondary. If you add the larger context of increasing demands towards the legislative procedure, e.g. due to the EU (cf. Grossman and Sauger 2007), suddenly article 38 appears to be a much more interesting option than before. In order to test this hypothesis it would be necessary to regress the classification of the party system and, for example, the workloads due to the EU against the relative use of articles 44.3 and 38. While going beyond the scope of this contribution, this clearly lays out directions for future research.

3.4 Conclusions

The evolution of executive politics under the Fifth Republic can be broken down into several major tendencies. Some elements have remained very stable, while others have changed rather rapidly. In this contribution we have analysed the major changes looking at different data both on the composition and on the practice of government under the Fifth Republic.

We showed that there is a clear pro-presidential bias in the institutional setting of the Fifth Republic. While this is well-known, we show that this institutional bias has been reinforced through the evolution of party politics and the role of the media during the Fifth Republic. In particular we stressed that while cabinet turnover has stayed more or less stable, this is not true for cabinet or portfolio experience, which has significantly declined over time.

The second half of the chapter looks at the instruments of executive authority and their evolution over time. We show that the much-debated package vote and confidence vote procedures are no longer as central as they used to be. Instead the long-forgotten or rather marginal empowerment statutes have become a central feature of French political-institutional life.

We argue that this may be explained by reasons related to the explanation of turnover and experience. Indeed, one may say that as political life is increasingly bi-partisan, the fundamental aim of article 44.3, i.e. preserving extra-parliamentary bargains, has become obsolete. In a context of increasingly complex policy-making, article 38 becomes a more interesting option.

All in all, then, while no major institutional change has taken place, some substantial changes in the institutional practice have changed the face of the Fifth Republic. It has become increasingly presidentialist and executive dominance is exerted through new instruments. Moreover, the five-year mandate inaugurated in 2002 may durably affect the party system. Finally, the proposals put forth by the 'Comité Balladur' on constitutional reform may make the Fifth Republic even more presidential (Balladur 2007). Yet it remains to be seen which of the proposed changes will actually be implemented, as major representatives of the parliamentary majority have voiced criticism.

Notes

1. There is, however, a recent test of the original Katz and Mair argument on cartel parties. Cf. Sauger (2007a).
2. 19 with the current prime minister, François Fillon, and counting Jacques Chirac twice, since he had two terms starting in 1976 and 1986.
3. 616 days on average (excluding governments bridging elections), 556 excluding cohabitation.
4. Of course, the last presidential election generated much speculation about what would have happened if François Bayrou, who came only third in the first round, had managed to get into the second round, which in that case he may have won, according to many prospective polls.
5. The rate of abstention was 69.8 per cent, which somewhat weakens any argument of the French being either in favour or against cohabitation.
6. Ben Clift provides a complete summary of the role of the media in French electoral campaigns and its evolution over time (Clift 2005).
7. Data for Figures 3.1 and 3.2 have been collected and formatted by the author.
8. Unlike Huber and Martinez-Gallardo, however, we have not included mandates during the Fourth Republic. Put differently, everybody starts with *no* experience in 1958. In their table Huber and Martinez-Gallardo show that a large fraction of the personnel of the early Fifth Republic had already served under Fourth Republic (Huber and Martinez-Gallardo 2004: 36).
9. In the parliamentary elections of 1973 the Gaullists had obtained 36.6 per cent of the votes (Gaullists and allies), as opposed to 16.7 for the group (*Réformateurs modérés*) of the future president, Valéry Giscard d'Estaing.
10. In fact, in a famous contribution, François Mitterrand accused de Gaulle in 1964 of allowing for a 'permanent *coup d'Etat*'. Yet, once president, he maintained a certain ambiguity on his own position towards article 16, even if he finally proposed to abolish it in 1993.
11. Article 49.3 reads: 'The Prime Minister may, after deliberation by the Council of Ministers, make the passing of a bill and issue of the Government's responsibility before the National Assembly. In that event, the bill shall be considered adopted unless a motion of censure, introduced within the subsequent twenty-four hours, is carried as provided in the preceding paragraph.'
12. For a more pragmatic stance, see Chapus, quoted in Quermonne (1987: 369).
13. The wording of article 38 is very restrictive:
    > In order to carry out its programme, the Government may ask Parliament for authorization, for a limited period, to take measures by ordinance that are normally a matter for statute. Ordinances shall be issued in the Council of Ministers, after consultation with the Conseil d'État. They shall come into

force upon publication, but shall lapse if the bill to ratify them is not laid before Parliament before the date set by the enabling Act.

At the end of the period referred to in the first paragraph of this article, ordinances may be amended only by an Act of Parliament in those areas which are matters for statute.

14. An interesting feature concerns the role of cohabitation for the use of empowerment statutes. Ordinances under article 38 are adopted by the Council of Ministers, which is presided over by the president of the Republic – even under cohabitation. In March 1986, shortly after being designated prime minister, Jacques Chirac announced the adoption of an empowerment statute under article 38. President François Mitterrand immediately declared that he would not sign an ordinance abolishing the administrative authorization for layoffs. In April, he refused to sign another ordinance concerning certain privatizations and, finally, he also opposed an ordinance regarding the reorganization of electoral constituencies. There was a much debate on whether the president was entitled to refuse his signature. Most legal scholars – and, of course, Prime Minister Chirac – considered that Mitterrand exceeded his powers. Yet, the government did not try to challenge his decision and eventually adopted the concerned ordinances as regular parliamentary acts (Chagnollaud 2005: 239; Chevallier et al. 2004: 335–7). The experience of 1986 apparently marked the successors of Jacques Chirac, since Edouard Balladur, prime minister during the second cohabitation (1993–95) did not even try to adopt ordinances of empowerment statutes. However, this fear was apparently dissipated during the third cohabitation, as the Jospin government (1997–2002) played a key role in the extraordinary increase of both statutes and ordinances.

15. Decision no. 76-72DC, 12 January, 1977.

Bibliography

Balladur, E. (2007). *Une Ve République plus démocratique*. Paris: Comité de réflexion et de proposition sur la modernisation et le rééquilibrage des institutions de la Ve République.

Bergounioux, A. and Grunberg, G. (2005). *L'ambition et le remords : les socialistes français et le pouvoir: 1905–2005*. Paris: Fayard.

Blyth, M. and Katz, R.S. (2005). 'From catch-all politics to cartelisation: the political economy of the cartel party'. *West European politics,* 28(1), 33–60.

Boyer-Mérentier, C. (1996). *Les ordonnances de l'article 38 de la Constitution du 4 octobre 1958*. Paris: Economica/Presses Universitaires d'Aix-Marseille.

Carcassone, G. (1994). 'Ce que fait Matignon'. *Pouvoirs* (68), 31–44.

Chagnollaud, D. (2005). *Droit constitutionnel contemporain*. Paris: Dalloz.

Chevallier, J.-J., Carcassone, G. and Duhamel, O. (2004). *La Ve République 1958–2004: histoire des institutions et des régimes politiques de la France* (11 edn). Paris: Armand Colin.

Clift, B. (2005). 'Dyarchic Presidentialization in a Presidentialized Polity: The French Fifth Republic'. In P. Webb and T. Poguntke (eds), *The Presidentialization of Politics – A Comparative Study of Modern Democracies*. Oxford: Oxford University Press, pp. 219–43.

Conley, R.-S. (2007). 'Presidential republics and divided government: lawmaking and executive politics in the United States and France'. *Political Science Quarterly*, 122(2), 257–85.

Delvolvé, P. (2005). 'Déclin ou renouveau de la lois? L'été des ordonnances'. *Revue Française de Droit Administratif,* 909–26.

Drago, G. (2006). 'Le Conseil constitutionnel, la compétence du législateur et le désordre normatif'. *Revue de droit public* (1), 45–64.

Duhamel, O. (2003). *Le pouvoir politque en France* (5 edn). Paris: Seuil.

Duverger, M. (1992). *Les partis politiques.* Paris: Seuil.

Elgie, R. (1999). *Semi-presidentialism in Europe.* Oxford: Oxford University Press.

Ellis, R.J. (1994). *Presidential Lightning Rods: The Politics of Blame Avoidance.* Lawrence: University Press of Kansas.

Gaudemet, Y. (2006). 'La loi administrative'. *Revue de droit public* (1), 65–84.

Grossman, E. and Sauger, N. (2007). 'Political institutions under stress? Assessing the impact of European Integration on French political institutions'. *Journal of European Public Policy,* 14(7), 1117–34.

Grossman, E. and Saurugger, S. (2006). 'Les groupes d'intérêt au secours de la démocratie?' *Revue française de Science politique,* 56(2), 299–322.

Grunberg, G. and Haegel, F. (2007). *La France vers le bipartisme? La présidentialisation du PS et de l'UMP.* Paris: Presses de Sciences Po.

Huber, J.D. (1996). *Rationalizing Parliament. Legislative Institutions and Party Politics in France.* New York: Cambridge University Press.

Huber, J.D. (1998). 'Executive decree authority in France'. In: J.M. Cary and M.S. Shugart (eds), *Executive Decree Authority.* Cambridge: Cambridge University Press, pp. 233–53.

Huber, J.D. and Martinez-Gallardo, C. (2004). 'Cabinet instability and the accumulation of experience: The French Fourth and Fifth Republics in comparative perspective. *British Journal of Political Science,* 34(1), 27–48.

Portelli, H. (2007). 'Les ordonnances: les raisons d'une dérive'. *Droits* (44), 3–8.

Quermonne, J.-L. (1987). *Le gouvernement de la France sous la Ve République* (5 edn). Paris: Dalloz.

Sauger, N. (2007a). 'L'UDF et la création de l'UMP: une logique de décartellisation?' In: Y. Aucante and A. Dézé (eds), *La transformations des systèmes de partis en Europe.* Paris: Presses de Sciences Po.

Sauger, N. (2007b). 'Un système électoral vecteur d'instabilité?' In F. Haegel (ed.), *Partis politiques et système partisan en France.* Paris: Presses de Sciences Po, pp. 359–90.

Sénat (2007). *Les ordonnances. Bilan au 31 décembre 2006.* Paris: Notes de synthèse du service des études juridiques du Sénat.

Shugart, M.S. (2005). 'Semi-presidential systems: dual executive and mixed authority patterns'. *French Politics,* 3(3), 323–51.

Skach, C. (2007). 'The "newest" separation of powers: semipresidentialism'. *International Journal of Constitutional Law,* 5(1), 93–121.

Vedel, G. (1997). 'Réformer les institutions… Regard rétrospectif sur deux commissions'. *Revue Française de Science Politique,* 47(3–4), 313–39.

Verpeaux, M. (2005). 'Les ordonnances de l'article 38 ou les fluctuations contrôlées de la répartition des compétences entre la loi et le règlement'. *Cahiers du Conseil constitutionnel* (19), 1–8.

Weaver, R.K. (1986). 'The politics of blame avoidance'. *Journal of Public Policy,* 6(4), 371–98.

4
Gone with the Wind? The National Assembly under the Fifth Republic

Eric Kerrouche

Whether one speaks in terms of 'decline' (Vandendriessche 2001), 'weakening' (Pezant 1977), 'domestication' (Lascombes 1997), 'subordination' (Chagnollaud 2001), or even 'crisis' (Boudant 1992), there is no lack of vocabulary to lament the role and status of the National Assembly provided for by the 1958 Constitution. Indeed, almost as soon as its provisions were put in place, commentators were already insisting on the fact that Parliament had been subordinated to the dictates of an all-powerful executive body. France went from a position in which the omnipotence of Parliament under the Third and Fourth Republics, so harshly criticized for encouraging chronic political instability and for depriving the executive of the ways and means of doing its job, was suddenly replaced by a situation in which the weakness of the French chambers and their incapacity to play their role to the full was decried. The Constitutional revision of 1962, which enabled the president of the Republic to be elected by direct universal suffrage, and the *fait majoritaire*, the concordance between the political leaning of the president with that of the majority in the National Assembly combined, to reinforce the impression of a weakened, almost useless legislative power, an impression borne out by the question that has become so commonplace: 'What use is Parliament?' (Chandernagor 1967). It seems that Parliament is no longer able to fulfil the three main functions to which any parliamentary institution should be devoted – legislating, controlling, and informing (Chatenet 1992). This criticism does not date from the creation of the Fifth Republic; in point of fact, the birth of the parliamentary system in France was accompanied by strong opposition and destabilizing criticism of all sorts.[1] But, ever since 1958, this criticism has reached new heights.

The 'declassification' of the National Assembly as the main role-player in the legislative process is even more clear when international comparisons are made.[2] Although comparative parliamentary studies are fraught with methodological pitfalls, researchers in this field are unanimous in classifying France's parliament as among the weakest, whether this be in the light of the influence it exerts over legislative production or as regards its ability to control the government (Best and Cotta 2000; Blondel 1973; Colliard 1978; Loewenberg and Kim 1978; Norton 1998). This situation has, in turn, affected academic studies on the National Assembly. While several hundred researchers devote their time and attention to studies on the American Congress, the French parliament fails to arouse much interest among political scientists, and its apparently inherent weakness seems so unambiguous that few researchers wish to pursue the question further. It almost seems nowadays as if politics in France happens on the margins – or outside the realm even – of this historically-entrenched institution of the French Republic. Even the most basic data on either the activity of the French chambers or the identity of their members is lacking. With the exception of a recent work (Costa and Kerrouche 2007), political scientists have published nothing of much scientific worth on the National Assembly or MPs for the last 20-odd years,[3] and what is available is often out of date or incomplete (Kerrouche 2004). The situation is even worse concerning the Senate. This has led to a number of important changes being neglected – the constitutional reform of 1995 for instance – despite the Senate having played a major role in partially transforming how the National Assembly functions. Above all, the work effectively carried out by MPs is seldom taken into consideration, which has had a very negative impact on how Parliament is regarded.

The aim of this chapter is to show that, even though a number of different factors have converged to challenge the legislative role of Parliament in the Fifth Republic, MPs do still play a key role in the French political system.

4.1   Has the French Parliament been dethroned?

The chapters by Elgie and Grossmann in this work eloquently illustrate how the government holds sway over the legislative process of Parliament, thus limiting MPs' scope for action and defining the institutional relations between government and Parliament under the Fifth Republic to the great detriment of the latter (Morin 1986; Latour 2000). The government is armed with constitutional power and is protected by its majority in the Assembly, thus depriving Parliament of its role as locus of legislative power and reducing its scope to that of a simple venue for raising contemporary problems and airing possible solutions. Parliament in this light is merely a centre for bureaucracy, with limited means to boot, where only a number of specialized MPs and high-ranking civil servants count. This is the result of two concomitant developments. First, the way in which power is exercised in France has changed greatly and this, in turn, has had a marked impact on Parliament. Secondly, this change was to take place within the institutional framework – largely unfavourable to legislative power – of the Fifth Republic.

4.2   The Assembly as a collateral victim of new modes of governance...

Globally, the National Assembly has borne the brunt of three concomitant changes: the rise to power of the executive, characteriztic of de Gaulle's republican vision; changes in new modes of governance; and the rise of new forms of law.

The Constitution set up under Charles de Gaulle was to refocus the exercise of power around the executive body (Frears 1990). In the postwar period, the 'modernizing' ideal embodied by de Gaulle, combined with his Caesarism, made serious inroads into Parliament's role in producing norms and, consequently, making public policy. In the 1960s, the myth of a 'rational' government reigned supreme and this, along with the continuous reinforcement of the role played by top civil servants in all positions of power in the state, meant that decision-making power lay within the immediate sphere of the government (ministries, major State administration departments, leading public companies) (Chagnollaud 1991; Dulong 1997). This refocusing process took place at a time when the political leaning of the president coincided with that of the majority in Parliament, giving rise to the *fait majoritaire*, all of which only served to further reinforce the grip of the executive. This configuration came into play in the mid-1960s and only three 'cohabitations'[4] were to disturb its tranquil supremacy – from 1985 to 1987, from 1993 to 1995 and, finally, from 1997 to 2002 (see Table 4.1).

At one and the same time, the history of the Fifth Republic also became enmeshed with changing modes of governance and the rise of new players on the political scene. The roles played by administrations, economic and financial lobbies, the recently-won clout of different federations (trade unions, new social movements), or indeed of the media, offset the generally accepted conception of Parliament as a privileged place for discussion and debate. Interestingly, the analysis of public policies has led to an increased number of hypotheses and theories concerning a number of new forms of regulation that remove political practice even further from the model of parliamentary democracy: dispersal of authority, multi-level governance, the increasing intervention of private players in public policy, the multiplication of debating arenas, the contractualization of public policy, the transversality of stakes, the marked attenuation of responsibilities, the deterritorialization of exchanges, the development of transnational links, and so on. The watershed of neoliberalism, globalization and the opening-up of decision-making processes to a variety of role-players thus spell out the end of central political institutions, including Parliament. In a polycentric world, Parliament is no longer in a position in to exercise unilateral control over the machinery of public policy-making. Parliament functions increasingly as a partner, in charge of co-ordinating a range of interests and judicial control, in a decision-making process that has become increasingly open and complex.

Table 4.1 Majorities and minorities in the French National Assembly, 1967–2007[a]

Legislature	'Left'			'Right'									Others	NAS	CS	AM
	PC/ PCR	FGD SPSR GPS	RCV	PDM	RDS/ UC	UC/ UDC	UDF/ NC	RI	UDR/ RPR/ UMP	RL	DL	FN				
III 04/67-05/68	73	121	''	41	''	''	''	42[b]	201	''	''	''	9	487	243	244
IV 11/68-04/73	34	57	''	33	''	''	''	61	293	''	''	''	9	487	354	244
V 04/73-04/78	73	102	''	''	51	''	''	55	183	''	''	''	16	491	238	246
VI 04/78-05/81	86	113	''	''	''	''	119	''	155	''	''	''	15	491	274	246
VII 07/81-04/86	44	285	''	''	''	''	62	''	88	''	''	''	12	491	329	246
VIII 04/86-05/88	35	212	''	''	''	''	131	''	155	''	''	''	9	577	286	289
IX 06/88-03/93	25	275	''	''	''	41	90**	''	130	''	''	35	12	577	275	289
X 03/93-03/97	23	57	''	''	''	''	215	''	257	23	''	''	5	577	495	289
XI 06/97-06/02	35	252	33	''	''	''	70	''	137	''	44	''	6	577	320	289
XII 06/02-06/07	21	141	''	''	''	''	29	''	365	''	''	''	21	577	394	289
XIII 06/07	24	187	''	''	''	''	20	''	311	''	''	''	8	577	331	289

Notes: NAS = National Assembly seats/CS = Coalition seats/AM = Absolute majority.
[a]For each main tendency, Left and Right, some columns contain more than one acronym because the party in question experimented with several names during the period under consideration. The initials for the Left forces are: PC, Parti communiste (Communist Party); PS, Parti socialiste (Socialist Party), the heir of FGDS (Fédération de la gauche démocrate et socialiste) and PSRG (Parti socialiste et radicaux de gauche); RCV, Radical, citoyen, Verts (which includes the French Greens). For the Centre and Right forces: PDM, Progrès et démocratie moderne (Centre-Right); UDF, Union pour la démocratie française (Centre-Right) which is the heir to RI (Républicains indépendants); UDC = Union du centre (centre-right, which is a result of the fragmentation of the UDF); RL, République et Liberté (Centre-Right); RPR, Rassemblement pour la République (Right) now UMP (Union pour un mouvement populaire); FN = Front National (Extreme Right); the 'Others' category is made up of MPs who do not belong to any party. The overall total of MPs may be different from the official number of seats in the National Assembly since some seats are sometimes left unoccupied for a variety of reasons (promotion to ministerial office, resignation, death and renewal of the seat, etc.).
[b]The grey cells depict the coalition in power. Dark grey represents the core coalition and light grey its temporary allies.

This questioning of how Parliament's role should be in the law-making process is also a result of the new powers devolved to the constitutional judge in France (cf. the chapter on this subject by Brouard). Although this jurisprudence has globally contributed to the extension of Parliament's legislative field of competence, it has not contested the grip that government has on the legislative process. At the same time, the general scope of constitutional control has been constantly increased. Since 1971 the constitutional judge has extended conformity control, provided for in article 61.2 of the Constitution, to include the content of laws, thus depriving Parliament of its sovereignty in the legislative sphere. The constitutional judge has also censured some laws with respect to stipulations outside the strict limits of the Constitution itself, as provided for in the foreword to the Constitution of 1946. Finally, the constitutional revision of 1974, which allows 60 MPs or senators to appeal to the *Conseil Constitutionnel* to contest the conformity of a law before it is promulgated, has led to a systematization of the control process being employed by opposition MPs who are behind 95 per cent of the cases referred to that body.

Lastly, and even more pervasively, the authority embodied in a law finds itself being whittled away by the increased number of other forms of law, whether this is through decrees imposed by the executive, local authority ordinances or European norms being directly or indirectly applied to EU member states. The 'displacement' of legislative power in favour of the authority of the EU or local councils, bolstered by new laws on decentralization and the development of inter-governmental relations, amplifies the phenomenon of loss of centrality affecting the legislative power in France. European construction, in particular, soon proved to be a field in which Parliament's influence would be strictly limited, even though article 88.4 of the Constitution obliges the government to submit all EU-related bills of a legislative nature to Parliament. Moreover, all these changes regarding the exercise of legislative competence have been compounded by the restrictive conditions applied to this self-same exercise.

4.3 ... and the institutional and regulatory machinery of the Fifth Republic

In practice, some of the stipulations of the Constitution and those emanating directly from the regulations of the National Assembly – as well as the Senate – jointly act to weaken the legislative role of Parliament. These dispositions concern the status accorded to the law within the text of the Constitution itself, procedures relating to rationalized parliamentarianism, as well as governmental control of the law-making agenda.

The first limitation is as symbolic as it is concrete. The 1958 Constitution was to challenge the central character of law-making. It was the 1958 Constitutional text which now attributed competence to Parliament – in complete contrast to what had previously prevailed during the Third and Fourth Republics – thereby challenging the central character of law. Over and beyond this, the domain of the law is itself defined by the Constitution (article 34), which also provides for an autonomous regulatory power parallel to that of Parliament (article 37). In concrete terms, this means that the principle laid down at the beginning of article 34 (Parliament votes the law) comes up against the stumbling block not only of article 38, authorizing the government to legislate using empowering statutes, but also of articles 3 and 11, which stipulate that the law may equally emanate from the people, via a referendum.

Measures concerning rationalized parliamentarianism find their expression in two specific articles of the French Constitution. Article 49.3, relating to the question of confidence, allows the government to oblige the National Assembly to make a clear choice – either voting for a law or voting to reject it. Article 49.3 is often resorted to along with article 45, which provides a way of getting round Senate opposition to a bill by allowing the National Assembly to have the last word (Foucher 1981).[5] As for article 44.3, it authorizes the government to impose a package vote on the entirety of a bill, thus excluding all possibility of Parliament then amending the law (Huber 1996). In practice, four other measures also limit the legislative power of MPs: article 40 stipulates that all propositions and amendments from MPs leading to a decrease in public resources, or to an increase in public payloads, are precluded;[6] article 41 allows the government to oppose a bill or amendment which pertains to regulation and not to law (art. 34 and 38); article 44.2 allows the government to refuse even to examine an amendment if it has not first been submitted to the competent parliamentary commission; finally, article 45.3 provides that no amendment to a negotiated text written by a commission with equal representation on both sides is to be accepted without prior governmental agreement, while the government itself could amend this document freely, at least until a recent limit to this right was established by the *Conseil Constitutionnel*.[7] All these measures allow artificial minority governments that are out of step with the legislative body to remain in power, as was the case during the 9th Legislature, thereby further relativizing the role of national representation in France.[8] This all boils down to a state of affairs in which Parliament is no longer in a position to really question or challenge governmental power. As if this battery of measures were not enough, other less visible obstacles appear in the Constitution or chamber regulations which impose even further restrictions on the possibility for MPs to intervene.[9] Both chambers are regulated by very strict organizational constraints, concerning for instance the number of parliamentary commissions (limited to six by article 43 of the Constitution) (Duprat 1996), the marginalization of enquiry or control commissions, or the ban on voting resolutions or petitions, which formed one of the key features of the two preceding Republics.

Even more fundamentally, the subordination of the National Assembly is shown by the way government wields control over the legislative calendar, in accordance with article 28. Until 1995 there were two parliamentary sessions – one lasting 80 days and the second less than 90 days.[10] Since 4 August 1995 there is now only one session, with a maximum length of 120 days. There are also internal time limits imposed on specific sectors of parliamentary activity. For example, article 47 of the constitution sets a time limit of 70 days for voting on the budget. Article 47.1 fixes a time limit of 50 days for voting on the social security budget. So not only is the parliamentary calendar governed by strict time limits, neither the National Assembly nor the Senate has control over their agenda, or over the timetabling of each parliamentary session. Article 48.1 of the Constitution stipulates that government bills have priority over those of Private Members. Although the Conference of Presidents is charged with organizing the timetable for each examination of a new law, the government nevertheless maintains its control over the legislative calendar since it can extend the National Assembly's scheduled deadline by permitting extra days for further debate. Moreover, the constitutional judge has defended the prerogatives of governmental control of the legislative agenda by allowing the government to make changes to the calendar scheduled by the Conference of Presidents and allowing it to introduce a new bill on the floor. Finally, according to the terms of article 45.3, the government may call upon the Conference Committee to settle a difference between the Senate and the National Assembly after only two readings in each chamber which means that the government is able to stop a Private Member's bill simply by not calling a conference committee. Other measures complete this array and put even further constraints on the legislative timetable. For instance, article 100.5 of the regulations of the National Assembly gives priority to discussion of government and commission amendments, and article 100.7 limits speeches in the chamber, on amendments other than those suggested by the government, to a maximum of five minutes. Conversely the government is not subject to constraints as regards extending the legislative process, since it can simply use article 29 which allows members of the parliamentary majority and the prime minister to call a special session.[11] In other words, it seems clear that if the main characteriztic of parliamentary time is that it is in short supply, MPs have no control over this state of affairs (Couderc 1981).

This complex network of constitutional constraints leads to dramatic results, as the data on legislative activity in France demonstrates. One example suffices to measure the full extent of this: under the 11th legislature (June 1997–June 2002), there were 784 governmental bills and 5103 Private Members' bills.[12] However, of the 432 laws promulgated during this period, 351 stemmed from the former and just 81 from the latter. Only 1.6 per cent of Private Members' bills were adopted compared with 45 per cent of governmental bills. Moreover, the laws were generally voted with very few modifications, as Figure 4.1 illustrates. Even though these figures include

66

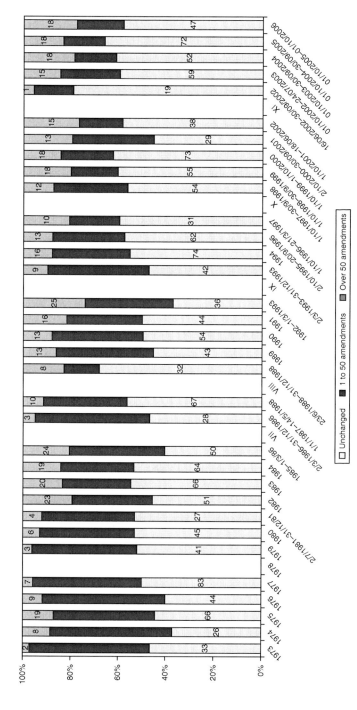

Figure 4.1 Proportion of modification of laws by amendments in France 1973–2006

ratification laws (and these, it must be borne in mind, may not be modified) it is still apparent that the government's control over the elaboration of legislation is substantial.[13]

4.4 The National Assembly, an institution in the process of becoming?

This picture of French institutional power relations seemingly condemns the National Assembly both in the role it is assigned, and in its capacity for action. However, some nuances to this rather stark appreciation of the facts may be highlighted. First, it should be recalled that the theme of lost parliamentary prestige (Carcassonne 1989) refers to a debatable notion, that of a traditional parliament presenting and voting on laws in an autonomous fashion and wielding control over the government. Such a presentation, inherited from an idealized vision of the English system was, in fact, only to be seen for a very few decades (Dorey 2004). Secondly, it is not necessarily true that the array of procedures described above would have the same impact in a system characterized by a clear separation of incessantly conflicting powers as it would in one characterized by the *fait majoritaire*, which establishes a distinction between the executive – legislative majority on the one hand and the opposition in the National Assembly on the other. Thus it is that the position of the National Assembly and its members has evolved down the years and has entrenched, or even accentuated, the indirect influence MPs have over legislative processes.

4.5 The new guise of legislative power

Two different types of factors came together to restore the National Assembly to some of its former glory: the institutions own, natural *sui generis* evolution and the effect of important constitutional reform which came into being in 1995.

Like all chambers in Western democracies, the National Assembly gradually obtained the means for handling the increasing complexity of public policy-making and addressing the difficulty of making sound decisions in areas where science and technology play key parts. A number of bodies were set up to bolster the control of Parliament over the executive and to keep MPs well informed. In this respect, an increasing number of offices, delegations and evaluation projects have appeared, especially since the late 1990s.[14]

Yet the most important changes have been seen in the constantly evolving means made available to MPs since 1958 (Gibel 1981). Over and above the improvements in their personal benefits (salary, pensions), material means, such as computers provided since 1986, have been afforded them, and this has had a very beneficial effect on how efficient they are in their parliamentary work. The most spectacular change came in the form of the staff they may now employ. From 1975 onwards MPs have been able to choose and employ a parliamentary assistant to support them in their work at the National Assembly and, in 1979, a second post was accorded to help them more specifically in their constituency work. Today, after successive reclamations, MPs now have access to an 'allowance' of 8859 Euros per month, which allows them to recruit up to five assistants.[15] These changes have had a profound effect on the way MPs exercise office. Formerly, they were obliged to 'improvise', but they now have a real team working with them, often composed of well-qualified individuals who have become professionals in this sphere (Fretel and Meimon 2005). These means may seem insignificant when compared with those available to MPs in other democracies, but they do allow French MPs to exercise true autonomy and work effectively over the whole area of their constituency.

The second significant change is linked to the 1995 Constitutional Reforms. The first, adopted on 31 July 1995, has modified the time constraint on parliamentary activity stipulated in article 28 of the National Assembly regulations, with one nine-month ordinary parliamentary session (from October to June) replacing two ordinary sessions of three months. The maximum authorized duration of the session is 120 days. One of the explicit motives for these organizational changes was to allow better control of government by means of a longer parliamentary session and by the inclusion of a compulsory session of 'Questions to the Government' each week (art 48.2). The same article also introduces one parliamentary reserved session (or '*niche parlementaire*') per month where priority is given to Private Members' bills.

At the end of 1995, a second constitutional reform took place. The way in which the social security system is financed and: above all, its effective financing having become a major stake, the Constitution stipulates that, from 1995 onwards, 'Parliament votes bills determining the financing of the social security system'. It is equally important to point out that the 1995 changes also gave France's assemblies a stronger role in scrutinizing both government and EU policies.

The National Assembly and the Senate each saw the scope of their formal competences extended. The Constitutional Revision of 19 February 1996 entrusted them with the management of social accounts, a role formerly handled jointly by the social partners (trade unions and employers) and the state. The chambers also vote laws on financing and voice their opinion on provisional revenues.

Although little research has been carried out into the effects of these reforms, Brouard has, nonetheless, provided a picture of contrasting consequences (Brouard 2005). In what concerns the switch to a single session, he shows the limited impact this was to have, while indicating that this is certainly not true in the case of parliamentary reserved sessions (or '*niches parlementaires*'). Although one might have expected that this measure, however much it encourages bills to be brought before the Assembly, would have had limited impact because of the very low number of texts presented by the government, the figures bear witness to a noticeable evolution – even if one must remain cautious as to the relative importance of this text or its real origin. Between 1969 and 1995 the average number of bills of non-governmental origin was 13.7 per year (12.8 between 1981 and 1995). Between 1997 and 2003 this figure reached 16.3. This is all the more surprising as over the same period of time the actual number of bills adopted dropped considerably: between 1997 and 2003 71 laws were adopted on average (against 86.6 between 1981 and 1995). The proportion of laws of parliamentary origin thus rose from 15.8 per cent between 1969 and 1995 to 24.6 per cent between 1997 and 2003. It seems reasonably clear that this rise is an expression of the combined effect of the new parliamentary reserved session with the more traditional 'complementary agenda', which allows Parliament to debate a text when the normal agenda has been exhausted yet some time still remains for Parliamentary work.

4.6   Reinforcing MPs' capacity for indirect influence

Despite some differences of opinion and vision, most MPs have a good grasp of the constraints weighing down on their legislative activities (Costa and Kerrouche 2007). Yet this does not therefore mean that their activity is null and void. On the one hand, MPs generally use the whole array of means made available to them, whatever the level of constraint weighing on these, as even the very possibility of initiating or amending a law is extremely restricted in France (Mattson 1995). On the other hand, MPs sometimes play an essential role in the legislative machinery, finding themselves at the crux of the push and shove of conflicting political powers. Equally, new means are in the course of being implemented.

The data available for France indicates that two main currents are at work as regards the means of control available to MPs. Left-wing and right-wing MPs do not use these means in the same ways. Left-wingers prefer the technique that involves proposing a law, while right-wingers mostly use the device of amendments. As Figure 4.2 shows, although these two techniques are the sole means available to the opposition to make their voice heard, the use of amendments only starts to become a major weapon from 1981 onwards. In other words, from this date on, amendments became a key tool for minority MPs, enabling them to remain part of the legislative process, either by slowing that process down or by using the amendments to air their opinions on the public stage and manifest their opposition to the key projects of the government in office (as was seen in the attempt to reform the social security system under the Juppé government of 1995–97).

A closer look at the total number of amendments set forward by the government and commissions illustrates the usefulness of this tool for MPs. Table 4.2 reveals first that only a minority of laws go on to be adopted without

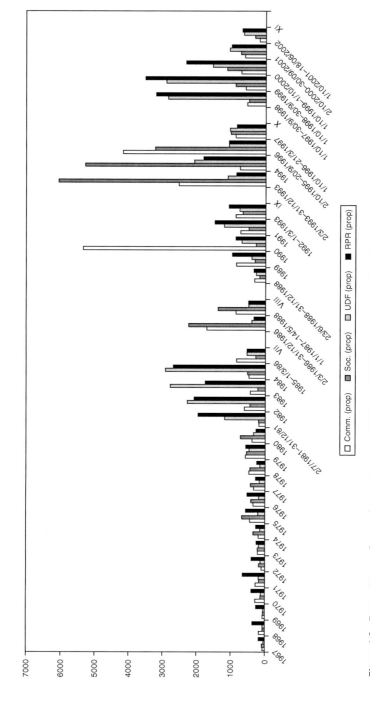

Figure 4.2 Propositions of amendments between 1967 and 2002 by the main political groups

Notes: For the Communists (Comm., Left), Socialists (Soc., Left), UDF (UDF, Centre-Right) and RPR (RPR, Right).

Table 4.2   Adopted amendments and amendment proposals in committees

Year	N° of Gvt amendments	N° of Adopted Gvt amendments	Ratio (%)	N° of Committee amendments	N° of adopted Committee amendments	Ratio (%)
1967	127	110	86.6	402	297	73.9
1968	147	134	91.2	487	332	68.2
1969	118	98	83.1	340	215	63.2
1970	263	212	80.6	1085	804	74.1
1971	417	336	80.6	1456	1005	69.0
1972	384	324	84.4	1057	685	64.8
1973	144	122	84.7	589	316	53.7
1974	189	160	84.7	687	416	60.6
1975	401	299	74.6	1508	957	63.5
1976	315	238	75.6	1166	755	64.8
1977	415	346	83.4	1261	879	69.7
1978	284	239	84.2	786	536	68.2
1979	339	269	79.4	884	611	69.1
1980	550	394	71.6	906	618	68.2
1981	457	317	69.4	1003	856	85.3
1982	1196	1051	87.9	3133	2603	83.1
1983	734	628	85.6	2942	2625	89.2
1984	780	676	86.7	2640	2323	88.0
1985	630	568	90.2	2304	2082	90.4
1986	295	271	91.9	614	409	66.6
1987	404	357	88.4	990	776	78.4
1988	318	273	85.8	900	691	76.8
1989	463	396	85.5	1788	1477	82.6
1990	515	438	85.0	1700	1467	86.3
1991	834	710	85.1	2807	2362	84.1
1992	1077	845	78.5	2769	2336	84.4
1993	422	332	78.7	1162	746	64.2
1994	575	474	82.4	1684	1195	71.0
1995–1996	476	397	83.4	1589	1173	73.8
1996–1997	402	329	81.8	1531	1047	68.4
1997–1998	552	446	80.8	2053	1745	85.0
1998–1999	596	502	84.2	2704	2317	85.7
1999–2000	653	581	89.0	3198	2773	86.7
2000–2001	844	705	83.5	2675	2402	89.8
2001–2002	449	410	91.3	1675	1476	88.1
2002–2003	440	400	90.8	2283	1934	83.0
2003–2004	701	613	87.4	2701	2127	78.7
2004–2005	547	481	87.9	2070	1583	76.5
2005–2006	388	345	88.9	2010	1654	82.3

amendments (only 680 out of 2227 laws were not amended between 1969 and 2003). Secondly, as was to be expected, government amendments are few in number compared with the total number of amendments set forward. Between 1969 and 2003, 6.9 per cent of the 245 311 amendments were

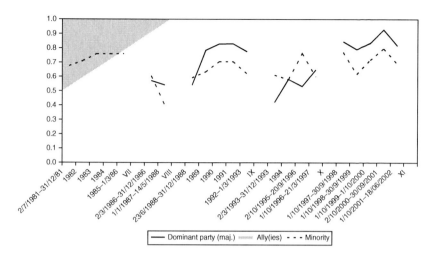

Figure 4.3   Rate of approval of amendments

introduced by the government. What is more surprising is that only 19.5 per cent of them were adopted. Last but not least, the success rate of government amendments from 1967 until 2007 (84%) is not so far to that of amendments originating from commissions (79.6%). However, this percentage is not applicable in the same proportions. Since 1967, the commissions of the National Assembly have set forward 63 539 amendments, three times the number of those of governmental origin (18 841). This shows that the government is not at the origin of the majority of amendments, since 76.2 per cent of amendments adopted come from commissions using this means to play their full role in the legislative process. This trend does not mean that amendments are never the result of negotiations between the executive and the legislative bodies, but even this bargaining process is in itself recognition of the role played by MPs and the power the amendment tool gives them. However, other factors also influence the room for manoeuvre that MPs enjoy.

An in-depth study of the Fifth Republic, from 1981 onwards, during which the use of the amendment tactic increased enormously, sheds light on the strategies the government adopted towards MPs. Thus, Figure 4.3 shows the number of adopted amendments in comparison with the number of proposed amendments from the main political parties. The higher the ratio, the more a government tends to adopt the proposed amendments. We have included only the dominant party of the majority, its partner(s) and the opposition groupings.

Yet even though 1981–86 was *prima facie* a period of confrontational politics, this should not disguise the fact that MPs from the minority parties (RPR and UDF) had more amendments adopted than was the case for PS and PC Members. This trend was, however, reversed at the end of the legislature, just before the elections. During the first cohabitation period, with its weak majority, Jacques Chirac's government was prudent in its handling of UDF members, accepting more proposals from them than from the RPR, the dominant party of the coalition. This was even more noticeable during the following legislature. Owing to their relative majority, governments of the Left tended to satisfy more requests from the dominant Socialist Party. The two other curves may reflect defiance towards the Communist Party and the fact that the centre is sometimes incorporated into the majority. Finally, the second cohabitation curves clearly indicate that political confrontation was less marked on the floor. More proposals from Socialist MPs were adopted than those from the Right. In other words, these evolutions show that even if the MPs are in a position of general weakness, the extent of this and the role they may therefore play in the legislative process does vary in accordance with the political context and its complexities.

Parliament also has more ordinary means for making its voice heard and controlling the activities of the government (Brouard and Rozenberg 2008). If we disregard enquiry commissions, two useful devices are available to MPs – oral and written questions.

Oral questions were the big winners of the 1995 revision of the Constitution, which greatly increased the number of sessions devoted to question time.[16] Although not all oral questions in the National Assembly give rise to debate, government question time is the most common form in which oral questions may be put to the executive. Introduced in 1974 to the National Assembly, this high spot of the parliamentary week only really came into its own with the 1995 reform, when its frequency and length was increased to two sessions of one hour per week on Tuesdays and Fridays. There has been no such similar increase, however, in the Senate, where question time was introduced in 1982.

Question time is especially significant because it is broadcast on television. This media coverage means that it is a prime opportunity for the opposition to manifest its disagreement with government policy. The opposition, which has little real status in the French system, uses question time as a means of restraining the government, especially within the National Assembly in which the most lively political confrontations often occur.

Written questions, the second means for exerting control over the government, have been used increasingly since 2000. In each chamber, any elected representative can send a written question to any minister, who has two months in which to reply. If no reply is received, the question is tagged and sent once again to the minister. Only a very small percentage of questions do not receive answers.

Since 1989 at least 11 000 written questions have been sent each year. The 12th legislature (2002–07) showed a steady increase in their number. A total of 32 000 written questions was reached in 2006, and this obviously put great

74

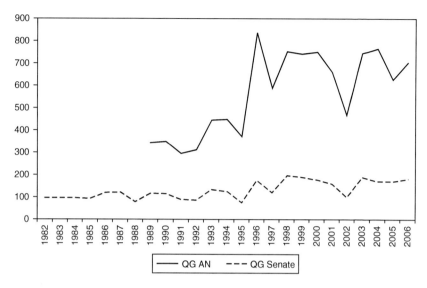

Figure 4.4 Number of 'topical questions to government' in the National Assembly and the Senate
Source: Brouard and Rozenberg 2008.
Note: Data for the National Assembly is not available before 1989.

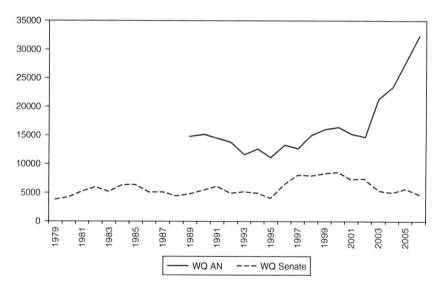

Figure 4.5 Written questions in the National Assembly and the Senate
Source: Brouard and Rozenberg 2008.
Note: Data for the National Assembly is not available before 1989.

pressure on ministerial departments. Although this boom can be explained in part by progress made in the field of information technology and the fact that written questions, which are not subject to a quota, benefit from a relatively simple procedure, other factors also come into play. Although of an intermittent nature, these questions are used to check government activity and to ensure that the government respects its promises and commitments either to its parliamentary majority or its allies. In this light the number of written questions serves as an indirect indicator of the level of trust between MPs and the government. The greater the trust, the fewer number of written questions, and vice versa.

4.7 Conclusion

When Carcassonne quotes the means available to the National Assembly to censure the government, he goes on to conclude that the Fifth Republic is a parliamentary and not a presidential regime (Carcassonne 2002). Yet, even in his example, it is the government to whom the constitution gives the upper hand (cf. art 49.2). This is an eloquent example of the paradoxical situation the French National Assembly has found itself in since 1958. The data we have studied above shows that in everyday reality the government rarely adopts the behaviour of a dictator but rather that of an 'agenda setter', putting forward its own best political options before a majority whose preferences may well be different from its own; a fact which means that compromises with majority MPs – and even those of the opposition – must sometimes be reached.

If the position of the National Assembly – and hence that of MPs – has improved over time – the effect of the reforms has been limited and the relationship between the government and the National Assembly has remained largely unchanged, still determined for the most part by the obligation of the parliamentary majority to support the government. As for the opposition, despite a number of limited changes, it suffers from a lack of real status and is often reduced either to silence or to obstruction strategies with little real scope (Carcassonne 1998). This situation shows that in France, as in other Western democracies, individual MPs have not been very effective as initiators of legislation (Andeweg and Nijzing 1995).

The current institutional reform project adopted by the Cabinet on 23 April 2008 and on which the majority and the opposition are still to reach agreement, could bring major changes in the role devolved to National Assembly and Senate alike. The text addresses a gap in the current constitution by officially specifying the tasks of Parliament – voting on laws and overseeing the action taken by the government. As in other Western democracies, it also allows the chambers to vote on resolutions. Moreover, one of the major limits of the current state of affairs – the restricted number of permanent commissions – would be partially addressed, with their number rising from

6 to 8. Finally, among other potentially important changes, opposition parties and groups would be granted specific rights. One day per month would be reserved for an agenda determined by the opposition. Other measures would allow a better balance to be established within the French regime by, for example, introducing the possibility of vetoing an emergency declaration made by government; fixing a mutual agenda with parliament and government equally determining this together; setting limits on the blocked vote laid down in article 49.3 on financing laws, and further limiting this to just one text per session and to certain kinds of bills (financial and social security); or introducing measures to control appointment procedures. It remains to be seen whether the need for institutional reform will not be nipped in the bud by political opportunism, as was the case in 1993 when the recommendations of the Vedel report were consigned to oblivion.[17] We may also hope that this reform of France's institutions will lead to a renewed interest for research into the French parliament, as so little has been done in this sphere in comparison with parliaments abroad and, in this light, the quasi-absence of studies on the Senate is even more revealing.

Notes

1. Michel Winock speaks in terms of right-wing, left-wing and even of a more general 'emotional' type of anti-parliamentarianism as being the structural basis of French political life from 1789 to the present day (Winock 1990).
2. This chapter deals more particularly with the situation in the National Assembly, which, as defined by the Constitution and the unequal bicameralism this provides for, is the main legislative arena in France – without, however, completely obscuring the role of the Senate.
3. There are several recent works on parliamentary and constitutional law. Anthropologist Marc Abélès has also devoted a book to the National Assembly, in which he highlights the lack of interest this institution arouses within the scientific community and confirms the misunderstandings that dog its image (Abélès 2000).
4. This refers to periods of coexistence when the president of the Republic is not from the same political party as the majority in the National Assembly and government.
5. Articles 44.3, 49.3 and 38 are discussed in detail in the chapter by Émiliano Grossman.
6. Between 1969 and 2003 about 12 000 amendments were rejected on the basis of article 40.
7. This is a body made up of MPs and Senators responsible for bringing together the respective positions of both houses.
8. These analyses concern cases in which the executive only has a relative majority, as was the case in the 9th Legislature, which had an immense negative impact on parliamentary practice.
9. The Conseil Constitutionnel has adopted a strict interpretation of the regulatory obligation of the Assemblies to respect the terms of the Constitution and, in doing so, has imposed draconian limits on the opportunities for MPs – whether they belong to the majority or the opposition – to hinder government policy. The judges have been particularly vigilant in ensuring that these resolutions

(internal regulations within the chambers) will not be deflected from their objective.
10. Cf. infra.
11. In this case, the special session has no fixed time limit, although it is limited to 12 days where members of the majority are concerned.
12. 'Statistiques, Bilan de la xı^e législature', *Bulletin de l'Assemblée Nationale*, 12 June 1997–98, June 2002.
13. Although this indicator is not the most refined or precise.
14. Worthy of note are: the Delegation for the EU (set up in 1979, after the first direct elections of Euro MPs, which thus cut the bond between them and national parliaments); the Parliamentary Office for Evaluating Scientific and Technological Choices (OPECST) (1984); the Parliamentary Office for Evaluating Legislation (1996); the Mission for Evaluation and Control (MEC) (1999); the Delegation for Women's Rights (1999); the Delegation for Planning and Sustainable Development in France (1999); the Parliamentary Office for Primary Health Care (2002); and the Mission for Evaluating and Controlling Finance Laws for the Social Security System (MECSS) (2004).
15. Along with this, political groups also began to form from 1981 on. At the close of the 12th Legislature (early 2007), MPs were split as follows: 35 in the UMP group, 37 in the Socialist group, 10 in the UDF group and 8 in the Communist and Republican groups.
16. 'At one sitting a week at least precedence shall be given to questions from Members of Parliament and to answers by the Government' (art. 48).
17. The 'Vedel report' is the generic name of the report submitted on February 1993 to the then president of the Republic, François Mitterrand, by the president of the Advisory Consitutional Reform Commission, Georges Vedel, former member of the Conseil Constitutionnel.

Bibliography

Abélès, M. (2000) *Un ethnologue à l'Assemblée*, (Paris: Odile Jacob).

Andeweg, R. and L. Nijzink (1995) 'Beyond the Two-Body Image: Relations between Ministers and MPs', in H. Döring (ed.), *Parliaments and Majority Rule in Western Europe*, (New York: St. Martin's Press).

Best, H. and M. Cotta (2000) *Parliamentary Representatives in Europe, 1848–2000: Legislative Recruitment and Careers in Eleven European Countries*, (Oxford: Oxford University Press).

Blondel, J. (1973) *Comparative Legislatures*, (Englewood Cliffs: Prentice Hal).

Boudant, J. (1992) 'La crise identitaire du Parlement français', *Revue de Droit Public*, n°5.

Brouard, S. (2005) 'The Role of French Governments in Legislative Agenda Settings', Paper presented at the ECPR joint sessions, Granada, 14–19 April 2005.

Brouard, S. and O. Rozenberg (2008) 'Parliamentary control in France: Three ways of *parliamentarisation* for the Vth Republic', working paper, CEVIPOF, 2008.

Carcassonne, G. (1998) 'La place de l'opposition: le syndrome français', *Pouvoirs*, n°85, pp. 75–85.

Carcassonne, G. (2002) *La Constitution*, 5th edn, (Paris: Le Seuil).

Chagnollaud, D. (1991) *Le premier des ordres. Les hauts fonctionnaires, 18ème–20ème siècle*, (Paris: Fayard).

Chagnollaud, D. (2001) 'La subordination du Parlement?', In *Droit constitutionnel contemporain*, T.2, (Paris: Dalloz).

Chandernagor, A. (1967) *Un parlement pourquoi faire?*, (Paris: Gallimard).

Chatenet, P. (1992) 'Les pouvoirs du Parlement', *Revue des sciences morales et politiques*, n°1.

Colliard, J.-C. (1978) *Les régimes parlementaires contemporains*, (Paris: Presses de la FNSP).

Couderc, M. (1981) 'La bataille parlementaire contre le temps', *Revue française de science politique*, 31(1), pp. 85–120.

Costa, O. and E. Kerrouche (2007) *Qui sont les députés français : enquête sur les élites inconnues*, (Paris: Presses de Sciences Po).

Dorey, P. (2004) 'Le Parlement en Grande-Bretagne', In O. Costa, E. Kerrouche, and P. Magnette (eds) *Vers un renouveau du parlementarisme en Europe?*, (Brussels: Editions de l'Universite de Bruxelles).

Dulong, D. (1997) *Moderniser la politique. Aux origines de la Cinquième République*, (Paris: L'Harmattan).

Döring, H. (ed.), *Parliaments and Majority Rule in Western Europe*, (New York: St. Martin's Press).

Duprat, J.P. (1996) 'L'évolution des conditions du travail parlementaire en France: 1945–1995', *Les Petites Affiches*, n°13.

Foucher, B. (1981) 'Le dernier mot à l'Assemblée Nationale', *Revue de droit public et de la science politique en France et à l'étranger*, n°5.

Frears, J. (1990) 'The French Parliament: Loyal Workhorse, Poor Watchdog', in P. Norton (ed.) *Parliaments in Western Europe,* (London: Frank Cass).

J. Fretel and J. Meimon (2005) 'La vie en coulisses. Les collaborateurs parlementaires à l'Assemblée Nationale (2002–2007)', In G. Courty (ed.), *Le travail de collaboration avec les élus*, (Paris: M. Houdiard), pp. 136–56.

Gibel, C. (1981) 'L'évolution des moyens de travail des parlementaires', *Revue française de science politique*, 31(1): 211–26.

Huber, J.D. (1996) 'Restrictive Legislative Procedures in France and the United States', *American Political Science Review*, 86(3): 675–87.

Kerrouche, E. (2004) 'Appréhender le rôle des parlementaires: étude comparative des recherches menées et perspectives', In O. Costa, E. Kerrouche and P. Magnette (eds), *Vers un renouveau du parlementarisme en Europe?*, (Brussels: Editions de l'Universite de Brussels).

Lascombes, M. (1997) *Droit constitutionnel de la Cinquième République*, (Paris: L'Harmattan).

Latour, X. (2000) 'Des rapports entre le parlement et le gouvernement sous la XI législature', *Revue de Droit Public*, n°6.

Loewenberg, G. and C.L. Kim (1978) 'Comparing the Representativeness of Parliaments', *Legislative Studies Quarterly*, 3(1): 27–49.

Mattson, I. (1995) 'Private Members' Initiatives and Amendments', In H. Döring (ed.) *Parliaments and Majority Rule in Western Europe*, (New York: St. Martin's Press).

Morin, M. (1986) 'La présence du gouvernement dans les assemblées parlementaires sous la Cinquième République', *Revue de Droit Public*, n°5.

Norton, P. (1998) *Legislatures and Legislators*, (London: Ashgate).

Pezant, J.L. (1977) 'Contribution à l'étude du pouvoir législatif selon la Constitution de 1958', in *Mélanges Georges Burdeau, Le Pouvoir*, (Paris: LGDJ).

Vandendriessche, X. (2001), 'Le Parlement entre déclin et modernité', *Pouvoirs*, n°99.

5
The French Party System: Fifty Years of Change

Nicholas Sauger

Over 50 years of history, the prominent feature of French political parties is change. None of the parties competing for the first legislative elections of 1958 still exists today, with the important exception of the Communist Party. And the current majority party – the UMP – was launched only in 2002. Parties have periodically changed their labels, organizations and strategies (Haegel 2005). This propensity to change indeed reflects the general weakness of party organizations in France in terms of resources and legitimacy (Mény 1996, Haegel and Lazar 2007), especially when compared to their European counterparts.

Focusing on the developments of the French party system under the Fifth Republic, this chapter posits two main arguments. First, there is a stable but not unchallenged pattern of party competition throughout the whole period, i.e. bipolarization. If defined in Sartori's terms (Sartori 1976), bipolarization is a type of limited pluralism (the number of parties is superior to two but does not exceed five), organized into two stable coalitions (or two blocks), with polarized party positions but a centripetal direction of competition. Secondly, within this context of bipolarization, the major characteristic of the French party system is instability. Even if periods of evolution can be delineated, the very institutional context of the Fifth Republic provides mixed incentives that largely explain the (otherwise) apparently erratic fluctuations within bipolarization.

Even if party change and party system change should not be mixed up (Mair 1997), the vulnerability of French parties to external and internal pressures have regularly led to changes in the structure of competition among parties. The emergence of the Greens and the extreme right *Front National* in the 1980s, the quasi-disappearance of the Communist, or the dramatic changes of strategies of centrist forces between independence and alliance with the right are obvious examples of such transformations. Despite evidence of change, the general picture remains quite confused at first sight. To take the words of Stefano Bartolini, 'the French party system presents inconsistent and mixed characteristics' (Bartolini 1984). The picture is all the more complicated by the very changing nature of electoral competition from an election to another. There is no linear evolution over the period of the Fifth Republic. Resembling sometimes more a stochastic process than a clearly identifiable trend, the transformation of the French party system has undergone both incremental change and sheer U-turns. The 2002 elections exemplify best this ambivalence with the first round of the presidential election representing the conclusion of a period of 20 years of fragmentation of the party system while the legislative elections held only a few weeks after led to the imposition of a quasi two-party system.

Deciphering the nature and dynamics of the French party system has led to important divergences among specialists. Among the vast literature on the subject, several ways of understanding contemporary changes have been proposed (for a review, see Knapp 2004, Bell 2000). The surge of the extreme right during the 1980s with the *Front National* has particularly represented the locus of debates. It has been viewed on the one hand as both the cause and the symptom of a dynamic of fragmentation of the system (Schlesinger and Schlesinger 1990, Ysmal 1998), eventually leading to a profound crisis of governmental parties (Cole 1990). On the other hand, French parties have been viewed as particularly resilient to the rise of challengers (Cayrol and Jaffré 1980), leading the whole system into the structures of a two-party system (Grunberg and Haegel 2007) and leaving the fundamental policy alternatives almost untouched (Andersen and Evans 2005).

The rest of this chapter is structured into four parts. The first section depicts the institutional framework of the Fifth Republic and its consequences on the structures of party competition. The following two parts depict the two main dimensions of the analysis of party systems (Klingemann 2006, Sauger 2008), that is to say, the fragmentation of the system on the one hand and the positions of parties in the policy space on the other. The last section concludes by discussing the question of the nature of change of the party system over time.

5.1   The institutional framework of the Fifth Republic and its consequences

Explanations of how the French party system is structured are largely heterogeneous. Students of the party system itself have often focused on the institutional constraints of the Fifth Republic, and especially on the direct election of the resident (since 1962) and the French exception of the two-round system used for both legislative and presidential elections (Bartolini 1984). The rationale is rather simple. Since the second round of the presidential election opposes only two candidates, it leads to the bipolarization of the party system.[1] In this perspective the first round leaves room for choice in each of these two camps to select the 'best candidate'. Of course the semi-presidential nature of the Fifth Republic reinforces the dynamics since the government should gain support of an absolute majority of representatives in the National Assembly, so that the cleavage between majority and opposition endures.

On the contrary, other authors have underlined the role of sociological and political logics structuring the system and its major evolutions. As Georges Lavau put it bluntly (against Maurice Duverger's argument about the role of electoral systems), parties reflect the *'réalités sociales'* (Lavau 1953). Recently the role of a major realignment at the beginning of the 1980s (Martin 2000), marked by the emergence of post-materialist issues, has been particularly emphasized as the key factor in understanding the rise of the National Front for instance. Naturally, many general accounts of the French party system insist on the plurality of the causes, encompassing also, besides those already mentioned, the strategies of the parties themselves and their organizations (Grunberg 2006). However, the indisputable contrast between the Fourth and the Fifth Republics is so important – there were 21 governments within the 12 years of the Fourth Republic, 19 in 60 years for the Fifth – that the role of institutions cannot be but central.

Yet institutions play an ambiguous role in shaping French politics. Many of the apparent incoherencies and inconsistencies emphasized by Bartolini (1984) are in fact the direct result of the working of the institutions. Inconsistencies stem for instance from the high disproportionality between electoral results in the first round of the legislative elections and the allocation of seats within the National Assembly. Disproportionality is up to 21.9 percent in the 2000s, outperforming thus all other countries in Europe (Grossman and Sauger 2007). The mixed character of the French party system is also the result of differences between legislative and presidential structures of electoral competition. This chapter claims this does not prevent the existence of a consistent and comprehensible underlying logic to the French party system, i.e. bipolarization. Concepts from comparative politics are central to understanding this logic, though, as will be shown, these concepts need careful application.

Furthermore, institutional change since the late 1970s has pushed further the divergences of incentives provided to political actors. Two reforms have in particular been viewed as playing an important role (Parodi 1997). First, new elections have been introduced in France, with the European election since 1979 and the regional elections since 1986. These two new elections have been organized with proportional representation, and not a majority electoral system.[2] This has provided clear opportunities for new parties to enter the game of French politics, the National Front, the Greens and eurosceptic parties all building their early success in such a context. The second major innovation in French institutions has been the introduction of a system of public funding for political parties and electoral campaigns since 1988 (Clift and Fisher 2004, François and Sauger 2006), substituting for the ban on corporate donations. The system of public subsidies has been designed so that both major and fringe parties benefit the most from it. These two reforms have contributed largely towards the fragmentation of the party system in the 1980s and 1990s and towards the discrepancy between electoral results and institutional representation.

5.2   Fragmentation and the politics of coalition

The principal dynamic of the French party system under the Fifth Republic has been that of the so-called 'bipolar quadrille'. By the end of the 1970s four parties of approximately equal strength – the Communist Party, the Socialist Party, the centrist UDF and Gaullist RPR – monopolized over 90 percent of the vote in their respective Left and Right blocs (Parodi 1991). Nevertheless, this end-state had taken 20 years to produce, concluding in fact only in 1978 with the formation of the UDF from different centre-right parties. It has also lasted only less than a few years. As early as at the beginning of the 1980s, two decisive evolutions appear clearly: the domination of one party within each bloc and the surge of 'anti-establishment' parties (Abedi 2004), namely the Greens and the *Front National*. These major evolutions are more precisely reviewed in the next three sections about the number of parties, the balance of forces and the challenges to bipolarization.

5.2.1   The number of parties

Counting the number of parties existing within a system has been the core activity of party system research from the 1950s (Ware 1996, Katz and Crotty 2006). This number has been historically viewed as a key to understanding government stability and the more general model of democracy to which a specific country belongs (Lijphart 1999, Powell 2000). Yet the task is far more complicated than what can be imagined at first sight. One of the main issues of the comparative literature on this question is the method of counting 'real' parties. Legal definitions of parties would for instance lead to acknowledging the existence of about two hundred registered parties,[3] among which 20, for instance, had claimed to be represented during the official campaign for the 2007 legislative elections. More classical definitions of parties, in terms of type of organization, goal and activity are not easy to apply to the French case. The UDF was the most obvious example of the difficulties of counting parties (Sauger 2003). The UDF was created in 1978 as an 'umbrella organization' representing the grouping of three still existent parties. Because its leader, the incumbent President Giscard d'Estaing, lost the 1981 presidential election against François Mitterrand, the process of consolidation of the new party was frozen at its early stage (Hanley 1999). It was then impossible to say whether the UDF or its component parts were the actual parties. More generally, the Fifth Republic has been characterized since the 1970s, one the one hand, by fairly stable electoral coalitions on the left (among communists, socialists and left-radicals), and on the right (between different centre-right parties and the different Gaullist parties), and, on the other hand, by sometimes highly factionalized parties. This simply means that one party can sometimes run more than one candidate for one office and sometimes run less than one candidate for an office. In 1988, for instance, the UDF ran in only half the legislative constituencies, because it filled in fact common candidates with the RPR for this election, but was represented in two different parliamentary groups at the National Assembly. Some of its representatives chose to have their own group which, besides, regularly supported the minority government of the socialist Michel Rocard.

Keeping this in mind, the number of French parties can be computed according to a number of indexes proposed by the comparative literature on the question, among which the most widely used is the effective number of parties by Lakso and Taagepera (1979).[4]

Figure 5.1[5] proposes a systematic application of this index for France, computing this index at four different levels to take into account the limitations mentioned before: the number of effective presidential candidates from 1965

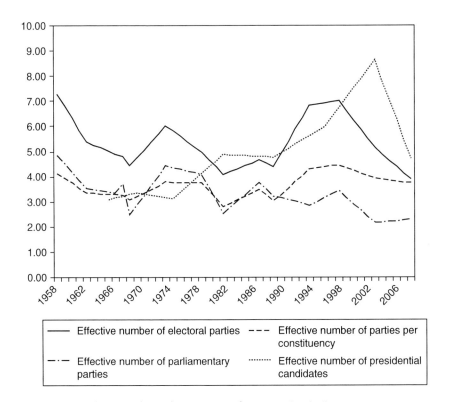

Figure 5.1   Evolution indices of party system fragmentation in France

to 2007, the number of effective parties from data about first-round votes for the legislative elections, the number of effective parliamentary parties from data about parties represented in the French *Assemblée Nationale,* and finally the average of the effective number of candidates by electoral constituency. What appears clearly on this figure is the important variation of the fragmentation of the French party system across indicators and over time.

Differences and variations of indicators of fragmentation of the party system are huge. In 2002, for instance, the effective number of parliamentary party was just above 2, the effective number of candidate by constituency is about 4, the effective number of electoral parties is equal to 5 while the effective number of presidential candidates is higher than 8. More generally, the number of parties at the national level is higher than the average number of candidates by constituency and higher than the number of parliamentary party. The former difference reflects the importance of electoral pacts. Parties frequently ally to present common candidacies for the first round, sharing the repartition of these candidacies at the national level. The latter characteristic is the result of the very high disproportional nature of the electoral system in France. The differences between presidential and legislative elections are on the contrary not systematic. From 1965 to 2002 the number of effective presidential candidates rose from three to eight. This underlines a clear discrepancy with the number of parliamentary parties that has followed a steady decline throughout the period. Meanwhile, the number of electoral parties for the legislative elections is more stable, with a high variability from one election to the other at the national level and certain permanence in constituencies. 2007 seems to show a rupture in these trends. The series of presidential and then legislative elections witnessed a clear convergence of the different indicators around an average number of three and a half parties.

These different results can be interpreted as proof of the strength of bipolarization of the French party system throughout the Fifth Republic. The differences between the number of effective electoral parties and the average number of effective candidates by constituency shows the importance of electoral alliances in the first round, at least until 2002. The difference between fragmentation in the first round of legislative elections and the composition of the National Assembly highlights the determinant character of alliances for the second round. No party outside a system of alliance has ever managed to secure a parliamentary group since the 1960s. What is however less clear from these results is the passage of a system with three partly confused sets of alliances (left, centre and right) until the 1960s to a system with only two sets of alliances (left and right) from the 1970s. The presidential contest is in this context an exception. The growing number of candidates from 1965 to 2002 can be explained by three factors. First, the institutional regime clearly underwent a tendency towards presidentialization (Clift 2005). This presidentialization of the working of the institutions has progressively led to the presidentialization of the parties and their strategies and hence of the electoral competition. Whereas the Communist party has accepted having a common candidate (François Mitterrand) with the socialists in 1965 and 1974, French parties have progressively all accepted the role of the president and considered the presidential election as the most important stake. Up to a certain extent the inability of the PC (because of its political position) and the UDF (because of its organization) to have credible presidential candidates is a central explanation for their current failure. This presidentialization has in turn led to the impossibility of forging alliances for the first round of the presidential election. Secondly, the logics of the two-round electoral system leave room for two possible equilibriums (Cox 1997). On the one hand, if a candidate is close enough to the threshold of the absolute majority in the first round, the only strategic incentive for voters is to choose if they wish a second round to take place. On the other hand, if no candidate is in this situation, there is room for at least three candidates since the real issue is the competition for the second and third place to determine which of these two candidates will make it to the second round. Thirdly, the conjunction of the dynamics of presidentialization and the multiplication of proportional electoral systems for regional and European elections (plus the 1986 legislative elections) has led to the 'proportionalization' of the first round of the presidential election (Parodi 1997). Because the presidential election is the only election with a coherent offer all over the territory and a high turnout rate, the results of its first round has been read as the opportunity to observe the real balance of powers among parties. It has been widely used in this perspective in negotiations among parties to form coalitions for the legislative elections. This proportional process of the first round has also led voters to send 'messages' to candidates and then influence parties' positions over issues by an 'inverted strategic vote' (Blais 2004). This explains why so many socialist voters in 2002 preferred to cast a vote for candidates of the extreme left despite their preference for the socialist candidate. Because they took for granted that Jospin would be qualified for the second round, they seized the opportunity to seek a more leftist and socialist programme. In other terms, the 'earthquake' of 2002, with Le Pen being in the second round, is explained by the fact that the four preceding elections have always opposed left to right in the second round and the more immediate polls predicting the repetition of this pattern (Durand et al. 2005).

5.2.2 The balance of forces

Having any number of effective parties in fact provides little information about the relative importance of those parties. If bipolarization is a characteristic of the whole Fifth Republic, the most significant trends deal with the relative balance of forces between each camp and within each bloc through the question of dominance.

The literature on party dominance provides numerous definitions of the concept of dominance. At a very abstract level, party dominance can nevertheless be shortly defined as a situation where the position of a party within a party system defines the properties of the system itself.[6] This definition comes from the duality of the concept of dominance, which applies both for a party and the pattern of interactions among parties (Sartori 1976). From this definition, a dominant party may be more precisely defined first as a party that holds the office or governmental position which is at stake in the competition and whose position cannot be defeated.

Dominance in France has been particularly viewed as the status of the Gaullist party, or more generally of the right, until the 1970s. Between 1958 and 1981 there was no alternation in power. The Gaullists controlled the presidency from 1958 to 1974 and were the most numerous forces within the National Assembly, although they did not control an absolute majority except once. The Gaullist hegemony collapsed during the 1970s. Unable to build a new leadership after the death of President Pompidou, the Gaullist party lost the presidency because of the support for Valéry Giscard d'Estaing by a number of dissidents led by Jacques Chirac. The legislative elections of 1978 then shed light on the strength of the left, which could have won this contest (Capdevielle et al. 1981). From 1962 to 1974 the Gaullist party was unequivocally dominant: no coalition could be formed without it and, more qualitatively, it had the capacity to 'identify with an epoch' (Duverger 1967).

The more debated issue is whether the UMP, formed around Jacques Chirac in 2002, will open a new era of dominance in France. This new right-wing party, created by merging the former RPR with part of the UDF (Haegel 2002), gained control of most of the different institutions of the Fifth Republic. President Chirac was elected in 2002 with more than 80 percent of the votes (in the second round of the presidential election). The following legislative elections gave a majority to the UMP in the National Assembly (the UMP won 365 out of 577 seats). A majority of members of the Constitutional Council were nominated by UMP members and a majority of local governments (regions, departments and cities) were controlled by UMP representatives. Moreover, for the very first time under the Fifth Republic, a single party had a majority in the Senate.[7] Such a parliamentary and executive dominance of a single party had never been achieved before. The congruence of the majorities among the executive (presidential majority), the National Assembly and the Senate is an exceptional feature. To a certain extent the 2007 elections have confirmed the possible domination of the UMP. The index of balance designed by Taagepera (2005) as a measure of dominance[8] (see Table A5.1) even shows its highest level in the whole period. However, the inability of the party to give good performances in intermediary elections prompts for more time before any definitive judgment.

Domination has besides never been verified at the local level. Using a technique of representation of the scores of the top two parties within each

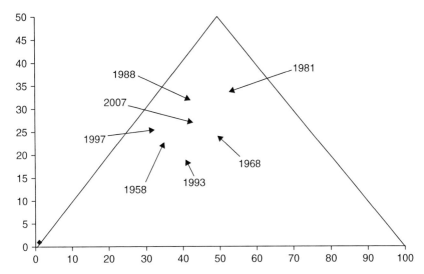

Figure 5.2 Competition in constituencies: average of the scores of the top two parties across districts for the first round of legislative elections (Nagayama triangle technique)

constituency borrowed from Nagayma[9] (Grofman et al. 2004), Figure 5.2 displays the average scores of top-finishing candidates in the first round of legislative elections from 1958 to 2007. What is striking is the quasi linear relationship between the scores of the top two candidates throughout the period. The average difference of scores is about 16 percent. The only election with a pronounced pattern of dominance is in fact 1968, in a very particular context.

From 1978 to 2002 no party was dominant in France. The systematic succession of alternation in power leaves no doubt about it. Yet, another transformation in the balance of power among parties took place during the period. The *'quadrille bipolaire'* has transformed into two blocks dominated by two parties. The two stories are however different on the left and right. On the left, the decline of the Communist party began in the mid-1970s, indeed long before the collapse of the USSR. In 1978, for the first time during the Fifth Republic, the Socialist party got a score almost equal to the Communist party (see Appendix for electoral results). Until this moment, the PCF had always been dominant on the left. Then, the Communist decline is pronounced. As early as 1981, the socialist pre-eminence is well established. On the right, the Gaullist party had been dominant until the mid-1970s. The unexpected victory of Giscard d'Estaing and the strategy of several centrist parties to enter into close alliance to balance the status of the RPR launched by Chirac in 1976 ended up in the formation of the UDF in 1978. The electoral start of the UDF was promising, performing as well as the RPR in 1978 and defeating it abruptly in the European elections of 1979. The 1981 defeat of Giscard d'Estaing provoked dramatic consequences for both the organization of the UDF and its standing in public opinion. From 1982 the RPR has taken over the UDF, progressively affirming an almost unchallenged leadership. This evolution ended with the creation of the UMP, gathering most of the important actors on the right of the political spectrum.

5.3   Challenges to bipolarization

If bipolarization characterizes the French party system under the Fifth Republic, this organization of party competition has not been unchallenged. To begin with, bipolarization has been progressively imposed over more than a decade. From 1958 to the mid-1970s, the system of alliances was rather confused. Bipolarization is in fact born from two related dynamics: the progressive alignment of most of the centre parties to the Gaullist party and the creation of a close alliance between the Communists and the Socialists. The alliance on the left is the result of both the evolution of the PCF in the 1960s towards a form of 'eurocommunism' (Ross 1992) and the strategy forged by François Mitterrand for the Socialists to favour the alliance with the PCF over any other kind of political collaboration. The victory of this strategy against a strategy more directed towards the centre was embodied by the Congrès d'Epinay in 1971. From then on the successive electoral victories of the Gaullists at their direct expense and the ideological impossibility of entering into a coalition with the Communists are the reasons why centre parties have been convinced they had to consider the Gaullist party as a partner.

As soon as a quasi-perfect bipolarization of the party system was achieved, at the end of the 1970s, this configuration of the party system was challenged. Parties from five different ideological horizons have appeared over the last three decades: the extreme right, greens, extreme left, eurosceptic and more recently the rebirth of a centre party in 2007 with the MoDem.

A significant party of extreme right was already present at the beginning of the Fifth Republic with the Poujadist. Reinforced briefly by those opposing the independence of Algeria, this political force soon disappeared at the beginning of the 1960s. Created in 1972, the FN had to wait ten years before meeting success when it performed an unexpected 11 per cent at the 1984 European election. Based on an anti-immigrant creed vehemently asserted, the FN became immediately one of the most successful extreme-right parties in Europe to the point when in 2002 its leader, Jean-Marie Le Pen, finally got to the second round of the presidential election. He suffered nonetheless a considerable loss in support in 2007. The FN has been characterized as an anti-system party, excluded from and refusing any form of coalition.

Some alliances were significant at the regional level, thus leading right-wing parties to dramatic turmoil in 1998 when a few local leaders have had agreement with it. Except 1998 and 2002, the impact of the National Front has nonetheless been limited on the working of the party system since its parliamentary representation has been almost non-existent after 1986 because the two-round uninominal electoral system leaves no opportunity for a party without any ally.

The Greens had a significant audience at the beginning of the 1990s as an autonomous force, refusing the left–right categorization. For the 1997 elections, the Greens chose the alliance with the socialists and hence the communists, to form what has been known as the 'plural left'. This strategy was heavily debated within the party, part of it preferring an influence on public debate rather than within institutions. Even if their alliance with the left enables the Greens to be represented in parliament and in government, it did not however recover its early electoral success in the 2000s.

The extreme left has gathered different parties from different inspirations. If the PSU had limited success in the 1970s, different parties from Trotskyst persuasion have enjoyed relative success since the 1990s. With the two successive popular figures of Arlette Laguiller (LO) and Olivier Besancenot (LCR), together they have achieved more than 5 percent of the votes in the presidential elections since 1995. These parties have until now refused to go along with any other party of the left even if some signs have gone in this direction since 2007.

A few eurosceptic parties have emerged in the 1990s in the wake of the ratification of the Maastricht treaty by referendum in 1992. On the right, the movements led by Charles Pasqua and Philippe de Villiers have contributed to the disorganization of the mainstream parties in the 1990s to the point where their list for the European election of 1999 took the advantage from the mainstream right list led by Nicolas Sarkozy. On the left, the creation by Jean-Pierre Chevènement of his own party has been considered as one of the important reasons for the defeat of Jospin in the first round of the 2002 presidential election. These parties have however been short-lived and their principal success has been limited to the European elections.

The most recent challenge to bipolarization has come from François Bayrou, leader of the UDF, who between 2002 and 2007 has evolved towards a more and more radical critique of his right-wing allies. Candidate in 2007, he decided to get rid of the enduring alliances between the two main right-wing parties. Positioning himself at the centre of the political spectrum, he has sent a number of signals implying that coalition with the Socialists is now possible. Despite a significant success in the first round of the presidential election, with more than 18 per cent of the votes, his decision to forbid any alliance for the legislative elections eventually led him to lose almost all his representatives in the National Assembly. The elite of the UDF refused such a choice, forming a new organization called New Centre in very close alliance with the UMP. Meanwhile Bayrou changed the name of the UDF to the MoDem (Movement of the Democrats).

To sum up, coalitions forged during the 1960s and 1970s have proved to be resilient until now. However, their change has been marked by two events: the progressive marginalization of the PCF on the left, the coalition having furthermore integrated a new partner with the Greens; and the transformation of the right coalition, with a fusion of its parts into the UMP. These coalitions show a remarkable capacity to control institutional representation, thanks to the electoral system. Yet, their control of the electoral market seems weaker. In other terms, bipolarization still pertains even if it endorses quite different faces in the 2000s from the 1970s.

5.4   Polarization and the dimensionality of policy space

Bipolarization refers not only to the logics of coalition but also to specific positions of political parties in the policy space. The left–right divide has been the most enduring cleavage in French politics. It subsumes many policy issues but is clearly focused on economic and social questions. Party positions on this dimension have already been described previously. This section systematizes then only what has been already said. The most important point is that cleavages have changed over this dimension, especially because of the existence or non-existence of centre parties in terms of functional role (capacity of alliance on both left and right) and not only position. More recently, a new cleavage has appeared in this dimension when the National Front has been opposed by a strategy of 'cordon sanitaire', i.e. exclusion from all possibility of alliance.

Figure 5.3 depicts the evolution of the positions of individual parties, according to data from the manifestos group (Budge et al. 2001). From a method based on counting the emphasis put on different issues, it is possible to infer the underlying left–right dimension in France (for a discussion, see Budge and McDonald 2006, Petry and Pennings 2006). Figure 5.3 does not reveal any important surprises in terms of position of individual parties. What is worth noticing however is the clear de-polarization of the system from the 1980s. Mainstream parties have clearly converged towards the centre of the left–right dimension. However, polarization of the system itself has experienced only a limited de-polarization over the period since the National Front, in particular, has occupied a polar position at the extreme right.

The left–right dimension has been recently discussed as the unique dimension of French policy space. From the 1990s a second dimension of political conflict has been described (Perrineau et al. 2000). It forms part of a broader change that Inglehart calls post-modernization (Inglehart 1997). It is anchored in attitudes and values about authority or libertarianism. Grunberg and Schweisguth (1997) have shown that Europe is part of this second dimension of French political space that ranges from universalism to

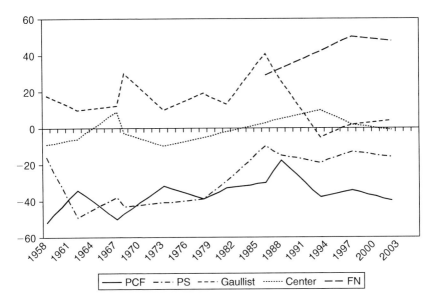

Figure 5.3 Party positions on the left–right dimensions according to CMR data

anti-universalism. Contrary to this thesis, other authors have demonstrated the stability of French political space (Andersen and Evans 2005). Building on the example of the role of the European issue, Belot and Cautrès (2004) claim that despite the fact Europe remains 'invisible', it contributes to redefine the whole meaning of political cleavages in France, transforming rather than substituting them. With finally quite similar conclusions, Evans (2007) shows that the limited impact of Europe on French electoral competition is explained because views about Europe simply replicate traditional delineations in social structures and mass ideological views. In other terms, the European issue is interpreted from the traditional frames of national politics.

This issue of the dimensionality of French political space can in fact be discussed from three points of view. First, from an historical point of view, more than one dimension of conflict has been present during the Fifth Republic. During its first decade, the issue of institutions and the issue of decolonization have been central, dividing particularly those accepting and those against the new Constitution and particularly the role it grants to the President. Following the same idea, Europe has been a divisive issue all over the period, cross-cutting the left–right cleavage since positions about Europe are in quadratic relation with this first dimension (Sauger 2005). Secondly, perspectives should be distinguished between parties and electorates. If this second dimension of political conflict is important, it is more important for electorates than for parties per se. One of the reasons for that is that even if

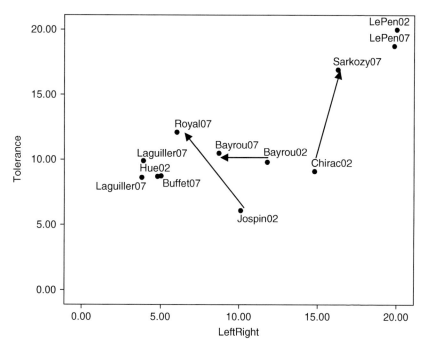

Figure 5.4   Main presidential candidates' positions using Wordscores technique, 2002–07

the National Front as a party can be easily located at the extreme right of the political spectrum, its electorate is spread all through it. Thirdly, the salience of a second dimension of political conflict has increased over the past two decades. That is why Figure 5.4, representing positions of the candidates of the contemporary period, uses these two dimensions.

Figure 5.4 is constructed from an automatic content analysis of party programmes, and, more precisely in this case, of presidential programmes according to the Wordscores technique (Laver et al. 2003). Building on a first application of this technique to the 2002 elections (Laver et al. 2006), this graph compares the positions of five of the main candidates in 2002 and 2007 according to an approximation of the two formerly described dimensions of conflict. The important results of this graph are twofold: on the one hand, candidates' positions are in fact lined up on an underlying dimension, reinforcing thus the idea of the redefinition of the left–right dimension by new issues; on the other hand, there is a clear trend in 2007 towards re-polarization of party positions. The socialist and the right-wing candidates follow a clearly centrifugal path, getting closer to extreme left or extreme right.

5.5 Conclusion: Instability and cycles

The Fifth Republic has been built on the idea of getting rid of the 'régime des partis' embodied by the Fourth Republic. Parties were under the accusation by de Gaulle of being the root of two related evils: absence of decision and general instability of the system. To a certain extent de Gaulle failed in his project. If the National Assembly has been actually dispossessed of most of its prerogatives, parties have flourished with an unexpected vigour. Furthermore, the configuration of the party system into a bipolar structure of competition has in fact been one of the most important reasons for the stability and efficiency of the political system as a whole. The initial ambition of de Gaulle has however left traces. Parties have remained weak organizations and instability within the framework of bipolarization has characterized the whole period.

Beyond instability, four phases of the party system can be distinguished. The initial phase, from 1958 to 1962, was the phase of consolidation of the system. Fragmentation was dramatically reduced and the system of alliances began to emerge. The period from 1962 to 1974 saw the time of the Gaullists' domination. As of 1974 the ideal-type of a bipolar *quadrille* is achieved until 1984, when a period of concentration ends to open up a new era of fragmentation of the party system. Yet, this fragmentation goes along with a relative depolarization of the system, the rise of the National Front compensating only partially the fall of the Communist Party. Fragmentation resulted in the shock of the 2002 presidential election. From the second round, a dynamic of concentration around two main parties has taken over, leading to a partial re-polarization of the system. These successive cycles of fragmentation and concentration on the one hand and polarization and depolarization on the other can be considered as the consequences of the dynamic of the system itself (the consequence of the fragmentation of 2002 is concentration) but also of the institutional system of the Fifth Republic. Presidentialization of the regime (Clift 2005) and the electoral system (Sauger 2007) can in particular be considered as a key to understanding these constant evolutions. The assumption is that the institutional system does in fact provide two kinds of contrary incentives: incentives for concentration around two main parties or coherent blocs but, at the same time, incentives for entry by new challengers.

Notes

1. The working of the two-round system is however more subtle, especially if applied to legislative elections (Sauger 2007).
2. Furthermore, the legislative elections of 1986 were also held with a proportional system and municipal elections have changed from a majority to a proportional system in 1983.

3. The *Commission Nationale des Comptes de Campagne et des Financements Politiques* recapitulates each year the organizations that have been registered by it. In 2003 (last available year) 244 organizations wanted to be registered, among which 195 actually were. Among these parties, 68 had benefited from public funding.
4. This index is the inverse of the index of fragmentation proposed by Rae (1969), i.e. $N = 1/\sum si^2$ where s is the proportion or seats or votes gained by the ith party or candidate.
5. Electoral results and accompanying values of the indexes are reported in the Appendix.
6. To a certain extent, this definition might however be viewed as marred by circularity.
7. This majority was the result of the merger of two groups (RPR and Independent Republicans, which also attracted members of both UDF or Liberal Democracy).
8. The index of balance is given by the formula $b = -\log(s1)/\log(p)$ where s1 is the largest share and p the number of seat-winning parties. It can range from 0 (total domination) to 1 (perfect equality among parties).
9. 'Nagayama triangles' are based on constituency level data. This kind of diagram is used to show the vote share of the largest party on the x-axis, and the vote share of second largest party on the y-axis. Because the second largest party must receive fewer votes than the largest party, the possible set of values in the diagram lies within a triangle bounded by the x-axis and segments of the line $x - y = 0$ and $x + y = 1$. These diagrams thus display information about the relative score of the two largest parties and information about the aggregated score of all the other parties (it is the distance between the plot and the nearest segment).

Appendix: Electoral results of presidential and legislative elections

Table A5.1   Presidential elections results (% of votes)

	1965 (%)	1969 (%)	1974 (%)	1981 (%)	1988 (%)	1995 (%)	2002 (%)	2007 (%)
Radical left	–	1.06	2.7[1]	3.41[1]	2.37[1]	5.30	10.44[1]	7.07[1]
PCF	–	21.17	–	15.35	8.86[1]	8.64	3.37	1.93
PS	31.72[2]	5.01	43.25[2]	25.85[2]	34.11[2]	23.3[2]	16.18	25.87[2]
Other left	1.71	3.61	0.69	2.21	–	–	7.65[1]	–
Greens	–	–	1.32	3.88	3.78	3.32	7.13[1]	1.57
UDF – Centre	15.57	22.31[2]	32.60[2]	28.32[2]	16.54	–	11.94[1]	18.57
Gaullist	44.65[2]	44.47[2]	18.28[1]	20.99[1]	19.96[2]	39.42[1,2]	19.88[2]	31.18[2]
Extreme right	6.35[1]	1.27	1.16[1]	–	14.38	20.02[1]	19.2[1,2]	12.67[1]
Effective number of candidates	3.09	3.35	3.13	4.88	4.77	5.97	8.63	4.70

Notes: [1]More than one candidate; [2]Second round candidate

Table A5.2 Legislative elections results (% of votes)

	1958 (%)	1962 (%)	1967 (%)	1968 (%)	1973 (%)	1978 (%)	1981 (%)	1986[1] (%)	1988 (%)	1993 (%)	1997 (%)	2002 (%)	2007 (%)
Radical left	1.2	2	2.2	4	3.2	3.3	1.2	1.5	0.4	1.7	2.6	2.74	3.44
PCF	18.9	21.9	22.5	20	21.4	20.6	16.1[2]	9.7	11.2	9.1	9.9[2]	4.91	4.62
PS	15.5	12.4	18.9	16.9	21.2	26.3	38.3[2]	32.8	37.6[2]	20.2	27.9[2]	26.67	27.67
Other left	5.8	5	–	–	–	–	–	–	–	–	–	–	–
Greens	–	–	–	–	–	2	1.1	1.2	0.4	11	6.9[2]	4.44	3.25
Centre	15	10.4	22.9[2]	20.5[2]	27.8[2]	–	–	–	–	–	–	–	–
UDF – Moderates	20[2]	13.8[2]	–	–	–	23.9[2]	–	–	–	–	–	5.52	7.76
Gaullist/UMP	20.6[2]	33.7[2]	33[2]	38[2]	24.6[2]	22.8[2]	42.9	44.6[2]	40.5	44.1[2]	36.2	38.35[2]	45.52[2]
Extreme right	2.6	0.8	0.6	0.1	0.5	0.8	0.3	9.9	9.9	12.9	15.3	12.2	4.7
Effective number of parties	7.29	5.38	4.79	4.42	6.04	4.96	4.08	4.64	4.39	6.84	7.01	5.15	3.87
Effective number of parliamentary parties	4.85	3.51	3.71	2.49	4.42	4.08	2.54	3.76	3.23	2.87	3.42	2.16	2.29
Effective number of parties per constituency	4.14	3.35	3.27	3.06	3.78	3.75	2.82	3.48	3.02	4.3	4.45	3.93	3.74
Index of balance	0.811	0.558	0.618	0.540	0.720	0.963	0.610	0.501	0.652	0.508	0.631	0.595	0.439

Notes: [1]Election with proportional electoral system; [2]Part of the new government coalition

Bibliography

Abedi, A. (2004) *Anti-establishment Parties: A Comparative Analysis* (London: Routledge).

Andersen, R. and J. Evans (2005) 'The Stability of French Political Space', *French Politics*, 3, 282–301.

Bartolini, S. (1984) 'Institutional Constraints and Party Competition in the French Party System' in S. Bartolini and P. Mair (eds) *Party Politics in Contemporary Western Europe* (London: Frank Cass).

Bell, D.S. (2000) *Parties and Democracy in France: Parties under Presidentialism* (Aldershot: Ashgate).

Belot, C. and B. Cautrès (2004) 'L'Europe, invisible mais omniprésente?' in B. Cautrès and N. Mayer (eds) *Le nouveau désordre électoral* (Paris: Presses de Sciences Po).

Blais, A. (2004) 'Strategic Voting in the 2002 French Presidential Election' in M. Lewis-Beck (ed.) *The French Voter: Before and After the 2002 Election* (Basingstoke: Palgrave Macmillan).

Budge, I. and M.D. McDonald (2006) 'Choices Parties Define: Policy Alternatives in Representative Elections, 17 countries 1945–1998', *Party Politics*, 12, 451–66.

Budge, I., H-D. Klingemann, A. Volkens, J. Bara, and E. Tanenbaum (2001) *Mapping Policy Preferences* (Oxford: Oxford University Press).

Capdevielle, J., E. Dupoirier, G. Grunberg, E. Schweisguth, and C. Ysmal (eds) (1981) *France de gauche, vote à droite* (Paris: Presses de Sciences Po).

Cayrol, R. and J. Jaffré (1980) 'Party Linkages in France: Socialist Leaders, Followers and Voters' in K. Lawson, (ed.) *Political Parties and Linkage: A Comparative Perspective* (New Haven: Yale University Press).

Clift, B. (2005) 'Dyarchic Presidentialization in a Presidentialized Polity: The French Fifth Republic' in P. Webb and T. Poguntke (eds) *The Presidentialization of Politics – A Comparative Study of Modern Democracies* (Oxford: Oxford University Press).

Clift, B. and J. Fisher (2004) 'Comparative party finance reform: the cases of France and Britain', *Party Politics*, 10, 677–99.

Cole, A. (1990) 'The Evolution of the Party System, 1974–1990' in A. Cole (ed.) *French Political Parties in Transition* (Aldershot: Dartmouth).

Cox, G.W. (1997) *Making Votes Count: Strategic Coordination in the World's Electoral Systems* (Cambridge: Cambridge University Press).

Durand, C., A. Blais and M. Larochelle (2005) 'The Polls of the French Presidential Election: An Autopsy', *Public Opinion Quarterly*, 68, 602–22.

Duverger, M. (1967) *Political Parties: Their Organization and Activity in the Modern State* (London, Methuen).

Evans, J. (2007) 'The European Dimension in the French Public Opinion', *Journal of European Public Policy*, 14, 1098–116.

François, A. and N. Sauger (2006) 'Groupes d'intérêt et financement de la vie politique en France: une évaluation des effets de l'interdiction des dons de personnes morales', *Revue Française de Science Politique*, 56, 227–54.

Grofman, B., A. Chiaramonte, R. D'Alimonte, and S.L. Feld (2004) 'Comparing and Contrasting the Uses of Two Graphical Tools for Displaying Patterns of Multiparty Competition', *Party Politics*, 10, 273–99.

Grossman, E. and N. Sauger (2007) *Introduction aux systèmes politiques nationaux de l'UE* (Bruxelles: De Boeck).

Grunberg, G. (2006) 'L'adaptation du système des partis : 1965–2006' in P. Culpepper, P. Hall and B. Palier (eds) *La France en mutation: 1980–2005* (Paris: Presses de Sciences Po).

Grunberg, G. and E. Schweisguth (1997) 'Vers une tripartition de l'espace politique' in D. Boy and N. Mayer (eds) *L'électeur a ses raisons* (Paris: Presses de Sciences Po).

Grunberg, G. and F. Haegel (2007) *La France vers le bipartisme ? La présidentialisation du PS et de l'UMP* (Paris: Presses de Sciences Po).

Haegel, F. (2002) 'Faire l'union : la refondation des partis de droite après les élections de 2002', *Revue Française de Science Politique*, 52, 561–76.

Haegel, F. (2005) 'Parties and Organizations' in A. Cole, P. Le Galès and J. Lévy (eds) *Developments in French Politics 3* (Basingstoke: Palgrave Macmillan).

Haegel, F. and M. Lazar (2007) 'France: Anti-System Parties vs. Governmental' in K. Lawson and P. Merkl (eds) *When Parties Prosper: The Uses of Electoral Success* (Boulder: Lynne Rienner).

Hanley, D. (1999) 'Compromise, Party Management and Fair Shares: The Case of the French UDF', *Party Politics*, 5, 171–89.

Inglehart, R. (1997) *Modernization and Post-modernization: Cultural, Economic and Political Change in 43 Societies* (Princeton: Princeton University Press).

Katz, R.S. and W.J. Crotty (eds) (2006) *Handbook of Party Politics* (London: Sage).

Klingemann, H.-D. (2006) 'Political Parties and Party Systems' in J. Thomassen (ed.) *The European Voter* (Oxford: Oxford University Press).

Knapp, A. (2004) *Parties and the Party System in France: A Disconnected Democracy?* (Basingstoke: Palgrave Macmillan).

Lakso, M. and R. Taagepera (1979) 'Effective Number of Parties: A Measure with Application to West Europe', *Comparative Political Studies*, 12, 3–27.

Lavau, G. (1953) *Partis politiques et réalités sociales: contribution à une étude réaliste des partis politiques* (Paris: Armand Colin).

Laver, M., K. Benoit and J. Garry (2003) 'Extracting policy positions from political texts using words as data', *American Political Science Review*, 97, 311–31.

Laver, M., K. Benoit, and N. Sauger (2006) 'Policy Competition in the 2002 French Legislative and Presidential Elections', *European Journal of Political Research*, 45, 667–97.

Lijphart, A. (1999) *Patterns of Democracy. Government Forms and Performance in Thirty-six Countries* (New Haven: Yale University Press).

Mair, P. (1997) *Party System Change: Approaches and Interpretations* (Oxford: Clarendon Press).

Martin, P. (2000) *Comprendre les évolutions électorales: la théorie des réalignements revisitée* (Paris: Presses de Sciences Po).

Mény, Y. (1996) 'La faiblesse des partis politiques français: une persistante exceptionnalité' in F. D'Arcy and L. Rouban (eds) *De la Ve République à l'Europe* (Paris: Presses de Sciences Po).

Parodi, J.-L. (1991) 'Le nouvel espace politique français' in Y. Mény (ed.) *Idéologies, partis politiques et groupes sociaux* (Paris: Presses de Sciences Po).

Parodi, J.-L. (1997) 'Proportionnalisation périodique, cohabitation, atomisation partisane: un triple défi pour le régime semi-présidentiel de la Cinquième République', *Revue Française de Science Politique*, 47, 292–312.

Perrineau, P., J. Chiche, B. Le Roux and H. Rouanet (2000) 'L'espace politique des électeurs français à la fin des années 1990: nouveaux et anciens clivages, hétérogénéité des électorats', *Revue Française de Science Politique*, 50, 463–87.

Petry, F. and P. Pennings (2006) 'Estimating the Policy Positions of Political Parties from Legislative Election Manifestos 1958–2002', *French Politics*, 4, 100–23.

Powell, G.B. (2000) *Elections as Instruments of Democracy: Majoritarian and Proportional Visions* (New Haven: Yale University Press).

Ross, G. (1992) 'Party Decline and Changing Party Systems: France and the French Communist Party', *Comparative Politics*, 25, 43–61.

Sartori, G. (1976) *Parties and Party Systems: A Framework for Analysis* (Cambridge: Cambridge University Press).

Sauger, N. (2003) 'The UDF in the 1990s: The Break-up of a Party Confederation' in J. Evans (ed.) *The French Party System* (Manchester: Manchester University Press).

Sauger, N. (2005) 'Sur la mutation contemporaine des structures de la compétition partisane en France: les partis de droite face à l'intégration européenne', *Politique européenne*, 16, 103–26.

Sauger, N. (2007) 'Un système électoral vecteur d'instabilité? L'impact du système électoral sur la structuration du système partisan sous la Cinquième République' in F. Haegel (ed.) *Les partis politiques en France* (Paris: Presses de Sciences Po).

Sauger, N. (ed.) (2008) 'Le changement des systèmes partisans en Europe', *Revue Internationale de Politique Comparée*, 14 (2).

Schlesinger, J.A. and M. Schlesinger (1990) 'The Reaffirmation of a Multiparty System in France', *American Political Science Review*, 84, 1077–101.

Taagepera, R. (2005) 'Conservation of Balance in the Size of Parties', *Party Politics*, 11, 283–98.

Ware, A. (1996) *Political Parties and Party Systems* (Oxford: Oxford University Press).

Ysmal, C. (1998) 'The Evolution of the French Party System' in P. Ignazi and C. Ysmal (eds), *The Organization of Political Parties in Southern Europe* (Westport: Praeger).

6

The Constitutional Council: The Rising Regulator of French Politics

Sylvain Brouard

The pre-eminence of parliamentary sovereignty in France, which was born with the French Revolution, forbade judicial review in the country for a long time (Stone 1992). In many respects, therefore, the creation of the Constitutional Council in 1958 was a break with French constitutional tradition. It was given a great deal of jurisdiction in three main areas: monitoring of national elections, of political incumbents, and of institutional activities. Conversely, the only role of the Fourth Republic's Constitutional Committee was to help both legislative chambers reach an agreement when they disagreed about the compatibility of a law with the constitution. When agreement was not possible, it proposed constitutional revision to take this into account.[1] In 1958, 'the need for an impartial institution in charge of scrutinizing the implementation of the constitution', according to the words of the first draft of the 1958 constitution, was acknowledged for the first time in France, following numerous examples abroad. Although popular approval of the new constitution was gained in October 1958, the Constitutional Council was effectively set up in March 1959 only. In fact, the Constitutional Council was the last institution to be created which symbolizes its second order status for the designers of the Fifth Republic. Fifty years later, the Constitutional Council plays a key role in regulating political competition in France. This new role enjoyed by the Constitutional Council in French politics constitutes one of the main changes ushered in during the Fifth Republic. Some scholars like Rousseau even attribute a 'supreme position' to the Constitutional Council in the French political system. This chapter will show that since 1958 the Constitutional Council has been the main engine for the 'judicialization of politics' in France despite its continuing politicization. In order to do that, it will look at the main changes in its role together with the reasons for these changes since the beginning of the Fifth Republic.

Since 1959, several (though not all) of the Constitutional Council's main institutional features have been modified. The first part of this chapter will describe these institutional settings and their partial transformation. The activities of the Council have also increased in number and developed in response to institutional change. The second part of the chapter will show how this pattern underscores change in the scope of the Council's role in the regulation of French political competition. Judges in France now play a new central role in politics. The dynamics of constitutional review also deserve special attention to allow a better understanding of this new role and the underlying reasons for it to emerge. Finally, some of the gaps in the study of the Constitutional Council will be identified and themes for future research will be suggested.

6.1   The partial change of institutional features

As the institutional features of the Constitutional Council have changed significantly, an analysis of these evolutions is essential to fully understand the new jurisdiction of the Constitutional Council in the regulation of politics in France. Although it initially had a significant amount of jurisdiction, there is no doubt that the constitutional designers in 1958 did not want the judges to play such a significant role in politics. Nevertheless, the powers granted to the Constitutional Council have been progressively extended. Furthermore, according to some scholars, the impact of the change in 1974, which allowed constitutional review to be instigated by a minimum of 60 MPs, is as important as the 1962 revision of the presidential elections (Philip 1988). Although further changes on access to the Constitutional Council continue to be discussed it is the appointment process itself which is under the strongest pressure to change. Change of the institutional features can only be described as partial as this latter dimension has not been modified since 1958. There is a sharp contrast between, on the one hand, the important changes in jurisdiction and access and, on the other hand, the fact that the appointment process has been untouched since 1959. The well-known related patterns – continuing politicization of the appointment process and consequently of membership – are now the main factors undermining the legitimacy of the Constitutional Council (François 1999).

6.2   The jurisdiction of the Constitutional Council

At the beginning of the Fifth Republic, the Constitutional Council was granted jurisdiction over many areas. Over the past 50 years two changes have occurred: new jurisdiction was added (for example, the constitutional amendment of 2008 granted the Court the power to control the use of article 49.3 within a prescribed period), and other types of jurisdiction were extended. The fields covered by the Constitutional Council can be divided into three different types (Table 6.1): supervision of national elections, of political incumbents and of institutional activities.

In three main articles (art. 58, 59 & 60), the constitution defines the core of the Constitutional Council's jurisdiction over national elections. As of

Table 6.1   Constitutional Council's jurisdiction

Monitoring national elections	Complaints about presidential elections (Constitution Art. 58)
	Request for a delay of the presidential election (Constitution Art. 7, al. 8C)
	Complaints about legislative elections (Constitution Art. 59)
	Monitoring legislative candidates' expenses and financial resources
	Complaints about referenda (Constitution Art. 60C et 50)
Monitoring political incumbents	Monitoring the incapacity of the president of the Republic (Constitution Art. 7 al. 4C)
	Monitoring the loss of mandate by an MP
	Monitoring registration of MPs' statement of patrimony
	Monitoring the compatibility between multiple electoral positions of MPs
	Monitoring the compatibility of MPs' other private or public roles with the functions of the mandate
	Monitoring of actions incompatible with the status of MP
Monitoring institutional activities	Legal status – statute or regulation – of legislative text (Constitution Art. 37, al. 2C)
	Control of excluded amendments (Constitution Art. 41 C)
	Monitoring the compatibility of an international agreement (Constitution Art. 54 C)
	Constitutional review of 'organic' laws and parliamentary rules (Constitution Art. 61, al. 1C)
	Constitutional review of laws (Constitution Art. 61, al. 2C)
	Legal status of legislative text for Polynesia, St Barthelemy and St Martin (Constitution Art. 73)
	Monitoring of local laws in New Caledonia (Constitution Art. 77 C)

1958, the constitution states that 'the Constitutional Council shall rule on the proper conduct of the election of deputies and senators in disputed cases'. In fact, the Fifth Republic broke the rule that only Parliament should judge claims about parliamentary elections. From a historical perspective, this was clearly an unambiguous step toward the regulation of political competition by judges. In 1962, with the introduction of a new and popular type of election for the French presidency by direct ballot, the task of monitoring the presidential election was also assigned to the Constitutional Council. Moreover, in 1976, the Constitutional Council gained new powers in the organization of the presidential election by being allowed to postpone the election in some cases (art.7). The monitoring of national referenda completes the panel of national elections scrutinized by the Constitutional Council. Finally, in 1990, a new dimension was added, that of monitoring the expenses and financial resources of the candidates. Judging compliance with the financial rules of political competition has once more broadened the scope of the role played by the Constitutional Council in national elections since 1958.

The Constitutional Council's second main task is to monitor political incumbents. For example, if a president is judged to be incapable, the Council's role is to deliberate on whether the judgment is permanent or not. In the same vein, it also statutes on the loss of position by an MP whatever the reasons might be (incompatibility, inappropriate behavior, court sentence, etc.). As a result of the adoption of the financial rules surrounding political activity by the parliament at the beginning of the 1990s and the increased limitation of the 'cumul des mandats' since the beginning of the 1980s, the Constitutional Court has gained new prerogatives in these domains.

At the beginning of the new regime, the Constitutional Council had a substantial degree of jurisdiction in monitoring its third main area – institutional activity. This was clearly a departure from French constitutional history. The best known of its new attributions was its empowerment to execute constitutional review of ordinary laws (art. 61). In France constitutional review is limited to abstract review and may only take place before a law is promulgated. Laws can be referred to the Constitutional Council only just before they are enacted, i.e. within 15 days after they are passed. The Constitutional Council must make a decision within a month or a week if the government declares the topic to be 'urgent'. If a law or part of a law is judged by the Constitutional Council not to comply with the constitution, it is simply erased. Further, the Constitutional Council was initially designed to play the role of referee between political institutions. With this in mind, the constitution granted the Constitutional Council compulsory review of 'organic' laws and of parliamentary rules. Moreover, the founding fathers of the Fifth Republic's constitution, M. Debré and C. de Gaulle, clearly thought that the Constitutional Council should guarantee the limits of parliamentary power and protect executive power. As a result, the Constitutional Council can monitor implementation of various aspects of 'rationalized parliamentarianism' such as the legality of the contested exclusion of an amendment (art. 41) or the legal status – statute or regulation – of a legislative text (art. 37). The Constitutional Court is also responsible for monitoring the compatibility of international agreements (art. 54). Finally, since 1998, the regulation of relationships between the national level and sub-national governments have also been attributed more and more often to the Constitutional Council along with the increasing 'federalization' of French territorial organization. The resolution of the New Caledonia crisis resulted in an important transfer of jurisdiction from the national to the local level. The Constitutional Council is now the body in charge of reviewing the constitutional validity of local laws voted in New Caledonia. Since the 2003 constitutional amendment and the autonomy given to certain overseas territories since 2004, the Constitutional Council is also in charge of monitoring to ensure national laws respect jurisdictions granted to French Polynesia, St Barthelemy and St Martin. Finally, the 2004 constitutional amendment empowered the Constitutional Council to scrutinize financial transactions between the state and sub-national government although this has not yet been exercised.

6.3 Easier but limited access to litigation before the Constitutional Council

The Constitutional Council is a specialized court in all domains it deals with, with the exception of national elections where it only intervenes on appeal. In the areas where it has jurisdiction, no other court can rule. One cannot understand its institutional role without understanding the question of access to the court and to whom this is reserved.

Access to the Court varies hugely according to the jurisdiction involved in a given case. There is a sharp contrast between scrutinizing an appeal in relation to a national election on the one hand and scrutinizing political incumbents and institutional activities on the other. In fact, access to judicial review is very wide in electoral matters. Virtually any registered voter in a constituency and any candidate can challenge the result of the election in their constituency. Conversely, access is restricted in both other matters.

Access to the court is restricted differently depending on the type of jurisdiction being appealed to. In certain cases access to the initiation process is extremely limited as, for example, in the case of MPs who have lost their mandate where only the Council itself can initiate the process. In other cases there exists a monopoly of initiation. For example, only the government may initiate a case before the Constitutional Council regarding the inaptitude of the president of the Republic to govern or the legal status of a legislative text. Following this logic, the legal status of legislative texts for Polynesia, St Barthelemy and St Martin may only be challenged by the president of a sub-national government.

At the beginning of the Fifth Republic, French constitutional review was one of the most closed systems in the world. Beyond the automatic referral of organic laws and parliamentary rules, only the French president, the prime minister, the president of the Senate and the president of the National Assembly were allowed to refer a law to the Constitutional Council. As was said previously, the French system is based on an *a priori* abstract review. So the time window for a challenge to the constitutionality of a statute is narrow. Consequently, the extent to which access to initiate such a challenge is open largely determines how effective the scrutiny will be. Initially, the Fifth Republic's constitution featured constitutional review with an *a priori* abstract review and restricted access, which allowed its designers to ensure that the Constitutional Council would only act as referee in judicial conflicts between the main political institutions.

However, in 1974, the new president, V. Giscard d'Estaing widened access to the initiation process of constitutional review. These were sweeping changes despite numerous criticisms at the time that they were of secondary importance. The constitutional amendment allowed a group of a minimum of 60 senators or 60 MPs to refer a law to the Constitutional Council. Since then at least one opposition party in parliament has always been able to set a review in motion. As will be explained later, the impact of this change on the regulation of the French political system has been huge. In 1992 a similar change took place on scrutinizing the compatibility of international agreements with the constitution. The right for a group of 60 senators or 60 MPs to initiate a review of an international agreement before the Constitutional Council was granted. Broadly open access to initiate review of local laws in New Caledonia was granted to political incumbents and was inspired by the 1974 reform of constitutional review.

The fact that access to judicial review by the Constitutional Council has been made easier is a central element of its enhanced role in the political system. Nevertheless, extended access to constitutional review is still limited when compared to countries like Hungary, Germany or Spain, for example. The possibility of allowing citizens to petition the Constitutional Council has been discussed since the end of the 1980s. Nonetheless, the latest proposal by the Committee for Institutional Reform to widen access to constitutional review follows a different line and recommends the introduction of concrete review, i.e. the possibility for citizens to initiate constitutional review during a case in Court.

6.4   The continued politicization of the appointment process and membership

More often than other constitutional courts, the French Constitutional Court is considered to be a political chamber for institutional reasons. 'The only major country without any restrictions to a purely politicized appointment process is France' (Tsebelis 2002). Every three years the president of the Republic, the president of the Senate and the president of the National Assembly choose a candidate who becomes a member of the Constitutional Council for nine years. There are no statutory constraints defining the skills or experience of the nominees. There are no hearings or votes on the candidates. No supermajority vote is required in the appointment process. Because there are no constraints the person who appoints a new member necessarily chooses someone whose preferences are known and similar to his/her own. Therefore, in France, members of the Constitutional Council are politicized and reflect the political orientation of the appointing authority.

Out of the 66 members nominated to the Constitutional Council between 1959 and 2007, 43 were ministers, MPs or holders of elected positions. Nearly two-thirds of the constitutional judges were politicians and had strong and public partisan commitments. If nominees who belonged to presidential or ministerial staff – often high-ranking civil servants – are also taken into account the level of politicization reaches 80 percent. Apart from two candidates (Michard-Pellissier and Monnerville), the political orientation of all nominees was consistent with that of the authority that appointed them (Stone 1992). Even in the case of members not officially committed to a political party, their political sympathies are nonetheless known. For example, Goguel, one of the fathers of political science in France, was a political adviser to de Gaulle.

Thus, the political slant of the members of the Constitutional Council is a basic feature of constitutional politics in France. However, the French case is by no means exceptional. The proportion of party members in Germany remained the same between 1983 and 2003. During this period, only 34 percent of constitutional judges had no partisan commitment. Moreover, 'an informal division of seats on the court has developed. Half of the seats are allocated to the CDU/CSU, the other half to the SPD' (Vanberg 2005). Every nominee in Germany is a party member or is supported by a political party. Compared with the Supreme Court in the US, the French case does not seem to be unique either as politicization is also the rule in the USA. 'More than 90% of all Supreme Court nominees are members of the President's party, which provides considerable empirical support for the view that, even among the world's most independent courts, the nomination process is highly partisan' (Helmke 2005).

As has been shown above, although the Constitutional Council is indeed highly politicized, it is far from being the only such Constitutional Court to be so. Nevertheless, on this basis, scholars regularly emphasize the contrast between the facts that the judges in France are politicians whereas they are judges everywhere else. Intuitively, one would imagine that being a politician does not necessarily correspond to being skilled in law. However, law degrees and employment in legal activities are widespread among Constitutional Court members. The proportion of judges without any legal background is small (14%). Only 19 percent of them have never been employed in a legal capacity. Thus, only 9.5 percent of Constitutional Council members are not qualified in law or have no experience in a legal area. Therefore, in spite of the fact that there are no specific qualifications in law required for the job, in actual fact the vast majority of nominees have such qualifications. In the light of this, claims that French constitutional judges are not qualified to do their job are often exaggerated. By contrast, what is particular to the way in which Constitutional Council members are appointed is the lack of a supermajority or at least of public scrutiny resulting from a public vote with the consequences this entails. This last feature seems rare in Western democracies. Some scholars underscore a stark contrast between the stability of the ideological balance in the German constitutional court and the situation in France, where 'the lack of supermajority requirements allows partisan appointments that significantly shift the aggregate composition of the Court as control of the Presidency, National Assembly, and Senate changes hands' (Vanberg 2005). The first obvious consequence is instability in the proportion of seats controlled by each party. Consequently, contrary to Germany, there is an imbalance in the proportion of right-wing and left-wing members. Moreover, there is no incentive to nominate moderate judges in France.

Regarding institutional features and changes to them, the idea of a French exceptionalism is supported only by the rules of the appointment process. This is increasingly perceived by French politicians as an anomaly or an anachronism. The committee in charge of proposing amendments to the French Constitution in 2007 took on board President Sarkozy's electoral promise of a parliamentary vote on appointments to the Constitutional Court, and now presidential appointments can be blocked by a 3/5 vote of the parliamentary committee. Further, 'in order to take the consequences of the judicialization of the role of the Constitutional Council into account' the committee has suggested a suppression of the rule which allows former presidents to be members of the Constitutional Council even though very few of them have been. With regard to other institutional dimensions, the Fifth Republic is fully part of the general trend towards an increased 'judicialization of politics'. The following analysis of the Constitutional Council's activity provides a clear illustration of the scope of this change.

6.5   The developing and changing activity of the Constitutional Council

In response to institutional changes, the developing and changing activity of the Constitutional Council underscores its growing role in the regulation of French political competition. Electoral decisions have remained the most important component of the Council's activity and have continued to grow since 1990. Among non-electoral decisions, the increase in the number of decisions relating to constitutional review is striking and is a direct consequence of the 1974 constitutional revision. The widening of access to the initiation process of constitutional review has increased the Constitutional Council's power of scrutiny over legislative politics. At the same time, the main and initial function – protecting the executive by enforcing a separation between regulation (made by government) and laws (made by parliament) – has decreased whereas the monitoring of MPs has increased in frequency. The changing content of non-electoral decisions exemplifies the new role of the Constitutional Council in France.

6.6   The Constitutional Council as an electoral judge

If analysed in terms of number of decisions, the Constitutional Council has primarily been an electoral judge until now. Three quarters of its activity has been dedicated to electoral decisions (Figure 6.1). Two-thirds of the total number of decisions concern litigation related to National Assembly elections, 4 percent concern presidential and senatorial elections and 1 percent

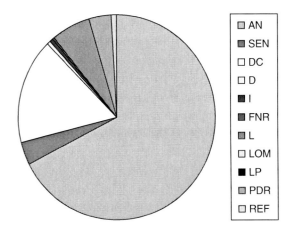

AN
SEN
DC
D
I
FNR
L
LOM
LP
PDR
REF

Figure 6.1   Type of decisions of the Constitutional Council 1959–2006

concerns referenda. Though often neglected in analyses, the dominant presence of electoral issues in the Constitutional Council's activities provides a larger than usual understanding of its regulatory role in French political competition.

Since 1993, the Constitutional Council has been an electoral judge in the fullest sense of the term (Figure 6.2). At that time, the number of claims increased eightfold compared with the previous legislative election. This increased number of cases was a result of the implementation of the new financial rules of political competition. In fact, since this peak, the level of litigation has remained substantially higher than before. The 2007 legislative election was also followed by a very large number of legal disputes. As the rules surrounding political competition have intensified, both the level of judicial litigation between the political players and the regulatory role of the Constitutional Court has increased. Moreover, beyond that, the content of non-electoral decisions has also greatly changed.

6.6.1   The changing content of non-electoral decisions

The increasing regulation of political competition by the Constitutional Council is also underlined by the growing number of decisions about political incumbents (Figure 6.3). Since the beginning of the 1990s the Constitutional Council has judged more cases about MPs than ever before. Conversely, since the end of the 1980s, the number of decisions on the legal status of legislative texts has decreased sharply. This dimension of the Constitutional Court's activity which was its second most important task for a long time, has been losing its pre-eminence. The way in which the institution works and the role it plays in the political system has clearly changed over time as a result of change in its institutional features.

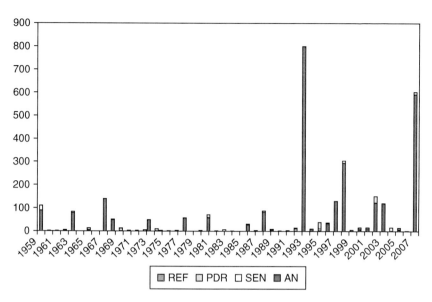

Figure 6.2 Constitutional Council's decisions about elections 1959–2007

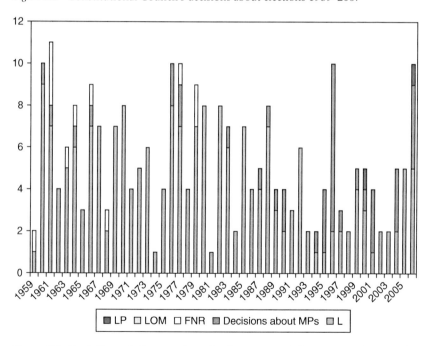

Figure 6.3 Evolution of the number of other types of Constitutional Council's decisions

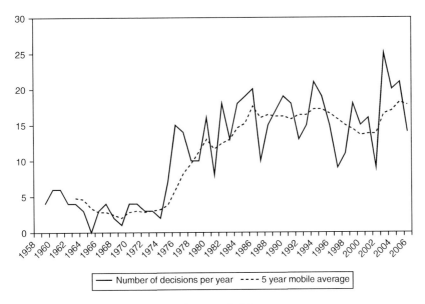

Figure 6.4 Number of constitutional review decisions

Apart from electoral decisions, the most spectacular increase in the Constitutional Council's activity is in constitutional review. Whereas the number of constitutional review decisions had seldom reached five per year before 1975, their number has almost never dropped under ten per year (Figure 6.4) since then. Since the 1981 alternation, the average is around 15 constitutional decisions per year. Undoubtedly, the fact that the minority may now initiate referrals has inflated their number and extended the regulatory function of the Constitutional Council beyond electoral competition to political decisions. As constitutional review activity has grown, other activities have totally disappeared. For example, the verification of contested amendments (FNR in Figure 6.3) was carried out for the last time in 1980. In fact, today, constitutional review includes verification of the validity of amendments and the resulting jurisprudence is unequivocal. There is therefore less cause for government and parliament to fight about them. The scope of the change and the importance of this for the dynamics of the Fifth Republic warrant a closer look at changes in French constitutional review.

6.6.2 The dynamics of constitutional review

The dynamics of constitutional review itself is a key element of the new central role of judges in French politics as is the reasoning behind this role. Beyond institutional changes, the Constitutional Council has succeeded in freeing itself from the initial role assigned to it by the constitutional designers by finding new ways of judging. The increasing use of restrictive interpretation has also been a creative way of diminishing the risks associated with being an aggressive counter-majoritarian institution preventing policy change. Nevertheless, the Constitutional Council has also vetoed much important legislation although constitutional rigidity in France is weak (Lijphart 1999). Fuelled by numerous referrals, the scope of constitutional review is wide in impact, and concerns a large number of different topics. But, despite the fact that appointments are so political, the politicization of constitutional review is limited.

6.6.3   New ways of judging

Although the 1974 reform radically changed the frequency of and logic behind constitutional referrals, the way judging was done had begun changing before that date. These changes have fuelled each other up until the present time and the dynamics of constitutional review also encompass three features related to the working of the Council itself.

First, a dramatic change in the definition of the 'constitution' itself occurred in 1971. Thanks to a referral by the president of the Senate, the Constitutional Council was called on to verify a law about freedom of association where the protection of citizens' rights was at stake. Because freedom of association was threatened, the statute was partially vetoed. The judges used two sources to defend their position: the content of the preamble to the 1958 constitution and the 'fundamental principles recognized by the laws of the Republic'. The Constitutional Council therefore acknowledged that the preamble was fully part of the constitution. By extension, this decision paved the way for the inclusion of the texts quoted in the preamble: the Declaration of Human and Civil Rights of 1789 and the preamble to the 1946 constitution. The content of the 'constitution' was hugely enhanced by this decision as were the resources available to protect the rights of citizens. Moreover, in the same 1971 decision, the Council established the constitutional value of the 'fundamental principles recognized by the laws of the Republic'. Even if this expression is explicitly written in the 1946 preamble, the constitutional source is not *de facto* constitutional because it is based on laws adopted before 1946. Through this innovation, the Council created a great deal of freedom for itself. In fact, since 1971 the Constitutional Council has been able to select laws which give birth to a fundamental principle from among the range of pre-1946 laws. Furthermore, in 1979, the Constitutional Council created a new set of constitutional rules, called 'principles with constitutional value'. These principles are not necessarily written in any specific text. The inviolability of the home, the right to lead a normal family life and the right to family reunification, safeguarding the dignity of the human person or protecting the health of mothers and children have been recognized by the Constitutional Council as principles with constitutional values. The extension of the content of the 'constitution' has been a major factor in the growth of the role of the Constitutional Council and of its judicial activism.

Secondly, the Constitutional Council has developed an intensive use of restrictive interpretation. It limits the way a law is implemented by defining how a law or part of a law should be applied so that it confirms the constitution. Since 1982 there has been an increase in the number of interpretations of laws by the Constitutional Council. The proportion of referred laws with restrictive interpretations has reached 50 percent of the total number of laws scrutinized by the Constitutional Court (Viala 1999). In order to escape the costly alternative between veto or agreement, the Constitutional Council *de facto* rewrites the laws and supervises their implementation without blocking them. The recent example on the use of DNA testing in the 2007 immigration statutes shows how the Constitutional Council may sharply restrict the implementation of a part of a law without necessarily vetoing it. When alternation occurs the use of restrictive interpretations is a way to decrease claims that the democratic process is being interfered with and, at the same time, to avoid being accused of deferring to the new government.

Lastly, the status of the Constitutional Council's decisions had been uncertain for a long time. Article 62.2 of the Constitution states that they 'shall be binding on public authorities and on all administrative authorities and all courts'. But the way to understand and apply this was debated intensely. The Constitutional Council itself was prudent on this issue. It defined its own position only slowly and implicitly in the content of several decisions, in 1962, 1979 and 1985. As often in judicial politics, the explicit statement in 1987 about the status of its decisions was used in a paradoxical context. The Salvan decision explained that the correction of a material mistake is not contradictory with the *res judicata* of the Constitutional Council. But it was the first time that this principle was explicitly written in a decision. Afterwards, on two occasions in 1988 and 1992, the Constitutional Council rejected referrals according to the *res judicata* principle.

The clarification of the status of decisions made by the Constitutional Council is a symbol of its new role within the French political system but also proof that its strategy of judicial activism has been successful. The scope and frequency of constitutional review provides another illustration of this.

6.6.4 The scope of constitutional review

As explained above, the Constitutional Council has considerably expanded the scope of its powers of scrutiny since the enlargement of the constitutional review initiative. The increase in the number of referrals has brought about a strong level of control over the drafting of new laws in France. Between 1986 and 2006, more than a quarter of French domestic laws (excluding constitutional laws and statutes ratifying international agreements and treaties) were under review by the Constitutional Council (Figure 6.5). During this period, the level of verification was seldom lower than 20 percent per year. Moreover,

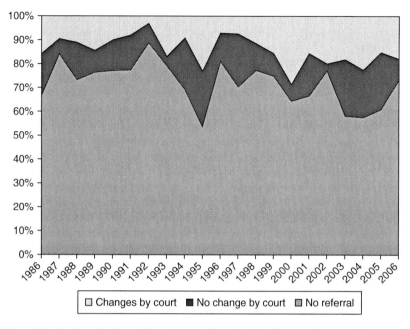

Figure 6.5   Level and effect of constitutional review (without ratifying and constitutional laws)

every contentious policy has been referred to the Constitutional Council for the last 25 years. For example, policies on both nationalization and privatization have been referred to the Council. In fact, the opposition is always motivated to contest majority policy when a high level of issue polarization occurs. Without these large numbers of referrals, the Constitutional Council would not have had the opportunity to develop such a level of judicial activism.

Conversely to most accounts of judicial politics, constitutional review of laws in France has brought about an unusual number of constitutional vetoes. From 1986 to 2006, half of the referred laws were totally or partially vetoed by the Constitutional Court. Nearly 14 percent of the domestic laws have been vetoed at least partially by the Constitutional Council. Figure 6.6 shows that the level of referrals and vetoes varies according to the policy sector. Four important policy sectors were scrutinized intensively and challenged by the Court. Nearly half of the policy proposals on Macroeconomics, Labour and Employment, Immigration and Space, Science and Technology were referred. Between 30 and 40 percent of them were ruled to be, at least partly, unconstitutional. At the other extreme, environmental policies have almost never been scrutinized until now by the Constitutional Court. But, with the addition of the Environmental Charter to the preamble of the Constitution in 2007, judicial activism by the Constitutional Council together with the amount of litigation on this issue should increase in the future.

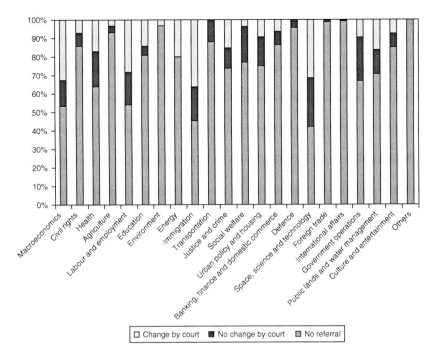

Figure 6.6 Level and effect of constitutional review by topics (1986–2007)

At an intermediary level, Justice and Crime, Energy, Urban Policy, Health and Education have been significantly ruled on by the Constitutional Council.

The number of referrals, of vetoes and of restrictive interpretations is very high in comparative perspective. Between 1986 and 2006 the proportion of ordinary laws with a partial or total constitutional veto greatly exceeded the 5 percent level associated with the strong German constitutional court. Thus, the French political system can no longer be characterized as a system with weak or limited constitutional review. Despite its politicization, the key role played by the Constitutional Council for years can no longer be neglected. Nevertheless, the impact of politicization needs to be estimated to understand the extent to which it has influenced constitutional review outcomes over the years.

6.6.5 The extent of the politicization of constitutional review outcomes

The politicization of the Council's judgments is an important question for comparative politics but also in French politics. Whatever their partisan commitments, French politicians, have a history of denouncing the Council as a political body. C. Pasqua, Minister of the Interior in 1993, said 'The Constitutional Council stops the government from creating its policy'. He argued that 'there are people in the Constitutional Council who are committed to politics (...) and this political commitment, in the majority, does not fit with today's [governmental] majority'. These positions are not specifically right-wing. Socialist leaders and supporters have often attacked the legitimacy of the Constitutional Court in very similar terms. In 1982, when the Constitutional Council invalidated the law on nationalization, the front page headline of *Libération*, a popular left-wing newspaper, described the Council as 'the gang of Monpensier Street' which is where the Constitutional Council meets.

Given the politicization of the appointment process outlined above, its effect on constitutional review outcomes is an important issue. Unlike what happens in the US Supreme Court, the secrecy of Constitutional Council decision-making precludes a study of the preferences of individual French judges (Stone 1992). Nevertheless, the strong politicization of these judges allows changes in the Constitutional Court majority to be tracked: the basic assumption is that there is a right-wing (left-wing) majority in the Constitutional Council if a majority of its members have been appointed by right-wing (left-wing) incumbents. Thus, it becomes possible to study the effects of the politicization of the appointment process by focusing on the consequences of divergence or convergence between legislative and Court majorities.

Historically, the Constitutional Council has more frequently been dominated by right-wing members. Since 1959 there has been a right-wing majority for a total of 40 years. The left has been in a majority for only nine years in total between 1989 and 1998. Since 1986 there have been seven cases of congruence between legislative and Court majorities, whereas divergence has occurred in four cases. On two occasions left-wing governments have had a divergent Court and on four occasions a congruent Court. Divergence between the Court and the government has concerned only two right-wing governments out of five.

The 'politicization hypothesis' assumes that the Court's response to the bills referred depends on the congruence or divergence between Court and legislative majorities. If the Constitutional Council's behavior is politicized, all else being equal, congruence between the legislative majority and the Constitutional Court majority should be associated with a lower level of veto. If the political factor is relevant, right-wing judges appointed by the right, for example, should be less critical of right-wing bills than left-wing bills. Divergence between the legislative majority and the Constitutional Court majority should be associated with a higher level of veto. If the political factor is relevant, left-wing judges have more incentives and motives for vetoing right-wing bills than left-wing bills.

Empirically, there are important variations in the rate of vetoes (out of the total number of referrals) by government since 1986 (Figure 6.7). The maximum is 60 percent and the minimum is 33 percent. The rate clearly changes according to the government in power. But there is no clear link between political orientation of government and number of vetoes per se.

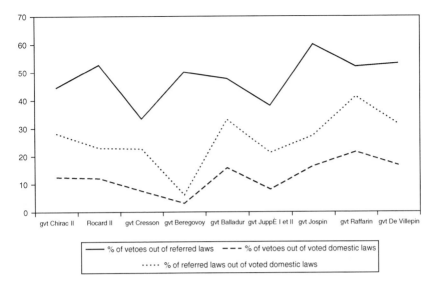

Figure 6.7 Constitutional Council's scrutiny per government 1986–2007

Conversely, there is no link between the majority in the Court and level of veto per se. The idea that a right-wing or left-wing majority in government or in the Court would be associated with specific behavior is not borne out. A left-wing Court does not seem to be more prone to judicial activism or self-restraint than a right-wing Court. In the same way, a right-wing government per se does not enact more constitutionally controversial statutes than a left-wing one. What does merit investigation is the pattern associating the different levels of the veto rate with the divergence or convergence between legislative and Court majorities.

The average number of partially or totally vetoed bills in a divergent Court (16.5) is higher than in a convergent Court (11.9). However, it is more significant to compare the veto rate to the total number of referrals. While the average rate of vetoes of referred laws per government is 45 percent when legislative and Court majorities converge, the proportion climbs to 57 percent when legislative and Court majorities diverge. Finally, without divergence between government and Court, 12 percent of the laws/bills passed are vetoed whereas with divergence, 14 percent of the laws/bills passed are vetoed. Thus, univariate analysis of Court behavior supports the politicization hypothesis. Whichever way they are computed, vetoes are more frequent when the Constitutional Council is controlled by the opposition. Outcomes of constitutional review vary according to convergence or divergence between Court and legislative majorities.

So there is clear indication[2] that the politicization hypothesis is supported but limited. The politicization of the appointment process does have an effect on the outcome of constitutional review. From this point of view, the Constitutional Council is undoubtedly affected by politicization. But what comparative statistics show is that a significant amount of vetoes (56 percent of the total amount of vetoes between 1986 and 2007) occurred when there was a congruent majority in government and Court. On average, 12 percent of domestic laws/bills passed when congruent majorities are in place are vetoed. 45 percent of laws referred in the same political context are also vetoed. Moreover, some of the founding decisions of the Constitutional Court took place in a congruent context. Even before the opposition was in a position to initiate constitutional review, the Council departed from a strictly political way of thinking with the breakthrough decision of 1971. In 1986 the privatization law enacted by the (right-wing) Chirac government was vetoed by the (right-wing) Constitutional Council applying the same reasoning as in 1981 for the nationalization law. The politicization of the highest judicial body falls far short of summing up the Constitutional Council's behavior and role in France. In many cases, the behavior of its members and indeed the institution itself has been shaped by factors other than politicization.

6.7   Conclusion and research agenda

Despite the enduring politicization of the Constitutional Council, its increasing jurisdiction, its institutional development and its changing activities have been the engines by which the 'judicialization of politics' (Stone 1992, Gaxie 1989, Favoreu 1988) has grown in France since the beginning of the Fifth Republic. Understanding the increasing regulatory role of the Constitutional Council implies, beyond constitutional review, taking into account the full scope of its missions including the most important dimensions of French politics, the monitoring of national elections and of political incumbents. An analysis of the almost 50 years of the Constitutional Council's history shows how the Fifth Republic has changed dramatically. The current French regime can no longer be characterized as one with limited or weak judicial review. Furthermore, regarding constitutional politics, the politicization of the Council is probably the only remaining element of French exceptionalism although the level of specificity should not be overestimated. It is the pattern in which Council members are politicized which is specific, not the mere fact of the existence or indeed the level of politicization. In the same way, describing the constitutional council as a political body making political judgments is far from the reality of the limited politicization of the Council's rulings. The divergence and the convergence between the Council's majority and the legislative majority do not offer an exhaustive understanding of veto politics in France.

Further research is needed to deal with this complex issue and to remove the discrepancies between existing literature and the empirical level of veto in France. A relevant research agenda might include a rigorous exploration of different hypothetical logics and factors in terms, for example, of the

Constitutional Council's audience or of selective defection, etc. A more general research agenda should also investigate the appointment process. There is a lack of data and studies on the way the appointment process has been organized and for what reason. Until now, there has been no equivalent in France to Yalof's book (1999) on the choice of Justices by US presidents. This would undoubtedly be a fruitful research agenda which would provide new perspective on well-known but unexplored topics.

Notes

1. There was one single referral, in 1948, to the Constitutional Committee.
2. An OLS regression analysis jointly testing the politicization hypothesis, the veto player hypothesis, the minority government hypothesis and the alternation hypothesis shows a statistically significant coefficient to the divergence variable. Ceteris paribus, divergence induces a veto rate 17% higher.

Bibliography

Bacquet-Bréhand, V. (2005) *L'article 62, alinéa 2 de la constitution du 4 octobre 1958. Contribution à l'étude de l'autorité des décisions du Conseil Constitutionnel*, (Paris: LGDJ).
Favoreu, L. (1988) *La politique saisie par le droit*, (Paris: Economica).
François, B. (1997) 'Le Conseil Constitutionnel et la Cinquième République', *Revue Française de Science Politique*, 47(3–4), 377–403.
François, B. (1999) 'La perception du Conseil Constitutionnel par la classe politique, les médias et l'opinion', *Pouvoirs*, n°105, 133–42.
Gaxie, D. (1989) 'Jeux croisés. Droit et politique dans la polémique sur le refus de signature des ordonnances par le Président de la République', in CURAPP, *Les usages sociaux du droit*, (Paris: PUF), 209–29.
Helmke, G. (2005) *Courts under Constraints*, (Cambridge: Cambridge University Press).
Jan, P. (1999) *La saisine du Conseil Constitutionnel*, (Paris: LGDJ).
Jan, P. (2001) *Le procès constitutionnel*, (Paris: LGDJ).
Philip, L. (1988) 'Bilan et effets de la saisine du Conseil Constituionnel', in O. Duhamel and J.L. Parodi, *La constitution de la cinquième République*, (Paris: Presses de la Fondation Nationale des Sciences Politiques), 408–21.
Stone, A. (1992) *The Birth of Judicial Politics in France. The Constitutional Council in Comparative Perspective*, (Oxford: Oxford University Press).
Stone-Sweet, A. (2000) *Governing with Judges. Constitutional Politics in Europe*, (Oxford: Oxford University Press).
Rousseau, D. (2006) *Droit du contentieux constitutionnel*, (Paris: Montchrestien).
Tsebelis, G. (2002) *Veto Players. How Institutions Work*, (Princeton: Princeton University Press).
Vanberg, G. (2005) *The Politics of Constitutional Review in Germany*, (Cambridge: Cambridge University Press).
Viala, A. (1999) *Les réserves d'interprétation dans la jurisprudence du Conseil Constitutionnel*, (Paris: LGDJ).
Yalof, D. (1999) *Pursuit of Justices: Presidential Politics and the Selection of Supreme Court Nominees*, (Chicago: University of Chicago Press).

7
Defence and Armed Forces: The End of the Nuclear Monarchy?

Bastien Irondelle

The Fifth Republic originates from the troubles of the Algerian War (1958 crisis) and the Defence policy of the Fifth Republic was launched by a divorce between the political order and the Army (the 1961 putsch). Under the leadership of General de Gaulle, the Fifth Republic gave birth to a 'nuclear monarchy', where the president benefits from a *domaine réservé* concerning defence and foreign policy, thanks to the president's nuclear privilege, and the existence of a political consensus on defence policy (Cohen 1986). Since 1958 France has been considered as the ideal type of a strong state in defence and foreign affairs (Katzenstein 1976, Risse-Kapen 1991).

Thus the first point that should be highlighted is that there indeed is a 'defence model' of the Fifth Republic, a particular trajectory in national defence policy after 1958, which distinguishes France from other European countries. The Gaullist legacy (Gordon 1993) has taken root progressively in France, to the point that it produced a 'defence consensus' (Dobry 1986). The fundamental orientations remained particularly stable until the mid-1990s. Since the middle of the 1980s this model has been confronted with numerous tensions and drivers for change that have resulted in a profound transformation of the French armed forces and a paradigm shift in defence policy.

7.1 Defence and the armed forces vis-à-vis the logics and dynamics of the Fifth Republic

On the one hand, policies on defence and the armed forces are exemplary of the logics and dynamics of the Fifth Republic: statism and economic interventionism, the weakness of Parliament, the power of the technocratic elite (*armament engineers*). On the other hand, the exceptionalism of national security policy in the French political system is in doubt: priority of defence spending; 'sanctuarization' of the military budget; political consensus; very short decision-making processes involving the president and a lack of interministerial negotiations. At the fiftieth anniversary of the Fifth Republic, the creation of the 'Balladur committee' represents an ideal landmark upon which to evaluate and discuss these changes. Indeed, President Sarkozy has proclaimed the end of the *domaine reservé* and his commitment to increase the power of Parliament in foreign policy and defence issues, notably concerning foreign military interventions.

Is the '*domaine réservé*' – meaning the presidential dominance and the weakness of the French Parliament – a myth? Is the Nuclear Monarchy still a relevant conception to speak of in French defence policy-making? Is it the end of the Gaullist legacy? What are the main and profound changes affecting French security policy? What dimensions of policy have changed and what parameters remain stable? Are the dynamics affecting defence and the armed forces the same as those affecting the French policy-making system as a whole?

In the following I argue that deep transformations have affected French defence policy since 1958. Since 1991 France has accomplished in a decade or so what some may consider a revolution in its defence policy (Bureau 1997) by the biases of progressive adaptation (1991–95) and substantial reform, brought about by President Chirac in 1996 (Irondelle 2003), which simultaneously affected nuclear strategy, military doctrine, the relationship with NATO, arms production, the organization of the armed forces, the transition to a professional army and the end of conscription. But the fundamental logic of the Fifth Republic, following the basic features of the Nuclear Monarchy (presidential dominance, parliamentary marginalization, political consensus, depoliticization of national security issues, civil–military relations) has remained particularly robust despite some inflexions. In contrast with the polity- and politics-levels, the policy- or sectoral-level has been more deeply affected by certain dramatic changes. The chapter underlines that some of the most important institutions and features of the Fifth Republic's defence policy do not derive from the constitution. It focuses on policy-making and institutional aspects of French security policy, somewhat leaving aside the military and strategic dimensions.

The next section analyses the genesis and the institutionalization of the *domaine réservé*. The following section study the Gaullist legacy of French security policy, while the final sections evaluate the changes that have affected defence policy by contrasting the transformation of the meso-level of policy-making with the robustness of the political and institutional features of the Nuclear Monarchy.

7.2   The 'hidden' logic of the Fifth Republic: Institutionalizing the domaine réservé

Although it has no legal basis – the notion does not appear in any official text – the 'reserved domain' is the most decisive institution for the elaboration of military policy. The reserved domain is both a regulatory mechanism for relations within the executive, and between the executive and legislative. Despite this dimension being neglected, the reserved domain is also a regulatory mechanism for relations between political power and the army.

7.2.1   The conflictual genesis of the Fifth Republic's military policy (1958–64)

The Fifth Republic originated in a time of divorce between the army and government. There were major traumatic events, such as the wars in Indochina and the state of crisis in Algerian civil–military relations, culminating in the 1961 military Putsch in Alger (Ambler 1966, Girardet 1964). The adoption of a nuclear deterrent strategy entailed the crisis of modernism in the armed forces. However, since 1962, civilian control over the military has firmly been established (Cohen 1994, Vennesson 2003). In a way similar to civil–military relations, the reserved domain emerged from conflict between the executive and legislative. I argue that the Nuclear Monarchy is a political construct that resulted from a conflict between executive power and Parliament at the beginning of the 1960s when the first two military program-laws were voted, due to restrictive legislative procedures. Indeed, on 8 July 1960 the government presented the first military program-law that defined procurement goals, notably concerning nuclear weapons in the National Assembly, thereby implementing the new orientation of defence policy, based on an independent nuclear '*force de frappe*'. According to Pierre Messmer, Minister of the Armed Forces (Ministre des Armées), the proposal of this law stems from two goals held by the executive. It is first to force Parliament to rally around the new defence policy, but also to impose a major reorganization of the army, as planned for by the policy. Many deputies from the majority feared that making the atomic weapon the utmost priority would engage France in a retreat from NATO and a disengagement from Algeria. The prime minister committed the government's responsibility during the three readings required to pass the law. The motion of censure was finally rebuffed.

This move toward greater control of defence policy in the hands of the executive was reaffirmed by a vote on the second military program-law in 1964, after the vote was blocked during the three readings in the National Assembly. Once again, parliamentarians had to choose between refusing the text and disavowing the direction of defence policy, as agreed to in 1960, or endorsing it and writing a blank check to the government. In contrast with the conclusions drawn by John Huber (1996),[1] the recourse to restrictive procedures results in a conflict between the executive and legislative on their preferences in regards to defence. Indeed, it is clear that in 1960, and to a lesser degree in 1964, the government was successful in imposing solutions on Parliament that are quite far from its preferences, closer to a maintenance of the status quo. Those two laws, and the way in which they were adopted, confirmed the president's supremacy and relegated Parliament to a subsidiary role. The failure of censure and the election of the president of the Republic in a direct popular suffrage in 1962 reaffirmed this supremacy. There is evidence to suggest that direct popular suffrage in the election of the president of the new Republic was linked to France's nuclear status. In 1963 Pierre Messmer wrote: 'Our military policy partly explains the recent evolution of the nation's political institutions... the Head of State exclusively holds power over the use of strategic nuclear forces (...) he must be elected by the whole nation to face such terrible challenges'.[2] The policy of nuclear deterrence is a strong dynamic in developing the institution of the presidentialization of the Fifth Republic.

7.2.2 Institutionalizing the 'domaine réservé': sanctioning General de Gaulle's legacy

An analysis of constitutional texts, namely the Constitution and the ordinance on the general organization of defence, does not provide a clear understanding of the president of the Republic's primacy in defence and foreign affairs. It only confers restricted powers upon the president. Article 13 relates to the nomination of military officers. Under Article 15, the president of the Republic has the role of commander-in-chief of the armed forces (*Chef des armées*) who 'shall preside over the higher national defence councils and committees'. The given title of *Chef des armées* is essentially an honorary one. As for the presidency of the Defence Council, whatever its importance, it does not legally set the president's primacy (Luchaire and Conac 1987, 529 and 577).

If the constitutional text does not set the foundations for presidential supremacy, the Constitution reserves important powers to the government. Under Article 20, 'the government shall determine and conduct the policy of the Nation' and affirms in the second paragraph that the government may 'have at its disposal the armed forces'. Under Article 21, 'the Prime Minister shall direct the operation of the Government. He shall be responsible for national defence'. The Ordinance of 1959 reinforces the prime minister's role, stipulating that 'the prime minister, responsible for national defence, exercises the general direction and the military direction of defence' (art. 9), and that the Ministre des Armées works 'under his authority' (art. 16). In other words, with regards to the ordinance of 1959, it is the prime minister who appears as the 'key to the whole organization of national defence' as the 'master of defence' (Chantebout 1962, 198–9).

More than in any other public policy field, the practical legacy of the Fifth Republic's founder is a determining factor in explaining the presidential leadership exercised over defence policy. On 8 February 1960 General de Gaulle made his view clear to Prime Minister Michel Debré: 'Issues involving Algeria, Defence, the armies, foreign affairs and the community must be directly taken up with me'.[3] General de Gaulle's institutional legacy gives Article 5 and 15 of the Constitution a meaning and resonance well beyond the original statement of the constitutional text. 'The President of the Republic "guarantor of national independence and the nation's integrity" being in charge of "the state's continuity", heading the "Defence Council", is the Commander in Chief of the forces. He decides either alone, within the Defence Council, or the Council of Ministers'.[4] In General de Gaulle's conception, the title of commander-in-chief of the armed forces or the presidency of a council cannot be understood as honorific or as collegial functions. 'During debates, I insist that opinions be expressed without reserve. At the end, I let my own opinion known. Often, there was a general agreement between members. I take note of it and all is said. If not, I take a decision that I deem right; and, it becomes that of the Council's'.[5] It is by presiding over the defence council that the practice of presidential primacy over defence policy is legally recognized with the orders of 18 July 1962, which profoundly changed executive powers.

Decree n° 62–808 relates to the organization of national defence and confirms the exclusion of the prime minister from defence policy-making: 'within the framework of general defence, defined by the Ministers' Council, defence councils or committees that are brought together and presided over by the President of the Republic, ensure the overall direction of national defence, and under specific circumstances, the conduct of war' while 'the prime minister ensures the implementation of government decisions'. More importantly, this decree formalizes the practice of the first few years of the Fifth Republic and cements presidential primacy in the elaboration of defence and military policy. It is reinforced by Decree n° 64–46 of 14 January 1964, by which the order for the use of strategic nuclear weapons is 'given by the president of the Republic, the president of the defence council and the commander-in-chief of the armed forces', upheld by article 15 of the Constitution.

7.3   The Gaullist legacy

The Gaullist legacy is built on political, diplomatic, strategic and industrial logics that are complementary and form a particularly coherent military model. This paradigm is based on several features:

- Strict political control over the armed forces with an uncontested subordination of the military to the president. Vertical organization of the Ministry of Defence with a formal (1982 decree), strategic (the three branches have nuclear weapons), budgetary and political equality among the three branches (Army, Air Force, Navy).
- The armed forces as an incarnation of national sovereignty: no integration in multinational forces, systematic national command structures, conscription. Defence policy is based on the political principle of national independence and the strategic principle of autonomy in

decision-making. It is guided above all by a political logic: defence policy in the service of the greatness of France and its rank in the world.

- At the military level, this policy rests on the implementation of a national nuclear deterrent strategy. The strategy and military tools are subordinated to the nuclear deterrent, cornerstone of French defence policy (Ruhl 1977, Yost 1994).
- An armament policy seeking autarchy through national production, particularly in the sectors considered decisive for strategic autonomy (nuclear, space, and aerospace). The system of arms production is based on administrative regulatory mechanisms organized by the *Délégation générale pour l'Armement* (DGA), the procurement directorate of the defence ministry. The DGA is the integrator of the French military system (Hébert 1995). Edward Kolodziej emphasizes this double feature of French experience in the military-industrial complex: it is statist and regulated by the 'oligarchy' of armament engineers (Kolodziej 1987). The creation of the *Délégation générale pour l'armement* in 1961 brought about the 'golden age of the military-industrial complex', until the end of the 1980s.
- Since its withdrawal from its integrated military structure in 1966, France has had a difficult relationship with NATO, especially in reconciling national independence and Atlantic solidarity (Bozo 1991, Menon 2000).

In 1974, the election of a centrist candidate to the presidency posed the question of the Gaullist legacy in defence policy, especially in regards to certain positions on nuclear deterrence or NATO. Giscard challenged the Gaullist dogmas and tried to introduce a change in the military doctrine in close collaboration with the chief of defence staff, Guy Méry. This challenge came with the 'enlarged sanctuary' of nuclear deterrence and participation to the conventional defence of Western Europe. The president's attempt at revising the Gaullist legacy failed (Rynning 2002), but Giscard did not change institutional practices and reaffirmed the reserved domain. The shifts of 1974 and 1981 did not lead to a readjustment of defence powers in favour of the prime minister or the parliament. The consensuses on defence, like the *domaine réservé*, were definitively solidified when the left came to power in 1981. François Mitterrand, the most vociferous adversary of the *Coup d'État Permanent*[6] designed by the institutions of the Fifth Republic, followed the example set by de Gaulle in terms of defence policy-making. François Mitterrand incarnated the Nuclear Monarchy when he proclaimed in 1983 that 'the main element in France's deterrent strategy is the head of state – that is myself' echoing Louis XIV's formula 'L'Etat, c'est moi'.

From an institutional perspective, but mostly from a practical perspective, the great axes of the defence consensus inspired by de Gaulle were created by presidential primacy, as well as a nuclear deterrent from weak to strong, which necessitates decisional unity, residing with one person. This translated into the primacy of nuclear deterrence in the French strategy, a policy of national independence, notably with regards to NATO, and a commitment to conscription. The convergence of political parties to this consensus can best be understood with reference to the presidential issue (Hanley 1984). The centrists' rallying to deterrence in 1974 may be the best example. From the middle of the 1970s participation in this consensus over defence and nuclear deterrence appears as the inescapable feature in the role of president: 'it [indeed] established the pragmatic rule according to which it is costly to markedly depart from it in the French political game' (Dobry 1986, 48). The official conversion to nuclear deterrence by the Socialist Party in 1978, and to a lesser degree, by the Communist Party in 1977, can be explained by these political actors' experience in proximity to power as well as both symbolic and electoral retributions.

7.4   A paradigm shift without trouble: The end of defence exceptionalism in the Fifth Republic

Between 1991 and 1996 French military policy underwent a paradigm change. A third order change occurred that can be described as a situation where 'not only were the settings of policy changed but the hierarchy of goals and set of instruments employed to guide policy shifted radically as well' (Hall 1986).

7.4.1   Priority shift: the end of nuclear primacy, the decline of military spending, and the end of conscription

The strategic changes that occurred in Europe in the early 1990s marked, for French military policy, a strategic rupture even deeper than the end of the Cold War. This was the first time since 1871 that military planning and definition of the force structure were not geared toward a major threat to national territory. The first words of the 1994 *Livre Blanc* sur *la défense* underlined that 'There are no more threats on France's borders'. Henceforth, the notion of war would give precedence to crisis management and French forces would be destined to take a greater part in foreign interventions. The missions of the armed forces evolved on two fronts: foreign military interventions and multinational cooperation within the United Nations, NATO or the European Union. French strategy experienced an inversion of priorities between the nuclear deterrent and conventional forces whose 'primary mission' would now consist in power projection and foreign interventions. Nuclear deterrence is no more the alpha and omega of French defence policy. The nuclear share of the defence equipment budget has declined from 40 percent to 20 percent since 1990 and the nuclear share of the defence budget has been reduced from 16.9 percent to 8.75 percent between 1990 and 1999 (Tertrais 2007). The share given to defence in the national budget and the deductions on national wealth have steadily decreased. From 5.2 percent of the GDP and 25 percent of the national budget in 1962, the budget for defence without pensions has changed to 2.5 percent and 13.21 percent respectively, for 1994 and 1.7 percent and 11.5 percent in 2005.[7] Despite military spending being reduced in the national budget, it has continued to increase in absolute terms and in francs until 1990.

Since 1958 the transformation of the French Armed forces is linked to its declining size. The maintenance of conscription conflicted with the accelerating decline of mass armies in Western democracies in the 1960s and 1970s (Martin 1977). The size of the armed forces decreased from 1 153 000 men in 1957 to 520 000 in 1992. Army personnel was the most affected, dropping from 700 000 to 260 000. The number of conscripts diminished regularly: from 275 000 in 1974 to 208 000 in 1994; while the length of the military service was reduced from 28 months at the time of the Algerian War to 10 months in 1992.[8]

To face up to the challenges entailed in the strategic environment and the evolution of the social context of conscription, between 1991 and 1995 France adopted a policy of incremental adjustment in the armed forces, with an emphasis on professionalism and modernized conscription, as part of the broader context of downsizing. On 22 February 1996, the newly-elected President Jacques Chirac decided in favour of voluntary armed forces. A few months later, on 28 May, he announced the end of compulsory military service. This was an epoch-defining change in a country where conscription was established by the 1798 *loi Jourdan*, and after a century of universal and compulsory military service according to the 1905 law.

7.4.2   A new balance of power within the defence networks

The military policy of the Fifth Republic rests on the implementation of the 'inflationist compromise' as the principal regulatory mechanism of defence policy (E. Cohen 1996). Until 1990 the constant increase in spending allowed for the resolution of structural conflicts inherent to the military system. This holds true for conflicts between the armed forces and industrialists, from either the private sector or the state; as well as between nuclear and conventional forces. These conflicts are mitigated by the implementation of a number of more-or-less institutionalized compromises. These are articulated through the dual function of integration and tutelage held by the DGA: the primacy of the industrial approach in armament cooperation, the absence of off-the-shelf purchasing, acquisitions by the French armed forces of materials to sustain exports, an allowance of higher intervention costs generated by the DGA and finally, an acceptance of the technological preferences of armament engineers.

For the first time in 1991 the Defence minister sees its available resources cut from the prior year. This breach with the inflationist compromise changes the power dynamics of military policy. This period marks the decline of the DGA's role in the elaboration of military policy (Genyes 2005). By emphasizing a trend which appeared during the *Livre Blanc*, work done by the strategic committee is affected by the DGA's weakened position. In March 1996 this translated into the departure of *Délégué général* Henri Conze and his replacement by a manager from the private automobile industry. 'The General Delegation for armament no longer appeared as the grand master of programming '.[9]

The reduced budget led to a financial framing of military problems which translated into a rise to power of budgetary specialists and authorities, within the Defence ministry. This development, internal to the defence ministry, echoed the increasing power of the Finance ministry at the governmental level, in the management of the military system. Within the staff headquarters, the military offices responsible for planning and finances together with the chief of staff, who supervises these questions, found their role considerably strengthened during that period. This trend can be seen in the evolution of career profiles leading to chief of defence staff appointments, where the technocratic model oversteps that of the soldier's (Hamelin 2003). From 1991 on, the civil Financial division (Direction des affaires financiers, DAF) grew in importance with regards to the department's activities and gained greater influence. This was compounded by the reforms undertaken by Minister Pierre Joxe after the Gulf War, reinforcing the role of transversal operations within the ministry: the renewal of the Secretary General of Administration (SGA) and the creation of the Policy division (Délégation aux affaires stratégiques, DAS).

Finally, in regards to the vertical distribution of power in financing defence policy, let us underline the greater role of the chief of the defence staff (Chef d'état-major des armées, CEMA) in planning and programming. Until recently, including the 1996 army reforms, the power of the CEMA and its arbitration role between the three branches were limited. The reform stemming from the 1982 order, which sets the attributions of the Chiefs of staff, changed this. The CEMA appears as the winner in this reform because it places him at the heart of the decision-making process linked to the allocation of resources, whether at the planning, programming or budgetary level. Article 1 stipulates that 'the CEMA is responsible for the preparation and the use of the forces, coherence in the capacities of armament operations and international military relations. He is also responsible for the elaboration of planning and programming work, jointly with the DGA and SGA'.[10]

This fundamental shift toward greater inter-army coordination truly begins in 1991. The lessons learned from the Gulf War lead to an adaptation of the Defence ministry's structure and chain of command to the management of international crises. Notably, Defence minister Pierre Joxe initiated those changes through the creation of DAS, Military Intelligence Division, Joint Headquarters, Special Forces Headquarters (Lanxade 2001). This process has led to an increasingly powerful role for the Chief of Staff of the Armies and the CEMA in the politico-military apparatus and in crisis management. Article 2 of the 2005 decree states that 'the CEMA has authority over the chiefs of staff for the army, navy and air force'. General Bentegeat, then CEMA, underscores that 'he has the authority, and I make this clear beyond the text, not only during operations or for operations, but on a permanent basis in all fields'. The 2005 decree is fundamental in the sense that it ensures the CEMA's primacy on the three forces and centralizes the representation of military interests and preferences in policy. Furthermore, it ensures the primacy of the CEMA and the EMA within the Defence ministry in relation to the DGA, the SGA and the DAS. General Bentegeat expresses this quite clearly when he says that 'this ministry, and I repeat this every time I have a meeting with the minister's cabinet, is primarily the Armies' ministry', an inconceivable speech in the age of triumphal deterrence.

7.5 The enduring relevance of the Nuclear Monarchy

7.5.1 Presidential dominance: the tests of cohabitation and reform

The first experience of cohabitation in 1986–88 represents the moment of truth for the reserved domain. This is true to the extent that the president of the Republic's primacy in the defence sector required both a docile and majoritarian parliament, as well as a prime minister inclined to consent. Cohabitation represented a battle between the president of the Republic and the government to control foreign policy and defence policy. Both executive figures clashed on high profile issues of defence policy. Each of these conflicts resulted in victory for the president of the Republic who rejected France's participation in the American Strategic Defence Initiative (SDI), despite the government's support. He also rejected any departure on the use of tactical nuclear weapons as suggested by the prime minister on September 1986, and opposed the development of a mobile strategic land-based missile (SX). In total, in the power game that emerged during cohabitation, defence and the management of the 'shared domain' belong, along with disarmament and Franco-German relations, 'to the sphere of presidential predominance' (Cohen 1989, 494). Marie-Anne Cohendet takes this paradox further and affirms that it is cohabitation which permits the 'advent' of the reserved domain, referring to the existence of a restrained sphere of state action where the president of the Republic determines policy, while his general competency as the ruler is challenged in every other sector. Until cohabitation these shared attributions of the presidency had never been as clearly defined. The president of the Republic's primacy over defence policy has typically been recognized by government and the prime minister. On 2 December 1986, after the public controversy over tactical nuclear weapons in the fall, the prime minister recognized that, in virtue of the constitution, questions related to defence 'are reserved for the appreciation of the head of state', even if the government is applying a policy upon which it was elected.[11] The 1993–95 cohabitation was reproducing, albeit in a more subdued climate, the scheme by which crises or disagreements between the president of the Republic and the government are settled by the predominance of the head of state's inclinations. This was notably the case for the nuclear tests, the renewal of nuclear components and NATO relations. This second cohabitation was marked by improved cooperation between the two executive heads. The third cohabitation (1997–2002) between Jacques Chirac and Lionel Jospin confirmed this co-management of military affairs between the president and the government, as seen during the war in Kosovo in 1999 or during the nuclear policy review in 1999–2001. In times of cohabitation the role of the president is weakened since he is compelled to find grounds for agreement with the government (Cohen 2003). In some cases the government opposed the president's preference, for instance, when the Jospin government refused to intervene militarily in the Ivory Coast when President Konan Bedié was removed by a *coup d'etat* in 1999.

The study of the main military reforms and policies undertaken recently, in a context where power between the president and the majority in Parliament is coincident, offers a different picture. Scrutiny of the decision-making process of the 1996 reform reveals that President Chirac imposed his resolution in favour of full professionalization upon reluctant militaries, which unanimously favoured the continuation of the 'mixed model', based on the preservation of conscription. When elaborating the 1996 reform, President Chirac used all the resources available through his policy leadership to ensure the change to a professional army against the initial wish of both the armed forces and the Defence ministry: choosing the officials, defining the agenda, mastering the calendar and organizing the decision-making process (Irondelle 2003). In sum, the president decides on the relationship between France and NATO, including the question of France's return to the military organization, as well as the main decisions about nuclear deterrence (nuclear testing, format of the *force de frappe*). The French policy over the Iraq War and the increase in the military budget, provided by the 2003–08 military programming law, confirmed that the president retains a very special role in French defence policy-making. These facts do not confirm the thesis that 'the Fifth Republic has witnessed the gradual erosion of the ability of the President to control defence policy' (Menon 1994, 86). The Chief of State has important resources at his disposal to maintain the presidential supremacy.

In addition to his constitutional prerogatives, the influence of policy-making traditions, and the support of public opinion, the president is considered the highest and legitimate authority by the actors of the military system. For the military officers, the president is the legitimate authority in matters of defence, since he is the commander-in-chief of the armed forces and the one making appointments to the high-ranking military posts, mastering the nuclear arsenal and deciding when to engage armed forces. An episode of the 'velvet cohabitation' clearly demonstrates this. Prime Minister Edouard Balladur, who was in favour of new nuclear testing, against the will of François Mitterrand who stopped it in 1992, remembers: 'I summoned

[Chief of Defence Staff] Lanxade to my office and I asked him "whom will you obey?" He answered without a moment's doubt "to the President of the Republic". That being the case it was no use going further'. In the daily practice, the Chief of Defence Staff, who is the government counsellor concerning military issues, is in fact the Head of State's direct interlocutor. Furthermore, the president has at his disposal a personal Chief of Staff who leads the president's private military staff, a small team of four senior officers, in charge of advising the president. As Louis Gautier underlines,

> The commitment to a defence consensus, the theory of the 'reserved' or 'shared' domain and the sanctuarization of the defence budget contributed to develop specific and very autonomous decision-making processes that all reinforce the President of the Republic (. . .) So the debate in parliament, the discussion inside the government and the inter-services dialogue at the interministerial level are deprived of much of their substances concerning defence issues. (Gautier 1999, 208)

But the president disposes neither of the administrative machinery nor of the concrete tools to implement his policy, both of which belong to the government, to the prime minister and the Defence minister. Therefore, there is no room for major disagreement between the president and the government: if such a situation should arise it is likely to lead to a resignation, as was the case of Jean-Pierre Chèvement, minister of Defence during the first Gulf War (1991). So as a general rule, the prime minister takes a back seat on defence, with the exception of budgetary and industrial issues, notably after the Cold War because of increasing financial constraints. Even during cohabitation, it is very difficult for Matignon to distance itself from, and even less to contradict, the Elysée.

7.5.2 Parliament: still out of the game

Comparative studies have underlined that the National Assembly is one of the most impotent parliaments in foreign and defence policies (Rozenberg 2001, Wessels 2002, Forster 2006). Defence represents an ideal-type in the way parliament has been marginalized in policy-making under the Fifth Republic. Symptomatically, John Huber, who tends to rehabilitate parliamentary studies, disregards defence and foreign affairs in his work because 'deputies generally approve defence and foreign affairs laws without recourse to amendments and with no significant debate' (Huber 1996, 72). Under Article 35 of the Constitution, Parliament authorizes the declaration of war. In practice this arrangement is not upheld in the case of foreign operations where the most significant feature of French policy-making is 'the evanescence of Parliament' (Hadas-Lebel 1991). In 1991, during the Gulf War, the government committed its responsibility before the National Assembly. However, the National Assembly's information report on parliamentary control of foreign operations states the exceptional nature of this event: 'Indeed, operations in the former Yugoslavia (Forpronu, IFOR and SFOR), in Albania (Alba 1997) and in Kosovo (allied forces and KFOR) were prompted, occurred and were renewed without Parliament taking part in those decisions' (Lamy 2000). The new version for article 35 of the Constitution, put forth by the Balladur committee, specifies that the government must inform Parliament of any foreign intervention, as well as its extension beyond the three-month period provided by the law. But when the president decided to increase French participation in the war in Afghanistan, Parliament was not initially consulted or even informed. Only the criticism from opposition parties and the media lead to a last minute debate at the National Assembly. The second method of parliamentary control resides in a posteriori control of external operations. The period of cohabitation between 1997 and 2002 was deemed auspicious in this way, with information-gathering missions in Rwanda and in Srebrenica (Delpa 2007). Whatever the limitations inherent in these two missions, they demonstrate unprecedented parliamentary intrusion at the heart of the reserved domain of the executive – with no sign of being reversed, for now. The French parliament is almost completely deprived of one of the usual resources of parliamentary control of defence policies, the budgetary procedure. Indeed, the opportunity to change the government's budget project (*Projet de loi de finances*) is severely restricted by the Constitution (art. 40). Furthermore, every major change initiated by members of Parliament is interpreted as an 'aggression' not only against the government, but also against the president.

7.5.3   The new consensus on defence: Is defence policy definitively non-political (persistence of depoliticization)?

The foundations of the consensus on defence (alliances, conscription, nuclear) were put in question at the end of the 1980s. But this consensus was reformed in the 1990s among the parties of government. The military reform of 1996, based on the professionalization of the armed forces and the elimination of military service, perfectly illustrates the dispersal of ideological debates and partisan division on defence. It shows that the army is no longer an ideological question, notably for the Left. There is a consensus uniting Right and Left on prioritizing military use for foreign interventions, building up European defence, and undertaking the neo-managerial reform (outsourcing and privatization of the armament industry). This seldom leads to controversial public debates (Gautier 2006). Since the mid-1990s, a 'European' paradigm has developed within the French decision-making elite (government, military, and diplomats) as a result of foreign military operations (the 1991 Gulf War and conflicts in the former Yugoslavia). This has been furthered by the development of the European Security and Defence Policy. The political and bureaucratic tensions between the defence and foreign ministries have not disappeared, but have smoothed out considerably in favour of the common and ambitious framework of the ESDP, to be pursued as autonomously as possible from the more pragmatic relations with NATO (Howorth 2004). Arguments abound to address and/or legitimize this depoliticization of defence questions: national security imperatives, international constraints, institutional configurations maintaining executive primacy, and the significance of passed experiences. Parameters of the electoral competition play a major role in producing the defence consensus. Michel Dobry has shown to what extent the proximity for a party to executive power is fundamental to explain the support of the socialists to the nuclear consensus at the end of the 1970s. This support is 'an attempt to avoid French nuclear forces to become a debate of the electoral campaigns and an issue of the socialist experience of power' (Dobry 1986, p. 52). Thus this consensus, and the idea that expressing a heterodox opinion concerning a major issue in defence policy is electorally and politically costly, limits the public debates on defence.

> By the mid-1980s, the French political class was – in private – more or less divided over almost every major issue of defence policy (...). These disagreements never crystallized into public debate, as no public figure was willing to claim responsibility for opening up this particular Pandora's box. (Menon 1994, p. 81)

The strength of the defence consensus and the absence of a clearly formulated political alternative cannot capture the complexity of the Right–Left divide. If we account for the strategies of political display, the Right–Left cleavage is much more effective. Symptomatically, since 1981 each government from the Right has launched a law on military program planning (Chirac in 1986; Balladur in 1993; Juppé in 1995; and Raffarin in 2002). Another indicator is that in 1997 the Jospin government did not prepare a new law on programming but reduced defence credits to finance youth employment and the 35 hour-week, an important argument on the legitimization of his actions and of his political leaning. The defence budget thus has broader meaning as it is linked to ideological and partisan orientations of governments, particularly for the right. In this way, the evolution of the defence budget corresponds to 'the theory of emblematic budgets' as suggested by Alexandre Siné (2006). According to this theory, and following an incremental framework, there exist only a limited number of budgets that may present themselves in a politically significant way, with enough emblematic importance to have an impact on the electoral market.

Furthermore, one may wonder to what extent the debate on NATO and the decision to increase the French contingent in Afghanistan, having entailed a motion of censure from the Socialist Party (April 2008), calls into question the consensus on defence, or if it is only temporary.

7.6   Conclusion and research agenda

The primacy of the executive in defence policy, instituted by de Gaulle's practice, is still crucial in contemporary France. Cohabitation periods favoured
a joint management of the reserved domain which then becomes more a
'shared domain' between the prime minister and the president, with a pre-
eminence of the latter. But the balance only takes place within the executive,
not with Parliament. The probable disappearance of cohabitation periods
will only reinforce the presidentialization of defence policy. This complete
presidentialization is suggested by the Balladur Commission in its revision
proposals: the president would 'define the policy of the Nation' (art. 5
revised) that the government would 'conduct' but no longer 'determine' (art.
20 revised). Article 21 would specify that in national defence matters, 'the
prime minister implements the decisions taken under the provisions of article
15' which stipulates that the president shall preside in the higher national
defence councils. President Sarkozy has decided to endow himself with a
Defence and National Security Council, equivalent to the US National Security Council. This presidentialization comes with a tendency to centralize the
bureaucracies in charge of national security policy: increasing the power of
the Defence Chief of Staff in the military domain, regrouping intelligence
services (Direction des renseignements généraux et Direction de la sécurité
du territoire) within the Direction of interior intelligence (Direction du ren-
seignement intérieur). Consequently, the elaboration of security and defence
policy might well be limited to a face-to-face between the president on one
side and the military establishment and intelligence services on the other.
The executive power thereby tends to deprive itself of one of its most efficient tools to control security policy: inter-services rivalry and diversification
of information chains.

The research agenda concerning the armed forces and defence policy in
France includes numerous tracks. I am concentrating on institutional aspects.
The role of the president has, justly so, focused research attention. Some holes
remain, particularly bearing on the presidential leadership and the impact of
each president. Although important research has been dedicated to defence
policy analysing it through presidency (Gordon 1993, Rynning 2002), we
know very little about comparison, variations and the diverse resources of
the president. It seems particularly useful to make a comparative analysis of
the executive powers in matters of defence and security, systematically comparing the French president with the British prime minister or the German
chancellor. The decision-making process of the Defence ministry and the
exact part played by its different branches, notably the military establishment or the Defence minister, are still ill known in France. The influence of
the French parliament, the evolution of parliamentary control of the armed
forces and intelligence services, the issue of democratic governance of the
armed forces should be explored. Systematic research, based on quantitative

data, concerning the value systems of military officers, analysing the potential gap between military and civilian values, comparing perceptions of the civilian and military elites regarding foreign policy, national security, and the role of the armed forces should be the core of the research agenda to renew the study of French civil–military relations. Last not but least, this research agenda should be comparative in essence. There is a need for deep comparative research in order to explain the variety of civil–military relations, the diversity of democratic control rather than 'insular case studies' (Allen Williams 2007, Born et al. 2004) and to understand better the French case of defence policy-making.

Notes

1. John Huber shows that the 'agenda-setting' and 'electoral' models explain the recourse to legislative procedures, rather than conflict.
2. Pierre Messmer, Ministre des Armées, 'Notre politique militaire', *Revue de défense nationale*, May 1963, p. 760.
3. Quoted in Pierre Messmer, *Après tant de batailles*, Paris, Fayard, p. 254.
4. Charles de Gaulle, *Lettres, notes et carnets*, 1961–63, pp. 273–4.
5. Quoted in *Ibid*, p. 223.
6. According to Mitterrand's book title published in 1960.
7. For the complete series of French military expenditures since 1958 see Baumgartner et al., Chapter 10 in this volume.
8. One must nevertheless underline that this stated length was dramatically shortened after the Algerian War (1962). Military service had been stabilized to 12 months since 1970.
9. Based on an interview with a high-ranking official from the Defence ministry, who took part in programming activities from 1991 to 1996, 26 July 2000.
10. Decree n° 2005–520 of 21 May 2005, fixing the attributions of the Chiefs of Staff.
11. *Le Monde*, 2 December 1986.

Bibliography

Allen Williams, J. (2007) 'Political science perspectives on the military and civil–military relations' in Caforio G., *Social Sciences and the Military*, London, Routledge, pp. 89–104.

Ambler, J. (1966) *The French Army in Politics, 1945–1962*, Columbus, Ohio State University Press.

Born, H., Haltiner, K. and Malesic, M. (2004) 'Democratic Control of Armed Forces: Renaissance of an Old Issue' in Born, H., Haltiner, K. and Malesic, M., *Renaissance of Democratic Control of Armed Forces in Contemporary Societies*, Bade, Nomos.

Bozo, F. (1991) *La France et l'OTAN. De la guerre froide au nouvel ordre européen*, Paris, Masson.

Bureau, J.-F. (1997) 'La réforme militaire en France: une mutation identitaire', *Politique Etrangère*, 1, Spring: 69–81.

Chantebout, B. (1967) *L'organisation générale de la Défense en France depuis la Seconde Guerre mondiale*, Paris, LGDJ.

Cohen, E. (1996) *La tentation hexagonale*, Paris, Fayard.

Cohen, S. (1986) *La Monarchie nucléaire*, Paris, Hachette.

Cohen, S. (1989) 'La politique étrangère entre l'Élysée et Matignon', *Politique étrangère*, Autumn.

Cohen, S. (1994) *La Défaite des généraux*, Paris: Fayard.

Cohen, S. (2003) 'Cohabiter en diplomatie. Atout ou handicap?', *Annuaire Français des Relations Internationales*, pp. 344–58.

Delpa, I. (ed.) (2007), 'Srebrenica 1995. Analyse croisées des enquêtes et des rapports', *Cultures & Conflits*, n° 65.

Dobry, M. (1986) 'Le jeu du consensus', *Pouvoirs*, 38: 47–66.

Forster, A. (2006) *Armed Forces and Society in Europe*, Basingstoke, Palgrave Macmillan.

Gautier, L. (1999) *Mitterrand et son armée*, Paris: Grasset.

Gautier, L. (2006) 'Le consensus sur la défense entre totem et tabou', *Défense Nationale*.

Genyies, W. (2005) *Le choix des armes*, Paris, Presses du CNRS.

Girardet, R. (ed.) (1964) *La crise militaire française: 1945–1962*, Paris, Armand Colin.

Gordon, P. (1993) *A Certain Idea of France: French Security Policy and the Gaullist Legacy*, Princeton, Princeton University Press.

Hadas-Lebel, R. (1991) 'La Ve Répulique et la guerre', *Pouvoirs*, n° 58: 5–24.

Hamelin, F. (2003) 'Le combattant et le technocrate. La formation des officiers à l'aune du modèle des élites civiles', *Revue française de science politique*, 53 (3): 435–63.

Hanley, D. (1984) 'The Parties and the Nuclear Consensus' in Jolyon Howorth and Patricia Chilton (eds), *Defence and Dissent in Contemporary France*, London, Croom Helm.

Hébert, J.-P. (1995) *Production d'armement. Mutation du système français*, Paris, La Documentation Française.

Howorth, J. (1992) 'The President's Special Role in Foreign and Defence Policy' in Jack Hayward (ed.) *De Gaulle to Mitterrand: Presidential Power in France*, London, Hurst & Company.

Howorth, J. (2004) 'Discourse, Ideas, and Epistemic Communities in European Security and Defence Policy', *West European Politics*, 27 (2): 211–34.

Huber, J. (1996) *Rationalizing Parliament. Legislative Institutions and Party Politics in France*, Cambridge, Cambridge University Press, 1996.

Irondelle, B. (2003) *Gouverner la défense. Analyse du processus décisionnel de la réforme militaire*, Thèse pour le doctorat en Science Politique, IEP de Paris.

Katzenstein, P. (1976), 'International Relations and Domestic Structures: Foreign Economic Policies of Advanced Industrial States', *International Organizations* 30 (Winter): 1–45.

Koenig-Archibugi, M. (2003) 'International governance as a new Raison d'Etat: the case of the EU common foreign and security policy', *European Journal of International Relations*, 10 (2): 147–88.

Kolodziej, E. (1987) *Making and Marketing Arms. The French Experience and Its Implications for the International System*, Princeton, Princeton University Press.

Lamy, F. (2000) *Contrôler les opérations extérieurs. Rapport d'information n° 2237*, Paris, Assemblée nationale.

Lanxade, J. (2001) *Quand le monde a basculé*, Paris, Nil éditions.

Luchaire, F. and Conac, G. (eds) (1987) *La Constitution de la République française*, Paris, Economica, 2nd edn.

Martin, M.-L. (1977) 'Conscription and the Decline of the Mass Army in France 1960–1975', *Armed Forces and Society* 5 (3): 355–406.

Menon, A. (1994), 'Continuing Politics by Other Means: Defence Policy under the French Fifth Republic', *West European Politics*, 17 (4): 74–96.

Menon, A. (2000), *France, NATO and the Limits of Independence, 1981–1997: The Politics of Ambivalence*, Basingstoke: Macmillan.

Risse-Kappen, T. (1991) 'Public Opinion, Domestic Structure, and Foreign Policy in Liberal Democracies', *World Politics*, 43 (3): 479–512.

Rozenberg, O. and Szukala, A. (2001) 'The French Parliament and the EU: Progressive Assertion and Strategic Investment', in Andreas Maurer and Wolfgang Wessels (eds), *National Parliaments on their Ways to Europe: Losers or Latecomers?*, Baden-Baden, Nomos Verlagsgesellschaft, pp. 223–50.

Rynning, S. (2001–02), 'Shaping Military Doctrine in France. Decisionmakers between International Power and Domestic Interests', *Security Studies*, 11 (2): 85–116.

Rynning, S. (2002), *Changing Military Doctrine. Presidents and Military Power in Fifth Republic France, 1958–2000*, Westport, Prager.

Ruhl, L. (1977) *La politique militaire de la Ve république*, Paris, Presses de la FNSP.

Siné, A. (2006) *L'ordre budgétaire*, Paris, Economica.

Tertrais, B. (2007) 'The Last to Disarm? The Future of France's Nuclear Weapons', *Nonproliferation Review*, 14 (2): 251–73.

Vennesson, P. (2003) 'Civil–Military Relations in France: Is there a Gap?', *Journal of Strategic Studies*, 26 (2): 29–42.

Wessels, W. (ed.) (2002) *The Parliamentary Dimension of CFSP/ESDP. Options for the European Convention,* Study submitted to the European Parliament.

Yost, D. (1994) 'France' in David Murray and Paul Viotti (eds), *The Defence Policies of Nations*, Baltimore, John Hopkins University Press.

8
France, Europe and the World: Foreign Policy and the Political Regime of the Fifth Republic

Richard Balme

8.1 Introduction

France's position in international relations arguably presents a number of specificities. These can be identified, first, with the wealth of its economy, ranked sixth behind the US, Japan, Germany, China and the United Kingdom with a 2005 total Gross National Income (GNI) of 2.2 trillion US dollars, and a market capitalization worth over 80 percent of its GDP. Such an economic prosperity supports the strength of its export industries, with 4.47 percent of world export of goods and services worth 26 percent of its GDP, and its attractiveness to foreign investors with net inflows of Foreign Direct Investment of 70.7 billion US dollars in 2005 (World Bank 2007). Wealth also entails important energy needs, and France, with an energy deficit of 55 percent (155.7 MTOE in 2005, Morss 2008), is in a position of client on energy markets, coming with both influence and sensitivity toward supplier countries.

Beyond this structural economic influence, a second characteristic of the French position in international relations lies with its military capacities, including nuclear forces, with 2006 military expenditures ranking third behind the US and the UK at 53.1 million US dollars, representing a share of 5 percent of world total military expenditures. Associated with this strategic potential is a flourishing defense industry, with 7.08 percent of arms sales at the world level between 1978 and 2006 (SIPRI 2007), as well as a capacity to develop and supply nuclear technologies. On a more political front, one should underscore its status of permanent member of the United Nations (UN) Security Council and, as such, its involvement in major international security issues; its role in the foundation of the European Communities, and more generally in the European integration process; the reputation and influence of its culture and technology beyond its own borders; and finally its relations with a number of developing countries, particularly in North and West Africa, and to a far lesser extent today in the Middle East and in South-East Asia, many of which carry, for better or for worst, a legacy of colonial past.

All of these resources allow France to matter in the world economy, to entertain important relations with major power-houses, and to benefit from a comparatively large area of bi-lateral influence supporting her significant position within international organizations. Other than geo-political delineations built through history, nothing is specifically French with international influence based on power resources. What makes France supposedly different is its reputation of commitment to independence and defense of its own values in international relations. More than in geo-politics, the French specificity in world affairs therefore seems to lie with a durable and long-term attitude of governments in the conduct of foreign policy.

Beyond France's image in international relations, this chapter explores the relations between the political regime of the Fifth Republic and foreign policy. Foreign policy can without doubt be accounted for within the frame of policy analysis, mobilizing such concepts as party politics, interest groups, bureaucratic politics, policy communities, agenda-setting and implementation. More specifically, foreign policy analysis developed its own toolbox within the field of international relations with approaches in terms of political psychology of leaders, group decision-making, national identity, domestic politics, and national attributes in the international system (Hudson 2007). We borrow here mainly from the domestic structure approach, with a special emphasis on the impact of national political institutions on foreign policy (Rosenau 1961, Katzenstein 1976, Shapiro and Page 1988, Eichenberg 1989, Russett 1990, Risse-Kapen 1991).

More than other government activities, foreign policy is directly linked to sovereignty, understood as the capacity for the executive to independently exert influence at home as well as abroad. From this perspective, foreign policy is constitutive of state-building. In the pursuit of diplomacy governments negotiate their capacity to stand on behalf of their own country, and for the state to behave, beyond domestic conflicts of interests and political changes, as a cohesive actor in international relations. The constitutional organization of the state affects foreign policy through relations between the executive, the legislative, political parties, the media, and the different bureaucracies (Foreign Affairs, Defense, Armed Forces, Industry and Trade, Interior with regard to migration) and interest groups (export industries, human rights groups, international NGOs, expatriate communities) involved. In establishing the moral foundations of the state, the constitution also durably orients foreign policy values and preferences for successive governments.

What we explore in this chapter is precisely how and to what extent the constitution of the Fifth Republic imposed some continuity in foreign policy to the different presidents in charge of the executive. By continuity we do not mean any absence of change between 1958 and 2007, but rather the capacity to develop successive policies adapting to changing contexts in line with the general orientations established with the foundation of the Fifth Republic. We also consider how, beyond changes in objectives and instruments, the major constitutional arrangements imposed constraints and limitations on the foreign policy decision-making process, and what were their consequences. We consider the period between the foundation of the Fifth Republic in 1958 and the termination of the second term of Jacques Chirac in 2007. We make use of a selection of key policy-events extracted from Fournié (2007) and more generally of the literature (particularly Grosser 1984, Aldrich and Connell 1989, Vaïsse 2004 and 2007), with a special emphasis on European Affairs, considered as a critical case-study for the understanding of French foreign policy. We argue that the characteristics of foreign policy under the Fifth Republic are more related to leaders' preferences and to the path-dependency of international relations than to the expression of specific citizens' preferences. We show that these characteristics have been amplified by the institutional features of the regime.

8.2   Early foundations of French foreign policy: the Gaullist period

With the Algerian crisis the birth of the Fifth Republic itself was directly related to external affairs. The constitution adopted on 4 October 1958 and revised in 1962 to allow for the election of the president through universal suffrage was precisely designed to overcome what de Gaulle saw as intrinsic and incorrigible weaknesses of a parliamentary regime dominated by a fragmented partisan system. The major features of the new constitution were indeed conceived by de Gaulle after France had been severely defeated by Germany in the initial stages of World War II, as a remedy to the incapacity of political leadership to face external threats and crisis of the 1930s. Only the Algerian crisis initiated in 1954 would allow for de Gaulle to return to power and to impose his constitutional ideas, giving wide room to the executive, in 1958. The origins of the Fifth Republic constitution are crucial to bear in mind to properly assess the constitutional influence on French foreign policy. We will return to this.

To a large extent, benefiting from his historical legitimacy and as the first president of the new Republic (1958–69), de Gaulle set the template of French foreign policy as it would be conducted by his successors Georges Pompidou (1969–74), Valéry Giscard d'Estaing (1974–81), Francois Mitterrand (1981–95) and Jacques Chirac (1999–2007). The French foreign policy style can be characterized by:

1) The search for leadership in international relations based on a policy of strict independence combined with strategies of influence through international aid, cooperation policy, cultural diplomacy, defining the so-called 'politique de grandeur'.
2) French foreign policy is expressed through diplomacy of movement, engagement and initiative, asserting the French presence on the

international scene. France does not depart from other countries when they pursue active diplomacies in that respect. However, although far from absent, structural resources such as the country's economic wealth, population size or natural resources, and military capacities, do not position France as a hegemon, but rather as a second-tier player among great powers. Such movement diplomacy is therefore all the more necessary to pursue international leadership as structural resources are comparatively limited. This owes French political leaders and diplomats some reputation in the art of conducting foreign policy. But it also sometimes puts diplomacy at risk of dramatic moves guided by strategies of position-taking more than real policy effectiveness, with diplomatic 'gesture' mobilized to fill the gap between position and ambition in international relations.

3) Finally, the French foreign policy style can be characterized by the strong personalization and concentration of prerogatives around the president. This is true internally, with the establishment of most of foreign policy as the 'domaine reservé' for the president, despite the absence of explicit constitutional provision on this matter, and the weakness in the role of Parliament, here more than in any other domain. Externally, French foreign policy has also been based on strong personal ties between the president and foreign leaders, particularly in the relations with Germany and with African countries, the practice of which was indeed established by de Gaulle.

Whatever the importance of de Gaulle's footprint on French foreign policy, a number of clichés need to be challenged (Gordon 1993, Paxton and Wahl 1994, Vaïsse 1998). First, with the noticeable exception of Algeria, there has been a fair deal of continuity in French foreign policy between the Fourth and the Fifth Republics. The Atlantic commitment in NATO dated back to 1949, and the Franco-German reconciliation was initiated in 1950 with the Monnet–Schuman declaration. The project to develop a French nuclear force was launched in 1955 by the government of Pierre Mendes-France, as well as decolonization in South-East Asia, Tunisia and Morocco. The recently ratified treaty of Rome was not questioned by the new Fifth Republic, while France had already expressed its unease with supra-national institutions with the rejection of the European Defense Community in 1954. France had also asserted its independence when defying the disapproval of the US and USSR together with the UK in the Suez crisis of 1956. From this perspective, the Empty Chair crisis of 1965 to oppose majority voting in the Council of Ministers and the two vetoes opposed in 1963 and 1967 to the adhesion of the UK to the EEC, the recognition of the People's Republic of China (PRC) in 1964, the decision to exit NATO integrated commandment in 1966, and the arms embargo against Israel in 1969 were indeed strong moves, emblematic of the Gaullist style of French foreign policy. But the overall foreign policy,

sometimes against de Gaulle's own preferences, had to assume a significant inheritance from preceding years, and was not in total rupture with
the precedent regime as it is sometimes assumed. In terms of independence,
these moves also have to be considered together with France's solidarity and
initiative during the Berlin crisis in 1960–61, and with the Franco-German
Elysée treaty of 1963 establishing the two countries as the political motor of
European integration for a long period. The real ruptures introduced with
the Gaullist period lie first with the resolution of the Algerian crisis, and
the termination of the colonial Empire by means of the French Community,
as provisioned by the new constitution, with Mauritania being the last former colony to access independence in 1960. To be effective such a change
in orientation required the conduct of external affairs to be supported by
a different constitutional setting, leaving a much larger room to the executive. The robustness of the new constitution from this point of view would
be tested in 1961, with the use of special powers provisioned under Art. 16
by the president to face the attempt of a coup in Algiers. Such a change in
French external policy nevertheless came at the cost of the marginalization
of the parliament, reduced to rubber stamping international treaties. The second major innovation in French foreign policy is therefore to be found in
policy-making itself, much more executive-led and long sighted than in the
previous period, but at the cost of weaknesses in public accountability.

The other major cliché about French foreign policy is the idea that few
changes have occurred in its orientations since these Gaullist origins. However, in many areas the de Gaulle period would remain an exception, allowing
for the transition between the ranks inherited from World War II and the
international dynamics of the late twentieth century.

8.3   France's European policy: in search of 'grandeur' by other means

Under many aspects, subsequent developments of French European policy
would prove the Gaullist period to be the exception rather than the rule.
In December 1969, a few months after de Gaulle's resignation from power,
Georges Pompidou, during the European summit in The Hague, implicitly
suspended the French veto to the UK membership, opening the way to the
1973 first enlargement to the UK, Ireland and Denmark, approved by a referendum in France in 1972. Valéry Giscard d'Estaing then actively promoted
European integration with the creation of the European Council calling for
regular meetings of European executive leaders (1974), with the use of direct
suffrage for the election of representatives in the European Parliament (EP,
first election in 1979), and with the creation of the European Monetary System and the related common currency denominated ECU (1979). After the
failure of the orthodox Keynesian policy of the first leftist government of

the Fifth Republic, and three consecutive devaluations of the French franc between 1981 and 1983, François Mitterrand in turn developed an active European diplomacy, supported by his proximity with the German chancellor Helmut Kohl and the activism of his former finance minister Jacques Delors as president of the European Commission (EC) starting in 1985. The convergence of views between these leaders formed the basis for a decisive coalition for agenda-setting in European integration, able to overcome the reluctance of the UK of Margaret Thatcher to successively yield the Shengen agreement suppressing borders between signatory countries (1985), the enlargement to Spain and Portugal (1986), the Single European Act preparing for the Single Market (1988), the Maastricht Treaty establishing the Economic and Monetary Union, and the procedure for European Social Dialogue designed to consolidate the social dimension of the EU (1992). These policy developments led by successive presidents issued from three different political parties significantly departed from the strict inter-governmentalist approach of the Gaullist period. Without ever turning into an openly federalist conception of Europe, they gave a considerable impulse to institutional developments at the supra-national level, which would in turn nourish the path-dependency of integration. As such they represented altogether a dramatic development, if not a change in orientation, in French European policy.

However, the early 1990s can also be seen as the end of this second period, where developments in European integration were claimed as an objective by French leaders, and where the activism of French diplomacy proved particularly successful in asserting its leadership on European affairs. On the domestic front, only a tight majority (51%) ratified the Maastricht Treaty in the referendum of 1992, after a difficult campaign where the president had to be involved, and where the Gaullist party appeared divided. The infamous 'permissive consensus' among public opinion, passively supporting integration carried by European elites, progressively eroded with the new saliency of EU policies and the greater exposure of citizens to European affairs. Two decades after the first oil shock, the 'wait and see' attitude of most French citizens granting leaders with political credit on European integration started to evaporate. The 1992 campaign for the referendum on the Maastricht treaty would have significant consequences for the party system and for public opinion cleavages (Balme and Woll 2003). With time passing, and with the incapacity to significantly reduce unemployment, the political-economy trade-off between today's national sacrifices and tomorrow's European better days became increasingly questionable. The support for integration, measured by the percentage of respondents thinking that France's membership to the EU is 'a good thing', eroded from over 70 percent in 1987 to 55 percent in 1992, and to 43 percent in 2004 (Sauger et al. 2007, p. 40). France's membership to the EU indeed entailed a number of significant domestic effects (Cole and Drake 2000, Rozenberg and Szukala

2001, Gueldry 2001, Balme and Woll 2003 and 2005, Grossman and Sauger 2007). However, the 'Europeanization' of policy-making is quite differentiated according to policy sectors. Policy domains experience different degrees of change and patterns of adaptation, while in no case apart from monetary policy the EU fully supplanted national decision-making. Comparative analysis suggests that regulative and redistributive policies were less conflicting with European integration than distributive policies at the core of the French welfare state, but that the latter have been also strongly resilient and resistant to radical changes. Patterns of policy changes are highly complex and diversified, and their 'path-dependency' is rooted in the political feasibility of public policy at the domestic level (Balme and Woll 2005). Therefore it is not the intensity of changes imposed by EU membership, but rather its incapacity to deliver significant improvements in the socio-economic situation as experienced by citizens, which progressively split public opinion on French European policy, and ended up with the rejection of the draft constitutional treaty with a significant majority of 55 percent in May 2005. It also significantly contributed to widening the distance between citizens' policy preferences and their perception of policy-making as carried out by political leaders, to the sharp decline in political trust, and to the crisis of political representation epitomized with the presidential election of 2002, where the Front National leader Jean-Marie Le Pen, openly opposed to European integration and to immigration, qualified for the second round. Such developments showed that the Europeanization of French policy-making came at the cost of significant domestic political tensions during the 1990s, and explain why European integration lost the prominent position it occupied on public policy agendas during the 1970s and 1980s.

French European policy in the last decade of the twentieth century was also deeply affected by external factors, at the forefront of which stand the aftermaths of the end of the cold war in Europe. During his first presidential mandate (1981–88), François Mitterrand actively worked with Helmut Kohl to strengthen the strategic dimension of the Franco-German engine, particularly in 1988 with the creation of a joint Council for Defense and Security, and the establishment of a bi-national brigade that would parade on the Champs Elysées on National Day (14 July, 1994). The relation with Germany could not however remain unchanged after the collapse of the Berlin wall. In the first place, the German reunification would definitely change the demographic weight and international status of the country. Connectively, the historical necessity to open the EU to central and eastern Europe countries, and the successive enlargements of 1995 (Austria, Finland, and Sweden) 2004 (Cyprus, the Czech Republic, Estonia, Hungary, Latvia, Lithuania, Malta, Poland, Slovenia and Slovakia) and 2007 (Bulgaria and Romania), bringing the number of member states to 27, would naturally dilute French influence in a larger Europe, and reinforce German attractiveness in an expanded neighborhood. Europe would also quickly have to face important security issues in the Balkans, where French and German diplomacies would prove in disagreement with the rapid recognition of Slovenia and Croatia by Germany in 1991. In such a context, Francois Mitterrand's foreign policy remained cautious, and aimed at anchoring Germany within the project of European Union. He seemed somewhat hesitant to face the perspective of rapid reunification for Germany, and bargained its support against the acceptance by Helmut Kohl of the monetary union at the European Council in Strasbourg in December 1989 (Vaïsse 2007).

The perspective of enlargement to central and east European countries also nourished some reservation among French leadership. The proposal for a European Confederation suggested by Francois Mitterrand in 1989 was interpreted as an attempt to keep former communist countries at bay from the European Community, and potentially under the influence of Russia, and as such was vigorously rejected in central and eastern Europe. France later sought to control the effects of the enlargement in preserving the capacity for deepening of European integration, along the momentum initiated during the 1980s. The Copenhagen criteria (1993) were designed to set the conditions for membership of the new members, while France's position in institutional reforms (Amsterdam treaty in 1997, Nice treaty in 2001, drafting of the constitutional treaty initiated in Laeken in 2002) aimed both at maintaining its institutional influence relative to Germany, and at preserving its advantages in the policy package included in the treaties.

The duration of the process of enlargement, the difficulties in adopting the related institutional reform, as well as the episode of rejection of the draft treaty in 2005 (while the German parliament had ratified the treaty), sufficiently prove that the development of integration in the new Europe was anything but smooth in this last period, and that the proactive French diplomacy in this area was significantly less effective.

In a less noticed development, France and Germany nevertheless succeeded in securing the financial conditions for the enlargement in 2002. The enlargement, with the accession of a large number of member states with lower standards of living, would either require to considerably expand the budget of the EU, or alternatively to deeply transform its policies. The whole policy structure of the EU, and the inter-governmental compromises they rely upon, were at stake here. At distance from public controversies on integration, the budgetary bargaining surrounding the enlargement was anything but trivial, and indeed conveyed highly political issues. Would 'new' member states be granted the same policy benefits as existing ones? Would 'old' member states contribute to the integration of newcomers? How would budgetary efforts and compensations be shared among different countries? Beyond its technicality, a budgetary agreement was a preliminary condition for the enlargement, and marshalling the political compromises it relied upon a major accomplishment.

After difficult negotiations, France (particularly sensitive to farmers as a pressure group, and the main recipient of agriculture policy) and Germany (the largest contributor to the budget) found a compromise through which agriculture expenditures would be capped to avoid the explosion of the global budget, and agriculture policy would be reformed to allow for a gradual increase of support to farmers of the new member states. On this basis, the European budget 2007–13 was stabilized in 2005. Through a reallocation of credits in regional and agriculture policies, the net balance (difference between payments and subsidies) of France's contribution to the EU budget should evolve from 0.15 percent of its annual GDP before 2005 to roughly 0.35 percent for 2007–13 (Lefebvre 2007).

Despite this increased contribution to the EU policies, French political influence and its strategy of grandeur through European integration somewhat eroded. While France had been at the geographical and political core of the EU with 12 member states (EU-12), its own position became more relative in EU-27. Its share of votes in the Council of Ministers would mechanically regress with a larger number of member states. The French leadership fought a long and uphill battle to maintain a parity of votes with Germany, despite a difference in population of more than 19 million, and made no concession on this issue, particularly during the negotiation of the nice treaty. The draft constitutional project and the reform treaty of Lisbon finally ratified by the French parliament in January 2008 eventually abandoned the parity with Germany, in exchange of a voting rule more favorable to the influence of member states with large populations, therefore granting France with a better influence on the whole decision-making process. There is no doubt however that French leadership in EU institutions, like for other early member states, has been diluted with the enlargement. The use of French language within European institutions also markedly declined during the 1990s, with English becoming the most widely used language in official documents in 1998.

The Franco-German engine remains pivotal, but does not benefit from the same political leverage on the whole of the EU. Jacques Chirac and Gerhart Schröder for instance failed to impose their favorite candidate Guy Verhofstadt as president of the Commission in 2004. Contrary to the Mitterrand–Kohl area, the developments in EU defense policy would later come from a Franco-British initiative, with the proposal to create an EU Fast Reaction Force at the Saint Malo summit in December 1998. In the area of security and defense, the new member states, most of which are in rupture with their communist past, were eager to secure their alliance with the US, and promptly applied for NATO membership. To the public dissatisfaction of Jacques Chirac, they also occasionally chose US rather than European suppliers for their arms contracts. As a result, the French concepts of 'Europe Power' (Valéry Giscard d'Estaing) and 'multipolar world' (Jacques Chirac), as well as the more general Gaullist aspiration to independence in defense policy, did not find much echo in the new Europe after the cold war. Very significantly, the French policy of opposition in the UN to the US and British invasion in Iraq in 2003, joined by Germany, was relatively isolated in Europe, with most member states openly supporting the US policy. In any case the French initiative, whatever the rightness of its position, remained at bay from building a consensus at the EU level, and did not even try to do so. In such a crucial international event and with such a strong move, French diplomacy had little political leverage on other European governments.

The post-cold war context obviously deeply transformed the parameters both of the relation with Germany, and of the capacity for France to exert its influence on a larger number of member states, many of which do not share the same aspiration to international leadership at the world level and independence in their relations with the US. The influence of French diplomacy within Europe was both more reactive and less effective than in the previous periods. Whether the proactive style of Nicolas Sarkozy will succeed in bringing France 'back' in European affairs, and whether this can be achieved without adopting significantly more atlantist positions, remain to be seen. The French presidency of the EU in the second semester of 2008 will probably be decisive in that respect.

8.4   Institutions and French foreign policy

What is true of French European policy, that is, the existence of significant changes despite some elements of continuity with the Gaullist period, and a more relative position particularly apparent since the end of the cold war, could also be shown regarding other areas such as the Middle East, Africa, or in cooperation policy. This does not come to an evaluation of French 'decline' and failure of French diplomacy, as is sometimes argued. Rather it shows that the increase in complexity of the international environment, introducing both new actors and new factors, deeply questioned French foreign policy, and requested adaptations uneasy to negotiate. We explore in this section the impact of the institutional design of the Fifth Republic on strengths and weaknesses of foreign policy.

The French constitution grants the president with the most crucial prerogatives in the conduct of foreign policy. He is indeed the warrant of national independence, of territorial integrity and respect of international treaties (Art. 5). He is the chief of the armed forces (Art. 15). He nominates and gives credits to ambassadors (Art. 14), negotiates and ratifies international treaties, and must be informed of negotiations of international agreements (Art. 52). In case of serious threats to the execution of France's international commitments, he can make use of special powers provisioned under Art. 16.

The constitution however also gives important powers in this area to the government, responsible for the conduct of the policy of the nation (Art. 20). The government is also explicitly responsible for national defense (Art. 21), and deploys the armed forces (Art. 20). However, as the president nominates the prime minister (Art. 8), and owing to the context of the foundation of the Fifth Republic, early governments spontaneously stood as subordinates to the president in the conduct of foreign policy, and accepted its establishment as a 'domaine réservé', the corner-stone of which is the exclusive control of the use of nuclear force by the president.

Although Parliament has to approve a declaration of war (Art. 35), the French president therefore benefits from a wide room for initiative and autonomy and the conduct of foreign policy, indeed more significant than most of his or her counterparts in other countries, including the US. The president can in particular send troops abroad in peace-keeping or security operations, including war situations such as Afghanistan or Kosovo, without receiving the former approval of Parliament (although the 2008 revision of the constitution requires a parliamentary vote on any foreign military action within four months). Article 53 of the constitution grants Parliament the capacity to ratify treaties negotiated by the government. But most military agreements established between France and other states were never submitted to the parliament. When parliamentary approval is explicitly required, the delay between the signature of the treaty and its submission to the two chambers of the parliament, as well as the political balance detrimental to legislative power, leaves the executive largely free from parliamentary control in the conduct of foreign policy.

The room for maneuver for the president is also very large within the executive branch itself. The government, via the Council of Ministers chaired by the president, is informed more than consulted on the definition of foreign policy. European affairs are somewhat specific in this respect, as the EU regulations interact on a day-to-day basis with domestic policies. Discussions in the Council of Ministers are therefore more frequent, as the government is directly involved both in the negotiations for agenda-setting within the EU Council of Ministers, and in the domestic implementation of EU regulations. The presidential leadership however remains strictly prominent on all critical issues. The government ensures the coordination of policy implementation through a number of inter-ministerial committees, such as the *Secrétariat général des Affaires européennes* (SGAE) for European affairs, the *Secrétariat général pour la Défense nationale* (SGDN) for defense issues, the *Comité interministériel pour l'étude des exportations de matériels de guerre* for arms exports.

The Ministry for Foreign Affairs, extremely influential under the Third and Fourth Republics, has seen its role deeply transformed and strictly subordinated to the president. While the composition of the government is proposed to the president by the prime minister, the custom was established for the president to personally select the Minister of Foreign Affairs, usually among his or her most loyal followers. The same roughly applies to the secretary of state for European affairs. The Minister and the Ministry also face the direct competition of the presidential staff, including the presidential headquarters for military affairs, the diplomatic task force, the 'African' task force, and a special councilor for G8 summits. Other ministries (Agriculture, Health, Justice and so forth), increasingly affected by international relations, also develop specific services for external affairs and directly interact with their foreign counterparts. The Ministry for Foreign Affairs remains crucial for marshalling policy alternatives available to the president and for implementing the conduct of diplomacy, but definitely in a less exclusive manner than in the past (Kessler 1999, Cohen 2007).

Such a concentration of power around the president allows for rapidity of decision-making, a strong capacity of policy adaptation in critical situations, and continuity based on the benefice of a rather long-term horizon in the conduct of foreign policy. However, it also entails a number of weaknesses. The first lies with the relative overload of the presidency, which does not benefit from full coordination with the different ministries involved, without disposing of an extensive staff of its own. As a result, French diplomacy seems excessively selective in defining its policy agenda, because of the saturation and deficit of coordination of its administrative capacities (Cohen 2007).

Another weakness of French foreign policy under the Fifth Republic lay with the 'cohabitation', or the situations of divided executive resulting from different presidential and parliamentary majorities. Such a situation requires the president to accommodate the policies of a prime minister and a government from another party. Cohabitation occurred in 1986–88 between François Mitterrand and Jacques Chirac, in 1993–95 between François Mitterrand and Edouard Balladur, and in 1997–2002 between Jacques Chirac and Lionel Jospin. While the competition between François Mitterrand and Jacques Chirac, experiencing the first cohabitation, was the most evident, tensions were also important between Jacques Chirac and Lionel Jospin. Practically, foreign policy during these periods was exerted as a shared rather than divided competence between the different components of the executive. François Mitterrand and Jacques Chirac worked in agreement for instance during the crisis in Chad and Lebanon, during the gulf crisis or 1987 or when authorization to fly over the French territory was denied to US forces to bomb Libya. The competition and hostility between the two leaders however was so evident that a double diplomacy developed in a rivalry of political communiqués clearly detrimental to foreign policy cohesion. Cooperation and coordination between the president and the prime minister were better with François Mitterand and Edouard Balladur. Generally speaking, the two branches of the executive are forced into cooperation. The president cannot send troops abroad independently of the government. Foreign policy initiatives are therefore based on converging views or on compromises between the protagonists. 'Turquoise', the military intervention in Rwanda in June 1994 was for instance the result of a bargaining between François Mitterrand supported by the Minister of Foreign Affairs Alain Juppe on the one hand, and the more skeptical Prime Minister Edouard Balladur and Minister of Defense

François Leotard on the other. In 1999 Jacques Chirac could not persuade the government of Lionel Jospin to make use of armed forces to support the evicted President Bedie of the Ivory Coast. Such a situation radically differed from the 'domaine réservé' characteristics of situations where the executive is not divided.

Although foreign policy alternated between hyper-concentration of power and diarchy within the executive itself, cohabitation nevertheless did not really prove a handicap in facing major crisis situations. It was even argued that it developed practices of consultation and consensus building of the conduct of foreign policy (Cohen 2003 and 2007). However, as in all cases protagonists would later compete in the presidential election, consensus with their main competitor was never a good political strategy, and contributed to somewhat water down the profile of French diplomacy. In the foreign policy game, the president and the prime minister indeed run the risk of being overtaken by their competitor, or alternatively of appearing too close to each other on foreign policy issues critical for presidential leadership. While the incumbent president had no incentive to enhance the international profile of his or her opponent, the later would equally be reluctant to appear as a subordinate in the conduct of a joint policy, and to restraint its capacity to offer an alternative for the next mandate. Crisis situations provided a different distribution of incentives, whereby the need to avoid a policy fiasco severely detrimental to both the presidency and the government would quite efficiently force the two branches to work together. Active cooperation however would not consolidate beyond the termination of such situations, analytically close to 'one-shot' games. In the longer term, when foreign policy is dominated by the need for planning in the promotion of objectives, and when it is subject to potential controversies among public opinion (as for the modernization of armed forces, relations with NATO, or relinquishing monetary sovereignty), cohabitation structurally imposed a context of mutual neutralization, if not impeachment, on the two branches of the executive, and eroded its capacity for leadership in international relations.

8.5   Conclusion

It would be wrong to claim that institutional constraints have been at the source of a lower profile for French diplomacy since the 1990s, indeed primarily located in the deep transformations induced by the end of the cold war in Europe and at the global level, and in the time needed for subsequent cognitive and strategic changes they imposed on French elites. But it also has to be acknowledged that the constitutional structure of the regime interacts with the international context to define the contours and the conduct of French foreign policy. While the extreme concentration of foreign policy on the presidential leadership allows for the infamous pursuit of 'grandeur' through bold diplomatic moves, situations of divided executive (cohabitation), regularly occurring between 1986 and 2002, also created a structural condition for passivity of French political leadership, all the more apparent as the international context in Europe became far less predictable, and urgently required policy adaptation. Institutional constraints became redundant with greater uncertainty in France's close international environment to somewhat mainstream the distinctiveness of French diplomacy. Another constraint of the constitutional structure lies with the relation between public opinion and foreign policy. The total de-parliamentarization of foreign policy, at least from a comparative perspective, indeed gives to the executive wide room for maneuver, and therefore a capacity for developing a long-term vision through salient moves and position-takings. However, this situation also leaves the conduct of foreign policy quite exclusively within the hands of the executive, with very limited public monitoring and democratic control. Such a lack of transparency occasionally leads French diplomacy to be involved in political imbroglios and sometimes tragedies, noticeably in Africa, such as the genocide in Rwanda for instance. But it is also detrimental to the domestic public debate on foreign policy. It is sometimes argued that French citizens are self-centered, not interested in international affairs, and particularly resistant to globalization. Such a claim would easily be challenged by comparative data, showing that French public opinion, despite some specificity, is no exception on international affairs. Rather, we believe that the marginalization of the parliament in the constitution channels the politization of foreign policy issues toward social movements, and is all the more likely to nourish opposing movements and protest behaviors that deliberation on foreign policy is atrophied. The prosperity of the anti- or alter-globalization movements in France, as well as the rejection of the draft constitutional treaty for the European Union in 2005, should be considered from this angle.

Bibliography

Aldrich, R. and J. Connell (eds) (1989) *France in World Politics* (London, Routledge).

Balme, R. and C. Woll (2005) 'Europe and the Transformation of French Policymaking', *Journal for Comparative Government and European Policy*, 3, 1–22.

Balme, R. and C. Woll (2003), 'France', in S. Bulmer and C. Lequesne (eds) *Member States and the European Union* (Oxford, Oxford University Press).

Cohen, S. (2007) 'Les acteurs de la politique étrangère', *Regards sur l'Actualité*, 332, June–July, 17–25.

Cohen, S. (2003) 'Cohabiter en politique étrangère: atout ou handicap?', *Annuaire français des relations internationales*.

Cole, A. and H. Drake (2000), 'The Europeanization of the French polity: continuity, change and adaptation', *Journal of European Public Policy* 7(1), 26–43.

Eichenberg, R. (1989), *Public Opinion and National Security in Western Europe* (Ithaca, N.Y., Cornell University Press).

Fournié, P. (2007) 'Chronologie', in J.C. Allain, P. Guillen, G.H. Soutou, L. Theys, M. Vaïsse (eds), *Histoire de la diplomatie française. II. De 1815 à nos jours* (Paris, Perrin) pp. 562–615.

Gordon, P. (1993) *A Certain Idea of France: French Security Policy and the Gaullist Legacy* (Princeton, Princeton University Press).

Grosser, A. (1984) *Affaires Extérieures: La politique de la France, 1944–1984* (Paris, Flammarion).

Grossman, E. and N. Sauger (2007) 'Political Institutions under Stress? Assessing the Impact of European Integration on French Political Institutions', *Journal of European Public Policy*, 14(7) (October), 1117–34.

Gueldry, M.R. (2001) *France and European Integration: Toward a Transnational Polity?* (Westport, CT: Praeger).

Hudson, V.M. (2007) *Foreign Policy Analysis. Classic and Contemporary Theory* (Boulder Co., Rowman and Littlefield Publishers).

Katzenstein, P. (1976), 'International Relations and Domestic Structures: Foreign Economic Policies of Advanced Industrial States', *International Organizations* 30 (Winter), 1–45.

Kessler, M.C. (1999) *La politique étrangère de la France: acteurs et processus* (Paris, Presses de Sciences Po).

Lefevre, M. (2007) 'La France et l'Europe', *Regards sur l'Actualité*, 332 (June–July), 27–38.

Morss, E.R. (2008) 'Global Energy: A Factual Framework for Future Research', in *New Global Studies*, 2(1), Berkeley Electronic Press, http://www.bepress.com/ngs/

Paxton, R. and N. Wahl (eds) (1994) *De Gaulle and the United States* (Berg).

Risse-Kapen, T. (1991) 'Public Opinion, Domestic Structure, and Foreign Policy in Liberal Democracies', *World Politics*, 43 (4) (July), 479–512.

Rosenau, J.R. (1961) *Public Opinion and Foreign Policy* (New York, Random House).

Rozenberg, O. and A. Szukala (2001) 'The French Parliament and the EU: Progressive Assertion and Strategic Investment' in A. Maurer and W. Wessel (eds), *National Parliaments on their Ways to Europe: Losers or Latecomers?* (Baden-Baden: Nomos), pp. 223–50.

Russett, B. (1990) *Controlling the Sword: The Democratic Governance of National Security* (Cambridge, Harvard University Press).

Sauger, N., S. Brouard and E. Grossman (2007) *Les Français contre l'Europe ? Les sens du referendum du 29 mai 2005* (Paris, Presses de Sciences Po).

Shapiro, R. and B.I. Page (1988) 'Foreign Policy and the Rational Public', *Journal of Conflict Resolution* 32(2), 211–47.

Stockholm International Peace Research Institute (SIPRI) (2007) *SIPRI Yearbook 2007: Armaments, Disarmament and International Security* (Oxford, Oxford University Press).

Vaïsse, M. (1998) *La grandeur. Politique étrangère du Général De Gaulle* (Paris, Fayard).

Vaïsse, M. (2004) *Les relations internationales depuis 1945* (Paris, A. Colin), 9th edn.

Vaïsse, M. (2007) 'La puissance ou l'influence? (1958–2004)', in J.C. Allain, P. Guillen, G.H. Soutou, L. Theys and M. Vaïsse (eds), *Histoire de la diplomatie française. II. De 1815 à nos jours* (Paris, Perrin), 429–562.

World Bank (2007) *World Development Indicators Database*, http://econ.worldbank.org accessed 19 March 2008.

Part II

Institutions and State–Society Relations

9
Economic Interventionism in the Fifth Republic

Ben Clift

9.1 Introduction

This chapter explores the evolution of state–market relations under the French Fifth Republic. It begins by charting the outline of the postwar French economic model, identifying France as the prime European exemplar of the 'Developmental State' (Amsden 2001; Woo-Cummings 1999; Shonfield 1969). Crucial to this was the French economic ideology of *dirigisme*, which denotes the French tradition of directive state intervention in economic activity. In contemporary parlance, France was, and is, a particularly statist variant (Schmidt 2003) of the 'co-ordinated market economy' variety of capitalism (Hall and Soskice 2001). The chapter considers the prevailing interpretation of the 1950s until the 1970s, with a successful, nimble state strategically pulling the levers of economic policy-making in order to steer France to strong economic growth. This conventional wisdom is interrogated through a reassessment of state–market relations and economic policy-making, asking how much of the credit for France's strong postwar economic performance was really due to economic interventionism.

The chapter then explores how, in the wake of the oil crises, breakdown of Bretton Woods, and world economic slowdown in the 1970s, economic intervention was no longer a sufficient condition of economic success. First, this was because certain policy levers, such as competitive devaluation, were no longer available. Second, it was because the kinds of interventions pursued did not have sufficient purchase upon apparently intractable economic problems (unemployment, inflation, industrial restructuring) that began to hurt the French trade and payments situation. As France's industrial and economic situation began to look less healthy, economic intervention took successive turns; first *dirigiste* 'redistributive Keynesianism', then a partial assimilation of anti-inflationary 'ordo-liberalism'.[1]

The U-turn of 1983 reset the parameters of French economic policy-making, jettisoning significant parts (though not all) of the postwar *dirigiste* heritage. The European single market, followed by the plans for economic and monetary union, provided partial justification for the dramatic changes in economic policy orientation. European economic integration was, after all, built upon some decidedly non-*dirigiste* economic foundations. The remainder of the chapter explores the challenges to the traditional French model of economic interventionism presented by international liberalization and Europeanization and asks how we should best characterize the French political economy in the contemporary period. French economic interventionism over the past 25 years has blended significant elements of liberalization with more modest doses of selective, targeted, novel *dirigisme*. France's quasi-*dirigiste* economic interventionism today is more market-conforming than in the first 20 years of the Fifth Republic. Economic intervention is more modest in scope, with state policy levers having less purchase on French capitalism than during the *trente glorieuses*. That said, French *dirigisme* has not disappeared. It remains important to the rhetoric and practice of state–market relations in France, as contemporary 'economic patriotism' demonstrates.

9.2 French postwar economic modernization and the Fifth Republic

In some respects the onset of the Fifth Republic was not as significant a break in state–market relations or economic policy (Cole 2003) as in other aspects of French politics. The institutions of indicative economic planning, established by Monnet and others in the wake of liberation, had been functioning relatively effectively in the 1950s, and continued to do so into the 1960s. While 1958–59 could not be described as 'business as normal', nevertheless the technocratic, elitist approach to planning gave it a degree of insulation from the political turmoil and seismic constitutional events of 1958. The same elites in planning ministries were still pulling the levers of economic policy-making. That said, the political and constitutional crisis which saw the demise of the Fourth Republic and the onset of the Fifth in 1958 was accompanied by economic and financial turbulence. The 'Pinay–Rueff' stabilization plan of 1958 (which was comparable to earlier such plans under the Fourth Republic) sought to do to the French political economy what de Gaulle was attempting with its polity – bring much needed stability.

Perhaps the two most significant developments for French state–market relations in the period occurred, by coincidence, in the same year as the Fifth Republic was born. The restoration of convertibility, which brought to an end the European Payments Union, changed the international context of the French economy, and its articulation with the international political economy in monetary and financial affairs. Meanwhile, where trade was concerned, downward pressure was being exerted on trade tariffs by the OEEC and the newly formed EEC. These set the parameters of what was to be an ongoing theme of French state–market relations throughout the Fifth

Republic – the compatibility (or otherwise) of statist French capitalism (and the French developmental state) with liberalizing international economic pressures and a changing international economic context.

In 1958, however, the French economy seemed well equipped to meet the challenges ahead. Economic modernization (along with social change – urbanization, and a population explosion) had proceeded apace since 1944, and in some ways the Fifth Republic took the credit for earlier achievements in restoring the French economy (Cole 2003: 18–19). The French economy grew at a very healthy annual average of 4.6 per cent between 1950 and 1959, with strong productivity gains and much improved living standards. In the 1950s, and indeed the 1960s, France enjoyed healthy growth and improving productivity compared to its key European competitors (Coates 2000: 1–20; Crafts 1997). Indeed unfavourable comparison of the UK experience to French economic dynamism sparked debates about UK 'decline' (English and Kenny 2000). Broadly speaking, French growth was strong, with full employment. The principle economic problem was inflation, and a balance of payments deficit (Chelini 2001: 102–3). Limited financial reserves and the uncertainties of the impacts of EEC trade liberalization gave policy-makers pause for thought as the Fifth Republic came into existence.

In terms of state–market relations, French policy-makers had already begun to prepare the ground for increased international competition. As Hall notes, 'French policy makers of the 1940s and 1950s used the resources of the state to encourage French industry and agriculture to increase the scale of production through mergers and acquisitions, to shift capital and labour into high-technology sectors, and to eliminate less efficient producers in favour of firms that could prosper on international markets' (2001: 173–4; see also Loriaux 1999: 241–7). De Gaulle enthusiastically endorsed such an approach, convinced that French 'national champions' in the economic field were a precondition of French military and political power on the world stage. In this he was echoed by the leader of the French employers' association, the CNPF, who noted 'the salient feature of this new phase of our economic development is the decisive role that states will be called upon to play. International competition will involve the whole nation. Left to themselves, firms cannot face this competition alone' (quoted in Hayward 1973: 152).

1958 also saw the onset of the third wave of French public sector expansion, the earlier waves being in the 1930s (e.g. SNCF), and immediately after the war (e.g. GDF, EDF). One feature of French statist capitalism is a comparatively large public sector. This time, rather than nationalizing existing firms, the Gaullist state created high-tech public firms in aeronautics, nuclear technology, and IT, as well as research facilities in telecoms and other strategic sectors (Loriaux 1999: 242–4). This was to be the state institutional infrastructure which would nurture de Gaulle's 'national champions' (Loriaux 1999: 259–60).

9.3   The French Fifth Republic: the archetypal 'developmental' state?

Alice Amsden (2001: 125) summarized the developmental state thus:

> The developmental state was predicated on performing four functions: developmental banking; local-content management; 'selective seclusion' (opening some markets to foreign transactions and keeping others closed); and national firm formation.... Two principles guided developmentalism: to make manufacturing profitable enough to attract private enterprise through the allocation of 'intermediate assets' (subsidies) and to induce such enterprises to be results-oriented and to redistribute their monopoly profits to the population at large.

This was the genus (predominantly associated with East Asia) of which French state–market relations at the time of the Fifth Republic were the European exemplar. According to Loriaux, 'the French developmental state is, in the simplest terms, the extension of the domain of competence of the Grand Corps from the problems of engineering and issues of hygiene to questions of economic policy' (1999: 257). Underpinned by the Republican *étatiste* tradition (Hazareesingh 1994, chs 3 and 6; Dyson 1980, 27–9), state intervention in economic activity in France has been predicated upon the state conceived as 'guiding force', providing capitalism with the necessary direction. This has a long pedigree within French politics, and 'French governments had for centuries alternated between policies of passive protectionism and active promotion – state-sponsored capitalism and state capitalism – based upon close collusion between the private sector and its public senior partner' (Hayward 1973: 152).

However, French *dirigisme* only took on recognizably 'developmental state' form in 1945, with the ENA, the planning apparatus, and the 'treasury circuit' of credit control transforming short-term deposits into long-term loans to finance industrial restructuring and public spending, all emerging simultaneously at the end of the war (Loriaux 1999: 245–7, 51). With the onset of the Fifth Republic, the executive dominance which transformed party politics and the polity itself (see Clift 2005: 221–45) also transformed the making of economic policy with increased technical expertise and support from an expanded *grand corps* operating within a number of influential ministerial *cabinets* (Hayward 1973: 159–88; Loriaux 1999: 259–60). Thus, 'it is under the Fifth Republic that the French developmental state achieved its full realization, burgeoning into what Pierre Birnbaum has called the "republic of civil servants"' (Loriaux 1999: 259).

As well as macroeconomic policies such as competition devaluation, as in 1957, 1969 and 1975 (Loriaux 1999: 262) and a broadly Keynesian set of fiscal and welfare state policies (Rosanvallon 1989), there was a panoply of instruments and institutions geared towards microeconomic interventionism in the French economy. The making of economic policy in the Fifth Republic was a source of national pride, widely credited as the reason behind France's *trente glorieuses* of economic growth and widening prosperity and affluence. Indeed, other European countries, notably the UK, sought inspiration from France's state-directed indicative economic planning in reshaping their own state–market relations in the early 1960s (Budd 1978: 87–8).

The French model was captured in Zysman's account of France's state-led industrial development (Zysman 1983), portraying an actively interventionist, *dirigiste*, 'player' state using its key agencies to steer the nation's economic development (Shonfield 1969: ch. 5; Hall 1986). The French *dirigiste* model was predicated upon a set of coordinating and steering mechanisms in the postwar era. The policy mechanisms included, firstly, price, credit and exchange controls. Secondly, there were norms of *tutelle* (or hands-on supervision) over key (public and private) industries, involving 'an intricate network of commitments on the part of private firms... all in return for favours from the state... [and] the habit of the exercise of power by public officials over the private sector of the economy' (Shonfield 1969: 86 and 128). As Hayward noted in 1973 'despite the dramatic industrial revolution through which France has been going in the last two decades, and is still undergoing, the weight of this long-standing *dirigiste* tradition still makes itself felt in the sense of dependence upon government, which French businessmen more or less explicitly acknowledge' (Hayward 1973: 152). The final element was state orchestration of industrial finance through the plan.

The comparatively large French public sector, noted above, was also used as a macroeconomic policy tool by *dirigiste* policy elites during the first two decades of the Fifth Republic. For example, prices of transportation and energy could be controlled in a bid to reduce supply-side costs and boost international competitiveness of French industry. As Loriaux notes, 'between 1959 and 1974, the prices of goods and services produced by the state sector actually diminished by 20 per cent relative to the prices of goods and services as a whole' (1999: 242).

Central to France's *dirigiste* interventionism was the state's role in providing funds for industrial investment (Zysman 1983). The centrality of 'institutionally allocated credit' from private and public banks, as opposed to 'asset-based credit' in the form of stocks and securities meant that in 1976, 85 per cent of credit to all firms and households came from institutional lenders (Loriaux 1991: 59). Industry's reliance, throughout most of the postwar era, on institutions directly or indirectly regulated by the state gives the French state a scope for leverage. The bottom line was that, 'capital would be strategic and cheap' (Loriaux 1991: 113). State loans tended to be conditional upon meeting specific restructuring targets, incorporating subsidiaries into parent companies, or merging with other big firms (Loriaux 1999: 259–60).

The state's centrality to the system of 'institutionally allocated credit' (as opposed to 'asset-based credit') from private and public banks gave the French state numerous levers it could pull. French public industrial investment was in some respects the motor of French economic growth (Hayward 1973: 166; Loriaux 1999: 244). In comparative terms, the degree of dependence of industrial and financial capital on the central state was highly distinctive (in the German co-ordinated market economy, for example, the key financial relations were more decentralized, between firms and local and regional banks). In addition to the 'economy of administered finance', a further characteristic of the French model was the 'inflationist social compromise' (Cohen 1995). This also contrasted with the German model, this time with its ordo-liberal sound money ethos. The French state's inability to control the inflationary growth of credit was compounded by 'the consensual refusal of the state, the trade unions, and the employers to control nominal changes in incomes and prices' (Cohen 1995: 26).

France's exceptional 'meritocratic' elitism was of central importance to the postwar *dirigiste* model, as exemplified by the central role of ENA. The coordinating role played by 'an interpenetration of state and business elites' (Maclean 1999: 101), whose schooling within the *grandes écoles* (many created by Napoleon) created a relatively homogeneous elite, has long been noted as a distinctive characteristic of French capitalism (Loriaux 1999: 237–41). Top civil servants, politicians, and bosses followed a similar educational path under the Fifth Republic, becoming part of the French *grands corps*. This informal community operated as a coordinating mechanism of French capitalism, in part through *pantouflage*, or the smooth passage, from higher civil service to the boards of major enterprises – public or private (Hayward 1973: 159–60; Hancké 2001: 313–14). These coordinating networks found institutional expression in the *noyaux durs*, or 'hard cores' of cross-shareholdings and overlapping board memberships of large French firms, which provided stability and coherence at various stages in the development and evolution of France's 'financial network economy' (Morin 2000).

What flowed from this model, these institutions, and these state traditions was a set of presumptions that have endured in some form throughout the history of the Fifth Republic on the part of administrative, economic and political elites, and on the part of the wider populace. These were that the French state could and should actively intervene in economic activity to deliver such public goods and economic growth, full employment and, in accordance with Republican values of equality and social cohesion, limited redistribution of wealth. The prevailing interpretation of the postwar experience of the 1950s until the 1970s was a successful, nimble state strategically pulling the levers of economic policy-making in order to steer France to a dramatic economic recovery with strong economic growth and improving living standards for most, if by no means all, of its population.

9.4 How successful was *dirigisme*?

This conventional wisdom is interrogated through a reassessment of state–market relations and economic policy-making between the late 1950s and early 1970s, asking how much of the credit for France's strong economic performance was really due to economic interventionism. An extensive literature questions the coherence of the picture advanced by Zysman, and a debate remains as to how much 'glorious' growth was really due to indicative economic planning and strategic interventionism in industry creating 'national champions' (see for example Hayward 1973: 180–7, 213–26; Hancké 2001: 309–12; Guyomarch et al. 1998: 161–8; Loriaux 1999: 241–7, 251–2; Levy 2000: 321).

The first issue is the coverage of *dirigisme* in terms of policy. Planning, as Loriaux notes, 'proved ineffectual with regard to achieving more abstract macroeconomic objectives, such as price stability, demand management, and employment which were sensitive to short-term pressures' (1999: 242). In addition, social security, a crucial aspect of economic and social policy, was controlled by the social partners, outside the Plan, and substantially outside the state's *dirigiste* lever-pulling grasp throughout the period (Palier 2002; Hayward 1973: 180).

The second issue is the assumed coherence and cohesiveness of the French state, which was not one and indivisible but deeply fragmented (Hayward 1973; 2006). Furthermore, the *dirigiste* technocrats were often not steering the tiller but being 'captured' by sectional interests within French industry (Hayward 1986: 13, 16, 101; Loriaux 1999: 264–5). While allowing politicians to avoid hard choices, this 'agency capture' ultimately restricted the French state's much vaunted autonomy.

Following on from this, a third issue is the assumed coherence of the economic rationale underpinning the decisions made. This criticism applies more to the 1970s than the 1960s or 1950s. For example, after 1971, the French government's complex credit rationing scheme (*encadrement du crédit*) controlled financial flows (Cerny 1989: 172), but did not always display the logic and virtues highlighted by Zysman et al. In the 1970s industrial policy 'turned its back on the plan and focused on the more immediate problems of preserving employment and propping up firms threatened by bankruptcy' (Loriaux 1999: 242; Berger 1981). It left many areas of the French economy undercapitalized, and hindered the development of capital markets. Often state funds did not feed a dynamic industrial core, but delayed lay-offs and restructuring in industries whose collapse was deemed too politically costly in the short term – such as steel. For example, in 1978, a handful of firms, most of them uncompetitive and many in declining sectors, were receiving more than 75 per cent of all public aid to industry (Levy 2000: 321). The French state was picking losers.

There was also a sense of a law of diminishing returns surrounding public exhortation to throw all hands to the planning pump. De Gaulle described the Plan as an 'ardent obligation', but it was not legally enforced, and by the Sixth Plan (1971–75), Hayward detected that 'the ardour has dissipated' (1973: 184–5). One reason for this was the harsher economic climate, and a sense of the flagging ability of planning to deliver the (internationally competitive) goods. The US, Japanese and German economies, for example, seemed to be weathering the storms of stiffer international economic competition and the global economic downturn better than France, and this reduced French *dirigiste* self-confidence. These problems were compounded by a growing fiscal crisis of the French state, leading many to question whether the French state could afford to play its traditional role, *even if* it were to be done effectively.

The reliance on institutionally allocated credit, the core of *dirigisme*, exposed 'the Achilles heel of capital in France – lack of private finance' (Boucek 1993: 76). Unlike the US and UK economies, where flourishing stock markets were key sources of industrial capital, in postwar France, financial markets had declined, not least because private sources of funding were 'crowded out' by cheaper and more readily available state capital investment funding. Thus, 'the new *dirigisme* of the 1960s and 1970s was mirrored by the stagnation of financial markets, seen as the outdated legacy of the Third Republic's *mur d'argent*' (Cerny 1989: 170; Loriaux 1999: 261).

French industrial modernization since the war had been over-reliant on public investment, and when this tap was turned off, the consequences were dire. The problem became acute in the wake of the 1974 industrial crisis. 'Reduced profitability and depressed markets provoked a sharp drop in investment; industrial investment fell by 15 percent between 1974 and 1977, to reach the level of 1970. The slight rally of 1978–1980 was followed by a new drop of 20 percent between 1980–1984' (Stoffaes 1989: 112–13). The chronic lack of investment in many areas led the French economy to be caricatured as 'capitalism without capital' (Stoffaes 1989: 122).

9.5   The French developmental state under duress

The oil crises and world economic slowdown in the 1970s exacerbated doubts about the coherence and effectiveness of indicative economic planning and strategic interventionism. Unemployment began to rise, making France's industrial infrastructure look less healthy. To this were added the question about the compatibility of the Fifth Republic's *dirigiste* approach to state–market relations with a changing global political economy. The breakdown of Bretton Woods meant certain policy levers, such as competition devaluation, were no longer available. The intractable problem of inflation began to hurt the French trade and payments situation.

Under Mitterrand in the early 1980s France attempted to buck the international liberalizing drift away from the developmental state model. The Socialist government's attempted response to economic problems was a *dirigiste* dose of reflation, nationalization, and planning. The Mitterrand era began in 1981–83 with an ambitious contra-cyclical 'redistributive Keynesian' (Hall 1986) demand-boost and a dash for growth in the context of a world slump. The Mauroy government was initially strongly committed to *dirigisme* in a wide range of industrial, economic, and social policy areas. This did not have the desired effect and led, within two years, to economic and financial crises. External pressures, perhaps most importantly in the form of commitments involved in staying in the EMS, demonstrated the incompatibility of this stance with the wider European and global political economy (see e.g. Muet and Fonteneau 1985; Cameron 1996).

This episode seemed to demonstrate decisively the incongruity of the *dirigiste* model with global financial markets, and the powerful external constraints they could impose on the economic policy of French governments. This was a salutary lesson of the need to rethink the nature of France's engagement with emergent globalization. The so-called *autre politique* option of 1983 offered a protectionist and *dirigiste* 'solution' which remained within the established referential of French economic policy-making, and Mitterrand received representations from both 'camps' right up until the paradigmatic decision was made. The *dirigiste* approach was rejected in favour of an 'ordo-liberal' (see Dyson 1999: 34–5), anti-inflationary and market-conforming solution, accepting European Monetary System (EMS) conditions for revaluation, and a distinctly German-influenced conception of what constituted sound macroeconomic policy, and indeed macro-policy-making institutions. Germany provided the model because its superior economic performance, combined with its sound money economic ideology of ordo-liberalism, ensured the Deutschmark was the EMS's anchor currency.

This policy choice engendered a paradigm shift of priorities in macroeconomic policy, relegating full employment to a distant future aspiration, and promoting tackling inflation to priority number one (see Lordon 1998; Blanchard and Muet 1993). Yet this came at a price in economic terms. The 'competitive disinflation' macroeconomic strategy pursued vigorously by left and right alike from the mid-1980s did nothing to alleviate a sizeable domestic unemployment problem. Wage de-indexation, undoubtedly a necessary step in tackling inflation, was vilified on the left as hurting those lower earners, and forcing the burden of adjustment on the shoulders of those least able to carry it. As the unemployment levels of lower-skilled workers increased, the sense that French industrial workers were paying for France's economic restructuring was pervasive.

The U-turn of 1983 reset the parameters of French economic policy-making, jettisoning significant parts (though not all) of the postwar *dirigiste* heritage. The neo-liberal Thatcher and Reagan administrations had already re-ignited debates about the appropriate balance between state and market, and Chirac's flirtation with neo-liberalism between 1986 and 1988 pushed further in the direction of market liberalization and privatization already plotted by 'modernizing' socialists Fabius and Delors between 1984 and 1986. Financial markets were reconstructed, and their role within French capitalism began to expand. In terms of state–market relations, France was becoming much more liberal in character. Zysman (1983) identified government direction of credit as central to industrial policy, but the deregulation of the French (and international) financial system fundamentally undermined this.

The revived process of European integration, which gathered momentum after the 1984 Fontainebleu summit, provided, for Mitterrand in particular, a 'heroic' transformative project, which became the focus of economic policy discourse. The European single market, followed by the plans for economic and monetary union, also provided partial justification for the dramatic changes in economic policy orientation, since European economic integration was built upon decidedly non-*dirigiste* economic foundations. The 1986 Single European Act, and the neo-liberal understanding of state–economy relations which underpinned it, had wide-ranging implications for French industrial and economic policy. Drawing heavily on US anti-trust laws, the new competition regulation framework saw state industrial subsidies, protected sectors, and preferential public procurement – all key weapons in the *dirigiste* arsenal – as trade-distorting practices. State aids were policed, prevented, and in some cases had to be returned to sender. Thus *dirigiste* industrial policy was decreasingly viable, given the weakening of traditional policy instruments, advancing Europeanization, and a Commission policing competition with increasing vigour. Meanwhile, other European political economies more aligned with the 'liberal market economy' than the 'co-ordinated market economy' ideal-type (Hall and Soskice 2001), such as the UK, found it easier to accommodate these market-conforming, liberalizing and deregulatory tendencies within European political economic change.

The undermining of the developmental state has been widely reported within international and comparative political economy. In part, this arises from the decline of its policy instruments (Perraton, 2002). Industrial policy – conceived as 'policy aimed at *particular industries* (and firms as their components) to achieve outcomes that are *perceived by the state* to be *efficient for the economy as a whole*' (Chang 1996: 60, emphases in original) – was a central plank of French state–market relations under the first three decades of the Fifth Republic. State activism in French industrial policy declined from the 1980s onwards in the face of fiscal crisis, Europeanization and globalization. It could be argued that countries with more established liberal elements within their political economic traditions, be it classical and neo-classical liberalism in the UK, or ordo-liberalism in Germany, were better placed to adjust to the adverse economic conditions of the 1980s after the oil shocks and the breakdown of Bretton Woods. This was in part because the tide of international economic orthodox opinion was turning against *dirigisme* and state interventionism in favour of neo-liberalism and freer markets.

Around the world governments in advanced post-industrial political economies have privatized state-owned enterprises and deregulated markets. Their ability to set trade barriers or subsidize favoured firms has been severely curtailed. Direct means of industrial support through trade protections, local content requirements, subsidies and tax breaks are now severely restricted by the WTO and regional trade agreements. France, like other countries, cannot systematically use trade policy to promote national industries as it once did (Ruigrok and Tulder 1995: ch. 9). Many of the *dirigiste* tools of industrial policy that were used by European and North American economies earlier in their history, and Japan and Korea in the postwar period, are no longer available because of global and regional trade rules (Chang 2002).

9.6   French state market relations in the 1990s: European constraint, macroeconomic policy, and structural unemployment

The European single market, followed by the plans for economic and monetary union, provided partial justification for the dramatic changes in economic policy orientation after 1983. European economic integration was one factor leading towards a rebalancing between state and market within the French political economy. There were also 'domestic' pressures for a change in state–market relations. Notably, from the 1980s onwards, the relatively generous set of welfare state institutions predicated on social insurance assuming full employment were, in the context of structural unemployment between 9 and 12 per cent, proving very costly (Palier 2002). French public debt stood at 20 per cent of GDP in 1980. It had reached 30 per cent of GDP in 1990, and continued to rise to around 55 per cent by 1997. Public debt levelled off before rising once more in the 2000s, reaching 66 per cent of GDP in 2005 (OFCE 2006: 85–7).

European constraints upon French macroeconomic policy-making were a recurrent theme of the 1980s, 1990s and 2000s. In the 1990s, as preparations for EMU progressed, high German interest rates, which France was constrained to emulate, proved very unhelpful in the French economic context. This deepened the recession in the early 1990s and the European-wide economic crisis of 1992–94. With no end of unemployment in sight, and the public finances deteriorating, in the 1995 presidential election campaign Chirac promised to heal France's 'social fracture' with an expansive *dirigiste* bout of state intervention and public spending which flew in the face of EMU commitments to the Maastricht convergence criteria. This discourse was soon replaced, after the election, by an abrupt turnabout to fiscal austerity and attempted welfare state retrenchment. The '*mouvement sociale*' of winter 1995 politicized European political economic constraints to a degree not seen before in France and demonstrated the strength of attachment to republican *acquis sociaux* in the field of welfare and labour market policy.

Two years later Jospin's Socialist government promised both a *volontariste* approach to economic policy-making and a critical but constructive engagement with European economic integration. Jospin's four 1997 election manifesto 'conditions' on passage to the Euro distilled diverse *dirigiste* elements. Jospin insisted that, next to the ECB, a European 'economic government' must be established, charged with coordinating Eurozone economic policies, and that the stability and growth pact be revised to favour more job creation and social cohesion policies. The Socialist government of 1997–2002 enjoyed some notable successes in economic policy terms, with some redistributive measures as well as welfare state reform, and apparent success in state-led responses to the unemployment problem.

Despite deterioration in the public finances, the Jospin government dedicated considerable financial resources to its state-led employment policy expansion, and to its redistributive and welfare reform aims. It also embarked on some dramatic tax cuts. However, the impression that too much political capital had been spent on the 35-hour week, which in turn had not had enough of a beneficial impact on the employment situation, began to gain ground with the world economic downturn in the early 2000s. This took the shine off the Jospin government's otherwise positive record as unemployment levels began to creep stubbornly, if slowly, back up.

The *dirigiste* instincts continued under Raffarin's Centre Right government, which from 2002 onwards pursued a sharply expansionary fiscal policy in 2002. French economic policy and particularly spending decisions were, it seems, made in the context of a pervasive assumption of the absence of harsh constraint, permitting the delaying (in relation to health insurance) or ongoing avoidance (in relation to pensions and civil service staffing levels) of tough spending reduction decisions (see e.g. Howarth 2004, 209–20). By 2004 French public expenditure was running at 53.3 per cent of GDP, 5 per cent above the EU zone average, and approaching Swedish levels (56.7 per cent) (OFCE 2006: 35).

There remained significant elements of statist interventionism, be it Chirac's promising to heal the 'social fracture', or Jospin's promise to recreate a full employment society in France. Such *volontariste* flourishes, at the level of discourse at least, remained and remain a crucial and recurrent element of economic policy discussion in France. Yet, more and more as the 1990s progressed, there was explicit and at times candid recognition of the new economic realities and of an underlying and significant shift in state–market relations in favour of the latter.

There was less recourse to the kind of 'heroic' (Hayward 1973; Schmidt 1996) defiance of the market economy and its rationale such as the rhetoric which accompanied Mitterrand's 1981 victory and the promised '*rupture avec le capitalisme*'. Increasingly, French state intervention went with the grain of the market economy. Within French socialism, for example, with the collapse of communism, and the acceptance of a 'new horizon' of a capitalist market economy in 1991, such 'transcendentalist' rhetoric appeared increasingly anachronistic. French socialism had undergone a 'secularization', involving a simultaneous shift away from extravagant maximalist programmes, and away from an analytical framework heavily influenced by Marxism (Clift 2003: 105–31). Perhaps the culmination of this process was Jospin's observations as Prime Minister that 'we no longer live in an administrated economy', and that 'the state cannot do everything'. That these banal statements of bald fact have subsequently drawn such critical attention, notably from the Left, indicates the difficulty with which French political culture 'accepts' the end of the heroic phase of *dirigisme*.

One reason for the reduced ambition on the part of the state was the sheer cost of *dirigisme*. French public spending and public debt were, in theory at least, hamstrung by the stability and growth pact (requiring public deficits below 3 per cent and public debt below 60 per cent of GDP). Both grew as a result of expansionary economic policies pursued by first the Jospin then the Raffarin governments, and deficit in particular exceeded the stability and growth pact's upper ceiling. Although less dramatic than 1983, or even 1995, once again the conflict over state–market relations between domestic political economic priorities and European obligations came to a head in 2003 as the European Commission sought to punish French profligacy and breach of the pact. Meanwhile, French budget plans continued to flout the stability and growth pact's budget balance requirements. France thus remained an 'unrepentant sinner' (Clift 2006; Mathieu and Sterdyniak 2005, 154, 159; Creel et al. 2002).

In response, at the Ecofin meeting of 24–25 November 2003, the French and German governments managed to secure the 'freezing' of the Excessive Deficit Procedures. In the wake of the Ecofin meeting, the stability and growth pact was in disarray. The revised pact which emerged from the crisis by early 2005 involved much greater interpretive flexibility. More account would be taken of specific national conditions, economic circumstances and the economic cycle. A political context of a Franco-German axis on deficit forgiveness, created areas of room to manoeuvre, notably in revising the interpretation and implementation of the pact to align more closely with French *dirigiste* preferences.

Success in changing the fiscal policy architecture contrasts, however, with the monetary policy situation. Here, the alignment of French preferences and European policy is less clear-cut. The first years of the Euro did nothing to allay concerns about the European Central Bank's deleterious impact on the French employment situation, as unaccommodating (tight) monetary policy saw the Euro rise, with the competitive position of many French firms adversely affected. Martin (2004, see also Martin and Ross 2004) puts the case forcefully for a significant part of the blame for French unemployment in the late 1990s and 2000s lying at the door of the European Central Bank, which has been insufficiently considerate of the French economy's growth and employment needs.

For years French politicians of Left and Right have argued that the German-inspired European Central Bank needed to be subjected to a 'political counterweight' to bring concern of jobs and growth to bear alongside its somewhat myopic focus on price stability (low inflation). At the Maastricht negotiations, French efforts to shift the goal posts of EMU, inserting more scope for *dirigisme* to counter the perceived 'monetarism' of the European Central Bank (ECB), crystallized into the proposal for an 'economic government' (EG) as a political counterweight to the ECB (Dyson and Featherstone 1999, 172–245). Although unsuccessful at the time, the desire for such an 'economic government' remained an undercurrent of French economic policy thinking (Clift 2006; Howarth 2001; 2002; Parti Socialiste 1997, 12–13). Yet this kind of major re-orientation of the European Central Bank and its monetary policy is unlikely. In this context, French economic interventionism in the 1990s and 2000s has focused more on microeconomic, rather than macroeconomic policy.

9.7   French microeconomic interventionism and economic patriotism

Whereas formerly French policy elites clung to their aspiration to enact their industrial strategy using the traditional arsenal of *dirigiste* policy instruments, they have found many of them blunted by liberalization, Europeanization and globalization. Yet the strength of the *dirigiste* reflex with 'statist' French capitalism (Schmidt 2003) is so strong that economic interventionism finds expression in new forms. Thus the contemporary political debate surrounding the restructuring of large French firms echoes earlier Fifth Republic themes. Although the term 'national champions' is no longer used, the idea behind it remains pertinent. In recent years the notion has found a new iteration, expressed in the term 'economic patriotism' coined by the de Villepin government in 2005. Economic patriotism has echoes in some interventionist policy initiatives and governmental rhetoric in other European political economies such as Italy and Germany. However, economic patriotism is arguably most developed, both as rhetoric and practice, in France where it aligns most closely with the statist economic policy traditions described above.

Earlier in the Fifth Republic French economic patriotism used to be sustained and pursued by the French state, through the 'hard cores' or *noyaux durs* of France's 'protected capitalism' (Schmidt 1996) exploiting its extensive range of holdings in large French firms, as well as a much wider set of informal links to elites throughout France's 'financial network economy'

(Morin 2000; Loriaux 1999). Through such links, by a variety of cajolery and moral suasion, the French state induced the emergence of a set of interlinked relationships in major French firms cemented by cross-shareholdings and interlocking board memberships. These were in many cases progressively broken up in the context of internationalization, mergers and acquisition strategies and restructuring in the 1990s. This meant that the French state lost some of its purchase over French capitalism.

The financial nexus of France's political economy changed as more large French firms, formerly significant players within the *noyaux durs,* relinquished significant stakes in each other, and each retained only those holdings they saw as essential to their core business. This shifted the logic within France's 'financial network economy' towards Anglo-Saxon shareholder value norms (Morin 2000: 37–41; Goyer 2003). These changes in the behaviour and capital structure of many large French listed companies undermined further elements of the traditional French *dirigiste* policy approach. The degree of erosion of *noyaux durs* is considerable but not complete.[2] Loriaux notes that 'the hard core now represents less than 30 per cent of the capital for half of France's blue chip, CAC 40 enterprises (France's top 40 firms), less than 20 per cent for fifteen of the forty, and less than 10 per cent for five of the forty' (2003: 116; see also Morin 2000: 39).

Not all large French firms have been transformed to the same degree, and one important differentiation is between those companies with close ties to the French state, and those without. Public procurement remains important (see Smith 2005), notably in securing close links with some of France's largest and most successful firms. Those large French firms with close links to the state, either by reliance on public purchasing and government contracts, or by being part state-owned, or by having until recently been part state-owned comprise more than half of the CAC 40, including Total, Suez, and Vivendi. There is, significantly, a much higher prevalence of *enarques* among the CEOs of those state-linked forms (more than half) compared with large French firms with more remote ties to the state, where fewer than a quarter are former students of the *grandes ecoles.*

Even as the hard cores began to unravel the 1990s amid the privatizations, and heightened merger and acquisition activity which was contemporaneous to a thorough internationalization of French capitalism, in certain cases the French state sought to leave the traces of the prior 'protected capital' era. Thus, in the negotiating of some privatizations, the French government was careful to retain 'golden share' holdings vested with sufficient voting rights to fend off potential takeover (Knudsen 2005: 510). This means of protecting its 'national champions' eventually attracted the EC's disapproving attention, and in the ECJ Golden Shares case of 4 June 2002, the French state was forced to sell off its 'golden share' in Elf-Aquitaine (Ipekel 2005: 345).

This suggests an enduring (although less significant) orchestrating role for the French state within France's 'financial network economy' between the 1960s and the 1980s. There is, as a result of the internationalizing and liberalizing political economic reforms that the same policy elite introduced over the last 20–25 years, a degree of disjuncture between the rhetoric and the reality of economic patriotism, between its theory and its practice. Many of the traditional *dirigiste* policy levers have become much less effective, and French policy-makers have sought to compensate for this by seeking new ones.

Thus, for the most part, the changing international political economic context means that economic patriotism finds expression in new policies and areas of regulation. In particular a central focus of economic patriotism in the new global economy is the need to protect France's economic and corporate patrimony from foreign 'raiders' on international capital markets. This is why the apparently technical issue of the regulation of corporate takeovers has acquired such political salience in recent years. A recurrent theme to the legislation and regulation of corporate takeovers in France has been the desire to carve out scope for *dirigiste* interventionism in relation to 'strategic' sectors. There were laws in 1996 and 2003[3] specifying that French state approval is required for takeover or investment in 'strategic sectors' such as national defence, public health or public order, including casinos.

It is significant that hostile takeovers are a relatively rare occurrence in France. Only 19 took place between 1991 and 2000 (Montagne et al. 2002), illustrating that the French market for corporate control remains underdeveloped. This is because a whole range of obstacles are put in the path of such manoeuvres. These take a variety of forms, some relating to provisions in company statutes, some to patterns of shareholdings (and understandings between shareholders), and some relating to differential voting rights. Through measures such as concentrated (often family-dominated) ownership of majority shares in 'safe' hands, the prevalence of differential voting rights securing effective control for 'insiders', and complex 'pyramidal' structures of ownership that lock up control, many large French firms are effectively insulated from hostile takeover (Enriques and Volpin 2007: 117–22).

Hostile takeovers are also the subject of often intemperate press coverage and political discussion. French state actors have in recent years re-engaged dramatically in the public debate surrounding such takeovers, as when rumours spread of a possible hostile takeover of Danone by Pepsi in July 2005. The Interior and Finance ministers vociferously opposed the move. Sarkozy said the government 'could not remain inactive when faced with a hostile takeover bid' for Danone. The public authorities had to 'do their utmost' and deploy all their 'powers of persuasion' to block the move.[4] The French state's open hostility to the planned bid may have been a key factor in scuppering the takeover, which never materialized.

With talk of 'economic patriotism' in spate as it gushed from the mouths of Prime Minister de Villepin and Finance Minister Breton from 2005 onwards, the range of interventions to help large French firms to arm themselves against hostile takeovers increased. The Breton Law of July 2005 created a further obstacle to certain hostile takeovers in requiring a bidder to also bid for overseas subsidiaries of a target parent company. In December 2005[5] when the economically patriotic de Villepin government introduced legislation allowing it to protect from hostile takeover national firms operating in 11 identified 'strategic' industries. In addition to which, the very substantial financial assets of the *Caisse des dépôts et consignation* CDC were to be deployed investing to preserve the national interest by buying up stakes in large French firms deemed strategically important.

Similar *dirigiste* motives explained Finance Minister Thierry Breton's orchestration, in March 2006, of the merger of Gaz de France with Suez to protect the latter from a potential hostile takeover by the Italian energy giant Enel.[6] As these large-scale takeovers were under discussion, the French state was finally in the process of implementing the EU Takeover directive. The directive designed to facilitate takeovers, when transposed into French law, in fact introduced new obstacles in the form of frustrating measures by target boards, disclosure requirements of potential bidders, and French 'poison pills'. French double voting rights, an important element in impeding hostile takeovers, have been retained. The new legislative context in place after the law transposing the EU Directive into French law paradoxically *expands* considerably the range of anti-takeover defences available to target boards.

As the French government's vocal opposition to Mittal's attempted (and ultimately successful) hostile takeover of Arcelor in January 2006[7] demonstrated, the government has limited powers to control the market for corporate control, and its more arms-length *dirigisme* cannot always protect French industrial patrimony as it would like. Nevertheless, in the range of legislative and regulatory measures available to it, French governments have in recent years pursued an economic patriotic agenda in relation to takeovers. The likely effect is that they will remain comparatively rare occurrences in France.

9.8 Conclusion

The French Fifth Republic has seen profound transformations in French state–market relations and the making of economic policy. However, the two stereotypical characterizations of these evolutions should be questioned. First, the conventional wisdom is that a rational, strategic and effective French developmental state steered France to economic prosperity in the postwar years and the first two decades of the Fifth Republic. As we have seen, there are considerable grounds for questioning parts of that assessment. The French state was intervening and spending, but seemed to be 'picking losers' as often as it was 'picking winners'.

Secondly, there is the assumption that, after 1983, the French political economy underwent a thorough neo-liberalization. This chapter has shown how 'the habit of the exercise of power by public officials over the private sector of the economy' (Shonfield 1969: 128) has in fact been a consistent strain within the Fifth Republic, running right through from the 1950s to the 2000s. The decline in industrial policy can easily be over-stated as states find innovative means to influence the economy. What *has* changed is that, in the 1950s and 1960s, this *dirigisme* took place in the context of a developmental state. By the 1990s and 2000s the French state had evolved into a market-supporting, or what Levy calls a 'constructive', state (Levy 2006: 367–93). The French political economy has shifted in a more liberal direction: the state plays a less central role, and its role is more market-conforming today.

The presupposition in favour of *dirigiste* interventionism has come under increasing threat in the last 25 years from structural changes in global financial markets, from the European Union, and from the ideological ascendancy of neo-liberalism. The limits of the possible in terms of *dirigiste* intervention has been scaled back by changing global and regional political economic governance structures. Furthermore, as the Arcelor case proves, even the best efforts of the French state cannot always prevail over powerful financial and industrial resources to protect French firms. Nevertheless *dirigisme* is not dead. Rhetorically, it remains a powerful undercurrent of French politics. In practical policy terms, the gap between 'economic patriotic' *dirigiste* rhetoric and the political reality varies according to policy sectors, and firms. Economic interventionism continues to play a significant part in political economic outcomes in France, but twenty-first century French *dirigisme* is much more selective and modest in scope than its precursor. French economic policy in the Fifth Republic's 50th year is thus an anachronistic, paradoxical amalgam which is at once liberalizing in some areas, and still staunchly statist and *dirigiste* in others.

Notes

1. Ordo-liberalism is a political science term referring to a German economic ideology which shares some common ground with Anglo-Saxon neo-liberalism. Rooted in the historical experience of hyper-inflation, ordo-liberalism prioritizes the constitutional enshrining of central bank independence and price stability (as with the German Bundesbank). More broadly ordo-liberalism favours market liberalization (of labour, product, and capital markets) and strict, enforceable rules of fiscal discipline (see e.g. Dyson 2002: 174–86, 193–7).
2. In 2002 networks of influence constructed around three big banks – BNP, Société Générale and Crédit Lyonnais remained in place, and 30 directors enjoyed between them 160 seats on the boards of major French firms.
3. 96/109 and Decree 2003 of 7 March accompanying ordinance.

4. 'Sarkozy et Danone: ni passivité ni nationalisation rampante', *Le Monde* 22 July 2005.
5. Decree 2005/1739.
6. 'Suez-GDF-Enel: le choc des patriotismes, le poids des réseaux', *Le Monde* 5 March 2006.
7. 'Le patriotisme, Arcelor et les PME', *Le Monde* 5 February 2006.

Bibliography

Amsden, A. (2001) *The Rise of 'the Rest': Challenges to the West from Late-Industrializing Economies* (Oxford: Oxford University Press).

Berger, S. (1981) 'Lame Ducks and National Champions: Industrial Policy in the Fifth Republic', in Hoffman, S. and Andrews, W. (eds) *The Fifth Republic at Twenty* (Albany: State University Press of New York).

Blanchard, O. and Muet, P.-A. (1993) 'Competitiveness through Disinflation: An Assessment of the French Macroeconomic Strategy', *Economic Policy*, 8: 11–56.

Boucek, F. (1993) 'Developments in post-war French political economy: The continuing decline of dirigisme?' in Sheldrake, J. and Webb, P. (eds) *State and Market* (Aldershot: Dartmouth), pp. 67–86.

Budd, A. (1978) *The Politics of Economic Planning* (Manchester: Manchester University Press).

Cameron, D. (1996) 'Exchange Rate Politics in France 1981–83: The Regime Defining Choices of the Mitterrand Presidency', in Daley, A. (ed.) *The Mitterrand Era: Policy Alternatives and Political Mobilization in France* (Basingstoke: Macmillan).

Cerny, P. (1989) 'The "Little Big Bang" in Paris: Financial Deregulation in a *Dirigiste* System', *European Journal of Political Research*, vol. 17: 169–92.

Chang, H.-J. (1996) *The Political Economy of Industrial Policy* (Basingstoke: Macmillan).

Chang, H.-J. (2002) *Kicking Away the Ladder: Development Strategy in Historical Perspective* (London: Anthem).

Chelini, M.-P. (2001) 'Le plan de stabilisation Pinay-Rueff, 1958', *Revue d'Histoire moderne et contemporaine*, 48(4): 102–21.

Clift, B. (2003) *French Socialism in a Global Era: The Political Economy of the New Social Democracy in France* (London: Continuum).

Clift, B. (2005) 'Dyarchic Presidentialization in a Presidentialized Polity: The French Fifth Republic', in Paul Webb and Thomas Poguntke (eds) *The Presidentialization of Politics – A Comparative Study of Modern Democracies* (Oxford: Oxford University Press), pp. 219–43.

Clift, B. (2006) 'The New Political Economy of Dirigisme: French Macroeconomic Policy, Unrepentant Sinning, and the Stability and Growth Pact', *British Journal of Politics and International Relations*, 8(3): 388–409.

Coates, D. (2000) *Models of Capitalism* (Cambridge: Polity).

Cohen, E. (1995) 'France: National champions in search of a mission', in Hayward, J. (ed.) *Industrial Enterprise and European Integration: From National to International Champions in Europe* (Oxford: Oxford University Press), pp. 23–47.

Cole, A. (2003) *French Politics and Society* (Pearson).

Crafts, N. (1997) *Britain's Relative Economic Decline 1870–1995: A Quantitative Perspective* (London: Social Market Foundation).

Creel, J., Dupont, G., Le Cacheux, J., Sterdyniak, H., and Timbeau, X. (2002) 'Budget 2003: Le pêcheur non repenti', *La Lettre de L'OFCE*, 224: 1–4.

Dyson, K. (1980) *The State Tradition in Western Europe* (Oxford: Martin Robertson).

Dyson, K. (1999) 'The Franco-German Relationship and Economic and Monetary Union: Using Europe to "Bind Leviathan"', *West European Politics*, 22(1): 25–44.

Dyson, K. (2002) 'Germany and the Euro', in Dyson, K. (ed.) *European States and the Euro* (Oxford: Oxford University Press), pp. 173–211.

Dyson, K. and Featherstone, K. (1999) *The Road to Maastricht: Negotiating Economic and Monetary Union* (Oxford: Oxford University Press).

English, R. and Kenny, M. (eds) (2000) *Rethinking British Decline* (Basingstoke: Macmillan).

Enriques, L. and Volpin, P. (2007) 'Corporate Governance Reforms in Continental Europe', *Journal of Economic Perspectives*, 21(1): 117–40.

Goyer, M. (2003) 'Corporate Governance, Employees, and the Focus on Core Competencies in France and Germany', in Milhaupt, C. (ed.), *Global Markets, Domestic Institutions* (New York: Columbia University Press), pp. 183–213.

Guyomarch, A., Machin, H. and Ritchie, E. (1998) *France in the European Union* (Basingstoke: Macmillan).

Hall, P. (1986) *Governing the Economy* (Cambridge: Polity).

Hall, P. (2001) 'The Evolution of Economic Policy', in Guyomarch, A., Machin, H., Hall, P. and Hayward, J. (eds) *Developments in French Politics 2* (Basingstoke: Palgrave), pp. 172–90.

Hall, P. and Soskice, D. (2001) 'An Introduction to Varieties of Capitalism' in Hall, P. and Soskice, D. (eds) *Varieties of Capitalism* (Oxford: Oxford University Press), pp. 1–70.

Hancké, B. (2001) 'Revisiting the French Model: Coordination and Restructuring in French Industry', in Soskice, D. and Hall, P. (eds) *Varieties of Capitalism* (Oxford: Oxford University Press).

Hayward, J. (1973) *The One and Indivisible French Republic* (New York: Norton).

Hazareesingh, S. (1994) *Political Traditions in Modern France* (Oxford: Oxford University Press).

Howarth, D. (2001) *The French Road to European Monetary Union* (Basingstoke: Palgrave).

Howarth, D. (2002) 'The France State in the Euro Zone' in Dyson, K. (ed.) *European States and the Euro-Zone* (Oxford: Oxford University Press), pp. 145–72.

Howarth, D. (2004), 'Rhetorical Divergence: Real Convergence? The Economic Policy Debate in the 2002 French Presidential and Legislative Elections' in Gaffney, J. (ed.) *The French Presidential and Legislative Elections of 2002* (Aldershot: Ashgate), pp. 200–21.

Ipekel, F. (2005) 'Defensive Measures under the Directive on Takeover Bids and their Effect on the UK and French Takeover Regimes', *European Business Law Review*: 341–51.

Knudsen, J. (2005) 'Is the Single European Market an Illusion? Obstacles to Reform of EU Takeover Regulation', *European Law Journal*, 11(4): 507–24.

Levy, J. (2000) 'France: Directing Adjustment?', in Scharpf, F. and Schmidt, V. (eds) *Welfare and Work in the Open Economy: Volume Two* (Oxford; Oxford University Press), pp. 307–44.

Levy, J. (2006) 'The State after Statism: From Market Direction to Market Support', in Levy, J. (ed.) *The State After Statism* (Cambridge: Harvard University Press).

Lordon, F. (1998) 'The Logic and Limits of Désinflation Competitive', *Oxford Review of Economic Policy*, 14 (1): 96–113.

Loriaux, M. (1991) *France After Hegemony* (Ithaca: Cornell University Press).

Loriaux, M. (1999) 'The French Developmental State as Myth and Moral Ambition', in Woo-Cummings, M. (ed.) *The Developmental State* (Ithaca: Cornell University Press), pp. 235–75.

Loriaux, M. (2003) 'France: a new "capitalism of voice"?', in Weiss, L. (ed.) *States in the Global Economy* (Cambridge: Cambridge University Press), pp. 101–20.

Maclean, M. (1999) 'Corporate Governance in France and the UK: Long-Term Perspectives on Contemporary Institutional Arrangements', *Business History*, 41(1): 88–116.

Martin, A. (2004) 'The EMU Macroeconomic policy regime and the European social model' in Ross and Martin (eds) *op. cit.* pp. 20–49.

Martin, A. and Ross, G. (2004) 'Introduction: EMU and the European social model', in Ross and Martin (eds.) *op. cit.* pp. 1–19.

Mathieu, C. and Sterdyniak, H. (2005) 'Pacte de Stabilité: la réforme impossible', *Lettre de l'OFCE*, 257: 1–8.

Montagne, S., Pernot, J.-M. and Sauviat, C. (2002) 'Corporate governance systems and the nature of industrial restructuring: France', *European Industrial Relations Observatory Online*, http://www.eiro.eurofound.eu.int/2002/09/word/fr0207107s.doc

Morin, F. (2000) 'A Transformation in the French Model of Shareholding and Management', *Economy and Society*, 29(1): 36–53.

Muet, P.-A. and Fonteneau, A. (1985) *La gauche face à la Crise* (Paris: FNSP).

Palier, B. (2002) *Gouverner la sécurité sociale* (Paris: PUF).

Parti Socialiste (1997) *Changeons d'Avenir: Nos engagements pour la France* (Paris: PS Presse).

Perraton, J. (2002) 'What's Left of "State Capacity"? The Developmental State after Globalisation and the East Asian Crisis', Paper delivered to the Political Economy of Development Conference, University of Sheffield.

Rosanvallon, P. (1989) 'The Development of Keynesianism in France', in Hall, P. (ed.), *The Political Power of Economic Ideas: Keynesianism Across Nations* (Princeton: Princeton University Press).

Ross, G. and Martin, A. (2004). *Euros and Europeans: Monetary Integration and the European Model of Society* (Cambridge: Cambridge University Press).

Ruigrok, W. and Tulder, R. van (1995) *The Logic of International Restructuring* (London: Routledge).

Schmidt, V. (1996) *From State to Market? The Transformation of French Business and Government* (Cambridge: Cambridge University Press).

Schmidt, V. (2003) 'French capitalism transformed, yet still a third variety of capitalism', *Economy and Society*, 32(4): 526–54.

Shonfield, A. (1969), *Modern Capitalism: The Changing Balance of Public and Private Power* (London: Oxford University Press).

Smith, M. (2005) *States of Liberalization: Redefining the Public Sector in Integrated Europe* (State University of New York University Press).

Stoffaes, C. (1989) 'Industrial Policy and the State: From Industry to Enterprise', in Godt, P. (ed.) *Policy-Making in France* (London: Pinter).

Woo-Cummings, M. (ed.) (1999) *The Developmental State* (Ithaca: Cornell University Press).

Zysman, J. (1983) *Government, Markets, Growth: Financial Systems and the Politics of Industrial Change* (Ithaca: Cornell University Press).

10
Patterns of Public Budgeting in the French Fifth Republic: From Hierarchical Control to Multi-Level Governance

Frank Baumgartner, Martial Foucault and Abel François

10.1 Patterns of public budgeting in the French Fifth Republic

The evolution of public finances during the Fifth Republic offers significant opportunities for analysis. First, budgets are one of the best measures of the choices made by policy-makers. Consequently, budget changes describe fundamental aspects of the evolution of the French political process. Second, budget patterns can be depicted for the three pieces of the French public administration (central state, local state and social security). This enables us to highlight strong interactions between the three administrative levels of the public policy implemented over 50 years. These trends show the decreased autonomy of the French state over time.

We review the growth and development of public spending and taxing since 1959. Evidence clearly demonstrates the increasing complexity of government sources of fiscal policy. Public authorities, of course, have grown dramatically since 1959, with public spending as a proportion of GDP being roughly double today what it was at the beginning of the Fifth Republic. At the same time as spending has increased, central state autonomy has declined. This is because of the creation of a more complex structure of multi-level governance, which we demonstrate here by looking at the share of public expenditure controlled by the central state, local government authorities, and the social security system. These last two sources of spending, once relatively minor players in the system, now constitute a majority of all public spending in France, with the central state itself only a minority player.

We demonstrate a number of important shifts over time and show the substantially different operation of French fiscal policies in the early decades of the Fifth Republic compared with the period since the late 1970s. Deficit spending has increased, transfer payments to individuals have become the single largest type of public expenditure, capital and infrastructure projects have declined dramatically, and power has been systematically fragmented. None of these trends appears to be affected by traditional partisan or ideological differences, as we see little to no effect of systematic relationships between these trends and the partisan composition of the government of the day. Rather, trends towards entropy (that is, fragmentation of authority) are consistent, inexorable, and long-standing. The result is a huge shift in political authority away from the hierarchical control of a single set of leaders at the top of the French state and towards the creation of a multi-level governance structure with multiple sources of power. The state is now bigger than at previous times in French political life. But it operates within a network of political institutions sharing power rather than at the center of a system where all eyes look to the state for leadership. These powerful shifts have occurred despite relative continuity in constitutional structures, suggesting that we need to understand much more than only the internal structures of the central state in order to understand its role in the economy.

Our analysis suggests that France has dramatically broken with its *dirigiste* past and now features a much more decentralized, socially embedded form of economic regulation. Jonah Levy (1999) called this strategy 'associational liberalism' because it combines a liberal aversion to the *dirigiste* state with a countervailing faith in the coordinating capacities of societal and local associations. Therefore, what Tocqueville decried almost two centuries ago – the all-importance of the central state – has now been replaced with a more complex institutional form of multi-level governance with a correspondingly less anesthetizing central state, but also one with less autonomy over the state of the economy. Over the terms of the Fifth Republic, the structure of state spending has indeed been transformed.

10.2 Taxing and spending over time

Figure 10.1 shows the evolution of overall taxing and spending rates over the period of the Fifth Republic. Tax receipts in 1959 were 142 billion Euros (all figures in this chapter are adjusted for inflation and reported in constant 2000 Euros); spending was 123 billion Euros. As a percentage of Gross Domestic Product (GDP), spending was 34 percent, and net tax receipts (e.g., prélèvements obligatoires, a more accurate assessment of the overall tax burden, subtracting out fees for service and internal state income transfers) were 31 percent of GDP.[1] In 2006 tax receipts had increased to 912 billion Euros, spending was 922 billion, spending represented 58 percent of GDP, and net tax receipts were up to 44 percent of GDP. Of course, the growth in the size of the state was partly due to population growth and partly due to growth in the size of the economy, but Figure 10.1 makes clear what comes as no surprise: The French state grew dramatically even as a proportion of a rapidly growing economy. Similar trends occurred in all OECD countries, of course. Net tax receipts in France have consistently been about 10 points higher in

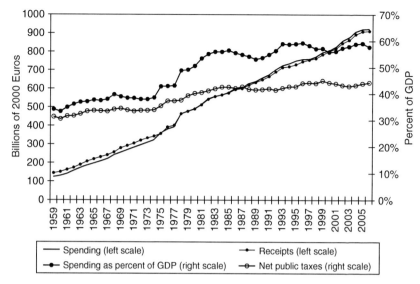

Figure 10.1   French government spending and receipts, 1959–2006
Note: The figure shows spending and receipts in billions of constant 2000 Euros (left scale) and spending and net public taxes as a percentage of Gross Domestic Product (right scale). Data include central public administration, local government, and social security. Net public taxes are tax receipts minus transfer payments among public authorities and are the best indicator of the overall tax burden.

France than the OECD average (these numbers increased from 25.6 percent in 1965 to 35.9 percent in 2004, the most recent year available).

State spending in 2006 was 6.5 times greater than in 1959, after adjusting for inflation. Largely, this was made possible by a dramatic increase in the size of the French economy. As a percentage of the economy, spending increased by a factor of 0.7, a significant amount to be sure but the growth of the state was made possible mostly by the huge increase in economic activity, not by devoting an increasing share of the economy to taxes.

10.3   The logic of state intervention

Of course, public spending is largely tied to the state of the economy. In Figure 10.2 we show how state spending can be partly explained as a reaction to the rate of economic growth. The figure displays the annual rate of change of GDP and the annual percentage change in public spending. We observe the reaction of the state to economic shocks. Standard economic theory since Keynes has suggested that in times of economic decline, increased state spending can stimulate the economy. These mechanisms may be so-called 'automatic stabilizers' (such as unemployment compensation, which

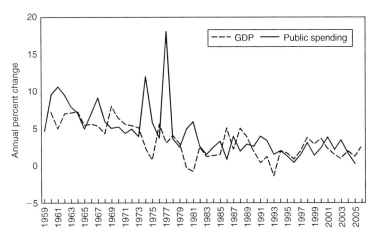

Figure 10.2   Annual rate of change in government spending and GDP, 1959–2006

naturally increase when economic activity declines), or they may be discretionary policy actions determined by governments in response to economic conditions. Whether the stabilizing activity is automatic or discretionary, we can expect to see an increase in spending (even in times of deficits) when economic growth is weak or negative, and indeed the figure makes clear that much of the growth, especially the sharpest spikes in state spending, can be explained by such reactions to economic crises. The huge spikes in 1974 and 1978 are easily explained by the effects of the oil crisis, for example. The budget automatically reacted strongly in these circumstances and the government also followed a counter-cyclical budget policy to offset the consequences of international shocks on its domestic market. The conservative government at the time (lead either by Prime Ministers Raymond Barre or Jacques Chirac) did not follow an ideological attitude (reducing taxes by cutting public spending), but rather followed standard economic theories widely shared on both the left and the right. Conversely, the later governments of Chirac (1986–88), Balladur (1993–95) and Juppé (1995–97) are characterized by large cuts in public spending during periods when GDP was not increasing. Since 1994 the size of the state has increased almost at the same rhythm as the growth of the domestic economy; it has neither grown as economic growth has made this possible nor has it reacted counter-cyclically to declines in the economy. Its hands have been tied.

Overall, the Figure 10.2 shows that the growth of the state follows a similar trend to that of the economy as a whole but that these patterns were clearer in the early decades than in more recent ones. The Fifth Republic has been characterized by strong economic variations to which public authorities have reacted differently at different times. During the first 15 years, both the economy and the state grew dramatically. Thus, Wagner's Law, which holds that increased economic wealth leads to greater public demand for state services (e.g., education, roads, and hospital services), is largely confirmed. Of course, we see evidence of Keynesian economics in play as well, though that evidence is mixed. Certainly in the 1970s state reaction to the oil crisis was very strong. Similarly in the 1980s we see increased state spending during periods of economic decline. Only in the 1990s do we see periods of serious economic decline (e.g., declining or even negative growth in GDP from 1989 to 1994) without a countervailing reaction by state authorities. In sum, we can see that the growth of the state was strongly related to the growth of the economy, as we suggested in discussing Figure 10.1, and that there is mixed evidence in France for the use of Keynesian economic stimulation policies. Whereas these were once standard and immediate, in the last 15 years they have become anything but automatic. One reason for this may be increased concern with the size of the deficit and the accumulated debt.

10.4   Surplus spending, deficit spending, and the debt

State spending in the early years of the Fifth Republic was often less than tax receipts; from 1959 to 1974 the state ran a surplus in all but two years (1967 and 1968). Such a situation has never recurred in France since the oil shock. Governments of each type have consistently run annual budgetary deficits in each year since 1974. Figure 10.3 shows the growth of the deficit and the related accumulated debt.

Consistent deficit spending in the 1980s and 1990s (reaching −5.9 percent in 1993) led to an accumulated public debt that surpassed 50 percent of GDP

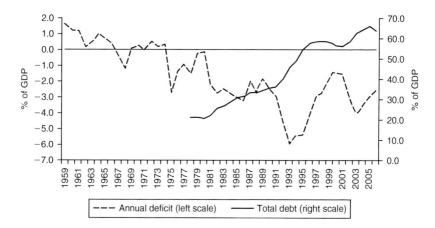

Figure 10.3   The annual public deficit and total debt, 1959–2006

Note: The figure shows the annual deficit (left scale) with the total accumulated debt (right scale; data not available before 1978). Figures are expressed as percentages of GDP.

in 1995 and which now is equal to approximately 65 percent of annual GDP. Since 1999, of course, European Monetary Union requirements put strong pressure on the French government to limit the deficit to less than 3 percent of GDP and the overall public debt to less than 60 percent. During the mid- to late 1990s serious efforts were made to reduce the size of the deficit (and Figure 10.3 shows that the debt declined slightly in the late 1990s). However, the figure makes clear that systematic public deficits have become the norm. France is consistently at the margin of conformance with EU monetary standards (often beyond the stated norms), and with its public debt now over 60 percent of GDP it may well face economic sanctions from its European partners.[2] We will see below (see Figure 10.8) that interest payments on the accumulated debt are consistently over 10 percent of total public spending in recent years; substantially more than capital investments, inverting the ratio between these types of spending that was established in the early years of the Fifth Republic.

Public finance has changed dramatically in the period since 1959. The economic crises after the 1970s caused massive adjustments to French spending patterns, with deficits replacing surpluses as the norm. Even more important transformations have taken place when we look not at the total levels of spending, but at the sources and structure of this spending, as we do in the next section. France has moved from a situation of relative clarity and state autonomy in the early period to one of decentralization, greater autonomy of local actors, and a huge transformation of state spending driven by the growth of social security spending and social transfer payments. It is no exaggeration to say that this has led to a dramatic decline in the autonomy of the central state.

10.5   The decline of the central state

The structure of public spending has changed dramatically over the Fifth Republic. In Figures 10.4 through 10.6 we show spending by three sources: The central state, local government authorities (regional, departmental, and municipal governments), and the social security administration. Figure 10.4 shows total spending by the three sources as a percent of GDP; Figures 10.5 and 10.6 show the percentage of total state spending and receipts respectively for the same three sources.

Figure 10.4 makes clear that while the central state grew dramatically over the Fifth Republic, growth was in fact much faster in local government and social security sectors. Figure 10.5 shows the percentages of total state spending. Central state spending (that is, the Parisian ministries and services controlled directly by them) declined from about 60 to 40 percent of total state expenditures. Local governments increased steadily in their importance, now representing roughly 20 percent of the total, and social security spending increased to be roughly equal to the size of the central state. Spending,

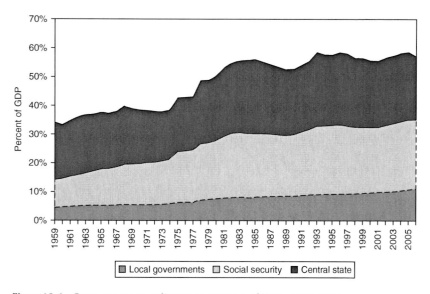

Figure 10.4 Government spending as percentage of GDP, 1959–2006
Note: The figure shows levels of spending by local governments, social security, and the central
state as percentages of Gross Domestic Product.[3]

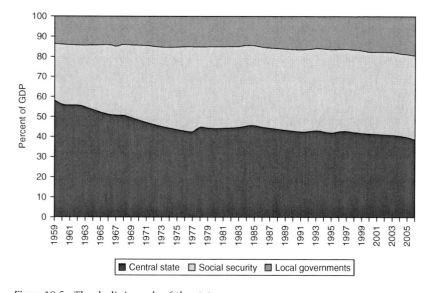

Figure 10.5 The declining role of the state
Note: The figure shows the percentage of total government spending by the central state, local
governments, and social security.

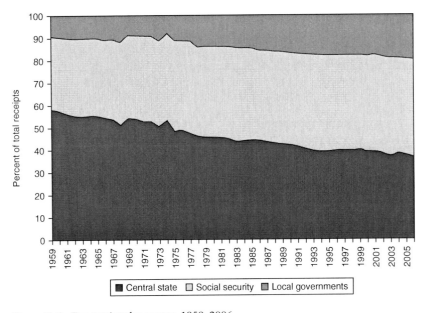

Figure 10.6 Tax receipts by source, 1959–2006

Note: The figure shows the percentage of total government receipts by the central state, local governments, and social security.

like receipts (see Figure 10.6) now represent a 40 / 40 / 20 split between the three sources; in 1959 the partition was more in the order of 60 / 25 / 15.

10.6 Sources of debt and deficit

Considering the rapid growth in spending by local governments and the social security system, one could think that the large structural deficits that have characterized the French state in recent decades might be due to imbalances in these spending accounts, especially social security. Figure 10.7 addresses this question. It shows that the public debt is largely a creation of the central state. Neither the social security accounts nor local governments accounts for more than a small proportion of the annual deficit. Local government administrations routinely accounted for a deficit on the order of 10 billion Euros during the period before the decentralization reforms of the early 1980s. Since then, new financial resources (local taxes and vertical transfers from the state) and new legal constraints (which have progressively limited the allowed levels of annual deficits for local communities) have improved their collective financial situation substantially and they slowly drifted between net surplus and deficit until 2006. In any case, local governments in France have consistently operated within a narrow range around

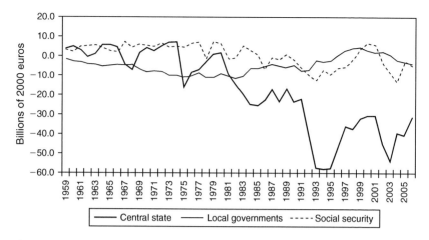

Figure 10.7   Annual surplus or deficit by source of public spending, 1959–2006

balanced budgets as the figure shows. The social security system generated regular surpluses during the 1960s and 1970s before declining substantially towards deficits on the order of 12 billion Euros by the mid-1990s. Demographic trends, medical technologies, and other factors have put tremendous pressure on the system, but several reforms (e.g., the Balladur reform in 1993 and the *plan Juppé* in 1995 increasing taxes and tightening conditions of eligibility for retirement) have reversed the trend towards increased deficits that were apparent during the 1980s and early 1990s. Since a constitutional revision of 22 February 1996, the French parliament has general authority over the state of social security accounts and is authorized to discuss and modify the content of social security accounts by the creation of social security finance laws. Neither social security nor local government administration is responsible for a significant proportion of the French budget deficit. Figure 10.7 makes clear that this is solely due to the budget of the central administration.

10.7   From services to transfer payments

Another aspect of the decline of the French state during the Fifth Republic is the growth, in relative terms, of direct transfer payments to individuals. Rather than being used to employ officials in centralized state administrations, an increasing share of the budget is directly transferred to individuals. Figure 10.8 shows spending across four categories: operating expenses, transfer payments, capital, and interest.

Huge shifts occurred in the structure of state spending in 1978, and these effects continue today. Before that period, state spending was largely focused on direct operating expenditures, with capital investments (e.g., building new

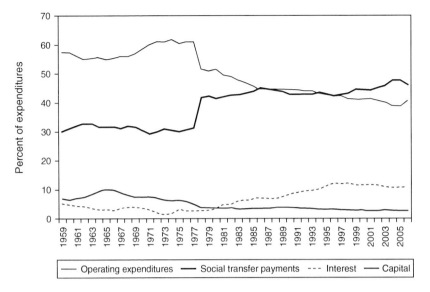

Figure 10.8   Central state spending, 1959–2006

Note: The figure shows four categories of central state spending; capital purchases (buildings, infras-tructure...), interest payments, social transfer payments, and direct operating expenses (salaries of civil servants, operating expenses of administrative agencies, etc.).

university campuses, highway construction, and other large infrastructure projects) reaching as high as 10 percent of the budget in the mid-1960s. Since 1978 direct expenditures have declined and capital spending has plummeted; spending on the debt has increased sharply and social transfer payments have become the largest single element in the budget.

10.8   Shifting tax sources

Figure 10.9 shows the changing structure of the French tax system across the Fifth Republic. Data show the five largest sources of tax receipts: Income tax, the Value-Added Tax (e.g., la TVA, implemented in 1954), other taxes on products (e.g., excise taxes not included in the TVA), social security con-tributions by employers and employees (shown separately here because they follow different patterns over time), with all other miscellaneous tax sources combined into a sixth residual category. (This last category includes all taxes which individually never made up more than seven percent of the total; it includes property, payroll, capital, and import taxes as well as production receipts and miscellaneous social contributions.)

The structure of the French tax system has never been simple, as the state has never relied on just a single form of taxation. Figure 10.9 shows how various taxes have risen and fallen, sometimes substantially, over time as a

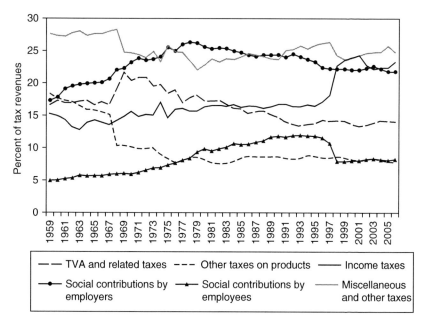

Figure 10.9   Tax revenues by type, 1959–2006

Note: The figure shows the percentage of total annual tax revenues for all French public administrations (central state, social security administration, and local governments) by source. For clarity
of presentation, sources that never generated more than 7 percent of total tax receipts in any year
have been combined into a single category called miscellaneous and other. The series sum to 100
percent in each year.

share of the total tax burden. Income taxes, which consistently represented
less than 15 percent of the total during the first decade of the Fifth Republic,
increased slowly in importance until the late 1990s when they moved substantially; today they are close to 25 percent of total receipts. Social security
payments by employers increased dramatically during the *trente glorieuses*,
riding a wave of economic growth and were the single largest source of
tax revenues by the mid-1970s. Since then they have declined in relative
terms. These shifts reflect the outcome of policies, implemented since the
1980s, designed to combat rising unemployment levels. These policies have
reduced the 'private' labor cost by transferring social security payments from
the employers to the central state. In contrast to the earlier period, today
the social security system is increasingly financed by the central state using
direct taxes on income such as the CSG (*Contribution Sociale Généralisée*) or
the CRDS (*Contribution au Remboursement de la Dette Sociale*).

Payments by employees increased when payments by employers were
reduced, but these payments declined sharply in the same period as income
taxes increased in the late 1990s. Sales and product taxes beyond the TVA

were substantial in the first ten years of the Fifth Republic but have declined significantly since the mid-1960s. The TVA itself, which represented over 20 percent of total receipts in the late 1960s, has steadily if slowly eroded in relative importance but remains at nearly 15 percent of the total in 2006. Note that the figures we discuss here are aggregate receipts, not tax rates. Income tax receipts increased dramatically in the 1990s, for example, not because of a change in individual tax rates but because of a sharp decline in unemployment. With more people working, income tax receipts rose. The overall mix of tax revenues by source is an important indicator of fiscal policy, however, and Figure 10.9 shows how its large structures have evolved over time.

10.9 Conclusion

Huge transformations have taken place in patterns of taxing and spending over the period of the Fifth Republic. When the new constitutional regime came into place and for the first decades of its operation, state spending grew dramatically as the economy expanded and the population grew. Governments regularly operated with a small annual surplus, the economy grew at an annual rate of more than five percent, and the state grew fast enough during this period that its share of GDP rose dramatically. The state became bigger as spending increased by a factor of more than six and the public sector expanded from approximately 30 percent of GDP to almost 60 percent. It also retained substantial autonomy. During periods of economic downturn, political leaders of the Right like those of the Left did not hesitate to spend in a counter-cyclical manner.

All this changed in the 1970s. We can point to three trends that have conspired to reduce the autonomy of the central state in France, producing a situation that might not be recognizable to those who governed France in the 1950s and 1960s. Further, none of these transformations that have reduced the autonomy of the state have any constitutional foundations. That is, the constitutional regime that Michel Debré and others has functioned as intended. Other trends, completely unrelated to constitutional design, have conspired, however, to reduce the power of the state. These are: 1) the rise of local authorities; 2) Europeanization; and 3) the functioning of the mature welfare state.

We saw in Figure 10.5 the declining proportion of public expenditures controlled by the central state. Spending by local authorities increased dramatically as a proportion of total public spending, as did social transfer payments through the social security program. Central state spending, once 60 percent of total public spending, was reduced to an equal footing with the social security program, about 40 percent of the total. Europeanization has strongly affected state economic planning as well, as EMU norms inhibit France from operating large annual budget deficits. While operating within a norm of public budget deficits no larger than 3 percent of GDP leaves considerable room for economic maneuver to French governments, in fact France had consistently been operating with this or higher levels of deficit spending for years; so in effect the European norms reduce the leeway and the options of French economic planners. This may be a good thing or a bad one, and leaders of the French state may find it sometimes to their advantage to point to the European strictures against certain fiscal policies. But, for good or ill, increased European oversight of domestic fiscal policies inevitably means reduced state autonomy. Some options are off the table. This was not the case back in 1968: in that year GDP declined to 'only' 4.3 percent and the government responded with the largest deficit spending up to that point −1.3 percent. In the following year GDP had grown to 8 percent and the deficit was replaced by a small surplus.

With a much greater proportion of public funds controlled by local authorities or in the social security system, and with reduced freedom to follow fiscal policies for fear of violating European norms, French leaders today operate with considerably less room for economic maneuver. While they may affect direct public spending by the state, they have little control over local government spending or the social security system. Further, since the largest share of public spending is direct transfers to individuals rather than operating expenses in government ministries, these programs are politically more difficult to revise. These changes are largely structural, have affected the system over the long term, and are relatively unrelated to questions of political ideology. That is, the arrival of a new government is rarely related to a structural break in the data series we have presented, including during those times when a government of the Left is replaced by one of the Right. Rather than responding to short-term political considerations, or to the decisions of autonomous state leaders, fiscal policy has evolved in the long term towards greater fragmentation of authority, with no turning back. Decentralization of political power was a major reform of the Mitterrand administration in the early 1980s and was given constitutional authority under the leadership of Prime Minister Raffarin in March 2003. Looking at the data presented in Figure 10.4 however, which show the amount of public spending by level of government, it is clear that fiscal decentralization has been a long-term commitment of French governments since the beginning of the Fifth Republic, and has progressed steadily. Similarly, the growth of the social security system is a symptom of a mature welfare state. Transfer payments have surpassed public operating expenses to become the largest form of expenditure for public authorities of all kinds, as we saw in Figure 10.8.

The result of the changes we have documented here is that the French state has lost considerable autonomy. Rather than being the single most important actor, by far, and regularly intervening forcefully in the economy, central authorities are now one of several important players. Others are local political leaders, European officials, and the administrators (and Members of Parliament) who oversee the social security system. Further, and perhaps more importantly, those funds that the state does spend are more likely to be transferred directly to individuals in the forms of pensions, unemployment payments, housing subsidies and other direct payments than they are to support the functioning of public agencies under the direct control of the government of the day. Michel Debré may be turning in his grave. And yet these transformations have little to do with the constitutional design he put in place. Rather, they provide powerful testimony to the idea that institutional design is only part of the picture. For fiscal policy, the Fifth Republic has seen huge transformations that have little if anything to do with the constitutional structure.

What long-run trends led the state to devolve power to a greater number of authorities? The key is government complexity and an accompanying trend towards entropy. Entropy is the idea that power will be spread increasingly among a greater range of relatively autonomous actors, and in France the evidence we have presented shows clearly these trends. In response to greater social demands and the ever-increasing complexity of social problems, autonomy for response to these questions is devolved to specialized agencies, or to local governments thought to be better able to respond to the particular nature of the issue in their own communities. We have looked at a macro-level in this chapter, focusing on just three sets of public actors: the central state, local governments, and social security. But we can see similar trends in the creation of specialized bodies (of which there are approximately 800 now at the central level, with more related to local governments, and still others attached to the social security system); all these things point in the same direction, the creation of a network structure rather than a single authority at the top. These trends have been consistent over 48 years of French fiscal history.

Entropy in the structure of government spending in France fits into a larger theme of Europeanization and the growth of multi-level governance. Increasingly, scholars throughout Europe have focused attention on the growth of complex relations among local governments, regional authorities, national governments and the European Union. While we have approached the question in a different way, focusing just on the French case, our findings fit nicely into this larger perspective. Policy-making and government leadership within a structure of multi-level governance is about networks of communication, shifting responses, and the evolution and dynamics of power structures. Leadership within Michel Debré's vision of the operation of the Fifth Republic was more related to constitutional authority and included both hierarchical controls within the state as well as economic *dirigisme* more broadly. This is particularly ironic as the size of the French state is actually larger now than at previous times in history. Why would the autonomy of the state decline even while its size increases? The answer is the entropy associated with the creation of new specialized bodies, Europeanization, and decentralization, all important factors of the new French political system and all constantly changing even while the constitutional structure of the Fifth Republic has remained the same.

10.10   Sources

Data reported in this chapter come from the French Census (Institut National de la Statistique et des Etudes Economiques, INSEE). INSEE has compiled time-series for national accounts between 1959 and 2006. Data were initially expressed in current Euros. We have used a consumer price deflator for the same period to present all data in constant 2000 Euros. Data are available from the INSEE web site at: http://www.insee.fr/fr/indicateur/cnat_annu/base_2000/finances_publiques/depenses_recettes.htm.

We used two different files: detailed public accounts (following the 1995 European System of Accounts presentation) and summarized accounts of spending and receipts. We have focused on three categories of public administration: Central public administration (state + related bodies), local public administration (local authorities + local bodies), social security administration (Social Security + related bodies). Related bodies are organizations with separate legal identities created by a public authority for a specific purpose. Examples of bodies related to the state at the central level are such things as the national libraries, the National Scientific Research Center (CNRS), National Geographic Institute, National Agency for Employment, public hospitals, nursery schools, regional committees of agriculture, regional committees of economic affairs, and high schools. Overall, there are some 800 organizations related to the central state.[4]

The first INSEE series yields simplified public accounts for the 1978–2006 period for the three levels of government as indicated above. As we investigated the evolution of both public spending and revenue during the Fifth Republic, we had to calculate the amounts of some categories of spending, and we did so by respecting the following equalities:

Revenue = Production revenue (including subsidies for production) + Property revenue (including interest) + Tax and social security contributions (including Tax on production and importations + Tax on income and property + Social security contributions of employees and employers) + Transfers.

Expenditures = Operating Expenditures (including intermediate consumption + Payroll + Tax on production) + Interest + Transfers (including social transfers + in-kind social transfers + subsidies + transfers between public administrations) + Gross Formation of Fixed Capital.

This method allowed us to establish comprehensive series for the entire period, except for two kinds of information. First, we do not have the level of current received transfers between public administrations for the period of 1959 to 1977 because these data were reported in a consolidated manner for the entire period. As a consequence, we underestimate the level of receipts from 1959 to 1977 by relatively small (but unknown) amounts. Second, we have estimated the balance of these transfer payments (that is, the difference between transfer payments received and transfer payments paid out) by interpolating backward in time from values available for 1978 to 2006. These missing values for transfers all concern only those transfers between the three main entities of interest: central state (and related bodies), local administrations (and related bodies), and social security (and related bodies). Neither of these adjustments should have a substantial impact on the trends we have reported.

Notes

1. The difference between state spending and net tax receipts is that net tax receipts exclude fees for state provided services. In France, such fees include tolls on autoroutes, public television licenses, and local trash collection fees. The total level of state spending therefore reflects the overall size of the state in the economy, but the net tax receipts better reflects the individual tax burden and is comparable with similar figures in other countries where private actors rather than public entities may provide certain services, similarly for a fee.
2. The European Stability and Growth Pact that coordinates the fiscal policy of the monetary union contains a fixed norm of public budget deficit but does not stipulate an explicit standard on the accumulated public debt standard.
3. Total spending differs from the sum of the three subtotals (shown here) by small amounts (average: -1.7%, minimum: -5.4%, maximum: 2.5% because of transfers and changes in budgetary accounting rules; the numbers were slightly positive before 1978 and slightly negative after that date when budgetary accounting rules changed.
4. The comprehensive list of such bodies is available at these urls: http://www.insee.fr/fr/indicateur/cnat_annu/base_2000/secteurs_inst/ex/ODAC_simple.pdf, and http://www.insee.fr/fr/indicateur/cnat_annu/base_2000/secteurs_inst/ex/ASSO_simple.pdf

Bibliography

Adam, François, Olivier Ferrand, and Rémy Rioux. 2003. *Finances publiques*. Paris: Presses de Sciences Po.

Arkwright E. et al. 2007. *Economie politique de la LOLF*. Rapport du CAE, Paris: La documentation française.

Baumgartner, Frank R., Martial Foucault and Abel François. 2006. 'Punctuated Equilibrium in French Budgeting Processes'. *Journal of European Public Policy* 13(6): 1986–1103.

Baslé, Maurice. 2004. *Le budget de l'Etat*, La Découverte 'Repères' n° 33.

Collectif (2005), Budget de l'Etat et finances publiques, *Cahiers français* n° 329, La documentation française.

Delorme, Robert and Christine André. 1978. 'L'évolution séculaire des dépenses publiques en France'. *Annales* 33(2): 255–78.

Delorme, Robert and Christine André. 1983. *L'État et l'Economie, essai d'explication de l'évolution des dépenses publiques en France*. Paris: Seuil.

Fonvielle, Louis. 1976. 'Evolution et croissance de l'Etat français: 1815–1969'. Cahiers del'ISMEA, Tome X, 9-10-11-12.

Leroy, Marc. 2007. *Sociologie des finances publiques*. Paris: La Découverte, n° 481.

Levy, Jonah D. 1999. *Tocqueville's Revenge. State, Society and Economy in Contemporary France*. Cambridge, MA: Harvard University Press.

Méreaud, J. 1995. *La dépense publique en France, évolution sur trente ans et comparaisons internationales*. Rapport du Conseil Economique et Social.

Monnier, Jean-Marie. 1998. *Les prélèvements obligatoires*. Paris: Economica.

OECD. 2006. *Revenue Statistics 1965–2005*. Paris: OECD.

Revue Française de Finances Publiques. 2002. numéro 77 (numéro spécial sur la dépense publique).

Revue Française de Finances Publiques. 2007. numéro 97 (numéro spécial sur La LOLF et la Vème République).

Sine, Alexandre. 2006. *L'ordre budgétaire. Economie politique des dépenses de l'Etat*. Paris: Economica.

Théret, Bruno. 1995. 'Régulation du déficit budgétaire et croissance des dépenses de l'Etat en France de 1815 à 1939'. *Revue Economique* 46(1): 57–90.

11
Rethinking Social Protection in the Fifth Republic: 'Buttressed Liberalization' in an Age of Austerity

Mark Vail

During the first three decades after World War II, France was widely viewed as a shining example of successful European economic reconstruction. In stark contrast to the political and economic failures of the interwar period, revamped political and economic institutions placed France at the vanguard of European economic development. France's success accelerated under the *dirigiste* Fifth Republic, as the country reeled off a string of astonishing economic achievements. Soaring growth rates, nearly full employment, and rising wages provided a testament to the capacity of politics to tame and direct the power of the market.[1] This 'changing balance of public and private power', in Andrew Shonfield's formulation (1965), took the form of an extensive role for the state in both shaping private sector economic activity and directly managing a large part of the economy (Hall 1986; Levy 1999). Perhaps more than in any other European country, France's economic success seemed to show that enlightened public policy and state guidance could create unprecedented levels of growth and prosperity, although, as Ben Clift demonstrates in his contribution to this volume, the image of the state as the sole author of France's postwar recovery has been significantly overdrawn.

Just as rapidly as it became a model of economic adjustment during the postwar era, however, France fell from grace in the 1970s, rapidly becoming an anti-model of economic stagnation and political dysfunction. Scholars and journalists alike increasingly came to view France as hopelessly sclerotic and as incapable of significant reform (Esping-Andersen 1996a; Pierson 2001, p. 448). As growth rates slowed unemployment rates increased and social expenditures exploded; conventional portraits of France as 'frozen' emerged that emphasized dysfunctional economic arrangements and political institutions that engendered recrimination and conflict rather than reform. As a result, observers claimed, France was incapable of meaningful economic adjustment, destined to become a fossil of a bygone era in which the supposedly irreconcilable goals of economic prosperity and social equity had achieved an impressive but fleeting synthesis.

191

Many critics have singled out the French welfare state and its effects upon the labour market as the key culprits in the system's inability to adjust (Esping-Andersen 1996b; Ferrera and Rhodes 2000; Esping-Andersen 1999). Such perspectives emphasize the country's payroll-tax-based social-protection system, which leads to high non-wage labour costs, thereby discouraging hiring and perpetuating high rates of unemployment. By reducing the number of contributing workers, high jobless rates in turn result in additional financial strains on the welfare state. Other versions of the prevailing wisdom of a 'frozen' French political economy blame the political institutions of the Fifth Republic, which concentrate power in the central state and marginalize interest groups such as employers' associations and trade unions, thereby creating dysfunctional relationships between state and society that undermine reform. Such political difficulties are seen as both the source and the product of many of France's ongoing economic problems, part of a vicious circle between dysfunctions in the labour market and the social-protection system. Still others, operating from quite a different set of assumptions and preferences, place the blame for France's political-economic sclerosis at the feet of the European Union, in particular the so-called 'Maastricht criteria' for European Economic and Monetary Union, which set tight official limits on public spending and indebtedness. Some suggest that France has struck a Faustian bargain in its efforts to maintain a position of leadership in the EU, leaving it with a set of constraints on fiscal policy that undermine the country's ability to adjust to new economic realities, in the interests of a set of political and geopolitical priorities which have changed dramatically during the past three decades. In a similar vein, others point out that France's ambiguous and often awkward relationship with the EU has left French leaders to cast about for a new role in (and for) Europe, even as they find themselves increasingly unable to meet pressing domestic economic and social challenges (Smith 2005).

In this chapter I show that such views of a 'frozen' French political-economic landscape are extremely misleading. In point of fact, French social and economic policy has undergone significant innovations during the past three decades, a process of rethinking and experimentation that has actually been more extensive in France than in many other Continental European countries. Far from an unchanging drag on the French economy, moreover, the social protection system and labour market arrangements of the Fifth Republic have actually been at the centre of the reform agenda. Stylized images of sclerosis both under-recognize the degree of change that has taken place and fail to recognize the shifting political dynamics that have generated these outcomes.

Below I detail some significant recent innovations in contemporary French social protection and argue that these changes reflect a largely unrecognized capacity of the French political economy to adapt and adjust. I argue that French reforms have followed a coherent, broad trajectory, to which I refer as *buttressed liberalization*.[2] The 'liberalization' component of this strategy has involved the loosening of labour market regulations, including protections on lay-offs and limits on overtime, and the promotion of non-standard employment arrangements such as defined-term contracts and part-time jobs. At the same time, however, authorities have dedicated significant economic and political resources to supporting job creation and workers' ability to compete in the labour market, while encouraging the unemployed to seek out and accept available jobs, thereby *buttressing* the process of liberalization for workers and employers alike. This policy trajectory has been marked by a shift away from traditional, passive labour market policies, including early retirement schemes, to 'active' policies designed to promote job creation, such as subsidizing employers' social contributions in order to reduce non-wage labour costs. This 'buttressing' has not been limited to the labour market, as governments have expanded the French network of anti-poverty and income support policies in order to help workers adjust to an era of high unemployment. Far from 'frozen', France has actually been among the more active European reformers, in terms of both the scope of policy change and degree of innovation that such change reflects.

In the following section I explore the sources of the misleading image of France's limited capacity for reform. I then analyse some of the most significant developments in French social protection during the past three decades, placing particular emphasis upon the labour market and anti-poverty programmes that have been central to the strategy of 'buttressed liberalization'. I end with a brief conclusion, where I explore the implications of these developments for the future of the French political economy, agendas for future research, and the lessons that French social protection reform offers to other advanced industrial countries.

11.1 Graven images: the orthodoxies of French social protection

Prevailing images of a 'frozen' French social protection system find their roots in the comparative welfare state literature. Scholars in this tradition emphasize several key characteristics of France's labour market and its linkages to the welfare state that are said to perpetuate high levels of unemployment. The first and most important of these characteristics is France's reliance on payroll taxes for funding the bulk of its social protection system. This 'Bismarckian' system was designed to share the burden of funding social benefits between the two parties who benefited from them – workers, who were protected against the predations of old age, ill health, and joblessness, and employers, who enjoyed social peace and a stable investment climate. This approach to funding social benefits was also consistent with traditions in many Continental European countries of occupational independence and of the idea known as 'subsidiarity' that the state should intervene only in situations in which other actors could not themselves successfully confront social or economic challenges (Baldwin, 1990; van Kersbergen, 1995).

This system worked extremely well during the postwar boom when rapid economic growth fuelled high levels of employment,[3] which in turn provided ample contribution bases for the social protection system and limited the number of workers forced to rely on it. One of the benefits of high levels of employment was that contribution rates could remain quite low, averaging, for example, around 1 per cent of GDP as late as 1970 (compared with 20.2 per cent in 1997) (Scharpf and Schmidt 2000, p. 363). These modest rates were adequate to ensure the solvency of social funds and were low enough so as to avoid any significant disincentives to job creation. This virtuous circle among high levels of employment, healthy social security accounts and low non-wage labour costs fuelled French economic prosperity while ensuring social peace.

By the late 1960s, however, these felicitous circumstances began to unravel, beginning with slowing growth rates and an increase in unemployment rates. Beginning with the first oil shock in 1973, previously modest pressures on the French welfare state and labour market intensified. From between 5 per cent and 6 per cent during the 1950s and 1960s, real GDP growth rates fell to 1.6 per cent by 1980 and, by the early 1990s, had stagnated at around 2 per cent. Trends in the unemployment rate were even more alarming, increasing to over 8 per cent in 1982 and hitting postwar highs of more than 10 per cent by the mid-1990s. As the number of workers contributing to social insurance funds declined and the number of benefit recipients increased, social contribution rates rose rapidly, as did total social expenditures, which reached around 30 per cent of GDP by the late 1990s (Scharpf and Schmidt 2000).

These stubbornly high rates of unemployment, rising social contribution rates and social expenditures, and sluggish rates of economic growth have led many recent observers to conclude that France is hopelessly mired in economic stagnation. Those reforms that have taken place are often dismissed as window dressing, papering over a 'self-reinforcing negative spiral' of 'welfare without work' (Esping-Andersen 1996b). As a result, systems such as France suffer from 'extremely high labour costs and labour market rigidities because the "insiders" are compelled to defend their employment security. As such, the labour market remains rigidly closed and incapable of major job provision' (1996b, p. 80).

Although economic in terms of mechanism, the ultimate causes of these dysfunctions are said to stem from the Fifth Republic's political system. France's 'poor capacity for reform' (Rhodes 1997, p. 16) is explained by the absence of functional bargaining frameworks between the state and social partners, itself the result of unions' and employers' historically antagonistic interactions with a dominant state. These relationships, together with the political liabilities inherently associated with welfare reform (Pierson 1996), are said to yield ambitious state initiatives that are often diluted or abandoned in response to social protest or undermined by the social partners' authority in welfare state and labour market institutions (Scharpf and Schmidt 2000, pp. 293–8). With levels of social spending that are among the highest in Europe, France is thus said to suffer from 'difficult, blocked' public debates (Crouch 2001, p. 117) and governments that are either unwilling or unable to enlist needed political support for policy change.

This view of deep political-economic dysfunction has been reinforced, and partially absorbed into, the literature on welfare regimes. The touch-stone of this body of work is Esping-Andersen's 1990 *Three Worlds of Welfare Capitalism*, which has inspired a cottage industry of modifications and qual-ifications (e.g., Bonoli 1997; Ferrera 1996; Huber and Stephens 2001; Castles and Mitchell 1993). Although the 'welfare worlds' literature provides useful comparative heuristics and highlights key differences among national sys-tems of social protection, it has also left behind a problematic analytical legacy for those wishing to understand the dynamics of welfare state adapta-tion. By focusing upon regularities of welfare states over time, rather than the ways in which they evolve, scholars in this tradition suggest that the 'worlds of welfare' are highly path-dependent and resistant to change. Coupled with the elevation of the 'welfare worlds' approach to a kind of orthodoxy, such perspectives have reinforced the erroneous belief of France as incapable of adjustment.

As I detail below, French social protection has exhibited a dynamic capac-ity that clearly contradicts these images of economic stagnation and political stalemate. As French authorities have pursued their strategy of 'buttressed liberalization' of social protection, they have loosened labour market regula-tions while subsidizing job creation, expanding active labour market policies, and increasing pressures on the unemployed to find jobs. At the same time, they have developed a comprehensive social safety net that fills important gaps in the protection provided by the postwar Bismarckian welfare state.

11.2 Buttressed liberalization in French labour market policy

The Gaullist strategy of economic modernization through labour exclusion and limits on wage growth had worked well in the felicitous economic con-text of the late 1950s and early 1960s. After 1965, however, increasing rates of inflation, declining real wage growth, and rising unemployment fuelled worker discontent, which exploded into the near-revolution of May–June 1968 (Howell 1992, pp. 61–73). In response, policy-makers turned their atten-tion from promoting rapid industrial growth to limiting its negative social and political side effects, as the 'technocratic considerations of economic modernization increasingly took a backseat to the political imperatives of regime preservation' (Levy 1999, p. 39). In the 1970s French authorities undertook a series of efforts to mute social unrest and preserve the Gaullist establishment's hold on power, which was also being challenged by an increasingly aggressive and coherent political Left (Levy 1999, pp. 41–3). During this period unemployment and inflation rates continued to increase and annual growth rates shrank to barely half their level during the postwar boom (Scharpf and Schmidt 2000, pp. 338–41). In less than a decade France had seemingly gone from an emblem of success and an object of admiration to an exemplar of inept economic management and social and political instability.

Following the failed experiment with Keynesian reflation under Socialist President François Mitterrand in the early 1980s, governments turned to new means to address the country's twin dilemmas of high unemployment and generalizing economic precariousness. As the dismantling of the edifice of *dirigiste* economic policy made traditional approaches such as sectoral industrial policy unavailable, and the postwar Keynesian consensus gave way to the neoliberal revolution of Margaret Thatcher and Ronald Reagan, market signals rather than state direction became the guiding principle of the French economy. At the same time, French authorities employing what Jonah Levy has called the 'social anaesthesia state' (Levy 2005, pp. 179–83), involving an expansion of traditional labour market instruments, such as early retirement schemes, in order to preserve social peace. Although instrumental in enabling France to shift away from *dirigisme*, such policies were quite expensive and did little to address the causes of unemployment.

Beginning in the early 1990s, French governments changed their adjustment strategy from subsidizing the unemployed to promoting their reinsertion into the labour market reducing unemployment. Tentative at first, the early stages of this strategy of 'buttressed liberalization' involved reorienting the expanded network of social protection that had been instrumental to enabling France to adjust to the demise of *dirigisme*. Growth in early retirement schemes was slowed significantly and new subsidies were introduced to reimburse part of employers' social contributions in order to encourage job creation.[4] As they turned their attention from expanding social policies to reforming these arrangements, French authorities focused on the problem of rising unemployment, which was undermining the economy's productive capacity and the financing mechanisms of the welfare state. No longer able to dictate labour market outcomes or to limit firms' recourse to lay-offs by administrative fiat, state actors were obliged to seek new ways to promote job creation against a background of growing demands on the state and a fragmented union movement unable coherently to represent workers' interests but quite capable of causing significant social unrest and economic disruption.

Beginning in 1993, newly elected conservative Prime Minister Edouard Balladur adopted a strategy that combined selective, targeted labour market liberalization with state subsidization of employers' social security contributions, in order to remove disincentives to hiring. The 1993 Five-Year

Law on Employment (*La loi quinquennale sur l'emploi*) permitted firms to negotiate work-time adjustments on an annual rather than weekly basis and offered partial contribution exemptions to employers who reduced (now annual) work time by 15 per cent combined with proportional job creation. The hope was that providing firms with this kind of flexibility in tandem with attractive social contribution exemptions would encourage firms to create jobs as they modified their workforces in response to fluctuations in demand (Join-Lambert et al. 1997, pp. 279, 305–7). Although its immediate impact was somewhat disappointing, the measure set an important precedent for future governments by breaking from the historical pattern of statist labour market regulation and served as a model for subsequent reforms.

In 1996 Prime Minister Alain Juppé's administration passed the *Loi Robien*, which reinforced the dual approach of subsidization and liberalization that had characterized the Five-Year Law. The law further liberalized the wage-bargaining process, permitting firm- and branch-level negotiations and reducing the mandated work-time reduction from 15 per cent to 10 per cent. It also provided more generous financial incentives to employers, offering a 50 per cent reduction in social security contributions the first year after an accord and 40 per cent each year thereafter, in exchange for a 10–15 per cent reduction in the number of hours worked annually and a proportional creation of new positions.[5] The law's first, or 'offensive', wing was aimed at firms that created jobs by reducing work time. The second, or 'defensive', wing applied to firms that avoided lay-offs, thereby preserving existing positions (Brunhes et al. 2001, pp. 17–18).

The pace of innovation in French labour market policy increased under the Centre-Left administration of Prime Minister Lionel Jospin. Following a surprise election victory in 1997, Jospin and Labour Minister Martine Aubry enacted a series of measures that aimed to facilitate social dialogue on matters of labour market reform, reduce levels of unemployment, and increase opportunities for workers across socio-economic groups. The centrepieces of the administration's labour market programme were two measures that reduced the working week to 35 hours while extending financial incentives to employers to create jobs. The first so-called Aubry Law, passed in 1998, increased social contribution exemptions to employers but made them conditional upon a firm's or sector's negotiation of a 35-hour weekly work-time limit, accompanied by proportional job creation.[6] The second law, adopted in 2000, introduced an exemption on social security contributions that rose with salaries up to 1.8 times the minimum wage (fixed above that level) and established generous annual limits on work time and overtime.[7] The laws aimed to create jobs through a combination of coercion and incentives, even as they conveyed an image of, in Aubry's words, 'the counter-current of ultra-liberalism'. Such rhetoric reflected the government's strategy to shore up support among its Leftist constituencies in the 'plural Left' Parliamentary coalition (composed of Socialists, Communists and Greens), even as they subsidized employers and granted them greater flexibility in order to reduce unemployment.

The reforms' appeal to the Left was reinforced by the heavy-handed manner with which the government introduced them, conveying a willingness to impose costs on self-serving employers. The government unveiled the first law as a sort of *fait accompli* at a 1997 conference among the new government, unions, and employers' associations, which had originally been called in order to demonstrate the government's commitment to social dialogue. In response, Jean Gandois, the president of the main employers' association (the CNPF, or *Confédération nationale du patronat français*) resigned in protest against a law that employers saw as authoritarian, expensive, and ineffective. Following Gandois's resignation, employers undertook a high-profile campaign against both the 35-hour laws and the government's broader policy agenda. This confrontational posture was reflected in the association's changing its name from CNPF to MEDEF, or the *Mouvement des entreprises de France*. By the late 1990s the organization had begun to act as a sort of ultra-liberal political party, working to influence both elections and a range of public policies.

Despite the acrimonious public conflict between MEDEF and the government, state authorities realized that the laws would have to compensate employers if the measures were to lead to significant job creation. Even as the Left scored political points through its confrontational rhetoric and by increasing the number of workers' annual vacation days,[8] the laws provided firms with both significant financial incentives and considerable flexibility over work-time allocation. Privately, employers even admitted that they objected primarily to the fact that the state had encroached upon their prerogative to negotiate wages and work time, rather than the actual substance of the measures, which they tended to support.[9] Not only did the laws increase employers' social contribution exemptions and offer them greater discretion over the use of labour, they accelerated a shift from national to sectoral and firm-level collective bargaining, a development that gives them greater influence in wage setting. By the end of 2000 the laws had created 265 000 non-agricultural positions, with an estimated 500 000 jobs created overall (Brunhes et al. 2001, pp. 9–10; OECD 2001a, p. 83).

The conservative government of Jean-Pierre Raffarin, which succeeded the Jospin administration in 2002, modified some aspects of the Aubry Laws but left the core of the measures intact. The *Loi Fillon*, named after the Labour Minister of the time, permitted some employers to negotiate a return to a 39-hour week, raised annual limits on overtime, and abandoned the application of the 35-hour week to those SMEs that had not already negotiated an accord. The administration resisted calls from MEDEF and other liberals to rescind the laws outright, however, leaving in place the firm-level and sectoral deals that had been negotiated under their auspices.

In the spring of 2006 the Centre-Right administration of Prime Minister Dominique de Villepin proposed a reform that was cut from the same cloth, the CPE, or *Contrat première embauche*, which made it easier to fire workers under the age of 26 in the hopes of encouraging firms to hire more of them in the first place. Though the law was rescinded after weeks of often-violent protest, it reflected a continuation of the strategy of the administration's predecessors, an approach that is likely to intensify following the election of Centre-Right candidate Nicolas Sarkozy to the French presidency in 2007 on an ambitious platform of liberalization and labour market reform. Broadly speaking, French governments of both Left and Right have continued the strategy of promoting job creation by subsidizing social contributions and liberalizing labour contracts that were central to the Aubry Laws.[10]

Such measures relating to work time and non-wage labour costs have dovetailed with a number of recent attempts to reshape the demand-side of the labour market, particularly with respect to unemployment insurance. The most significant recent changes in this area came out of MEDEF's so-called *Refondation sociale*, involving demands for a series of reforms of French social protection. While clearly part of an effort to influence the trajectory of reform, the campaign also reflected MEDEF's attempt to combat what it viewed as the government's growing intrusion into the purview of the social partners. In the words of Denis Kessler, the intellectual father of the *Refondation*, the campaign was also about a 'quest for rules' governing social dialogue and a clarification of the respective responsibilities of the state and social partners.[11]

In June 2000, MEDEF and the CFDT trade union agreed to limit access to benefits and imposed significant new obligations upon job seekers. The *Plan d'aide et de retour à l'emploi* (PARE) made benefits contingent upon a signed contract obligating job seekers to work with the ANPE, the national employment office, in a personalized job-search (the *Projet d'action personalisé*, or PAP). Following the conclusion of union-employer negotiations, the government refused to ratify the agreement, arguing that the measure insufficiently extended coverage and that, in any event, defining rights to benefits was the state's sole prerogative. Aubry's objections, however, were more jurisdictional than substantive, since she and her closest advisers supported the basic policy direction represented by the deal. After a series of often-acrimonious negotiations, the final law was passed in the autumn of 2000, representing the most significant reform of French unemployment insurance since the beginning of the Fifth Republic in 1958.

The strategy of 'buttressed liberalization' in French labour-market reform has begun to pay significant dividends. A large share of total jobs created (832 000 between 1997 and 1999 alone) have been the products of labour-market reforms, with 50 000 resulting from increased part-time employment, 106 000 from reductions in social-security contributions, and, as early as 1999, an estimated 67 000 from reductions in work time.[12] Part-time jobs as a share of total employment increased from 12.2 per cent in 1989 to 14.7 per cent in 1999 (OECD 2001b, p. 18), as did the share of temporary jobs (OECD 2001a, p. 32). Although France continues to confront significant labour market difficulties, these difficulties are clearly not the product of a moribund policy-making process. Indeed, labour market policy has witnessed some of the most intense innovation of any area of French policy-making, as governments continue to confront a climate of economic austerity with aggressive and novel policy instruments.

11.3   Expanding the French safety net: income support in an age of liberation

The second central component of the French strategy of buttressed liberalization has involved an expansion in the social safety net designed to protect those who have fallen through the cracks of the Bismarckian, contributory welfare state. During the 1970s rising levels of unemployment highlighted the plight of the country's poor and led observers to question the assumption that the rising tide of economic prosperity of the *trente glorieuses* had lifted all boats in French society. Although the near-revolution of May–June 1968 had raised concerns about the social costs of such economic inequities, it was the aftermath of the first OPEC oil shock in 1973 that converted poverty from a relatively marginal issue into a central concern (Palier 2002, pp. 283–7). The ensuing period of slowed growth and rising joblessness also highlighted the weaknesses of the postwar Bismarckian social insurance system, whose equation of 'workers' and 'citizens' had been predicated upon an assumption of full employment and continued economic growth.

In response, governments began to make tentative steps towards the erection of a network of means-tested anti-poverty benefits, managed and funded by the state rather than by the social partners. At the time the only benefit was the *Minimum vieillesse*, a programme instituted in 1956 to provide basic pensions to elderly citizens whose inadequate contribution histories left them without coverage from the basic or complementary regimes.[13] In the mid-1970s governments under President Valéry Giscard d'Estaing instituted additional income support programmes, such as the 1975 *Allocation pour adulte handicapé* (AAH), which provided an income equal to that provided by the *Minimum vieillesse* for disabled workers. In the same vein, in 1976, the government created the *Allocation de parent isolé* (API), which provided a means-tested benefit to single parents, until their children reached the age of three. Although such measures reflected a growing recognition of the need for income support programmes, their purview was rather limited and left many vulnerable groups unprotected.

It was with Socialist President François Mitterrand's abandonment of *dirigisme* in 1983 that the expansion of French anti-poverty benefits began to gather significant momentum. As the authorities struggled to cope with the spike in unemployment and the mounting economic precariousness attendant to the repudiation of 'redistributive Keynesianism', they embarked upon a broad expansion of anti-poverty programmes. For example, in 1984, the government instituted the *Allocation de solidarité spécifique*, or ASS, which provided benefits for unemployed workers having exhausted their rights to unemployment insurance, and the *Allocation d'insertion* (AI), a short-term benefit for people in periods of transition into the labour market, such as freed prisoners, citizens returning from abroad, and applicants for political asylum. As the government turned to the market as the organizing principle of the political economy, it thus – somewhat paradoxically – moved towards state-managed anti-poverty programmes as the income guarantors of last resort.

The post-1983 expansion of incomes policies found perhaps its clearest expression in 1988, with the creation of the *Revenu minimum d'insertion*, or RMI. During his 1988 election campaign, Mitterrand issued an open letter to the French population, in which he emphasized that 'a means of living, or, rather, of surviving, must be guaranteed to those who have nothing, who are unable to do anything, who are nothing. This is the condition of their reinsertion into society' (cited in Palier, 2002, p. 300).[14] This explicit linkage of anti-poverty benefits and 'social reinsertion' pointed to the RMI's dual character. On the one hand, all French residents over the age of 25 whose income was below a fixed ceiling (adjusted for the number of family members) would henceforth be entitled to a flat-rate monthly benefit (Huteau and Le Bont 1997, p. 380). In addition, recipients were entitled to other forms of social assistance, including increases in housing benefits, assistance with medical expenses, and exemption from the French residence tax. The law's second component was an ensemble of professional support and job placement services, which were organized on the level of the department.[15]

This connection of social assistance with employment reflected the social and economic preoccupations of the time. With the demise of *dirigisme* in the early 1980s French unemployment rose dramatically, from 8.3 per cent in 1983 to 10.5 per cent in 1987, and poverty and homelessness had become serious social problems (Levy 2000, p. 328; Scharpf and Schmidt 2000, p. 341). By the late 1980s the notion of *exclusion* had become a central preoccupation and was addressed in a growing number of scholarly and popular works (Palier 2002, p. 284). Such concerns reflected the deteriorating social situation in many parts of the country, particularly the poorer suburbs of Paris and deindustrialized areas, many of which had substantial immigrant populations living side by side with disaffected whites. The RMI was conceived in part as a response to such social and economic problems, and its unanimous approval by Parliament demonstrated the political consensus behind such policies. Moreover, the rapid increase in the number of beneficiaries reflected pent-up demand for such a measure, which expanded the reach of earlier, targeted benefits and partially replaced the former, spotty system of locally administered anti-poverty benefits (Levy 2000, p. 328). The annual rate of increase in the number of recipients grew from 14.2 per cent in 1991 to 21.2 per cent in 1993, with 1.1 million beneficiaries and 2.2 million people covered, including family members and dependent children, by the end of 2003 (Palier 2002, p. 300; de Montalembert 2004, p. 188).[16]

Between 1997 and 2002 the Jospin administration further extended the social safety net in ways that were consistent with its prioritization of labour market activation and 'making work pay'. This strategy informed the 2001 *Prime pour l'emploi*, or 'employment bonus'. The *Prime* is essentially an income-tax break for low-wage workers (similar to the American 'earned-income tax credit') that grants an annual payment to all workers earning between 0.3 and 1.4 times the SMIC but below an income ceiling (€1311 per month in 2003). The benefit, which in 2003 was €228.70 for a single worker with no dependants whose wages were equal to the SMIC, increases with income starting at 0.3 times the SMIC, peaks at the level of the SMIC, and then decreases to zero at 1.4 times the minimum wage. This measure dovetailed with the government's other initiatives aimed at reducing unemployment, such as intensified job-search requirements for unemployment benefits.

The cornerstone of Jospin's expansion of anti-poverty benefits was a programme of universal health insurance, the *Couverture maladie universelle* (CMU), which took effect in 2000. The law created a universal right to health insurance, irrespective of one's contribution and employment history. The law offered free health insurance to all those earning less than FFr 3500 (€533.60) per month. The CMU also provides complementary insurance to those who have rights under the basic system but who cannot afford secondary coverage. Like the basic benefit, this complementary coverage is financed largely by the state, which pays premia on behalf of beneficiaries to France's sickness funds and, in some cases, to private insurance companies (Palier 2002, p. 252). Despite concerns that this the measure represented a state intrusion into corporatist social protection institutions and the opposition of the Centre-Right, the policy's popularity and a large majority on the Left ensured its passage through Parliament.[17]

Although less ambitious than that of the Jospin administration, the Centre-Right administration of Jean-Pierre Raffarin (2002–05) continued the expansion of anti-poverty benefits. For example, in November 2003 the government created the *Revenu minimum d'activité* (RMA), a complementary anti-poverty benefit paid to those in receipt of the RMI for one year or more. The benefit, equal to a weekly minimum of 20 times the SMIC, obligated recipients to work at least 20 hours per week for up to 18 months. In June 2003 the government also announced an unusually generous 5.3 per cent nominal increase in the SMIC, representing a 3.7 per cent rise in real terms. Although for some, notably minimum-wage workers affected by the 35-hour week, the increase would be less, the measure significantly boosted incomes for low-wage workers, with more than a million standing to receive the maximum increase (*Les Echos* 2003).

Over the last 25 years, French governments have supported labour market liberalization with a major expansion of anti-poverty programmes. The extension of social rights gained significant momentum in the late 1980s, culminating in a series of new benefits under the Jospin administration between 1997 and 2002. Although the scope of such reforms has been greater under governments of the Left, it has been far from an entirely partisan affair. Not only did the 1988 RMI enjoy unanimous support by Left and Right, governments of the Right have devised new policies, and increases in the real value of the minimum wage have tended to be as generous under governments of the Right as under those of the Left.[18] As successive governments have extended anti-poverty policies, they have furthered, although later and under a different guise than he might have imagined, the realization of Pierre Laroque's dream of a universalistic French welfare state.

11.4   Conclusion: Beyond the frozen welfare state

The past two decades have witnessed some of the most significant innovations in French social protection in the history of the Fifth Republic. Since the early 1980s governments have shifted away from traditional approaches towards a strategy of 'buttressed liberalization' of social protection. This policy approach has involved two major components. The first has entailed a broad process of labour market liberalization supported by the creation of novel instruments to reduce unemployment. Authorities have significantly loosened labour market regulations, increased subsidies to employers, expanded active labour market programmes, and increased pressure on the unemployed to seek out and accept available work. The second component has involved a steady expansion of anti-poverty programmes designed to promote economic adjustment by protecting workers who fall through the cracks of France's Bismarckian welfare state. Together these two policy trajectories have created a much more active dynamic labour market even as they have protected large segments of the population from poverty, and represent meaningful steps towards reconciling equity and economic vitality.

These patterns of dynamism and innovation bear little resemblance to the images of sclerosis and self-serving parochialism that have come to dominate contemporary images of France. These portraits are misleading on two levels. First, they vastly under-recognize the degree of change that has taken place in the French social protection system. Second, they mischaracterize the political dynamics that are blamed for France's putative sclerosis, as reforms have been driven by a significant shift in the country's policy-making dynamics. No longer a paragon of dominant (in the 1950s and 1960s) or dysfunctional statism (since the 1970s), French policy-making has actually involved a good deal of give and take between governments and interest groups, particularly MEDEF and moderate unions. Such developments in both policy trajectories and the politics of adjustment clearly contradict prevailing images of a 'frozen' French welfare state and political economy.

Although this chapter has shown that there are significant reasons for optimism about France's economic performance, there remain areas of concern. For example, unemployment continues to run high, particularly for groups such as the young and the long-term unemployed.[19] The country continues to resist, more or less explicitly and in ways that are often politically problematic, the fiscal policy strictures of EMU and the hard currency regime that it has created, which represent significant, though not insuperable, obstacles to the kinds of strategic deployment of resources described in this chapter. These obstacles noted, the kinds of innovation outlined above have clearly begun to pay dividends in the form of reducing unemployment and social expenditures.[20] They also show that robust active labour market policies and the devotion of significant state resources can help to reduce unemployment, even in the face of perhaps unwelcome limits on governments' ability to tax and spend, a lesson backed up by a growing body of economic evidence (e.g., OECD 2005, section 4).

More generally, the French strategy of 'buttressed liberalization' suggests important avenues for future research for students of comparative political economy and social policy. Perhaps most important, it shows that a robust welfare state need not be inimical to economic performance. In the right circumstances it can support economic adjustment by preserving social peace and governments' legitimacy in the wake of economic downturns. Those who point to high levels of French social spending as evidence of failed adjustment, therefore, are not only mischaracterizing the state of health of the French political economy, they are also misidentifying the cure. Rather than engaging in the false choice between neoliberalism and stagnation, scholars of European politics need to provide systematic comparisons of national strategies for economic renewal. Doing so will require an openness to alternative conceptions of economic success, in which both equity and efficiency are important values. It will also require an awareness of how linkages between the welfare state and the broader political economy, and between domestic political economic arrangements and the institutions of the European Union, govern economic performance and adjustment. If France has confronted many unique challenges under the Fifth Republic, then, the development of its social protection system offers important lessons that go far beyond its borders.

Notes

1. Between 1953 and 1973 annual economic growth averaged 5.3 per cent, and annual productivity growth averaged between 4 and 5 per cent. See Boltho 1982, pp. 10, 22.
2. For a more detailed analysis of this strategy in the context of French labour market reform and a comparison with recent developments in Germany, see Vail 2008.

3. Between 1959 and 1969 unemployment averaged 1.8 per cent. See Sautter 1982, p. 449; and Glyn et al. 1990, p. 47.
4. The limitation of early retirement programmes has had a significant impact on the rate of labour market exit of workers aged 60–64. Between 1970 and 1985 the number of such early retirements grew by an annual average of 7.46 per cent. Between 1985 and 2003 the number *declined* by an annual average of 0.17 per cent (Ebbinghaus 2006, p. 107).
5. By contrast, the 1993 law provided for only a 10 per cent reduction in work time and failed to specify social security exemptions, which were negotiated on a case-by-case basis.
6. The incentives to employers involved a FFr 9000 (€1372) per worker annual subsidy offered in exchange for a 10 per cent reduction in work time against a 6 per cent increase in payrolls, and a FFr 14 000 (€2134) payment for a 15 per cent reduction in time against a 9 per cent increase in the number of workers. These subsidies were cut by FFr 1000 (€152) per year until they reached FFr 5000 (€762) in 2002.
7. In July 2000 these exemptions averaged FFr 21 500 (€3278) for workers earning the minimum wage, declining to FFr 4000 (€610) at the ceiling of 1.8 times the minimum wage (DARES 2002, p. 10).
8. In many cases firms granted workers additional days off rather than actually shortening the number of hours worked per week. This 'annualization' of work time was among the reforms' most appealing aspects for French employers.
9. In the words of Denis Kessler, then second-in-command at MEDEF and the architect of the *Refondation*, the intrusion of the state represented by the Aubry laws reflected the continued 'atrophy of civil society'. Interview, 15 May 2002.
10. The resulting reduction in payroll taxes has been partially compensated by the *Contribution sociale généralisée*, or CSG, a tax on incomes and returns to capital that has funded an increasing share of social benefits.
11. Interview, 15 May 2002.
12. Data taken from author's calculations and Pisani-Ferry, 2000, p. 29.
13. The fact that this benefit was created so long before other anti-poverty programmes was a testament to the urgency of the problem of old-age poverty in the immediate postwar era. In 1958 and 1959 the benefits of nearly 59 per cent of those who enjoyed a basic pension under the auspices of the *régime général* were low enough to entitle them to the new, means-tested programme (Join-Lambert et al. 1997, p. 459).
14. Author's translation into English.
15. These job placement services included offers of public sector jobs and internships in the private sector. See Join-Lambert et al. 1997, pp. 632–3.
16. The number of RMI recipients has remained relatively constant, declining by 11 000 in 2006 to 1.102 million at the end of the year (*Les Echos* 2007).
17. By mid-2001 the policy already had 6.5 million beneficiaries, 1.2 million for basic health insurance and another 5.3 million for complementary coverage. By mid-2003 the number of recipients of the basic insurance benefit had increased to 1.5 million (Palier 2002, p. 252).
18. In part, this bipartisan support derives from such policies' popularity. In 1999, 69.6 per cent of those surveyed expressed 'support' or 'sympathy' with protests in defence of 'social rights', including incomes policies as well as a broad array of other social programmes (Muxel 2001, p. 73).
19. In 2004 standardized overall unemployment rates were 9.7 per cent in France, while rates for those aged 15–24 were 21.3 per cent (OECD 2005, pp. 237, 241).

20. In October 2005, for example, due in part to the effects of active labour market policies, French unemployment dipped below 10 per cent and the number of registered unemployed declined for the sixth consecutive month. See *Le Monde* 2005.

Bibliography

Baldwin, P. (1990) *The Politics of Social Solidarity: Class Bases of the European Welfare State, 1875–1975* (Cambridge: Cambridge University Press).

Boltho, A. (1982) 'Growth' in A. Boltho (ed.) *The European Economy: Growth and Crisis* (Oxford: Oxford University Press).

Bonoli, G. (1997) 'Classifying Welfare States: A Two-Dimension Approach', *Journal of Social Policy* 26(3), 351–72.

Brunhes, B. et al. (2001) *35 heures: Le temps du bilan* (Paris: Desclée de Brouwer).

Castles, F.G. and D. Mitchell (1993) 'Worlds of Welfare and Families of Nations', in F.G. Castles (ed.) *Families of Nations: Patterns of Public Policy in Western Democracies* (Brookfield, Vt.: Dartmouth University Press).

Crouch, C. (2001) 'Welfare State Regimes and Industrial Relations Systems: The Questionable Role of Path Dependency Theory', in B. Ebbinghaus and P. Manow (eds) *Comparing Welfare Capitalism: Social Policy and Political Economy in Europe, Japan and the USA* (London: Routledge).

DARES (Direction de l'Animation de la Recherche, des Etudes, et des Statistiques) (2002) 'Le passage à 35 heures vu par les employeurs', *Premières Synthèses*, April.

Ebbinghaus, B. (2006) *Reforming Early Retirement in Europe, Japan and the USA* (Oxford: Oxford University Press).

Esping-Andersen, G. (1996a) 'After the Golden Age? Welfare State Dilemmas in a Global Economy', in G. Esping-Andersen (ed.) *Welfare States in Transition: National Adaptations in Global Economies* (London: Sage).

Esping-Andersen, G. (1996b) 'Welfare States without Work: The Impasse of Labour Shedding and Familialism in Continental European Social Policy', in G. Esping-Andersen (ed.) *Welfare States in Transition: National Adaptations in Global Economies* (London: Sage).

Esping-Andersen, G. (1999) *Social Foundations of Postindustrial Economies* (Oxford: Oxford University Press).

Ferrera, M. (1996) 'The "Southern Model" of Welfare in Social Europe', *Journal of European Social Policy* 6(1), 17–37.

Ferrera, M. and M. Rhodes (2000) 'Recasting European Welfare States: An Introduction', in M. Ferrera and M. Rhodes (eds) *Recasting European Welfare States* (Portland, Ore.: Frank Cass).

Glyn, A. et al. (1990) 'The Rise and Fall of the Golden Age', in S.A. Marglin and J.B. Schor (eds) *The Golden Age of Capitalism: Reinterpreting the Postwar Experience* (Oxford: Clarendon Press).

Hall, P.A. (1986) *Governing the Economy: The Politics of State Intervention in Britain and France* (New York: Oxford University Press).

Howell, C. (1992) *Regulating Labor: The State and Industrial Relations Reform in Postwar France* (Princeton, N.J.: Princeton University Press).

Huber, E. and J.D. Stephens (2001) 'Welfare State and Production Regimes in the Era of Retrenchment', in P. Pierson (ed.) *The New Politics of the Welfare State* (Oxford: Oxford University Press).

Huteau, G. and É. Le Bont (1997) *Sécurité sociale et politiques sociales*, 2nd edn (Paris: Armand Colin).

Join-Lambert, M.-T. et al. (eds) (1997) *Politiques sociales*, 2nd edn (Paris: Presses de Sciences Po et Dalloz).

Kersbergen, K. van (1995) *Social Capitalism: A Study of Christian Democracy and the Welfare State* (London: Routledge).

Le Monde (2005) 'Le chômage recule grâce aux emplois aidés', 29 October, 1, 6.

Les Echos (2003) 'La rémunération des smicards augmentera de 1,6% à 5,3% selon les cas au 1er juillet', 24 June, 3.

Les Echos (2007) 'RMI: La baisse de 1% du nombre de bénéficiaires en 2006 n'efface pas un bilan décevant pour la majorité', 8 March, 3.

Levy, J.D. (1999) *Tocqueville's Revenge: State, Society, and Economy in Contemporary France* (Cambridge, Mass.: Harvard University Press).

Levy, J.D. (2000) 'France: Directing Adjustment?', in F.W. Scharpf and V.A. Schmidt (eds) *Welfare and Work in the Open Economy*. Vol. II, *Diverse Responses to Common Challenges* (Oxford: Oxford University Press).

Levy, J.D. (2005) 'Economic Policy and Policy-Making', in A. Cole, P. Le Galès, and J.D. Levy (eds) *Developments in French Politics 3* (Basingstoke: Palgrave Macmillan).

de Montalembert, M. (2004) *La protection sociale en France* (Paris: La documentation française).

Muxel, A. (ed.) (2001) *Les Français et la politique*, Series *Problèmes et politiques sociaux*, no. 865 (Paris: La documentation française).

OECD (2001a) *OECD Economic Surveys: France* (Paris: OECD).

OECD (2001b) *OECD in Figures: Statistics on the Member Countries* (Paris: OECD).

OECD (2005) *OECD Employment Outlook* (Paris: OECD).

Palier, B. (2002) *Gouverner la sécurité sociale: Les réformes du système français de protection sociale depuis 1945* (Paris: Presses universitaires de France).

Pierson, P. (1996) 'The New Politics of the Welfare State', *World Politics* 48(2), 143–79.

Pierson, P. (2001) 'Coping with Permanent Austerity: Welfare State Restructuring in Affluent Democracies' in P. Pierson (ed.)*The New Politics of the Welfare State* (Oxford: Oxford University Press).

Pisani-Ferry, J. (2000) *Plein emploi*. Rapport du Conseil d'Analyse Economique (Paris: La documentation française).

Rhodes, M. (1997) 'Southern European Welfare States: Identity, Problems and Prospects for Reform', in M. Rhodes (ed.) *Southern European Welfare States: Between Crisis and Reform* (Portland, Ore.: Frank Cass).

Sautter, C. (1982) 'France' in A. Boltho (ed.) *The European Economy: Growth and Crisis* (Oxford: Oxford University Press).

Scharpf, F.W. and V.A. Schmidt (2000) 'Statistical Appendix', in F.W. Scharpf and V.A. Schmidt (eds) *Welfare and Work in the Open Economy*. Vol. I, *From Vulnerability to Competitiveness* (Oxford: Oxford University Press).

Shonfield, A. (1965) *Modern Capitalism: The Changing Balance of Public and Private Power* (London: Oxford University Press).

Smith, A. (2005) 'The Europeanization of the French State', in A. Cole, P. Le Galès, and J.D. Levy (eds) *Developments in French Politics 3* (Basingstoke and New York: Palgrave Macmillan).

Vail, M.I. (2008) 'From "Welfare without Work" to "Buttressed Liberalization": The Shifting Dynamics of Labor-Market Adjustment in France and Germany', *European Journal of Political Research*, 47(3), 334–58.

12
Local/Regional Governments and Centre–periphery Relations in the Fifth Republic

Patrick Le Galès and Gilles Pinson

During most of the Fifth Republic conventional wisdom relating to centre–periphery relations (or in more recent terms, the organization of local and regional governments) stated that France was highly centralized. The common sense about France is still that the relationships between 'Paris', i.e. the central power on one hand, and the 'provinces', i.e. local powers, have been and remain asymmetrical, which is no surprise within a unitary state. The central state is still a very important actor in public policies and economic development but the French institutional system has been transformed through a decentralization process during the last 25 years.

There is no unequivocal account of what the Fifth Republic has brought about or changed in the field of local government and centre–periphery relations. On one hand, the regime contributed to the reinforcement of centralization and of the state control on peripheries. Indeed, the new Republic was founded in a context within which the formal institutional organization was centralized and the room for manoeuvre of local governments in policy-making very narrow. However, thanks to the possibility of holding multiple offices at local and national levels, local elected officials were able to control national policies and influence their implementation. The new regime was able to marginalize the local elected officials in policy-making. It strengthened central state control on policy design and implementation through the reinforcement of the central bureaucratic apparatus and the reassertion of the power of the prefect, the state local representative, on local elected officials and in policies implementation.

On the other hand, the tide of centralization went on the ebb; the Fifth Republic paved the way for the emergence of new territorial powers, the regions and large cities that have gradually become important institutions in policy-making and public investment. The Fifth Republic was also changed by a major set of decentralization reforms (which began with the 1982–83 decentralization Acts) quite unique in the French institutional history. Since the constitutional reform of 2003, the first article of the Constitution states that the organization of the Republic is decentralized. The Republic has also

208

increasingly accepted differentiated powers and legal organization for over-seas territories and Corsica, paving the way for a more plural conception of state unity.

The evolution of central–local relationships is not unambiguous. For the sake of clarity the chapter contrasts two periods and stresses a central ten-sion/conflict essential to understanding the ambiguity of the change over time. The first period, the incoming tide of centralization, runs from the start of the Fifth Republic in 1958 to the mid 1970s. This period sees increas-ing power of central government and the bureaucracy over local authorities in policy-making. There is also an ongoing attempt to marginalize tradi-tional local elected officials together with the promotion of alternative local elites at the regional and, to a lesser degree, the metropolitan level. The second period starts in the mid-1970s, characterized by the increasing polit-ical and policy-making role of the three levels of local, departmental and regional government together with the gradual retreat of the state's local representatives. The latest decades have also seen drastic evolutions in the power hierarchy between these levels: the regions, once the weakest level, have gradually reinforced their position; more significant is the rise of city-regions, i.e. inter-municipal cooperation institutions (*communautés urbaines, communautés d'agglomération*) and the increased responsibility of *départements* to manage social services.

Obviously, the contrast between two periods simplifies too much what never was a steady, continuous and consensual process. Rather, those changes have occurred through – and in spite of – a constant conflict between two blocs of political and institutional interests. The first bloc represents the rural areas and tries to defend the traditional organization of local government that objectively favours rural interests. It is composed of the main part of the municipal elected officials in small communes (500 000 officials for 36 000 communes), the départements and the Senate. The second bloc represents urban interests and the new political, administrative and economic elites that see in large city-regions institutions and the regional level a way to bypass the rural interests and their representatives. The confrontation and the balance between these two blocs have in large part determined the evolution of the system of local governments and centre–periphery relationships.

12.1   1958–75: Bureaucratic modernization and the marginalization of resistant local traditional elites

In 1958, despite deeply entrenched centralization (pursued by absolute monarchs and revolutionary Jacobins alike), France was a country where local elected officials, mayors of small rural communes, together with MPs and ministers, were the keystone of the political system. Local *notables*, i.e. offi-cials recruited in the social elites and exerting an undisputed and long-lasting political domination on small and most often rural constituency, were the central figures of the Third and Fourth Republics. The first period of the new regime was characterized by political and bureaucratic centralization leading to the conflict between the new administrative and political Gaullist elite that monopolized central positions in the government and the traditional local political elites that hold powerful positions in Parliament. The former tried to marginalize the latter, seen as the principal obstacle to the modernization of the country.

12.1.1   Centralized modernization: the rise of new bureaucratic elites and the development of national territorial public policies

Despite the strong resistance of French 'notables', the Gaullist policy of forced modernization gradually changed the face of the country and centre–periphery relations. The coming age of the Fifth Republic led to the rise of a new type of political and administrative elite (Suleiman 1995), made of more politicized technocrats, top civil servants trained in the elitist '*grandes écoles*' and more particularly, the old *Ecole Polytechnique* and the new *Ecole Nationale d'Administration* created by Michel Debré and Charles de Gaulle (Dulong 1997; François 2008). They wanted to modernize France through industrialization and urbanization. They were convinced that only the technical elites could achieve this vision by colonizing the central state apparatus at the expense of the Members of Parliament and local notables. The so-called Gaullist modernizing elites used public expenditures, the national planning mobilization (Hall 1986) and large firms to fulfil their project (Jobert and Muller 1987). The break with the Malthusian and ruralist vision of the 'notables' was clear and a battle started soon to marginalize those in Parliament, in the *Conseils Généraux* and in town halls who opposed the modernizing project. The aim of the Gaullists was to replace them by '*forces vives*', i.e. new political and economic elites that were not represented by the old notability system.

Territorial public policy was used to redefine central local relations. First, postwar national economic planning was reinforced as a state-led industrial meccano. Local economies were dismantled; local notables became economically more dependent upon Paris. Once structured not only by large firms but also by a myriad of local industrial systems, networks or familial SMEs protected by the state, the French economy became structured by large vertical firms and the systematic demise of SMEs and local or regional production systems (Aniello and Le Galès 2004). Ever since, integrated vertical large firms based in Paris have organized economic growth and dominated the French economy. Most firms' and banks' headquarters left places such as Lyon and Lille for Paris (Veltz 1996).

Secondly, the modernization imperative translated into the creation of the '*Politique d'Aménagement du Territoire*', the French heroic voluntarist version of regional policies which, as elsewhere in most European countries, was a mix of sticks and carrots. A new agency, DATAR (*Délégation à l'Aménagement du Territoire et à l'Action Régionale*) was founded in 1963 and led the decentralization of industrial plants in rural regions, in particular in the west and south west of France and to a more limited extent in industrial regions in crisis such as Lorraine, St Etienne or Marseilles. About 400 000 jobs were transferred to those regions paving the way for long-term growth in the west of France in particular. Large firms used cheap, low-qualified, non-unionized labour leaving rural areas. Foreign investment was oriented towards Bordeaux, Montpellier or Grenoble. Thirdly, urban policies were implemented to develop cities. The DATAR (*Politique des métropoles d'équilibres*) supported urban mayors who took advantage of the state modernist strategy to take the lead in urban development (in Grenoble, Bordeaux, Strasbourg, Rennes, and so on). Massive investments were made to create various infrastructures, schools, universities, research centres, cultural centres, hospitals. Sleepy provincial towns gradually turned into dynamic regional capitals. Urbanism was profoundly restructured through the creation of new tools for high density urban planning, social housing and new transport systems. Innovative *Ingénieurs des Ponts et Chaussées* led the creation of the *Ministère de l'Equipement* in 1966 and the development of infrastructures and urban planning in most cities. The Ministry of Finance and the French-owned public bank *Caisse des Dépôts et Consignation*s created a French version of public (state, dominant) public (local) partnership with private status but rarely private capital: the *Société d'économie mixte*. After 1958 a new organization, the SCET (*Société Centrale d'Equipement du Territoire*), created local branches in most cities to undertake large-scale urban renovation and development schemes, including the famous new neighbourhoods on the outskirts of cities providing housing for the working class. Finally, in parallel to DATAR, an interventionist urban policy was designed and implemented mainly for the Paris region, leading to a major strategic Plan in 1965 and the creation of new towns and new transport infrastructure.

The *département* was the key level of administration for state external services. In contrast to the hands-off policy in the UK, the French state has developed its administrative machinery within all corners of France to directly control and integrate the territory. Major ministries like the ministries of housing, infrastructure, agriculture, later health and social services, and of course the ministry of finance (*Trésorier Payeur Général*) are organized on a hierarchic basis with offices in each *département*. Last but not least, state services in the *département* are supposedly under the supervision of the powerful representative of the state (attached to the Ministry of Interior), the all-powerful *Préfet*, symbol of French centralization. The prefect has power of control over local politicians, and also some financial power to control local authorities (with the representative of the ministry of finance). Local authorities are in the hands of the prefect and state external services in gaining access to money and to technical expertise. The state modernized the country in a centralized way, building alliances with new urban and regional elites.

12.1.2   Beyond centralization: 'Jacobinisme apprivoisé'

In 1958 the influence of local elected officials, especially those representing the interests of rural France, was guaranteed thanks to the 36 000 communes, the *départements* (about 100) and the Senate. The power of the *notables* stemmed from the rural nature of French society and from the ambition of the fathers of the Republic to entrench the regime in the dense network of rural communities. Later, this power was reproduced by a central institution of the French Republic: multiple office-holding.

Rurality and agriculture have often been presented as the elements that gave its identity and stability to the French Republic, while cities were seen both by conservatives and Republicans as places of instability and political unrest. As Agulhon has shown (1970), the rural commune and its mayor symbolized the Republican values of France with its town hall, war memorial, local school and central square. The myth of rural France gave long-lasting political legitimacy to the political actors representing those rural areas.[1]

The Republican model, celebrating rural France and the communes, let local elected officials have key political roles maintained by via multiple office-holding. Until the limitations of '*cumul des mandats*' in 1985 it was possible for a politician to be both mayor, *conseiller général* (i.e. member of the *département* assembly), deputy/senator or to hold a ministerial position. The *cumul* was essential to gaining political influence; it enabled a politician to maintain a local electoral clientele, to inlfuence central decisions and direct investments towards his constituency. This enabled both the centre to integrate the peripheries and the peripheries and the representatives of localities to influence national government's policies (Grémion 1976; Tarrow 1977; Mabileau 1994).

During the first period, the rising tide of centralization did not lead to reform of local government. The government failed to rationalize the map of communes and was in conflict with the Senate. Despite attempts to rationalize the French communal map, the number has not changed much since the Revolution. On 1 March 2008 there are still 36 568 communes in metropolitan France run by as many mayors and about 500 000 local councillors. Mayors have powerful legitimacy within the system; they solve problems through face-to-face interactions with the population (Lorrain 1981), through personal contacts with state services in the *départements* (including the prefect) or through access to national civil servants via powerful notables holding several political offices. The *commune* is the heart of French democracy, of French politics. It is the level for the making of associations, for the mobilization of many interests, for the politicization of conflicts in parallel to the national scene. The national association of mayors (*Association des Maires de France*) is a powerful lobby (Le Lidec 2001), with huge influence in Parliament and is present in all debates concerning local authorities.

In 1958 all communes were deemed equal, having the same legal status to guarantee communal autonomy and an a priori right to address important local issues. The Republican regime has always feared the rise of urban powers; hence the systematic lack of specific rights and powers for cities and urban governments. Paris epitomized those fears. It is therefore slightly misleading to assume there was no exceptional legal status for cities: Paris was directly run by the state and not by an elected mayor.

The 100 '*départements*' created by the Revolution is the other stronghold of 'notables' and the second institution that gives rural interests predominant power in the country. Elections for the departmental assemblies are based on an old division, the *canton*, bringing together a small town and a series of small communes. Inhabitants elect a member of the departmental assembly named '*conseiller général*', usually the mayor who will have access to resources (grants for equipments such as roads for instance). The organization in *cantons* structurally undermined the political weight of cities. The world of *conseiller général* is also a world of face-to-face interaction with the inhabitants and small organizations in the area. Over time, with the rise of urban areas, conflicts between *départements* and cities (regional capitals in particular) have become a structural feature of the French political system and the allocation of resources.

Local and departmental elected officials elect senators. If the 1958 Constitution rationalized parliamentary life, it did not modify the election rules for senators. The election is organized at the level of the *départements*. Senators are thus mainly elected (for nine years) by the representatives of rural and often conservative interests. It follows that the right-wing majority of the Senate has never been threatened. In 1958, and ever since, the left was marginalized and major conflicts have arisen over time with the Gaullists, proponents of a state-organized modernization of the country, and the centrists eager to maintain their position.

The central position of local politicians holding both local and national offices nuances the centralist view of French politics. Grémion and the sociologists of Michel Crozier's *Centre de Sociologie des Organizations* named that complex system of relationships '*Jacobinisme apprivoisé*' (tamed Jacobinism) (Grémion 1976). In this system, the prefect held most of the resources to implement policies. In the name of the 'general interest', he was the chief operator of national programmes and held most of the financial and technical resources. By contrast, mayors were deprived of any significant technical services or financial resources and the *département* officials of any executive power.

Nevertheless, thanks to multiple office-holding and to their political legitimacy, local politicians negotiated the content of state policies implemented in their constituencies. Their national mandates enabled them to access ministries in order to exert pressure on their prefects or on the executive of state field services, or to channel specific investments towards their constituencies. Rather than a relation of unilateral domination, the relations between '*le préfet et ses notables*' (Worms 1966) were relations of interdependency. Furthermore, working on a daily basis at *département* level with the mayors and the *conseillers généraux*, the prefects and the heads of state field services were likely to become the representatives of local interests as much as those of the central government. The arrangements with the national norms were thus the rule in terms of policy-making.

The political weight of local notables was made visible with the 1969 referendum failure to create, and the unsuccessful policy of, municipal amalgamation launched in 1971. First, the direct election of the president in 1962 led to a lasting conflict between de Gaulle and the Senate. In 1969, for legitimacy reasons also, de Gaulle organized a referendum to reform the Senate and the election rules for senators, and to create regions. The failure of the referendum marked the departure of de Gaulle. It also made unthinkable any plan to reform the Senate and it postponed decentralization reforms for 13 years. Secondly, in 1971 the Minister of Interior, Raymond Marcellin, himself a leading multiple office-holding notable of the Republic, proposed a reform to limit the number of small communes by amalgamating them into larger communes, following the rationalizing trend which led to the reform of local government in most European countries. Resistance to the drafting of the law and to its implementation gave evidence of the capacity of the French territorial system to resist any rationalization imposed by the government. The law created financial incentives for the amalgamation of communes but completely missed its target: the number of communes declined only from 37 700 to 36 400 between 1971 and 1977.

12.1.3   The slow emergence of the 'modernist' couple of French territorial politics: the city and the region

The Gaullist regime faced the resistance of local interests. It therefore aimed, in territorial matters as in culture or agriculture policy, to promote new groups of interests and new territorial levels to implement and support the modernization strategy. The region and large cities benefited from the support of the Gaullist modernizing elites.

The region, which was traditionally seen as a symbol of the monarchist and conservative right, was brought back to life by the Gaullist modernists against the notables. That meant state sponsored regions promoted in a centralized modernization scheme. Nothing could be more alien to the French centralist tradition than federalism. When some regionalist thinkers started to play with the idea in the 1960s, the political and administrative elite reacted strongly, as federalism was then the symbol of the anti-Revolution faction, the enemy of the Jacobin state, the symbol of division and chaos.

However, in management terms, as early as the late 1950s, once the interventionist territorial policy on the way was in the firm hands of state bureaucracy, it appeared helpful in reinforcing the regional level as a level of coordination for mobilizing some interest groups and prioritizing public investments. The region was a weak level of administrative coordination under the leadership of a prefect. In the name of administrative rationalization, 21 regions were established in 1959 and then 1964 under the bureaucratic names of *Circonscriptions d'action régionale* and *Commissions de développement économique régionales* (CODER). With the end of colonization, social regionalist movements or lobbies in Brittany or Alsace also played a role. A section of the non-communist left progressively also supported the idea. The 1969 referendum would have been the normal step forward leading to the quasi-linear institutionalization of a proper region, mobilizing a new political elite and bypassing local interest, if it had succeeded.

The idea was not abandoned but the very slow march of regionalism (Mény 1974) led to the creation in 1972 of public regional agencies with limited powers, under the control of *département* elected representatives and the executive leadership of the prefect. In some regions the impact of that new body was not significant. In other regions, either because it attracted councillors and administrators strongly in favour of the region (as in Alsace, or Britanny) or because it had to face economic crisis and industrial restructuring (Nord Pas de Calais, Provence Alpes-Côte d'Azur), there was a strong mobilization, the organization of policy networks, serious discussion of national industrial strategies for the region or mobilization of regional economic interests.

In parallel, the urban level of government was making serious progress. Although the rationalization of the map of communes had failed, the state managed to create authoritatively inter-municipal cooperation structures in large cities (*communautés urbaines*) in only 12 cities and nine new towns in the Paris region. If the political functioning of these new structures was most often quite chaotic, each mayor being eager to conserve his prerogatives, they nevertheless gradually became the frame for prospective reflections and strategic planning.

Nevertheless, an invisible revolution started to occur in large cities. In the absence of radical institutional reform, communes invented new forms of cooperation. Single or multi-purpose(s) inter-municipal cooperative bodies (*syndicats intercommunaux*) were created to manage utilities and services. Those organizations allowed for economies of scale and without the creation of supra-municipal institutions which would have threatened the legitimacy and political visibility of the mayors. Besides, the largest cities started to develop their own capacity to design and implement their own policies in the sectors neglected by state field services. Mayors like Pierre Pfimlin in Strasbourg, Jacques Chaban-Delmas in Bordeaux, Henri Fréville in Rennes for the right, Hubert Dubedout in Grenoble, Gaston Defferre in Marseille or Pierre Mauroy in Lille for the left, progressively abandoned the passive stance of most local elected officials and began to develop urban bureaucracy, to hire highly educated civil servants in order to design and implement their own urban strategies and policies, and to attract inward investments. From the mid-1960s onwards, the number and qualification of the managers surrounding urban mayors started to increase (Lorrain 1989).

In the early 1970s the situation was ambiguous. From a 'policy-making' perspective, the centralization trend is obvious. The new regime saw the promotion of new political and administrative central elites concentrating much of the initiatives and resources in the field of economic and territorial policies, the reinforcement of state field services and the gradual marginalization of the traditional local elites. Nevertheless, 'notables' were still able to defend their institutional positions, to resist institutional modernization.

12.2   1975–2008: ebbing centralization and the making of a more plural territorial organization of the Republic

The slow rise of cities and regions was accelerated by the economic crisis of the mid 1970s which signalled increasing public expenditure (see Baumgartner et al. in this volume) but also the contestation of the state and the transfer of resources. The ongoing decentralization dynamics leading to the institutional innovations is therefore the result of political pressure and social and economic tensions which prevailed and gained in legitimacy during the centralization period and the crisis.

12.2.1   Political pressures and the gradual move towards decentralization

By the mid 1970s most of the national modernizing territorial policies were in retreat. DATAR could not allocate growth poles in a period of economic crisis, the Paris economy also had to gain support and the main rapid phase of urbanization was over. Also, a slow transfer of resources was in the making: money and expertise were gradually shifting from the centre to the periphery, paving the way for successful decentralization reform a decade later.

After the failure of the 1969 referendum on regionalization, the Pompidou government created 21 '*Etablissements publics régionaux*' with the 5 July 1972 Act: embryo regions, weak administrative bodies under the control of state representatives but with their own budget and a board of local elected officials and business representatives debating state regional policy. The creation of these embryonic regions gave rise to expectations among local economic elites, organized in regional lobbies.

In the left-wing parties and social movements, the proponents of decentralization and regionalization also gained an increasing influence during the 1970s. After 1968 part of the Left contested centralization, the bureaucratization and the authoritarianism brought about by Gaullist elites' takeover of policy-making. This protest gave rise to the rebirth of regionalist movements supported by some fringes of the non-communist left such as the *Parti Socialiste Unifié* (PSU). Many then joined the newly created *Parti Socialiste* (PS), founded by François Mitterrand in 1971. Inside the new party, against the dominant centralist tendency, they allied with the representatives of municipal socialism such as Gaston Defferre (Marseilles) and Pierre Mauroy (Lille).

The municipal elections of 1977 were a crucial moment for spreading the support for decentralization among left-wing parties. Surfing on public discontent due to the deepening of the economic crisis and the rise of unemployment rates, the Left enjoyed a major electoral success during these elections winning important cities. Socialist/communist coalitions tried to resuscitate municipal socialism, but they were often hampered by the opposition of prefects who tended to sue these initiatives in administrative courts. This experience eventually convinced the Left that it was crucial to give more autonomy to local and regional governments. Many policies were implemented more or less legally and decentralization was in the making. Indeed, one of the last actions of the Giscard d'Estaing presidency was to introduce the *'Dotation générale de fonctionnement'* – a system of state financial transfer to local governments – and to give the power to communes and *départements* to determinate the rate of local taxes in 1980.

Decentralization reforms were on the cards. The political historic change of 1981 paved the way for a lasting large-scale sequence of decentralization reforms that fundamentally changed the relations between the state and regional and local governments. The first decentralization Act, voted in August 1981 by the National Assembly and promulgated on 2 March 1982, transformed the *'Etablissements Publics Régionaux'* in terms of regional government. After a transition period the new regional councils were to be directly elected in 1986. In addition, the law proclaimed that the communes, *départements* and regions would be freely governed by their elected councils. The executive power for these three tiers was to be transferred from the prefects to the presidents of the councils of each level. As important was the removal of the financial and administrative a priori control on the local and regional governments' decisions, replaced by a formal/legal a posteriori control (Mény 1992; Thoenig 1992). Another law, voted in July 1982, created the regional audit courts (*Cours régionales des comptes*), endowed with the responsibility to control the finances of regional and local governments (Benoit 2003). Other laws were voted in the following years, reorganizing the system of French indicative planning, creating special statutes for Paris, Lyons and Marseilles, organizing the system of right and duties for local governments and civil servants.

Under the Jospin government (a Socialist-Communist-Green coalition 1997–2002) a series of three laws[2] were passed that reinforced cooperation between municipal governments, created a more competitive conception of territorial development, and legitimized the formulation and delivery of policy along new territorial lines. Together, often in contradictory terms, they organize the territorialization of state priorities, the making of collective strategies for different types of territories, the institutionalization of intercommunal bodies (*communautés*), and the redistribution of social and spatial responsibilities and powers on a different scale. Lastly, a constitutional reform, or Act II of decentralization, was pushed forward by the Raffarin government (2003) to include the rights of local authorities to organize the transfer of 150 000 civil servants to local and regional authorities, to oversee the transfer of powers to different levels of government (i.e. roads, social aids, and waste disposal to the *départements*; and aid to firms, training, regional strategic planning, and public equipment to the regions), and to grant the right to experimentation in terms of organization and public policy.

Regions mainly deal with economic development, training, the building of secondary schools, culture, environment, and now, increasingly, railways. *Départements* have special power and resources to manage social services, transport and roads. Communes mainly deal with social services, their own roads and primary schools, basic services, environment, sports and culture. Inter-communal *communautés* mainly work on utilities, waste management, transport, economic development and water. However, each level of government feels free to intervene in any domain: all have policies for the environment, culture or economic development, for instance; hence a considerable amount of overlap. The world of local and regional government comprises 500 000 elected members and 1.8 million public sector employees, which constitutes about 30 per cent of the French public service. But the appearance of a clear distinction is misleading: in the absence of hierarchy, each level is more or less legitimate in developing policies in most sectors. On top of this, the system has been made even more complex by the possibility given to local and regional governments to exert discretionary functions. Indeed, municipalities can add to their mandatory functions policy initiatives in various matters such as economic development, culture, tourism, housing, health, etc. Since the last Constitution reform (28 March 2003) local and regional governments have a right to experimentation, which is also a way of both recognizing and regulating the ability of local governments to be the most effective political level in addressing new needs.

12.2.2   Political competition between levels of government, overlapping powers and finances and state regulations

All in all, the French territorial system has been profoundly transformed because once centralization went out of favour, the decentralization dynamics led to never-ending cycles of decentralization reforms every four or five years. More resources, technical expertise and political legitimacy were gradually transferred to local and regional administrative and political elites creating a more differentiated and plural polity altogether.

These legislative moves paved the way for a profound restructuring of government at the subnational level. Three contradictory images emerged from three decades of reforms: the slow erosion, adaptation and firm resistance of the old system: communes/*départements*/Senate; the coming of age of metropolitan and regional governments; and a reshaping of state organization, with a progressive retreat from day-to-day management to a more strategic role at the regional level. Slowly, cities and regions are becoming a more important locus of organization of interests, decisions and implementation of public policy, and creation of collective strategies.

Intense political battles take place both in Parliament and between national associations of local government. These groups are permanently engaged in a ceaseless struggle to develop transfers of power from the state and to prevent other levels of government from benefiting at their expense. This competition between groups of politicians from different levels of government is an important competitive dynamic over time, even within political parties. The collision between the former systems (communes/*départements*/Senate) versus the urban/regional system reinforces the dynamics of decentralization. The success of the 1999 Act reforming local intercommunal organizations has much to do with local patterns of leadership, stabilized forms of political exchange, and organizational learning through previous or pre-existing forms of cooperation (Baraize and Négrier 2001). Inter-municipal governments offer new opportunities for local leaders willing to establish local strongholds on a wider scale: a large majority of *communautés* are chaired by mayors, often the mayor of the central city around which the *communauté* was built. Mayors are reinforcing their authority on a larger territorial basis at the expense of *départements*. Lately, the Raffarin decentralization reform also reflected the power relations in the new right-wing party, the UMP. Although the prime minister managed to strengthen the role of the regions in the Constitution, he could only do so by giving more resources and powers to the *départements* and by increasing the role of the Senate in local matters.

The French state is no longer a uniform state; it is a unitary state with regions and local authorities. A more complex picture of local government has emerged, a mosaic-like pattern resembling the situation in other countries throughout Europe and very different from the previous well-organized state-view of local government: uniform, controlled by civil servants, and enshrined within financial and legal constraints set by the state.

The last constitutional reform, during the Raffarin government, gave regions a constitutional status and a right to experiment in new domains like universities, professional training, and management of ports, airports and roads. Already, some 'voracious regions' regions have proved very ambitious claiming their legitimate competence in domains such as the management of ports, traditionally a dominion of the central state, on the basis of their success in development of regional railways networks. Some are also contesting with Chamber of Commerce or *départements* the management and development of airports. Here again, the regional level is favoured by the state which tends to reorganize its services – traditionally organized at the *département* level – and to foster strategic planning and inter-institutional negotiations at this level (Pasquier 2004). As a result, regions are also threatening the *département* as a key political level. Regional mandates tend to compete with those of *départements* in political career plans.

Formally, there still is a single legal status for both tiny rural communes and large urban communes in the French system of local government. Nevertheless, the great winners of decentralization have been the large cities rather than rural communes. They gain the same things in terms of functions: urban planning and land use regulation, housing and transportation. But only the large urban communes have been able to fully benefit from the functions transfer because they have the financial resources, expertise and technical capacity to implement. With a larger fiscal base and relatively healthy economy, the largest cities have fully benefited from the decentralization. They were able to emancipate themselves from the state's field services resources and expertise and to develop policies well beyond their statutory competences.

Today the impressive progress of inter-municipal cooperation in urban areas has accentuated a process of differentiation of the forms of local governance in urban and rural areas that started with the growing urbanization of the country in the 1960s. This movement towards internal differentiation has intensified during the last two decades with, on one side, increasingly powerful urban inter-municipal cooperative structures gaining an increasing autonomy and political capacity, while on the other side rural communes are increasingly dependent on upper tiers, be they *départements*, regions or state field services. Indeed, metropolitan institutions are bringing together an increasing number of resources and functions and have recently developed considerable political capacity. For instance, in 2006 the *Grand Lyon*, i.e. the *communauté urbaine* of Lyons could count on a €1484 billion budget, compared with the €679 billion budget of the City of Lyons, the €1332 billion budget of the *département du Rhône* and the €1877 billion budget of the region *Rhône-Alpes*. Of this budget 31 per cent is dedicated to investment, which makes the metropolitan institution the major actor in urban policy-making, especially in fields such as transportation, urban planning and economic development. Metropolitan areas have become essential places for planning and setting visions. In elaborating and implementing their policies, metropolitan institutions can rely on an increasingly competent and professionalized staff. Municipal officials were known in the 1960–70s for their low educational and professional profile. Nowadays, the emergence of powerful metropolitan institutions with more functions requiring greater professional skills has given a new impulse to the professionalization of local government. Not only do these institutions attract the best qualified staff from the communes, they also attract the administrative and technical elites of the state field services.

12.2.3 Not a federal Republic but an increasingly differentiated legal territorial organization in part regulated by the Conseil constitutionnel

Once the tide of centralization has retreated, the political endogenous dynamics of territorial differentiation of the Fifth Republic has become the key factor in explaining the transformation of centre–periphery relations. However, another explanation, possibly more speculative, should be explored.[3] The territorial differentiation that has been underlined is also well documented by lawyers pointing to the increasing territorialization of law in France (Auby 2006). Within the Republic experiments in new forms of territorial organization and regulation have been tried out in overseas territories, the territorial inheritance from the colonial empire. Historically, within the French Constitution, the territorial differentiation of law was considered for overseas territories.

In the 1946 Constitution (Fourth Republic), overseas territories were organized into two categories; the old ones (Martinique, Guadeloupe, Guyane, Réunion) were already organized as *Départements d'outre mer (D.O.M)*. The 1958 Constitution reinforces the 'normalization' of those territories and creates a slightly different legal status for the others, the *Territoires d'outre-mer (T.O.M)* including Mayotte, St Pierre et Miquelon, Wallis et Futuna, Nouvelle Calédonie and the jewel in the crown of the Republic, French Polynesia. For reasons not explored here, a massive uncoordinated movement of differentiation has been taking place in particular since the 1980s. There is no space here to relate each particular story.[4] Briefly however, St Pierre et Miquelon, once a TOM, became a proper département in 1976, a normalization process that might have been seen as the last push of centralization, but then gained a special status of '*collectivité territoriale*' in 1985. The most dramatic and conflicting story of New Caledonia reached some high points during the Chirac government (as prime minister). NC also gained some special status in 1985 but the dramatic events led to more negotiation. The Noumea agreements of 1998 leading to the constitutional revision of May 1999 are a bizarre construction from a legal point of view. The new Title XIII of the Constitution nearly gives legislative power to the Assembly and includes specific legal arrangements for the elections (and rights to vote for different communities) (Fabereau 2005). In this case, the idea of association is floated around, hence the dynamics of federalization mentioned by some commentators (Lévy 2000). French Polynesia has also been through political strife and increasing differentiated legal provisions with its autonomy pushed towards the extreme limits within the French state.

This constant pressure and dynamics of fragmentation paved the way for a major constitutional revision (28 March 2003), rewriting part of the

Constitution. Articles 73 and 74 now deals with all those overseas territories. What is remarkable however is the fact that there is no attempt to harmonize legal status. By contrast the Constitution gives some sort of procedural tool box to create new local and regional authorities with specific legal status and normative powers. The Constitution now states that new types of local or regional authorities can be created within the Republic, therefore acknowledging the increasing pluralization of French territorial order. The new DROM (*Départements et regions d'outre mer*) and COM (*Collectivités d'outre mer*) have increasingly more differentiated resources, competences and organizations.

In his chapter Sylvain Brouard convincingly documents the fact that the Constitutional court has become increasingly involved in resolving disputes in the interpretation of the law concerning New Caledonia. Riots and violence in the 1980s led to the negotiation of 'special territorial status', which had to be made more precise over the years because of the interpretation of the Constitutional council. The case of Corsica is even more interesting (Vallet 2004). Again, following years of violence, special status was negotiated for Corsica at more or less the same time as the Noumea agreements for New Caledonia. Beforehand, Corsica had already been granted particular fiscal and economic advantages and a specific Assembly. A first law in 1991 had been rejected by the Constitutional court because of the mention of the famous sentence stating that there was such a thing as '*un peuple corse, composante du peuple français*'. Ongoing violence during the following decade culminated with the assassination of the Prefect, Claude Erignac. After years of negotiation between the Jospin government and nationalist organizations, a law was passed in December 2001. The Constitutional court has then had the opportunity to make a detailed assessment of the law, validating some key points but rejecting some elements in terms of normative power in particular. After 2002 the new Minister of Interior Nicolas Sarkozy put forward a sophisticated legal status for Corsica in 2003. This included a unique regional authority with extensive powers and autonomy and a different electoral system. Although supported by the nationalist and the French governments, the referendum organized in Corsica in July 2003 was narrowly defeated and the special legal status was abandoned, at least for the time being.

During all these debates three points are worth emphasizing: 1) the Constitutional court plays an increasing role in assessing what is acceptable or what is constitutional, thus reflecting the increasing juridicization of centre–periphery relations in the Fifth Republic; 2) in the process, major transformation has taken place and a surprising differentiated legal and political territorial order with more normative power granted to local and regional authorities – centre–periphery relations become more diverse and asymmetric; and 3) although more evidence should be sought, the dissemination logic of increased differentiation in overseas territories has some impact on the decentralization debate in France. This should be traced more precisely through networks of politicians, administrations and judges but clearly some Corsican representatives have in mind what happened with New Caledonia and French Polynesia. Similarly, the debate in Alsace is not without reference to what takes place in Corsica.

12.3 Conclusion: The end of the decentralization cycle?

France is not becoming a federal Republic but politics in France is and remains profoundly territorially rooted within regions, rural communes, small towns and cities. This deep territorialization continues to have an impact on the way in which society and the economy operate. As in most continental European countries, conflicts about redistribution, norms of political behaviour or public policy implementation remain rooted in contrasting regions and localities.

We divided the Fifth Republic into two main periods. On wonders whether a third period is likely to start right now because 25 years after decentralization reforms, state elites are finally learning the rule of the new polity and reorganizing their policy instruments together with a more hands-off policy to pilot public policy implementation. In a way, the French state is in part, slowly, moving towards a more regulatory role, structuring the rules of the game, and leaving more autonomy to the actor to deliver policies. The decentralization debate is also entering a phase where, for the first time in more than three decades, local and regional authorities appear as non virtuous and inflationists. The debate on the high level of public deficits and the debt (63 per cent of GDP) is stirring an important public debate. As reform proves difficult owing to powerful local and regional interests rooted in Parliament (and sometimes in the most conservative sense as in the Senate), one temptation is to rule through macro financial indicators to impose cuts. It may also be an appealing solution for state elites to govern an increasingly mosaic-like territory. The golden age of decentralization may be over. The new phase may be organized around more local and regional pressure to experiment new normative powers and legal status within a stricter set of legal and financial rules. In short, a more plural but re-centralizing state?

Notes

1. The Third Republic was presented as the '*République des petites patries*' (*Politix* 2001), a regime sustained by a federation of municipal and departmental officials eager to exert strict control on state action through Parliament.
2. 1999 Voynet Act on regional planning and sustainable development (ministry of environment and regional policy), 1999 Chevènement Act on inter-municipal cooperation (ministry of interior), and the law '*Solidarité et Renouvellement Urbain*', (ministry of planning, housing, infrastructures) 2000.
3. The authors are grateful to Sylvain Brouard for suggesting this line of research.
4. For an overview see the special issue of *Pouvoirs*, no.113, 2005.

Bibliography

Agulhon, M. (1970) *La République au village*, Paris: Plon.

Aniello, V. and Le Galès, P. (2004) 'Between large firms and marginal local economies: the making of systems of local governance in France', in C. Crouch, P. Le Galès, C. Trigilia, H. Voelzkow *Local Production Systems in Europe, Rise or Demise?*, Oxford: Oxford University Press.

Auby, J.B. (2006) *La Décentralisation et le droit*, Paris: LGDJ.

Baraize, F. and Négrier, E. (eds) (2001) *L'invention politique de l'agglomération*, Paris: L'Harmattan.

Benoit, O. (2003) 'Les chambres régionales des comptes face aux élus locaux: les effets inattendus d'une institution', *Revue Française de Sciences Politique* 53(4): 535–58.

Blériot, L. (2005) 'Les départements et régions d'outre-mer, un statut à la carte?, *Pouvoirs* no.113: 73–93.

Borraz, O. (2000) 'Le gouvernement municipal en France. Un modèle d'intégration en recomposition', *Pôle Sud*, 13: 1–26.

Borraz, O. and Le Galès P. (2005) 'Local government in France: intercommunal revolution and new forms of governance', in Bas Denters and Larry Rose (eds) *Comparing Local Governance: Trends and Developments*, Basingstoke: Palgrave Macmillan.

Clinchamps, N. (2005) 'Les collectivités d'outre mer et la Nouvelle Calédonie: le fédéralisme en question', *Pouvoirs* no. 113: 73–92.

Cour des comptes (2003) *La déconcentration des administrations et la réforme de l'Etat*, Rapport Public, Paris: Les éditions des journaux officiels.

Douillet, A.C. and Faure, A. (eds) (2005) *L'action publique et la question territoriale*, Grenoble: Presses Universitaires de Grenoble.

Dulong, D. (1997) *Moderniser la politique. Aux origines de la Ve République*, Paris: L'harmattan.

Duran, P. and Thoenig, J.C. (1996) 'L'Etat et la gestion publique territoriale', *Revue Française de Science Politique* 4: 580–622.

Fabereau, J.Y. (2005) 'La France et son outre-mer. Même droit ou droit différent?', *Pouvoirs* no.113: 5–22.

François, B. (2008) *Le régime politique de la Ve République*, Paris: La Découverte.

Grémion, P. (1976) *Le pouvoir périphérique*, Paris: Le Seuil.

Hall, P. (1986) *Governing the Economy: The Politics of State Intervention in Britain and France*, Cambridge: Cambridge University Press.

Hayward, J. (2006) *The State and the Market Economy*, Brighton: Wheatsheaf Books.

Jobert, B. and Muller, P. (1987) *L'Etat en action. Politiques publiques et corporatismes*, Paris: PUF.

Le Galès, P. (2006) 'The ongoing march of decentralisation within the post Jacobin state', in P. Culpepper, P. Hall, B. Palier (eds) *Changing France: The Politics that Markets Make*, Basingstoke: Palgrave Macmillan.

Le Lidec, P. (2001) *Les maires dans la République. L'Association des Maires de France, élément constitutif des régimes politiques français depuis 1907*, PhD dissertation in Political Science Politique, Université de Paris I.

Le Lidec, P. (2007) 'Le jeu du compromis: l'Etat et les collectivités territoriales dans la décentralisation en France', *Revue Française d'Administration Publique*, no.121–122: 111–30.

Le Saout, R. and Madore, F. (eds) (2004) *Les effets de l'intercommunalité*, Rennes: Presses Universitaires de Rennes.

Levy, J. (1999) *Toqueville's Revenge. State, Society and Economy in Contemporary France*, Harvard: Harvard University Press.

Levy, J. (2000) 'République fédérale de France Acte I', *Pouvoirs Locaux* no.47.

Linginbé, P. (2003) 'Le changement institutionnel du DROM: les marges de manœuvre', *Semaine Juridique. Administrations et collectivités locales*, no.7: 171–5.

Lorrain, D. (1981) *A quoi servent les mairies*, Paris: Fondation des villes.

Lorrain, D. (1989) *Les mairies urbaines et leurs personnels*. Paris: La documentation française.

Lorrain D. (1991) 'De l'administration républicaine au gouvernement urbain flexible', *Sociologie du travail*, no.4.

Luchaire, F. (2002) 'La Corse et le Conseil constitutionnel', *Revue du droit public*, no.3: 888–902.

Mabileau, A. (1994) *Le système local en France,* Paris: LGDJ.

Matutano, E. (2005) 'Actualité d'une notion en mutation: les "lois de souveraineté"', *Revue Française de droit constitutionnel*, 7(63): 527–37.

Mény, Y. (1974) *Centralisation et décentralisation dans le débat politique français: (1945–1969)* Paris: LGDJ.

Mény, Y. (1992) 'La république des fiefs', *Pouvoirs*, 60.

Négrier, E. (2005) *La question métropolitaine: les politiques à l'épreuve du changement d'échelle territoriale,* Grenoble: Presses universitaires de Grenoble.

Pasquier, R. (2004) *La capacité politique des régions*, Rennes: Presses Universitaires de Rennes.

Pontier, J.M. (2000) 'Les avancées toujours renouvelées de l'autonomie local: le cas des TOM', *Revue Administrative*, 53 (313): 66–75.

Politix (2001) 'Le temps des mairies', no.53.

Suleiman, E. (1995) 'Les élites de la Vème République', in E. Suleiman, H. Mendras (eds) *Le recrutement des elites en Europe*, Paris: La Découverte.

Tarrow, S. (1977) *Between Centers and Peripheries*, New York: Yale University Press.

Thoenig, J.C. (1973) *L'ère des technocrats,* Paris: Editions de l'organisation.

Thoenig, J.-C. (1992) 'La décentralisation. Dix ans après', *Pouvoirs* 60.

Vallet, E (2004) 'L'autonomie corse face à l'indivisibilité de la République', *French Politics Culture and Society,* Fall, 22(3): 51–75.

Veltz, P. (1996) *Mondialisation villes et territoires,* Paris: PUF.

Worms, J.-P. (1966), 'Le Préfet et ses notables', *Sociologie du Travail*, 3: 249–75.

13
The Demise of Statism? Associations and the Transformation of Interest Intermediation in France

Cornelia Woll

France has long been considered as the ideal type of statist interest intermediation, despite some elements of weak neo-corporatism. With a strong central government and a highly technocratic tradition, interest groups had but a marginal role to play in the policy-making process. Mistrustful of intermediary bodies that were considered to distort the expression of the public interest, France tellingly outlawed associations at the end of the eighteenth century and only re-established associational freedom in 1901. In keeping tradition with Jean-Jacques Rousseau's beliefs in the nuisance of private groups to public life and with the negative experience of war corporatism under the Vichy Regime, the Fifth Republic was built around a strong executive removed from parliamentary pressures and with little interest in the consultation of non-governmental stakeholders. Many authors have labelled this particular type of state–society relations 'statism'.

Yet state-led and centralized policy-making came under pressure in the 1970s and 1980s. *Dirigiste* economic policy-making broke down after François Mitterrand's failed Keynesian experiment in 1983. The concurrent drive towards decentralization that the new left-wing government had undertaken in 1982–84 underlined the necessity to include local actors in the governance networks at the regional level. The late 1980s and 1990s were a period marked by attempts by the French government to empower a diverse set of social groups as political actors in their own right. The simultaneous explosion of interest intermediation at the European level that followed the Single European Act in 1986 and the Single Market project in 1992 provided a further venue for interest groups eager to circumvent the tutelage of the French state. In particular regional and economic actors have been able to benefit tremendously from these new opportunities and to exert pressure on their home government by passing through the European Union (Ladrech 1994; Schmidt 1996b; Grossman and Saurugger 2004; Weisbein 2005). In line with developments elsewhere, 'civil society' has become the *mot d'ordre* for politicians and bureaucratic decision-makers in France (see Smismans 2006). Grossman and Saurugger (2006) speak of the 'participatory turn' to highlight how central the concept of 'participatory democracy' has become in the discourse and initiatives of public decision-makers.

Over one hundred years after the law of 1901 and at the 50th anniversary of the Fifth Republic, we are at a good moment to evaluate these changes. What are the consequences of the reshuffling of the state–society relations? Has the French government abandoned its statist relations with social actors and established more open and participatory policy regimes? Is statism still a pertinent category to speak of interest intermediation in France? In particular, one may ask if civil society has been able to rise to the challenge and seize the new opportunities offered. While Vivien Schmidt (1996a) has demonstrated how economic actors and in particular entrepreneurs contributed to redefining the political economy of France, others remain more pessimistic. Jonah Levy's (1999) study of regional economic policy-making shows that governmental actors tried to implement what he calls 'associational liberalism' but largely failed. Indeed, compared with their European counterparts, even economic actors, such as the national employer association, the *Mouvements des enterprises de France* (Medef), remain relatively weak policy-actors, despite intense public relations campaigns in recent years (Culpepper 2003; Woll 2006).

But this is precisely the paradox of the recent transformation of interest intermediation in France. While traditional groups such as trade unions and employers' organizations struggle to adapt to the new modes of representation and partially fail to do so, a multitude of new associations flourish and actively take part in policy deliberation and local administration (Saurugger and Grossman 2006). One million groups are estimated to be active in France today, twice as many as in the mid-1980s (Decool 2005). Opposition to established parties and new social values such as environmentalism, feminism, or personal liberties are fought for and defended by associations, which play a crucial role in organizing protests and shaping the atmosphere of electoral campaigns. In 2004 the French government assigned the first ever ministerial title for associational life to Jean-François Lamour and organized a National Conference for Associational Life in 2006 to decide on ways and means to support the participation of groups in policy-making. On a great number of issues, and especially in regional governance, associational networks have become essential, but only if and when the government has invited them to take part in the policy process.

In the following I argue that interest intermediation in France has transformed profoundly, but statism still remains a pertinent category to understand the range of these changes. Interest group consultation only supplements bureaucratic decision-making and the central government has considerable room for manoeuvre to escape pressures put on specific policy proposals. However, civil society groups do take part in the implementation of policy projects and contribute to the atmosphere in which the objectives become defined. Indeed, associations increasingly take over functions that were previously the domain of political parties (Manin 2007). They are the pillars of policy communities and create allegiances that allow for issue-specific identity politics. As such, the semi-institutionalized forms of associational participation are part of the particular equilibrium that is slowly establishing in response to the representational crisis that has affected the Fifth Republic (Grossman and Saurugger 2006; Berger 2006).

The chapter divides into two parts. The first section opposes the elements that earned France a reputation for being statist with the growth and vivacity of associational life. A second section then asks if these changes are only superficial. Despite the difficulties of the traditional social partners to drive socio-economic reform in France, I argue that groups have become an important part of the French system of representation, especially as forums for deliberation and the implementation of policy projects and institutionalized feedback mechanisms for governmental initiatives.

13.1   The rise of associations in statist France: French Statism

Political thinkers from James Madison (2004 [1787]) to Alexis de Tocqueville (1966 [1835/1840]) recognized that associations promised the liberty of expression for individual citizens but also posed a threat to political stability, as they could turn into hotbeds or 'violent factions'. Yet, for Jean-Jacques Rousseau (2006 [1762]), associations were undesirable even if they did not turn to violence. As 'societies within society', they affected the interests of their members and therefore prohibited the free expression of the general will. The state could not represent the public interest of all citizens, if several organized in groups and influenced public decisions. In the aftermath of the French Revolution, this philosophy was put into law through the Décret d'Allarde of 2 March 1791, which abolished corporations, the Le Chapelier law of 14 June 1791, which outlawed professional associations and a decree on 18 August 1792 against religious groups. These restrictions were continuously debated in the later half of the nineteenth century, but it was not until 1884 that professional groups were allowed and until 1 July 1901 that associational freedom was fully re-established (Barthélemy 2000: 38–57; Belorgey 2000: 15–26). However, the authorization of associations was not simply a liberal act meant to empower civic groups, but also a way of controlling those that have been properly registered and setting them apart from others, in particular religious groups (Belorgey 2000: 19).[1]

After a period of wartime corporatism under the Vichy regime, the Fifth Republic maintained associational freedom, but preserved a great degree of mistrust towards all forms of organized groups. Yet over time French law became increasingly supportive of associations. In 1971 the associational freedom granted in 1901 became a constitutional clause. Additional legislation followed, either to facilitate voluntary work or to help specific groups, such as associations of the elderly in 1977 or athletic school clubs in 1986.

Associations of foreigners, the last remaining ones to be restricted under the Fifth Republic, became legal in 1981.

However, the deep-seated defiance against intermediary bodies in political life is not only manifest in legal arrangements concerning these groups directly; it also plays out in the organization of government. Frank Wilson (1987) argues that at several institutional arrangements contribute to the exclusion of intermediary groups in policy-making in the Fifth Republic. First, the strong role for the political executive allows the French president to control the legislative calendar together with the prime minister. Moreover, through the use of package votes (which do not allow for amendments) and votes of confidence (which require a motion of censure to block a government bill) the government can limit parliamentary control over its proposals and thus restrict the influence of lobbyists who seek to affect the wording of a bill.

Second, party cohesion in the legislative tends to insulate individual representatives from constituency pressure. Representatives often vote the party line, even if regional differences should lead them to disagree on policy content. Frank Wilson also highlights the importance of ideological cleavages, which make it difficult to argue over the technical details. However, these voting patterns noted in the late 1980s may not persist over time or apply to issues with both high and low political salience. The attempt of the French legislative to propose a bill to regulate lobbying in the National Assembly indicates that interest group pressure on the legislature has increased considerably in recent years.[2]

A third element of French statism is the strength of state bureaucracy and technocratic policy-making. Traditionally, the generalist training of French bureaucrats in the *grandes écoles* made them somewhat hostile to external consultation procedures and counter-expertise provided by interest groups. The main policy orientation in the government bureaucracies springs from the educational backgrounds of individual administrators, their *corps*, and not their contacts with outside stakeholders. And yet stable consultation procedures and institutions jointly managed by the government and the social partners exist within the French bureaucracy, especially in social policy areas or agriculture, which has led some authors to speak of corporatism '*à la française*' (Jobert and Muller 1987).

Finally, the centralization of the French political system is a fourth element weakening the role of political groups. As everywhere else, regional and departmental governments are generally more accessible for local stakeholder groups but they have traditionally lacked power relative to the national government. The moves towards decentralization since the 1970s have therefore contributed to empowering local groups and led to a 'more pluralist, competitive and negotiated polity' (Le Galès 2006).

This review of the traditional model of state–society relations in France highlights the fact that many of the central elements of statism have evolved

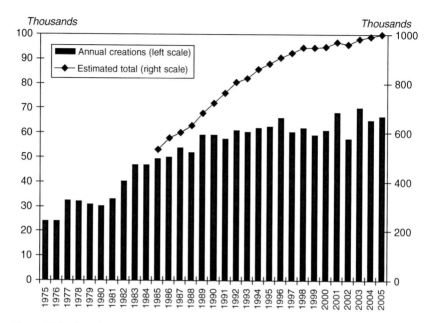

Figure 13.1   Associations in France, 1975–2005
Source: CNVA (2007) and Decool (2005) for estimation of total number of associations.

over time. Despite the deep-seated mistrust of the potential nuisance of groups, French law and the political institutions in France moved towards acceptance and incorporation of intermediary bodies into policy-making processes.

13.1.1   The associational explosion

Decision-makers increasingly acknowledged the social benefits of associational life and started encouraging and promoting them. Whether they are politically active as interest groups or not, associations have become a visible feature of French society in the second half of the Fifth Republic. To begin with, the steep rise in the number of associations in France is striking. One million are estimated to exist in France today, which is twice as many as in the mid-1980s. Figures are most precise for the creation of associations, which are recorded to average around 60 000 annually in recent years, up from around 25 000 creations per year in the mid-1970s (see Figure 13.1).[3] 21.6 million French aged 15 or older – over 45 per cent of the population of France – held at least one associational membership in 2002. Because of multiple memberships associations throughout France were able to count 35.6 million members (Febvre and Muller 2004).

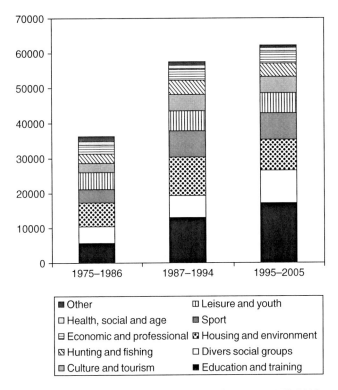

Figure 13.2 Total of association creations by sector of activity, 1975–2005
Note: Metropolitan France, with the exception of the Alsace-Moselle region.
Sources: CNVA (2003) and Bilan 2000–2002.

A breakdown by sector of activity of associations created each year indicates that a large part of these associations are not primarily political groups but cover issues such as education and training (e.g. parent–teacher associations or specialized education), local social activities (e.g. family, health or old age), housing (e.g. neighbourhood associations), athletic activities or leisure activities (see Figure 13.2). One may suspect that creations per year do not give a complete picture of the associational landscape, because these figures cannot indicate differences in longevity according to sector. Professional groups, for example, might have a longer life span than neighbourhood associations or sport and music clubs. But even when one looks at the membership percentages in French society, associations promoting leisure activities remain at the top. As Table 13.1 indicates, only 5 per cent of all French aged 15 or older are members of a trade union or a professional association, while 19 per cent belong to a sports club.

Table 13.1   Membership by association, 2005

Associations	%
Sport	19
Culture	9
Trade unions and professional unions	5
Elderly	4
Alumni and veterans	3
Town and local	3
Leisure / party	3
Parents–teacher	3
Church	2
Health	2
Community service	2
Humanitarian	2
Education	1
Political parties	1
Consumers	1
Environment	1
Other	3
Total	43

Note: Metropolitan France, age 15 or older. Percentages do not add up due to double membership.

Source: INSEE, permanent survey on life conditions, 2005.

Grouping associations according to the motivation of the participants, the National Institute for Statistics and Economic Studies (INSEE) distinguishes between groups formed in the pursuit of specific activities (sport and culture), social interaction between like-minded groups (elderly, church, local, alumni, veterans and retired people) and the defence of interests (unions and professional associations, humanitarian, parent–teacher or housing). In 2002 sport and cultural associations accounted for 37 per cent of all membership, principally from the younger sections of the population, associations aiming for social interaction accounted for 27 per cent of memberships and interest representation amounted to 36 per cent of all membership (Febvre and Muller 2003). To be sure, these distinctions are somewhat artificial, as the defence of interests presupposes the existence of a group of like-minded people. Most prominently, Mancur Olson (1965) points out that lobbying is often a side effect of groups constituted for an entirely different purpose. With its 38 million members, the American Association of Retired Persons (AARP), for example, has often been called one of Washington's most powerful lobbying groups (Morris 1996). One should therefore be careful not to dismiss the associational explosion as a phenomenon that might improve only the French social tissue but which has little political consequence. Since political activity is quite hard to separate from other associational activities, we will deal with associational life as explicitly or implicitly political, even if a majority of groups engage primarily in leisure activities (Lelieveldt and Cainani 2007).

The political aspects of associational life become evident when one considers the new political discourse on democratic policy-making. Politicians today appeal explicitly to associations as the legitimate setting of deliberation, arguing that they give a voice to different sectors of French society. The centennial anniversary of the law of 1901 was an occasion to publicly praise the benefits of associational freedom.[4] In 2004 the Ministry for Youth and Athletics became the Ministry for Youth, Athletics and Associational Life, giving France for the first time in history a minister charged with the development of associations, Jean-François Lamour.[5] In a speech to the Economic and Social Council, Lamour interprets this decision as a desire by the president and the prime minister to acknowledge publicly that intermediary groups have become 'essential to the exercise of democracy and the development of social ties'. His mission is thus to 'make participatory democracy meaningful, by going beyond strictly administrative debates in order to create a true civil dialogue in the public interest'.[6] These declarations epitomize a turnaround in French attitudes towards associations that began over two decades ago. Already in 1983, the National Council for Associative Life (*Conseil national de la vie associative* – CNVA) was created as a consultative body under the auspices of the prime minister to survey and facilitate the work of associations in France. In a speech at the CNVA in 2004 Prime Minister Jean-Pierre Raffarin had expressed his belief that decentralization needed to be accompanied by the social cohesion that association can provide. According to him, 'the legitimacy of civil society' is crucial for a 'representative and participatory democracy'. This implies 'not only to consult, but also to share the public interest'. In opposition to traditional French thought, he stresses that 'the state does not have the monopoly of the public interest'.[7] This is a remarkable break with the past, when French politicians insisted that groups are a threat to democracy and the expression of public interest.

Indeed, public administration under the Fifth Republic has put an increasing emphasis on group consultation. Consultation happens not only in the Economic and Social Council, which Appleton (2005: 57) calls the 'lynchpin of the Gaullist vision of a political process of *concertation*', but also in an impressive number of councils, commissions and committees open to participation from representatives of different stakeholder groups. In 1971 the number of consultative organs was estimated at 500 councils, 1200 commissions and 3000 committees, whereas a recent government estimate that Appleton cites puts the total number at 20 000, including 645 national councils. In line with this new vision, French politicians set out to clarify and institutionalize the role of associational participation in politics. In January

2003 the French government organized the first ever National Conference of Associational Life, which aimed at recognizing the role of associations in the civil dialogue, institutionalizing relations with public actors and facilitating voluntary service within associations.[8]

The associational explosion and the new discourse on participatory democracy indicate that France has indeed undergone a 'participatory turn', comparable with other European democracies (see Maloney and Roßteutscher 2007). However, this does not mean that France has adopted a pluralist model of state–society relations. In fact, not all groups have been able to benefit from the new political opportunities. As Saurugger and Grossman highlight, the 'participatory turn' in France comes with a paradox: while many new associations find an open political opportunity structure, traditional groups such as employer organizations or trade unions have not be able to expand their role in policy-making (Saurugger and Grossman 2006).

13.2   Tocqueville's revenge?

For Jonah Levy the passiveness of the social partners in shaping regional policy responses was due to the burden of history: after decades of excluding intermediary groups for policy-making, decision-makers were unable to mobilize their relevant partners in the last part of the twentieth century. He called this phenomenon 'Tocqueville's revenge'. Although Tocqueville advocated the benefits of groups, it was the Rousseauian rejection of groups that was implemented in French history. According to Levy, this now comes to haunt French politicians who would like to rely on strong social intermediaries to coordinate and implement policies.

The analysis proposed in this chapter is more nuanced. Associations have spread and play an important role in French politics, but not all of them and not everywhere. Levy is therefore right to insist on the legacies of statism, which help in particular to understand the weak role of the social partners that are so central to the neo-corporatist arrangements of other European countries. The rise of associational liberalism in France nonetheless transformed policy-making and opened up new political opportunity structures for previously marginalized groups of French society.

13.2.1   Weak social partners

Assessing the role of employer associations and trade unions in France has always been difficult in international comparisons, particularly those that sought to rank countries on a scale from pluralism, where many groups compete for influence, to neo-corporatism, where the social partners enjoyed privileged ties to the government and played a central role in the coordination of socio-economic institutions. Depending on the measures used, France appeared as moderately to weakly corporatist and sometimes fell off the scale altogether (Siaroff 1999). The contradictory picture led many authors to put

France in a category of its own: even though the social partners are able to determine wage levels and other aspects of labour issues since the 1950 law on collective bargaining, the French state maintains a strong role in the coordination of socio-economic issues. What characterized industrial relations in the first half of the Fifth Republic was, first, the predominance of protest politics: labour relations were represented and experienced a class conflict in mass actions organized by trade unions. Second was the high institutionalization of the social partners in consultative committees and joint management councils (*paritarisme*) that govern important aspects of social policy such as unemployment, retirement or social security. Despite the lack of consensual policy-making at the national level, individual policy sectors therefore display a very high degree of corporatist management. A third feature of the French model is the firm-level management of job stability and career advancement (see Van Ruysseveldt and Visser 1996; Lallement 2006). With heavy government intervention in socio-economic areas, associations of employers and workers concentrated on labour law and protest movements rather than collective negotiation capacity.

Starting in the 1980s, this postwar order was challenged by political and market pressures for greater flexibility. French firms lobbied individually for new policy solutions at the European and the national level and partially circumvented both the bureaucratic state and the encompassing employer organizations (Schmidt 1996b). French trade unions, which had always been ideologically divided into several competing organizations, were unable to respond to these changes collectively. Trade union density, traditionally one of the lowest in European comparison, fell from 20 per cent in the early 1970s to 8 per cent in the present (see Ebbinghaus and Visser 2000). What is already a low figure hides important disparities: over half the unions are in the public sector, which has a unionization level of about 15 per cent, while only 5 per cent of workers in the private sector (which accounts for 70 per cent of employment) are unionized. In other words, trade unions have almost no influence over important parts of the French economy, but remain strong in distinct 'fortresses' of unionization, such as the transport sector (Andolfatto and Labbé 2006b: 290). The privatization of public companies during the 1980s was therefore a further blow that contributed to the fall of trade union influence (Culpepper 2006). Figure 13.3 shows that strikes in the private sector have fallen sharply since the 1970s. Although strikes remain a feature of French politics, they now affect mainly the public sector.[9]

The reform of working time in the 1990s revealed the weakness of the organized social partners. Both the Robien Law of 1996 and the Aubry Laws of 1998 and 2000 encouraged firm-level negotiation over working time. Moreover, the government-imposed 35-hour week implemented by the Aubry Laws was experienced as a political embarrassment to employers (Woll 2006). Trade unions, in turn, found it difficult to organize effectively at the firm level: most of their past efforts had gone into the institutionalized bi-partite

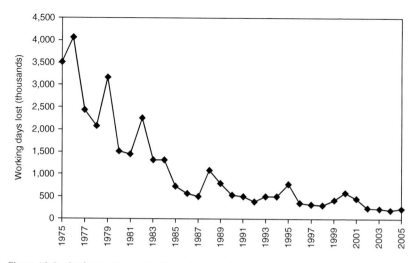

Figure 13.3   Strikes in France in the private sector
Source: French Ministry of Employment / DARES.

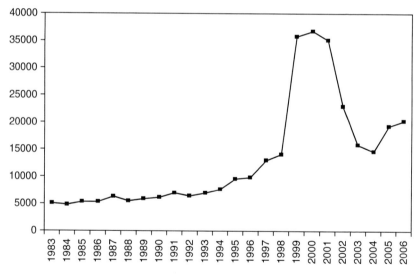

Figure 13.4   Evolution of collective agreements at the firm level
Source: French Ministry of Employment / DARES.

institutions and large-scale protest. A set of legal exemptions introduced in
the 1980s and capped by the 2004 law on social dialogue steadily replaced
sectoral negotiations with firm level negotiations, which experienced an
important increase in the late 1990s (Jobert and Saglio 2004), as Figure 13.4

shows. Although the number of national and branch agreements has remained stable over the last 30 years, this development profoundly undermines the importance of collective bargaining in French labour relations.

A financing scandal of over €19 million withdrawn in cash by Denis Gautier-Sauvagnac, president of the Union des Industries et Métiers de la Métallurgie (UIMM), to 'smooth social relations' sheds further doubts about the capacity of the traditional social partners to renew themselves and reinvent their role in the social dialogue.[10] The battle that has broken out between the peak organization Medef (*Mouvement des enterprises de France*, formerly the *Conseil national du patronat français*) and UIMM over the consequences of this scandal illustrates how central the reform of industrial relations is to the cohesion of the French business associations. Unity among trade unions is no less difficult. Since the 1980s new unions and associations have been created to challenge the old pillars of French industrial relations. The state-recognized representative unions *Confédération générale du travail, Confédération française démocratique du travail, Force ouvrière, Confédération française des travailleurs chrétiens* and *Confédération générale des cadres* now compete with others that have split away, such as the *Union nationale des syndicats autonomes*, the *Fédération syndicale unitaire* and a group of ten trade unions under the label G-10 SUD.[11] The diversification on the employer side is comparable, even though the Medef can claim to represent about 60 per cent of French firms (see Woll 2006).

However, while internal fragmentation and de-unionization has undermined the collective bargaining capacities of the social partners, it has not kept them from contributing to public debates and challenging government initiative. The most noted initiative of Medef, the 'social refoundation' launched in 1999 and the successful large-scale protests orchestrated by trade unions against a new employment contract (the *contrat première embauche*) in the fall of 2006 even led Mark Vail (2007) to speak of 'competitive interventionism' in France, where the state competes with the social partners for control over the direction of socio-economic reform. Whether the social partners compete indeed on equal footing with the state is doubtful, but it is true that the French government focuses on structured dialogue with societal stakeholders in recent years and delegates parts of its programmes to societal groups for implementation. It is now more and more likely that governmental projects will be submitted for discussion with the social partners to assure some sort of consensus, but many observers highlight that 'discussion' does not imply 'negotiation' (e.g. Andolfatto and Labbé 2006b: 285). By controlling policy initiatives and shifting its actions from direct intervention to enabling policies, the government remains central in shaping socio-economic institutions in France. The social partners have largely failed to become institutionalized pillars of some form of neo-corporatist governance at the national level. However, as forums for dialogue and deliberations, the traditional trade unions and employer associations, just like their new competitors, have become part of the policy networks that influence the evolution of individual issues. To see how this is possible, we have to turn to the new role of associations in French politics more generally.

13.2.2   The functions of associational representation

In his survey of the evolution of industrial relations in France, Michel Lallement (2006: 50) highlights that recent changes are based on a trend towards the 'contractualization of society'. By this he means that the French government no longer prescribes policy solutions, but oversees the negotiations between stakeholders over the rules, practices and relationships that define social life. With the aim of a consensual outcome, these procedures encourage stakeholders to be constructive and autonomous, but nonetheless bind them by contractual solidarity. This trend towards consensus-oriented negotiations applies not just to industrial relations but to state–society relations in France in general. To avoid extensive protest and ensure effective governance the French government increasingly privileges stakeholder groups as partners in the elaboration and implementation of policy initiatives. In this framework associations play an important role as forums for deliberation, as identity communities and as implementation networks. Let us consider each of these in turn.

Numerous scholars have pointed out the rising importance of deliberation as an element of democratic decision-making.[12] By emphasizing inclusion, compromise and transparency, deliberative decision-making implies greater openness to groups that can define themselves as stakeholders. In doing so the consultation with associations increases the legitimacy of the policy process and appears to provide a partial remedy to the 'crisis of representation' noted by many observers of the French political system (e.g. Berger 2006).

However, deliberation does not mean that outcomes are necessarily consensual. Grossman and Saurugger (2006) distinguish between competitive and cooperative deliberation to clarify this point. Under competitive deliberation, associations express their often conflicting opinions on a policy issue in a public debate and use media or mass communication strategies to sway public opinion. Ultimately, citizens or their elected representatives act as judges in determining the public interest. The new strategy of the employer association Medef epitomizes this trend. Breaking with its rather secretive and informal public intervention of the CNPF, Medef has concentrated on extensive media campaigns and outreach programmes aimed to affect public opinion.[13] Other social actors actively contest the propositions made by Medef on socio-economic issues in equally public campaigns. The objective of these campaigns is not to reach a compromise, but to make one's opinion heard and to determine the terms of a debate, with the ultimate goal of swaying legislators by means of public opinion pressures (see Manin 2004).

Cooperative deliberation describes procedures that aim to define a policy strategy all actors can agree on. Grossman and Saurugger (2006: 311) note that cooperative deliberation was the objective of two series of legislation in France in the 1990s. Consultation with and information of local stakeholders became central to urban and regional policy in the early 1990s. In 1995 the Barnier law made consultation obligatory and created the National Commission for Public Debate (*Commission nationale du débat public* – CNDP). In the late 1990s several government bills opened up policy processes to interest groups, in particular regional and sustainable development and urban policy. Associations become thus an increasingly institutionalized part of public deliberation procedures, even in areas that were not marked by sector-specific corporatism.

A second function of associations in political life in France comes with the first. Since associations now participate in politics on behalf of very diverse sets of groups in French society, they act as identity communities that allow for a heterogeneous representation of French citizens. Political parties no longer contribute to the mass integration of well defined social groups. As they have turned into parliamentary and campaign organizations that are largely candidate-centred, identification with political parties and party loyalty are declining (Manin 1997: 193–235). In this context, associations seem to provide an alternative to what some criticize as outdated ideological cleavages. Participation in sector and issue-specific groups is seen as an instrument to 'modernize politics', to bring it closer to citizens and their preoccupations (Barthélemy 2000: 92). Put differently, associations allow for a representation of what is experienced as the new structure of French society. According to Alain Touraine (1991), the vertical organization of society around the capital/labour conflict is being replaced by a horizontal organization of society around a centre of insiders that are integrated into the labour market, surrounded by a periphery of excluded outsiders. Unlike the traditional social partners and political parties that are still marked by the vertical cleavages of society, associational representation promises to give a voice to those that would otherwise be left out of the system of representation. The associations of 'withouts', those without citizenship rights (*les sans papiers*), employment or housing, are an example of this trend. Just like economic exclusion, political exclusion is one of the primary reasons for political engagement: in many cases, associations form to politicize issues that its members consider to be insufficiently treated in the established political process, such as gender relations, racial discrimination, homosexual rights, child protection or ecological issues.

However, while associations serving as identity communities perform an important function, one should be careful not to overestimate their capacity to create trust and civic engagement more generally (see Mayer 2003), a hypothesis often put forward by the social capital literature. Where political representation is experienced as a failure, associational participation does little to remedy political conflict, as one might argue in light of the recurrent outbreaks of violence in the French suburbs.

A final function of associations is their role as local networks to which the French government delegates important implementation and surveillance tasks. As Grossman and Saurugger (2004: 211) note, the new state–society equilibrium results in 'increased auto-regulation of a number of public policies'. Depending on the sector and the issue, it is not uncommon to see private actors govern different elements of public policy without any or with only limited intervention from the state or the traditional social partners. In the context of decentralization, Le Galès (2006: 203) highlights the fact that associations act as quasi-services for local government by running festive or social services, and that private–public partnerships are common in the provision of environment, transport or housing services. This echoes Lallement's insistence on the contractualization of French society: where they appear to represent legitimate stakeholders in a policy process, associations may be called upon to assure new forms of regulation for the issues that concern them.

13.3 Conclusion

The rise of associations clearly responds to changes in the French state–society relations. Many of the central elements of statist policy-making are transforming and have moved towards greater inclusion of non-governmental actors. While Levy (1999) rightly noticed the partial incapacity of the traditional social partners to rise up to these new opportunities, it is difficult to argue that the statist tradition has stifled associational participation in all aspects of French political life. On the contrary, associational life is striving and non-governmental groups participate actively in both the elaboration and the implementation of new policy initiatives.

Announcing the advent of pluralism and a retreat of the state would nonetheless fail to capture the current French model of state–society relations. By organizing and monitoring the contractualization of society, the French state remains in control over socio-economic reforms and paces both the agenda-setting and the schedules of reform. This applies to associational participation as well as the relationship with the traditional social partners. A recent reform proposal of French labour contracts was given to the social partners for discussion, but Nicolas Sarkozy tellingly announced that the French government will take over the policy initiative if the negotiating parties failed to develop an agreement by the end of 2007.[14]

Furthermore, by decentralizing negotiations and multiplying the forums for deliberation, the French government has actually increased its autonomy from societal groups. If negotiations advance at different speeds in separate forums, it becomes much harder to organize nation-wide resistance, even on issues which apply in a similar manner to a diverse set of stakeholders. By orchestrating protest into competitive or cooperative deliberation and by including associations as stakeholders that it can partially delegate policy tasks to if it so chooses, the French state firmly remain in the driving seat of socio-economic governance.

In comparison, the developments in France illustrate two more general trends that have been observed in a number of countries. First, governments now orient their policies to encourage associations in order to foster social capital. Despite the traditional mistrust in France towards all forms of civil groups, the French government now supports associational life and increasingly consults with stakeholders and interest groups. This participatory turn leads to an extensive and lively association tissue and presents a move towards pluralist policy-making. Second, neo-corporatist institutions are increasingly under pressure, even in a country which was always a mixed case with a special emphasis on jointly management sectoral governance. The paradox of the participatory turn comes from these two simultaneous movements. The social partners are least able to benefit from the changes in French state–society relations, because they have to straddle an old system that many argue should be reformed and new opportunities, which they will only be able to seize if they can reinvent themselves.

Notes

1. The heated debates surrounding state–church relations explain why over 30 proposed laws on associational freedom had failed to pass between 1870 and 1901. Four years later, France formally separated state and church through the law of 9 December 1905.
2. See Assemblée Nationale, 'Proposition de résolution tendant à modifier le Règlement de l'Assemblée nationale pour établir des règles de transparence concernant les groupes d'intérêt', 13eme Législature, No. 156, 29 October 2007.
3. Since no information is supplied when associations cease to operate, the total of existing associations in France relies on various estimation procedures. See Decool (2005: 9–12).
4. Summaries of events organized at the National Assembly, the Senate, the Economic and Social Council, the Constitutional Court, the European Parliament or at regional institutions in 2001 can be found in Conseil national de la vie associative (2003: 11–38).
5. This arrangement only lasted until May 2007. Following the merging of several responsibilities, the Ministry is now in charge of health, youth and athletics.
6. Jean François Lamour's speech of 8 July 2004 is reproduced in Conseil national de la vie associative (2007).
7. Jean-Pierre Raffarin's speech of 10 March 2004 is reproduced in Conseil national de la vie associative (2007).
8. The measures adopted or initiated at this conference included an increased reliance on consultation and information, increased financial aid to associations, as well as recognitions and rewards for voluntary service. A complete list can be found in Conseil national de la vie associative (2007: 65).
9. Working days lost to public sector strikes have now overtaken private sector strikes, with much noticed peaks in 1989, 1995, 2000 and 2007. Starting in 1996, transport sector strikes are excluded from the private sector statistics and grouped with public sector transport strikes. For further discussion, see Lallement (2006: 63).

10. 'Patronat et organisations syndicales: un système à bout de souffle', *Le Monde Economie*, Dossier Spécial, 30 October 2007: i–viii.
11. All of the new unions are not recognized as representative organizations, even though each of them represents more members than some of the smaller recognized ones. See Andolfatto and Labbé (2006a).
12. For discussion and a French perspective, see Blondiaux and Sintomer (2002).
13. The election of Laurence Parisot, CEO of a French public opinion research institute, as president of Medef in 2005 confirms the importance of this strategy.
14. Remi Barroux, 'Contrat de travail unique: la négociation ou la loi', *Le Monde*, 7 September 2007.

Bibliography

Andolfatto, Dominique and Dominique Labbé (2006a). *Histoire des syndicats, 1906–2006.* (Paris: Seuil).

Andolfatto, Dominique and Dominique Labbé (2006b). 'La transformation des syndicats français: vers un nouveau "modèle social"?' *Revue française de science politique* 56:2, 281–98.

Appleton, Andrew (2005). 'Associational Life in Contemporary France', in: Alistair Cole, Patrick Le Galès and Jonah D. Levy (eds), *Developments in French Politics.* (Basingstoke: Palgrave Macmillan, 54–69).

Barthélemy, Martine (2000). *Associations: Un nouvel âge de la participation?* (Paris: Presses de Sciences Po).

Belorgey, Jean-Michel (2000). *Cent ans de vie associative.* (Paris: Presses de Sciences Po).

Berger, Suzanne (2006). 'Representation in Trouble', in: Pepper D. Culpepper, Peter A. Hall and Bruno Palier (eds), *Changing France: The Politics that Markets Make.* (Basingstoke: Palgrave Macmillan, 276–91).

Blondiaux, Loïc and Yves Sintomer (2002). 'L'impératif délibératif', *Politix* 15(57): 17–35.

Conseil national de la vie associative (2003). *Bilan de la vie associative 2000–2002.* (Paris: La documentation française).

Conseil national de la vie associative (2007). *Bilan de la vie associative 2004–2007.* (Paris: La documentation française).

Culpepper, Pepper D. (2003). *Creating Cooperation: How States Develop Human Capital in Europe.* (Ithaca: Cornell University Press).

Culpepper, Pepper (2006). 'Capitalism, Coordination, and Economic Change: The French Political Economy since 1985', in: Pepper Culpepper, Peter A. Hall and Bruno Palier (eds), *Changing France: The Politics that Markets Make.* (Basingstoke: Palgrave Macmillan, 29–49).

Decool, Jean-Pierre (2005). *Des associations, en général... vers une éthique sociétale.* Rapport au Premier Ministre. Mission parlementaire auprès de Jean-François Lamour, Ministre de la Jeunesse, des Sports et de la Vie Associative.

Ebbinghaus, Bernhard and Jelle Visser (2000). *Trade Unions in Western Europe since 1945.* (New York: Grove's Dictionaries).

Febvre, Michèle and Lara Muller (2003). 'Une personne sur deux est membre d'une association en 2002', *INSEE Première*: 920, www.insee.fr/fr/ffc/ficdoc_frame.asp?ref_id=ip920.

Febvre, Michèle and Lara Muller (2004). 'La vie associative en 2002: 12 millions de bénévoles', *INSEE Première* 946, www.insee.fr/fr/ffc/ficdoc_frame.asp?ref_id=ip946.

Grossman, Emiliano and Sabine Saurugger (2004). 'Challenging French Interest Groups: The State, Europe and the International Political System', *French Politics and Society* 2:2, 203–20.

Grossman, Emiliano and Sabine Saurugger (2006). 'Les groupes d'intérêt au secours de la démocratie?' *Revue française de science politique* 56(2): 299–321.

Jobert, Bruno and Pierre Muller (1987). *L'Etat en action: politiques publiques et corporatismes*. (Paris: Presses Universitaires de France).

Jobert, Bruno and Jean Saglio (2004). 'Ré-institutionaliser la négociation collective en France', *Travail et Emploi*: 113–27.

Ladrech, Robert (1994). 'Europeanization of Domestic Politics and Institutions: The case of France', *Journal of Common Market Studies* 32(1): 69–88.

Lallement, Michel (2006). 'New Patterns of Industrial Relations and Political action since the 1980s', in: Pepper Culpepper, Peter A. Hall and Bruno Palier (eds), *Changing France: The Politics that Markets Make*. (Basingstoke: Palgrave Macmillan, 50–79).

Le Galès, Patrick (2006). 'The Ongoing March of Decentralisation within the Post-Jacobin State', in: Pepper Culpepper, Peter A. Hall and Bruno Palier (eds), *Changing France: The Politics that Markets Make*. (Basinstoke: Palgrave Macmillan, 198–219).

Lelieveledt, Herman and Manuela Cainani (2007). 'The Political Role of Associations', in: William A. Maloney and Sigrid Roßteutscher (eds), *Social Capital and Associations in European Democracies*. (London: Routledge, 175–91).

Levy, Jonah D. (1999). *Tocqueville's Revenge: State, Society, and Economy in Contemporary France*. (Cambridge, Mass.: Harvard University Press).

Madison, James (2004 [1787]). 'Federalist Paper No. 10', in: Alexander Hamilton, James Madison and John Jay (eds), *The Federalist Papers*. (New York: Pocket Books).

Maloney, William A. and Sigrid Roßteutscher (eds) (2007). *Social Capital and Associations in European Democracies: A Comparative Analysis*. (London: Routledge).

Manin, Bernard (1997). *The Principles of Representative Government*. (Cambridge: Cambridge University Press).

Manin, Bernard (2004). 'Déliberation et discussion', *Revue suisse de science politique* 10(4):180–93.

Manin, Bernard (2007). 'Post-Script to the German Edition', in: Bernard Manin (ed.), *Kritik der Repräsentativen Demokratie*. (Berlin: Matthes und Seitz, 486).

Mayer, Nonna (2003). 'Democracy in France: Do Associations Matter?' in: Dietlind Stolle and Marc Hooghe (eds), *Generating Social Capital: Civil Society and Institutions in Comparative Perspective*. (Basingstoke: Palgrave Macmillan, 43–66).

Morris, Charles R. (1996). *The AARP: America's Most Powerful Lobby and the Clash of Generations*. (New York: Times Books).

Olson, Mancur (1965). *The Logic of Collective Action: Public Goods and the Theory of Groups*. (Cambridge, Mass.: Harvard University Press).

Rousseau, Jean-Jacques (2006 [1762]). *The Social Contract*. (New York: Penguin Books).

Saurugger, Sabine and Emiliano Grossman (2006). 'Les groupes d'intérêt en France: transformation des rôles et enjeux politiques', *Revue Française de Science Politique* 56(2): 197–203.

Schmidt, Vivien A. (1996a). *From State to Market? The Transformation of French Business and Government*. (Cambridge: Cambridge University Press).

Schmidt, Vivien A. (1996b). 'Loosening the Ties that Bind: The Impact of European Integration on French Government and Its Relationship to Business', *Journal of Common Market Studies* 34(2): 223–54.

Siaroff, Alan (1999). 'Corporatism in 24 industrial democracies: Meaning and Measurement', *European Journal of Political Research* 36(2): 175–205.

Smismans, Stijn (2006). *Civil Society and Legitimate European Governance*. (Cheltenham, UK: Edward Elgar).

de Tocqueville, Alexis (1966 [1835/1840]). *Democracy in America*. 1st Perennial classics. Auflage. (New York: Harper & Row).

Touraine, Alain (1991). 'Face à l'exclusion', *Esprit* (February): 7–13.

Vail, Mark I. (2007). 'The Evolution of Bargaining under Austerity: Political Change in Contemporary French and German Labor-Market Reform', *MPIfG Discussion Paper* 07:10, http://www.mpi-fg-koeln.mpg.de/pu/mpifg_dp/dp07-10.pdf.

Van Ruysseveldt, Joris and Jelle Visser (1996). 'Contestation and state intervention forever? Industrial relations in France', in: Joris Van Ruysseveldt and Jelle Visser (eds), *Industrial Relations in Europe: Traditions and Transitions*. (London: Sage Publications, 82–123).

Weisbein, Julien (2005). 'La vie associative and the State: unequal partners in the French debate on Europe', in: Helen Drake, ed., *French Relations with the European Union*. (London: Routledge, 146–63).

Wilson, Frank L. (1987). *Interest-Group Politics in France*. (Cambridge: Cambridge University Press).

Woll, Cornelia (2006). 'National Business Associations under Stress: Lessons from the French Case', *West European Politics* 29(3): 489–512.

Part III
The Republican Universal Model as Institution

14
Republican Universalism Faces the Feminist Challenge: The Continuing Struggle for Gender Equality

Eléonore Lépinard and Amy G. Mazur

As this book shows more generally, the republican universal model has been an important institution in French political life under the Fifth Republic. In this chapter we examine the implications of that model for the political pursuit of gender equality under the Fifth Republic through a range of state actions by the various actors that have mobilized around demands for improved women's rights, equality between the sexes and the reduction of gender-based hierarchies that contribute to those inequities. Using a rich, multi-disciplinary literature in English and in French, including the French results of a cross-national study of women's policy agencies and women's movements, we argue that despite ongoing efforts by the individuals and groups that have mobilized around feminist issues both inside and outside of the state, a gender-biased universal model continues to be an important impediment to achieving authoritative policy in this area and making progress towards achieving equality between the sexes. Across a variety of domains, women's status and condition still lags significantly behind men's; in some areas women's socio-economic status has failed to progress or has even worsened in recent years.

The first part of the chapter presents the notion of gender-biased universalism and traces the interplay between gender and the republican model from its consolidation in the 1960s to its resilience in the face of the rise of second-wave feminist movements in the 1970s and, in the 1980s, the emergence of relatively strong state-based policy agencies charged with promoting women's rights and gender equality. In the second part we take a closer look at the interplay between policy formation and the gender-biased republican model from the 1970s to the early 2000s through examining the 'symbolic reform dynamic' in gender equality and gender-related policy through, first, the French results of an international study on state feminism and, second, published research on feminist policy formation in the early 2000s. In the last section we present the two issues that have shaped recent reconfigurations in gender politics: parity and diversity. From a close reading of the wealth of scholarship on gender and politics in France, we challenge the conventional wisdom about the weakness of the French women's movement and the women-friendly nature of left-wing governments. We also emphasize the importance of Europe and the EU integration process for the pursuit of gender equality as well as the need to look outside of Paris-based politics to fully understand the evolution of gender equality politics under the Fifth Republic.

14.1   Taking a gendered approach to the universal republican model

The French state has been characterized by scholars as the champion of 'republican universalism'. The term can designate alternatively or simultaneously a political doctrine, a political culture or a conception of nationhood and citizenship (Rosanvallon 1992; Brubaker 1992; Schnapper 1994). It commonly refers to the revolutionary roots of the French political system and to the idea that granting rights and equality to individuals as abstract figures, not as concrete group members, is a potent tool for emancipation (Rosanvallon 1998). Feminist scholars have shown that republican universalism implies a specific gender bias: the necessity to ignore citizens' social, economic and status differences in order to grant them individual rights, freedom and equality. It also led to the exclusion of those who were perceived as 'different', namely women, from the public space (Landes 1988; Scott 1996; Fraisse 1989, 1996). The universal abstract figure of the citizen therefore hides, since the French Revolution, a masculine persona and state policies define women as a *particular* group marked by a difference – gender – that needs specific policies that tend to reinforce traditional gender roles and create a dual citizenship (Lewis 1992; Siim 2000). Here we discuss how this model evolved under the Fifth Republic to be an important obstacle in the articulation of gender equality claims and policy, a force that still drives gender politics and policy today.

The impact of republican universalism on gender relations, feminist mobilization and gender equality policies has been explored through various lenses. Several features of the Fifth Republic's institutions have been characterized as gender biased: the system of political representation that favors the election of men despite its formal gender neutrality (Sineau 2001), family policies which have oscillated between reinforcing traditional gender roles and promoting women's autonomy (Commaille 1993; Jenson and Sineau 2003; Revillard 2006), and even equal employment policies or *égalité professionnelle* (Lanquetin et al. 2000; Laufer 2003; Mazur 1995a).[1] In each policy domain, formal neutrality and abstract universalism on one hand makes it difficult to raise issues of gender difference which are crucial to any treatment of sex-based inequalities and, on the other, hides a differential treatment of women, who are often confined to their traditional gender role in the private sphere. Despite major victories for gender equality since 1958, Republican institutions, public policies and political discourses have therefore curtailed feminist gains. What is more, both-right wing and left-wing governments have contributed to the development of the gender-biased model. Indeed, despite important differences in their approaches – one can contrast for example François Mitterand's 1965 platform for women emphasizing their autonomy with de Gaulle's labeling of a women's bureau as a 'ministry of knitting' – as early as 1984 Mitterrand abandoned his commitments in favor of women's rights (Jenson and Sineau 1995) and right-wing President Valéry Giscard d'Estaing established the first cabinet level office for 'women's status' in 1974 against his own political camp.

This double language of universalism and gender difference has also affected the way women mobilize under the Fifth Republic to gain new rights. French feminists, as well as femocrats – the bureaucrats who work for state-based agencies charged with gender equality and women's rights – have also been trapped since the 1950s in this dilemma (Jenson 1985; Jenson and Sineau 1994). The interplay between gender and republican universalism has moved through three distinct periods: during the 1960s the gender-biased model was consolidated, especially in the domain of family policies, despite the simultaneous emergence of activist women's policy agencies. From the 1970s to the mid-1980s the gender-biased model was challenged both by an autonomous feminist movement and a stronger women's rights administration. In the 1990s, the last period, as radicalism faded away, the women's movement has contributed to the stability of state feminist institutions, despite severe cutbacks, hence providing a continuous challenge to the gender biased model. We examine the evolution of this model up through the 1980s in the rest of this section to set the stage for our analysis of feminist politics and policy that follows.

14.1.1   The institutionalization of gender-biased universalism in the 1960s

Governments of the Fifth Republic became interested in gender through two different approaches: familialism and women's work. Familialism was the official doctrine of the Republic, and quite incompatible with women's rights as individuals. The constant fear of depopulation and the postwar re-establishment of a traditional gender order combined to incite women to leave the workforce and benefit from generous family policies (Offen 1984; Jenson 1986; Commaille 1993; Revillard 2006). Women's associations mainly mobilized around the same issues: maternity provisions and benefits, and women's roles and rights as mothers. Simultaneously, the preoccupations with women's work, a consequence of women's increased participation in paid labor, was reflected in the creation in 1965 of the first women's bureau, dedicated to women's employment: *le Comité du travail féminin*. The *Comité* paved the way for a new approach inside the Republic's institutions. Despite the usual ambivalences vis-à-vis the 'difference' of women and the necessity for women, and not men, to reconcile work and family, the *Comité* initiated a critique of the previous governmental policies and changed the approach from women's protection through social and labor policies, to women's promotion, slowly emphasizing the need to encourage women's active participation in the workforce.

14.1.2   The critique of gender-biased universalism in the 1970s and 1980s

The 1970s opened a new era, both for women's mobilization and for the Republic's response to women's demands. The second-wave feminist movement decisively broke with the familialist and maternalist approaches, by directing its actions on sexuality, abortion and contraception. This new focus emphasized women's autonomy as individuals rather than as mothers and in that particular domain the feminist movement challenged the Republic's gender bias: for the first time women obtained new rights *as* women, not as mothers, rights that were not protections but tools for emancipation (Jenson 1985). The French second-wave women's movement was characterized by a strong revolutionary component that eschewed reform-oriented activities and coalition building with the left-wing parties and unions (e.g., Duchen 1986; Jenson 1990). However, despite the pronounced anti-system tendency of the second wave of French feminism, a strong feminist presence developed simultaneously within the state through the women's policy offices. Responding to pressure from the street, as well as to international pressure preceding the 1975 United Nations Conference on Women in Mexico, President Giscard d'Estaing created a low-level cabinet position in charge of the 'women's question' in 1974. The office was upgraded to a delegate ministry in 1978 under the center-right Barre government and continued under the Socialist government when the left arrived in power in 1981 with Socialist, Yvette Roudy's, Delegate Ministry of Woman's Rights (Mazur 1995b; Revillard 2006).

For the first time a major law in favor of equal employment for women was adopted in 1983. Despite this symbolic victory equal employment policies remained confronted with steadfast opposition, from both state institutions based in the Ministries of Employment/Social Affairs and trade unions, as well as from indifferent employers (Mazur 1995a). Similarly, the attempt of Socialist MP and feminist activist Gisèle Halimi to introduce a quota in favor of female candidates on municipal election lists met with fierce resistance. The quota amendment proposed by Halimi was rejected by the Constitutional Council in the name of republican universalism; positive differential treatment for women henceforth could not be considered as a tool to achieve gender equality.

14.1.3 Resisting and recovering: from 1985 onwards

During the first half of the 1980s the powerful feminist Roudy Ministry under the Socialist government built many bridges with the women's movement, and the anti-system stance held by some of the women's movements of the 1970s led way to more open cooperation. This new alliance helped the women's rights administration survive from 1985 up to the end of the 1990s when it was threatened by political instability and low funding. Despite a period of low mobilization in the 1980s, with women's movement activity primarily located in the political parties and trade unions through women's commissions, each time governments downgraded state feminist institutions the movement mobilized to ensure their durability (Revillard 2007). This collaboration shows progressive penetration of the state machinery by feminists and femocrats and a better representation of women's interests despite the permanence of the gender-biased model that was an important force in the way gender issues were dealt with across a range of policy issues from the 1970s to the late 1990s and in the formation of feminist policy in the early 2000s, to be examined in the next section.

14.2 How the Fifth Republic resists: The symbolic reform imperative, 1970–2000

As research on feminist policy in France and other western democracies has shown, 'feminist' government action – defined as policies that aim to promote women's rights and/or strike down sex-based hierarchies – tends to have a 'symbolic reform' imperative (Mazur 1995a; 2002). Building from Edelman's (1971) notion of symbolic politics, symbolic reform has come to mean policies that have clearly stated goals, with little 'policy feedback' where governments make little or no effort to implement policy and few groups are interested in seeing that the policies are implemented and enforced; in other words, policy 'outputs' without policy feedback. The analysis in this section examines the symbolic imperative from two different vantage points: in an overview of the French results from the study conducted by the Research Network on Gender Politics and the State (RNGS) in five policy areas from the 1970s to 2000 and a summary of an assessment of explicitly feminist policies adopted from 2000 to 2005.

14.2.1 Gender and public policy from the 1970s to 2000: The RNGS results on France

The Research Network on Gender Politics and the State is a research group of over 40 members founded in 1995 to systematically study the impact of women's policy offices and women's movements on government action in 17 western post-industrial democracies. RNGS assessed the impact of women's policy machinery across four different policy areas that have the potential to affect gender relations – job training (JT), abortion (AB), prostitution (PT), political representation (PR) – as well as a fifth policy area of high priority within a given country on a 'hot issue' (HI). The group developed a multi-stage research design and administered the study over ten years, producing a book on each issue area, a dataset and a capstone book on all five issue areas.[2]

For each issue area in each country in the study experts analysed the impact of women's movements and women's policy machineries in three policy debates and the formal decisions that ended them, usually but not always legislation. The three debates selected for study had to represent the range of policy debates in that area over time and at different levels of government. For each debate RNGS researchers used 'process tracing' (McKeown 2004) based on archival research, interviews and an exhaustive consultation of secondary sources to analyse to what degree 1) the women's policy agencies (WPAs) during the debate advanced women's movement demands and changed the terms of the debate to focus on gender – men's and women's identities in relation to each other or 'Women's Policy Agency Activities', and 2) the women's movement actors (WMAs) participated in the debate arena and their demands were contained in the final state decision or 'State Response to Women's Movement Activism'. RNGS combined the two dimensions to assess the level of women's movement – women's policy agency alliances in each debate studied.

Table 14.1 presents the pattern of alliances in 15 French policy debates across the five policy areas.[3] The most successful alliances between women's policy agencies and women's movements, INSIDER/DUAL RESPONSE, are those where the agencies support women's movement positions and gender the debate and women's movement actors actively participated in the debate and their demands become incorporated in the final decision, usually a law. The least successful cases, SYMBOLIC/NO RESPONSE, are those where the agency neither supports the demands of the women's movement nor introduces a gender frame into the debate and women's movement actors are absent from the debate and the decision contains no WMA demands. As Table 14.1 shows, there are few complete successes or complete failures in France.

In two out of the five debates, both in the 1980s, the relatively powerful Minister for Woman's Rights, Yvette Roudy, under the Socialist Mauroy government for the abortion debate and the Deputy Secretary for Women's Rights in the Rocard Socialist government successfully gendered the debate frame, supported women's movement position in the debate; women's movement actors participated in the debate and were able to have some demands included in the final decision – the reimbursement of abortion expense in the first case and the rejection of discussion of regulating prostitution which included a feminist approach to prostitution in the second. In the case of the single failure the same Minister of Woman's Rights neither supported the demands of MP Halimi to insert the quota for women on municipal electoral

Table 14.1 Patterns of WM–WPA alliances in France

INSIDER/DUAL RESPONSE:	
AB: Reimbursement of abortion expenses (L)	1981–83
PT: Public health/AIDS (L)	1989–90
INSIDER/PREEMPTION:	
AB: Penal sanction for anti-abortion protesters (L)	1991–93
PR: Parity reform (L)	1995–2000
MARGINAL/ PREEMPTION:	
JT: Representation of workers' interests (L)	1982–84
PT: Penal code reform of pimping and solicitation (L)	1991–92
HI: 35-hour work-week reforms (L)	1997–2000
MARGINAL/ NO RESPONSE:	
JT: Youth training and placement (R)	1978–80
PR: Reform of national electoral system (L)	1985
JT: Employer job training contribution (L)	1991
JT: Job training and reinsertion (R)	1993
JT: Job training and decentralization (R)	1993
NON ALLY or SYMBOLIC/PRE-EMPTION:	
PT: Prostitutes' rights and law enforcement (R)	1972–75
AB: Reaffirmation of legal abortion (R)	1979
SYMBOLIC/ NO RESPONSE	
PR: Reform of municipal electoral system (L)	1981–82

Notes: L = Left-wing governing majority; R = Right-wing governing majority.

lists, nor attempted to introduce any gender concerns into the debate. The rate of failure in France is similar to other countries in the study, between 5 and 10 per cent; however, the rate of success in France (13 per cent) was lower than in Canada (40 per cent), Finland (30 per cent), Great Britain (50 per cent), and Italy (40 per cent).[4]

While it is clear that the less successful alliances occurred in the 1970s under right-wing governments – in the case of the debate on prostitutes' rights in the 1970s and the 1978 law to re-affirm abortion, women's policy agencies were absent from the debates and women's movements had some success, but were not present in the debate – there was neither a linear movement toward successful alliances across-time nor a record of alliance success under left-wing governments. On one hand debates on parity and abortion rights in the 1990s witnessed near successful alliances under left-wing governments, with only the absence of significant women's movement participation. On the other hand, the three job training debates in the 1990s, one under a left-wing government, displayed lower levels of alliances success with agencies supporting women's movement demands but unable to change the terms of the mainstream employment debates and no evidence of any women's movement impact. A similar dynamic of resistance occurred in the late 1990s in the case of the 35-hour work week reforms adopted by the Socialists, except that the final reforms contained stipulations that reflected women's movement demands to a certain degree. The low level of alliances in the 1990s even under left-wing women friendly governments points to the resilience of the gender-biased model, particularly in the employment arena where the policy subsystem was firmly closed to women's movement actors and the dominant actors there, trade unions, employers and representatives from the Labor ministry, were opposed to taking on board ideas of gender equality in any serious manner.

The symbolic reform imperative can be identified here too; one which appears to be still prevalent at the end of the 1990s. Out of the 15 cases, seven debates ended with a decision that reflected the women's movement demands without any women's movement participation, PREEMPTION, a form of symbolic reform. In three of these more symbolic debates the WPA also presented women's movement demands in the debate and gendered the debate – indicating more WPA involvement and policy change, moving the policy away from purely symbolic reform. In the remaining symbolic cases, however, the WPA either failed to gender the debate (MARGINAL), in three cases, or failed to support women's movement actors (NON ALLY), in the 1979 law to reaffirm legal abortion, or did neither in the case of the debate on prostitutes' rights and law enforcement that led to the Pinot Report in 1975 (SYMBOLIC). There is neither a pattern away from symbolic reform over time – the least symbolic cases of INSIDER/DUAL RESPONSE occurred in the 1980s – nor is symbolic reform associated with a given policy area – PREEMPTION occurred in all of the policy areas.

14.2.2   The dynamics and determinants of feminist policy formation, 2000–2005

Following on from where the RNGS data left off, an examination of five key areas of explicitly feminist policy in the early 2000s, and not just policies that have the potential to affect gender relations, shows that the grip of the republican gender-biased model began to be loosened with the development of a more gendered approach to public policy beginning in 2000; an approach that has become increasingly accepted by policy actors and decision makers both inside and outside of the state.[5] An unprecedented culmination of five contextual factors created a favorable environment for the development of more concrete policies on women's rights and gender equality, what Kingdon (1995), Keeler (1993) and others have called a policy window or for social movement scholars, like McAdam et al. (1996) a favorable Political Opportunity Structure.

The first important factor was that while the differences between men's and women's status and condition persisted, and researchers and the media drew attention to the persistence of sex-based inequities, public opinion polls showed that the French were becoming more open to gender equality and the need to close the sex gap. For example, with regards to women's status in paid labor, women's unemployment was the same in 2000 as in 1990 around 11 per cent, compared with men's unemployment rates of 6 per cent in 1990 and 7.6 per cent in 2000 (Eurostat 2002, p. 182). The sex gap in salaries has been stalled since the 1980s – in 2000 women still earned 80 per cent of what men do overall (Laufer 2003). The percentage of working women in part-time jobs increased from 24 per cent in 1990 to 29.9 per cent in 1999, and since the 1970s women have continued to make up over 80 per cent of all part-time work, among the highest levels of women's share of part-time work among the OECD countries (OECD in O'Connor et al. 1999, p. 72).

Second, the women's movement became revitalized in the mid-1990s through the emergence of active reform-oriented groups around specific issues such as sexual violence, reproduction rights, sexism and parity in Paris and in the provinces in large cities like Marseille, and in less urbanized areas like Brittany (e.g., Mazur 2007a). These groups became active partners with women's policy machineries at national and sub-national levels to achieve a certain level of success in feminist policy under governments of the Left and the Right. This broad range of women's movement activities in the 1990s inside and outside of Paris challenges the stereotype of the French women's movements as being anti-system, deeply divided and Paris based.

A third important factor was the consolidation and increasing institutionalization of the women's policy machinery during this period. The strength of the women's policy administration was arguably at its high point in 2000, with a ministerial level office and large staff, a separate administrative bureau with five separate divisions one of which oversaw a territorial administration at the regional and departmental levels, three different commissions, an autonomous 'Observatoire de la parité', and newly established commissions on women's rights in the Senate and the National Assembly. Moreover, when a right-wing government came to power in 2002, the women's policy machinery was given the same, and arguably increased, support. For example, the Raffarin government upgraded the ministerial office for women's rights to a full-fledged ministry under Nicole Ameline in 2002.

A fourth important factor that set the stage for more concrete feminist policy formation was the ever-increasing pressure from the European Union and the integration process. EU gender equality policy was an important tool used by French femocrats and other feminist actors to convince recalcitrant policy makers to support women's rights policy. During this period, as femocrats interviewed for the study asserted, the new approach of the European Union to women's rights – gender mainstreaming where the treatment of gender equality is introduced across all policy sectors – became an accepted and much used policy tool in feminist policy circles.

A final contextual factor to be considered in the development of this 'macro reform window' (Keeler 1993) is the presence of a women-friendly left-wing government under Lionel Jospin from 1997 to 2002, a government that placed many of the policies examined here on the government's 'decision agenda' (Kingdon 1995). At the same time, the extent to which these policies were not just continued but elaborated upon under the right-wing Raffarin government and the Ameline ministry, as we show below, puts into question the conventional wisdom that left-wing governments are more women-friendly than their right-wing counterparts.

In the context of the particular combination of these five factors around 2000, feminist policies that had previously displayed quite symbolic imperatives, where formal texts and principles had been at best partially implemented (if not completely ignored) were suddenly given new attention, support, and resources by the government usually through the collaboration among women's policy offices, women's groups and feminist actors. In the area of reproduction, responding to the demands of feminist groups, the Jospin government pursued a new campaign on abortion rights and adopted a law that addressed the more blatant gaps in abortion rights. The right-wing Ameline ministry continued the implementation of these programs in collaboration with the women's groups through its inter-ministerial commission on reproduction and sexual information and the elaboration of the Equality Charter.

The Charter, defined by the Ameline ministry as a major instrument of gender mainstreaming, was a 280-page document that outlined detailed government plans, by sector and ministry. For the most part the measures included in the Charter reflected the earlier work of the women's rights administration and the various commissions; hence to a certain degree the positions of feminist groups and experts that were partners with the women's policy agencies. Over 300 representatives of non-feminist groups, ministries, and agencies signed the final charter which was presented to the public in March 2004. Each of the four other areas of feminist policy was specifically covered in the charter in the same systematic and detailed manner as reproduction policies.

A new equal employment law adopted under the Jospin government by the Minister of Women's Rights and Job Training, Nicole Péry, shored up the gaps in the implementation of equal employment plans in firms by making them required and creating a penalty for non-compliance. The Ameline ministry also adopted a more authoritative law on salaries to address the persistent gap between men's and women's salaries which had actually widened since the 1980s. The right-wing minister instituted a new equality label to be given to gender equality friendly firms. Reflecting the limits of this policy, only 30 firms received the label to date, instead of the hundreds expected by the Ministry. In the important feminist area of reconciling family and work obligations, governments of the Left and the Right had developed a relatively generous family leave policy that has increasingly provided incentives for women to either stay at home to raise their children or to pursue part-time work (Jenson and Sineau 2003). While formally the policy is designed for both men and women, in reality, as studies show, it reinforces gender roles and is taken up primarily by women. In this period, to address the slow take-up of family leave by men, a new daddy leave policy was instituted by the socialist government and in 2003 50 per cent of fathers took advantage of the new policy (Revillard 2007).

In the area of violence the left-wing Perry Ministry contracted a systematic study of domestic violence which was the first study of its kind to identify the incidence of domestic violence within marriage. New feminist groups from a younger generation also brought unprecedented attention to sexual violence (Ni Putes Ni Soumises) and sexual harassment in universities (Clasches). At the same time, when compared to other areas of feminist policy, more than any new authoritative policies it was the identification of the problem as a legitimate issue for government that was an important development during this period. As studies show (e.g., Saguy 2003), anti-sexual harassment policy remains highly contested both in terms of the issue of sexual harassment and how to end it. The 2000 parity laws, covered in greater detail in the next section, also were a result of the open reform window. On one hand, the principle of equal access to elected posts between men and women was codified for the first time in law and the constitution; on the other, efforts to implement the new policies have been circumscribed with relatively disappointing results (Lépinard 2007a)

Thus, in examining these five areas of feminist policy, we see that the symbolic reform imperative has been reduced, but not completely broken, with the adoption of more authoritative policy and a certain degree of interest on the part of the government and various groups in implementation. At the same time, policy implementation has remained circumscribed and women's status has not significantly increased (and in some areas has worsened) particularly in the feminization of poverty (e.g., Laufer 2003).

14.3 Parity and diversity: The dismantling of the republican model?

The effect of the republican model on feminist claims and gender politics is nowhere more apparent than in the domain of political representation and anti-discrimination/diversity policies. The parity reform deserves specific attention: because it took so long from the time the notion of parity appeared on the public scene in 1992 and its implementation in the 2001 municipal elections, because of its scope – the parity reform entailed a revision of articles 3 and 4 of the Constitution – and because of its impact in terms of women's numerical representation in elected offices (see Table 14.2). Is it a landmark in the history of gender politics under the Fifth Republic? To what extent has it gendered the Republic's institutions, its representatives and its policies? This section argues that despite its promise to undo gender-biased universalism, the parity reform consisted of piecemeal and incremental change rather than a broad-reaching reform. Diversity policies emerging at the turn of the twentieth century may have picked up the problem where parity reform left off; however, this broader scheme, which targets discrimination across several criteria (ethnic or racial origin, disability, age, religion, sexual orientation and gender) also risks diluting gender equality claims and policies.

14.3.1 Parity: Unfinished reform and partial gendering of the Republic

The parity claim initially challenged the gender bias at the core of the Republic's abstract citizenship model. Drawing on historical and philosophical premises parity advocates argue that the Republic had excluded, until 1945, women *qua* women, and therefore had to include them as women, not as abstract citizens. Denouncing the continuing exclusion of women from political office as a by-product of a masculine bias which regulates the political sphere, parity proponents claimed that only through positive action, a 50 per cent gender quota that would ensure women's equal presence with men in elected bodies, could women have access to fair political representation.[6] Hence parity aimed at redefining the legal terms of gender equality in the political sphere and challenged the republican doctrine of equality: contrary to formal equality, parity defines gender equality as equal presence, equal numbers, and this new substantive definition of equality implies affirmative action measures.

After several years of only relative successes in lobbying political parties to present more female candidates (Bereni 2006), the parity campaign gained momentum when Lionel Jospin, head of the Socialist Party, became Prime Minister in 1997 (Giraud and Jenson 2001). His commitment to parity, as well as President Chirac's long-awaited approval,[7] put the reform on the political agenda and the Constitution was revised in 1999 to enshrine in its article 3 the 'promotion of men and women's equal access to electoral mandates and functions', and to incite, via an amendment to its article 4, political parties to promote that new goal. Several laws to implement the new goal of gender equality in political representation were adopted in 2000.

As Table 14.2 shows, in 2008, after nearly a decade of implementation the results of the parity reform show a partial feminization of elected political elites. Unsurprisingly, the parity reform proved very efficient for list elections for which a 50/50 balance strictly applies to candidates' lists, and much less so for elections for which parity applies only partially (as for the Senate) or through financial incentives for political parties (as for legislative elections). Moreover, despite the explicit mention of all elected offices in the revised article 3 of the Constitution, no regulation was adopted by the National Assembly to ensure women's equal presence in executives of elected offices, which was implied by the new wording. The absence of any effort to promote women's presence at the head of elected councils effectively leaves in place a glass ceiling for women in the political sphere. Hence, parity has not

Table 14.2 Percentage of women in elected offices

	Before Parity	After Parity
Parity laws strictly apply		
Town Councils – cities over 3500 inhabitants	25.7 (1995)	47.4 (2001)
Regional Assemblies	27.5 (1998)	47.6 (2004)
European Parliament	40.2 (1999)	43.6 (2004)
Parity laws partially apply		
Legislative Assembly	10.9 (1997)	12.3 (2002) – 18.5 (2007)
Senate	10.9 (2001)	16.9 (2004)
Parity laws do not apply		
Town Councils – cities under 3500 inhabitants	21 (1995)	30 (2001)
General Councils	9.2 (2001)	10.4 (2004)

Data source: Observatoire de la parité – Ministry of Interior.

yet clearly challenged the gender bias inherent to the political system, the recruitment of its elites or the interests it represents.

As Table 14.2 indicates, some indicators point in the right direction: women constitute a growing critical mass of locally elected representative, new institutions, such as parliamentary commissions for women's rights in the National Assembly and the Senate and the Parity Observatory have taken root in the bureaucracy. In addition, for the first time in 2007, the Socialist party designated a woman, Ségolène Royal, as its candidate for the presidential elections. However, this shift in gender politics is not a change of tides. The political system still contributes to excluding women, especially those who already work a double shift as working mothers, and it remains difficult to evaluate how women's presence affect the content of public policies, that is, women's substantive representation in politics (Achin et al. 2007).

Beyond the increase in the number of women lies the question of the impact of the parity reform on republicanism as an institution: has parity challenged gender-biased universalism? Parity activist efforts to reclaim a share of abstract universalism in the name of women's difference have been confronted by the steady resistance of top level government decision makers as well as republican institutions such as the Constitutional Council. Indeed, the 1982 decision of the Constitutional Council rejecting the gender quota for local elections constituted a precedent that determined the fate of the parity claim: it forced parity activists to demand a revision of the Fifth Republic Constitution (a delicate exercise demanding that three-fifths of the deputies and senators agree on the reform). The 1982 decision also constrained parity activists to challenge core principles of the Republic as the article to be revised had to be the article in the name of which the Council first rejected the idea of gender quotas for political representation, which is article 3 on national sovereignty. However, this challenge to one of the core articles of the Constitution articulating that sovereignty is indivisible and cannot be broken up into various social groups or categories, ended up reinforcing republican doctrine.

Indeed, to create the necessary political consensus parity advocates have worked to show the compatibility of their claim with republican ideals, arguing that granting gender quotas did not imply the recognition of separate categories (women/men) within the nation, but rather the recognition of a universal difference, sexual difference, which mirrored republican universalism (Bereni and Lépinard 2004; Scott 2005; Lépinard 2007a). This republican twist secured parity's final victory over the Constitutional Council but also legitimized republican doctrine and the political marginalization of other social groups marked by a 'difference' that could not be framed in terms of gender difference. In other words, the breach in the doctrine of abstract citizenship that allowed the recognition of gender difference and legitimized positive measures for women cannot include beneficiaries from other marginalized groups based on ethnicity, culture or religion (Lépinard 2007b). Does this caveat mean that the republican doctrine has been left undisturbed by the parity reform? Or was parity the first act in a broader scenario, that of the emergence of diversity politics? We turn to the issue of links between gender equality and ethnic politics through diversity in the next section.

14.3.2   Diversity and discriminations: New concepts and new challenges

Since 1997 policy approaches to immigration and inequalities have drastically changed in France, mostly under the impetus of the European Union,[8] paving the way for the emergence of diversity and anti-discrimination policies which focus on minority groups, especially ethnic ones although they are not defined as such (see Chebel d'Appolonia's chapter in this volume, and Guiraudon 2005). This new approach has not only changed the framing of the issue at stake, now focusing on the government's responsibility to ensure fair treatment of members from minority groups as well as their promotion through some form of positive measures and diversity plans. It has also led to the creation of new institutions in charge of anti-discrimination policies such as the recent HALDE (*Haute autorité de lutte contre les discriminations et pour l'égalité*), a new all-encompassing anti-discrimination legislation in 2001, as well as a larger mobilization of minorities based on their identities, as is the case with the *Conseil Représentatif des Associations Noires* (CRAN) in which identity is defined along color lines.

This shift away from the traditional assimilationist model (Brubaker 1992) certainly challenges the republican doctrine, although, as with the parity reform, the process is not a linear one (Guiraudon 2005). However, as far as gender is concerned, this shift raises new challenges for femocrats and feminists. Indeed, if the rise of diversity as a legitimate policy objective might help to soften republican universalism, it might also be fraught with the threat of diluting gender equality concerns within too broad a framework. As the parity reform showed, at the time feminists favored the single goal of women's political representation over a broader critique which would have included other minority groups.[9] Today the new challenge, at both the European and the national level, lies in the possibility to include women in diversity policies without losing what has been toughly won (Squires 2005 and Woodward 2008).

In France the feminist bureaucracy has not been directly threatened by the new focus on diversity; however, its political supervision, the former state secretary for women's rights and parity has disappeared since 2007. From interviews conducted in Spring 2008 it appears that femocrats in the Women's Rights Service and bureaucrats in the HALDE are working together to a certain degree. At the same time a recent article in *Libération* asserting that with women being able to take discrimination cases to the Halde, the still existing women's right administration has lost its raison d'être (*Libération* 2-7-08), foreshadows the potential for its disappearance, particularly in the context of the apparent relentless government down-sizing of the Sarkozy administration. In this new institutional and political landscape the future of gender equality will depend on the durability of the new institutions that have emerged at the turn of the century, such as the Parity Observatory, the parliamentary delegations for women's rights, on the active presence of a strong women's movement, on European initiatives and on the ability of these various actors to enshrine in efficient, rather than symbolic, legal provisions and public policies new gains for women, gains which are compatible with rather than in competition with gains for other minorities.

14.4 Conclusion

Looking back on 50 years of gender politics under the Fifth Republic, one can state that the Republic has not been an obvious ally for women. Its gender bias has actively contributed to their exclusion from the economic sphere, especially in the 1960s, as well as from the political sphere up until the 1990s. In many circumstances republican doctrine has nevertheless provided feminists with a vocabulary to articulate their claim, a language of universalism and equality for all. However, the crucial language of women's autonomy has been imposed the hard way by the second-wave women's movement, against an official doctrine – endorsed by both right- and left-wing parties – promoting traditional gender roles. The incremental institutionalization of women's policy agencies, despite its fluctuating political visibility, has secured the gains made by feminist and femocrats over the years – breaking the imperative of symbolic reform without achieving a complete gendering of the Republic. While feminist policies have become more concrete, many pitfalls still block the authoritative implementation of an array of feminist policies, not least of which is the current unprecedented threat by the Sarkozy/Fillon government. It is still unclear the degrees to which the new diversity policies will incorporate the gender dimension as well as build from the strengths of the women's rights administration.

Moreover, the story of this continuing struggle cannot be understood within the limits of the Fifth Republic. Indeed, at each step, since the creation of the *Comité du travail féminin* to equal pay legislation, the parity reform and anti-discrimination politics, European institutions and legislation have played a crucial role. French femocrats and feminists have consistently relied on their European counterparts to influence their reluctant national government (Mazey 2002) and have used the European window of opportunity to chip away national gender-biased universalism. In the context of this incremental process of change two stereotypes have been debunked once and for all – that the French women's movement is only radical, anti-system and Paris-based and that there is a clear partisan division for support for women's rights. In the final analysis a central tenet of social science analysis applies, the dynamics and drivers of gender politics under Fifth Republic France are complex and multiform – no single monolithic cause or process can be identified. Instead, this assessment of a wide range of research on gender politics in France has shown the resilience of the gender-biased universal model as a major Fifth Republic institution and incremental change through women's policy agency and women's movement collaboration that has brought clear, yet limited, advancements in feminist policy and women's status; advancements which may very well be in the process of being reversed under the current Sarkozy administration and in the context of an EU policy that is no longer focused on gender equality as a top priority.

Notes

1. *Egalité professionnelle*, mainly, if not exclusively, refers to gender equality in employment. Since the beginning of the 2000s, equal employment for ethnic minorities is referred to as 'diversity policies' or 'equal opportunity policies'.
2. For more details on the network, the study, and to download the RNGS dataset and codebook go to http://libarts.wsu.edu/polisci/rngs.
3. For more detailed analysis of the results collected by the French team and financed by a French Ministry of Social Affairs grant see Mazur (2001) on job training; Robinson (2001) on abortion, Mazur (2004) on prostitution; Baudino (2005) on political representation and Mazur (2007) on the hot issue.
4. Thirteen countries were covered in the RNGS study. In nine countries at least four of the five areas were analysed: in Austria, Canada, Finland, Great Britain and the Netherlands four out of five areas were covered; in France, Italy, Spain and the US all five areas were covered. Across these nine countries the most meaningful comparisons can be made, since some issue areas tend to display more degrees

of success than others – political representation has the highest rate of alliances success and job training the lowest.

5. This section summarizes a more detailed study of these five policy areas in Mazur (2005) and Mazur (2007). The research for this study was conducted from 2003–05 and included extensive archival research and 12 open-ended interviews with policy actors. Relevant English and French language literature was also extensively consulted, some of which is cited in this chapter.

6. The literature on the parity reform includes, among many others, Bereni (2007), Bereni and Lépinard (2004), Gaspard (2001), Lépinard (2006 and 2007a and b), Mossuz-Lavau (1998), Opello (2006), and Scott (2005).

7. On French right-wing parties' attitude towards parity, see Opello (2006).

8. The 2000 EU Council 'race directives', 43/2000 and 78/2000, have introduced new legal provisions and institutional requirements for France in the domain of anti-discrimination policies (Geddes and Guiraudon 2004).

9. On the practical consequences of such a tension between parity and minority groups' political representation see, for example, Bird (2001).

Bibliography

Achin, Catherine et al. (2007) *Sexes, genre et politique* (Paris: Economica).

Baudino, Claudie (2005) 'Gendering the Republican System: Debates on Women's Political Representation in France' in J. Lovenduski (ed.) *State Feminism and Political Representation* (Cambridge: Cambridge University Press) 85–105.

Bereni, Laure (2006) 'Lutter dans ou en dehors du parti? L'évolution des stratégies des féministes du Parti socialiste (1971–1997)', *Politix*, 19 (73), 187–209.

Bereni, Laure (2007) 'French Feminists Renegotiate Republican Universalism: The Gender Parity Campaign', *French Politics*, 5(3), 191–209.

Bereni, Laure and Eléonore Lépinard (2004) ' "Les femmes ne sont pas une catégorie": Les stratégies de légitimation de la parité en France', *Revue française de science politique*, 54 (1), 71–98.

Bird, Karen (2001) ' "Liberté, égalité, fraternité, parité...and diversité?" The difficult question of ethnic difference in the French parity debate', *Contemporary French Civilization*, 25 (2), 271–92.

Brubaker, Rogers (1992) *Citizenship and Nationhood in France and Germany* (Cambridge MA: Harvard University Press).

Commaille, Jacques (1993) *Les stratégies des femmes. Travail, famille et politique* (Paris: La Découverte).

Duchen, Claire (1986) *Feminism in France, from May '68 to Mitterrand* (London, Boston and Henley: Routledge and Kegan Paul).

Eurostat (2002) *The Life of Women and Men in Europe: A statistical portrait of women and men in all stages of life*. October.

Fraisse, Geneviève (1989) *Muse de la Raison: La démocratie exclusive et la différence des sexes* (Paris: Editions Alinéa).

Fraisse, Geneviève (1996) *La différence des sexes* (Paris: Presses Universitaire de France).

Gaspard, Françoise (2001) 'The French Parity Movement', in J. Klausen and C.S. Maier (eds) *Has Liberalism Failed Women? Assuring Equal Representation in Europe and the United States* (New York: Palgrave).

Geddes, Andrew and Virginie Guiraudon (2004) 'Britain, France, and EU Anti-Discrimination Policy: the Emergence of an EU Policy Paradigm', *West European Politics*, 27 (2), 334–53.

Giraud, Isabelle and Jane Jenson (2001) 'Constitutionalizing Equal Access: High Hopes, Dashed Hopes?' in J. Klausen and C.S. Maier (eds) *Has Liberalism Failed Women? Assuring Equal Representation in Europe and the United States* (New York: Palgrave), 69–88.

Guiraudon, Virginie (2005) 'Immigration Politics and Policies', in A. Cole, P. Le Galès and J. Levy (eds) *Developments in French Politics 3* (New York: Palgrave Macmillan), 154–69.

Haussman, Melissa and Birgit Sauer (eds) (2007) *Gendering the State in the Age of Globalization. Women's Movements and State Feminism in Postindustrial Democracies* (Lanham, MD: Rowman and Littlefield).

Jenson, Jane (1985) 'Struggling for Identity: The Women's Movement and the State in Western Europe', *West European Politics*, 8 (4), 5–18.

Jenson, Jane (1986) 'Gender and Reproduction: Or, Babies and the State', *Studies in Political Economy*, 20, 9–46.

Jenson, Jane (1990) 'Representations of Difference: The Varieties of French Feminism', *New Left Review*, 180, 127–61.

Jenson, Jane and Mariette Sineau (1994) 'The Same or Different? An Unending Dilemma for French Women', in B.J. Nelson and N. Chowdhury (eds) *Women and Politics Worldwide* (New Haven: Yale University Press), 243–60.

Jenson, Jane and Mariette Sineau (1995) *Mitterrand et les françaises: un rendez-vous manqué* (Paris: Presses de la FNSP).

Jenson, Jane and Mariette Sineau (eds) (2003) *Who Cares? Women's Work, Childcare and Welfare State Redesigned* (Toronto: University of Toronto Press).

Keeler, John (1993) 'Opening the Window for Reform: Mandates, Crises, and Extraordinary Policy-making', *Comparative Political Studies*, 24, 433–86.

Kingdon, John (1995) *Agendas, Alternatives and Public Policies* (New York: Harper Collins).

Landes, Joan B. (1988) *Women and the Public Sphere in the Age of the French Revolution* (Ithaca and London: Cornell University Press).

Lanquetin, Marie-Thérèse, Jacqueline Laufer and Marie-Thérèse Letablier (2000) 'From Equality to Reconciliation in France', in L. Hantrais (ed.) *Gendered Policies in Europe: Reconciling Employment and Family Life* (London: Macmillan), 68–88.

Laufer, Jacqueline (2003) 'Equal Employment Policy in France: Symbolic Support and a Mixed Record', *Review of Policy Research*, 20 (3), 423–42.

Lépinard, Eléonore (2006) 'Identity without politics: how cultural politics shaped the implementation of the sex-parity law in French local politics', *Social Politics, International Studies in Gender, State, and Society*, 13 (1), 29–58.

Lépinard, Eléonore (2007a) *L'égalité introuvable. La parité, les féministes et la République* (Paris: Presses de Sciences Po).

Lépinard, Eléonore (2007b) 'The Contentious Subject of Feminism: Defining "Women" in France from the Second Wave to Parity', *Signs*, 32 (2), 375–404.

Lewis, Jane (1992) 'Gender and the Development of Welfare Regimes', *Journal of European Social Policy*, 2 (3), 159–73.

Lovenduski, Joni (ed.) (2005) *State Feminism and the Political Representation* (Cambridge: Cambridge University Press).

Mazey, Sonia (2002) L'Union européenne et les droits des femmes: de l'européanisation des agendas nationaux à la nationalisation d'une agenda européen? in R. Balme, D. Wright and V. Chabanet (eds) *L'action collective en Europe* (Paris: Presses de Sciences Po), 405–32.

Mazur, Amy G. (1995a), *Gender Bias and the State: Symbolic Reform at Work in Fifth Republic France* (Pittsburgh: University of Pittsburgh Press).

Mazur, Amy G. (1995b) 'Strong State and Symbolic Reform in France: le Ministère des Droits de la Femme', in D. McBride Stetson and A.G. Mazur (eds) *Comparative State Feminism* (Thousand Oaks, CA: Sage Publications), 76–94.

Mazur, Amy G. (2001) 'Republican Universalism Resists State Feminist Approaches to Gendered Equality in France', in A.G. Mazur (ed.) *State Feminism, Women's Movements, and Job Training: Making Democracies Work in the Global Economy* (New York: Routledge), 155–82.

Mazur, Amy G. (ed.) (2001) *State Feminism, Women's Movements, and Job Training: Making Democracies Work in the Global Economy* (New York and London: Routledge).

Mazur, Amy G. (2002) *Theorizing Feminist Policy* (Oxford: Oxford University Press).

Mazur, Amy G. (2004) 'Prostitute Movements Face Elite Apathy and Gender-Biased Universalism in France', in J. Outshoorn (ed.) *The Politics of Prostitution. Women's Movements and the State* (Cambridge: Cambridge University Press), 123–43.

Mazur, Amy G. (2005) 'Gendering the Fifth Republic', in A. Cole, P. Le Galès and J. Levy (eds) *Developments in French Politics* (Basingstoke: Palgrave Macmillan), 212–29.

Mazur, Amy G. (2007a) '35 Hour Work-week Reforms in France, 1997–2000: Strong Feminist Demands, Elite Apathy, and Disappointing Outcomes', in M. Haussman and B. Sauer (eds) *Gendering the State in the Age of Globalization. Women's Movements and State Feminism in Post Industrial Democracies* (Boulder and London: Rowman & Littlefield), 121–46.

Mazur, Amy G. (2007b) 'Women's Policy Agencies, Women's Movements and a Shifting Political Context: Toward a Gendered Republic in France?', in J. Outshoorn and J. Kanotla (eds) *Changing State Feminism: Women's Policy Agencies Confront Shifting Institutional Terrain* (Basingstoke: Palgrave Macmillan), 102–23.

McAdam, Doug, John D. McCarthy, and Mayer N. Zald (1996) *Comparative Perspectives on Social Movements: Political Opportunities, Mobilizing Structures, and Cultural Framings* (Cambridge: Cambridge University Press).

McBride Stetson, Dorothy (ed.) (2001) *Abortion Politics, Women's Movements and the Democratic State: A Comparative Study of State Feminism* (Oxford: Oxford University Press).

McKeown, Timothy J. (2004) 'Case Studies and the Limits of the Quantitative World-view', in H.E. Brady and D. Collier (eds) *Rethinking Social Inquiry: Diverse Tools, Shared Standards* (Boulder: Rowman & Littlefield), 139–67.

Mossuz-Lavau, Janine (1998) *Femmes/Hommes, pour la parité* (Paris: Presses de Sciences Po).

O'Connor, Julia S., Ann Shola Orloff, and Sheila Shaver (1999) *States, Markets, Families: Gender Liberalism and Social Policy in Australia, Canada, Great Britain and the United States* (Cambridge: Cambridge University Press).

Offen, Karen (1984) 'Depopulation, Nationalism, and Feminism in Fin-de-Siècle France', *American Historical Review*, 89 (3), 648–76.

Opello, Katherine A.R. (2006) *Gender Quotas, Parity Reform and Political Parties in France* (Lanham: Lexington Books).

Outshoorn, Joyce (ed.) (2004) *The Politics of Prostitution: Women's Movements, Democratic States, and the Globalization of Sex Commerce* (Cambridge: Cambridge University Press).

Revillard, Anne (2006) 'Work/Family Policy in France: From State Familialism to State Feminism?', *International Journal of Law, Policy and the Family*, 20 (2), 133–50.

Revillard, Anne (2007) 'Stating Family Values and Women's Rights: Familialism and Feminism within the French Republic', *French Politics*, 5 (3), 210–28.

Robinson, Jean C. (2001) 'Gendering the Abortion Debate: The French Case', in D. McBride Stetson (ed.) *Abortion Politics, Women's Movements, and the Democratic State* (New York: Oxford University Press), 87–110.

Rosanvallon, Pierre (1992) *Le sacre du citoyen, histoire du suffrage universel en France* (Paris: Gallimard).

Rosanvallon, Pierre (1998) *Le peuple introuvable, histoire de la représentation démocratique en France* (Paris: Folio histoire, Gallimard).

Saguy, Abigail C. (2003) *What is Sexual Harassment? From Capitol Hill to the Sorbonne* (Berkeley CA: University of California Press).

Schnapper, Dominique (1994) *La communauté des citoyens. Sur l'idée moderne de nation* (Paris: NRF essais, Gallimard).

Scott, Joan W. (1996) *Only Paradoxes to Offer. French Feminists and the Rights of Man* (Cambridge, MA: Harvard University Press.

Scott, Joan W. (2005) *Parité! Sexual Equality and the Crisis of French Universalism* (Chicago: University of Chicago Press).

Siim, Birte (2000) *Gender and Citizenship. Politics and Agency in France, Britain and Denmark* (Cambridge: Cambridge University Press).

Sineau, Mariette (2001) *Profession: femme politique. Sexe et pouvoir sous la Cinquième République* (Paris: Presses de Sciences Po).

Squires, Judith (2005) 'Is Mainstreaming Transformative? Theorizing Mainstreaming in the Context of Diversity and Deliberation', *Social Politics*, 12 (3), 366, 388.

Woodward, Alison (2008) 'Est-il trop tard pour une approche intégrée de l'égalité?', *Cahiers du genre* No 44.

15
Race, Racism and Anti-discrimination in France

Ariane Chebel d'Appolonia

The civil unrest that started in Clichy-sous-Bois in October 2005 and spread throughout 15 other urban areas once again pushed the theme of the 'crisis in the Republican model of integration' to the top of the agenda. There was nothing new about the riots; they had been recurring since the 1980s. The theme of the crisis in the French model was not new either. It also emerged during the 1980s, notably with the 'headscarf affair', culminating controversially in the debate over the ban on the wearing of 'conspicuous religious symbols' at school in 2004. These events have served to structure the current discussion around two basic positions.

For the defenders of traditional republicanism the riots illustrated the dangers of communitarianism, defined as a form of tribalism and associated with religious and ethnic fanaticism. From this perspective, there is a need to restore the authority of the Republic in the suburbs (*banlieues*) (characterized as 'no-go' areas) and to protect the values of Jacobean republicanism against the delinquency and '*incivilities*' of young rioters (characterized as '*la racaille*' or scum). The only appropriate short-term response is to further establish the authority of the 'moral order', by implementing a 'zero tolerance' policy towards urban violence. Proponents envisage this approach, in the long term, as key to the re-invigoration of republican principles. The very notion of French citizenship has been restated: all French citizens should enjoy the same rights, and all French citizens (but notably those of foreign origin) should respect the duties that come with their civic status. In the same spirit, the 'integration contract' now requires newcomers to endorse the 'grand principles of the Republic', as well as 'the values of French society'.

An alternative reading of the 2005 riots has been developed by those who argue that the rebellion of young people in the *banlieues* (characterized as marginalized neighborhoods or deprived areas) expressed deep-rooted problems, such as racial discrimination, unemployment, and exclusion from 'Frenchness' – despite the fact that they are predominantly French citizens. Moreover, in this view, the French model is not able to address these issues, which, furthermore, are a direct result of the French republican form of abstract universalism. According to proponents of this position, the denial of the 'rights of minorities', coupled with the insistence on cultural assimilation, fuels discrimination and legitimizes a form of differential racism, which, in turn, fosters resentment among those who suffer from discrimination. A vicious circle thus ensues.

It is worth noting that these two opposite perspectives share many of the same premises. They both view France as a multi-ethnic society characterized by increasing cultural and religious diversity. They also both focus on the figure of the 'North African', or alternatively the 'French Muslim', as a major test of the viability of the integrative capacity of French society. Finally, these two perspectives both seek to address the same series of questions although they offer divergent responses to these questions: Is the republican model of integration still relevant in dealing with diversity? Should this model be seen as a source of 'emancipation' (to use the notion initially embedded in the republican project) through the promotion of individual rights? Or rather, should it be viewed as an exclusionary ideology aimed at rendering invisible (in policy terms) the visible minorities intent on remaining ignorant of discriminatory processes? Ultimately, can republican universalism be balanced with the recognition of particular minority groups in order to combat racism and discrimination effectively?

The central puzzle to be addressed in this chapter is how and why the principle of 'indifferentiation', embedded in the French model of integration, has become a vehicle for both inclusion and exclusion. This will be done by assessing the basic policy principles included in this model, and by evaluating its capacity to deal with the main concerns that currently challenge the explicit goal of republican integration.

The first section examines the special emphasis placed on the historical and political evolution of republican principles. In contrast to the traditional republican mantra which tends to dismiss the realities of (past and present) racism by providing a fictional rosy picture of previous immigration and integration, I argue that the French republican model was not initially designed to integrate immigrants. On the contrary, the objective was to achieve the integration of nationals (Bretons, Corsicans, etc.) though a more rigid distinction between French citizens and foreigners. When viewed through historical lenses, this model has proved to be unexpectedly successful.

The second section will evaluate how anti-racist and anti-discrimination public policies are formulated and implemented. Clearly, the legal arsenal available to the French state to combat racism and discrimination is quite impressive. Yet, while support for racist beliefs is declining, the number of racist acts of violence is increasing. This puzzle raises two questions: Does the denial of the category of 'race' undermine the fight against racism? Conversely, does the introduction of 'race policies' susceptible to combat prejudice more efficiently? In the same vein, a brief assessment of the new anti-discrimination framework highlights a series of difficulties faced by the

French republican model. How can the Republic respond to ethnic discrimination if there are no reliable data about ethnic minorities? Might the introduction of ethnic categorization strengthen the ethnicization of public policies and, subsequently, legitimize ethnic discrimination?

Beyond the controversy over the production of ethnic data and the introduction of some degree of *'positive discrimination'*, the reformulation of republicanism in France raises crucial issues, especially in the aftermath of the terrorist attacks that occurred in the US and Europe. The last section of this chapter addresses the current challenges republicanism is facing. Concerns about the sustainability of the French integration model have been fuelled by certain socio-economic problems (notably, high levels of unemployment), combined with the political malaise that has characterized France since the mid-1980s. With regards to the visibility of 'others', notably immigrants and nationals of North African origin, the so-called 'changing character of immigration' is admittedly related to the increasing dysfunction of the traditional tools of integration (such as education, housing policy, and the labor market). Furthermore, persistent socio-economic exclusion and a rampant Islamophobia prior to 9/11 undermined the integration of migrant and minority groups. Since then, it is the republican model itself that is threatened by the securitization of integration issues. The framing of ethnic and religious diversity into a security issue generates suspicion, resentment, and social tensions.

15.1   The French republican model: Historical perspectives and political myths

Republicanism in France consists of five key components: equality before the law; individual emancipation (commonly understood as a rejection of any form of communitarianism); a universal understanding of citizenship, based on a mix of *jus solis* and *jus sanguini*; secularism (especially since 1905); and cultural assimilation. With regard to immigrants and minority groups, these principles were included in a 'color blind', or 'ethnic blind' approach to integration that can be summarized by four principles:

- The integration of immigrants must be in keeping with the secularization of the state;
- It is individuals rather than groups that integrate, and at no time can the process of integration contribute towards the constitution of particular communities;
- Integration presupposes rights and duties (an immigrant must respect French law and, in return, the law respects the culture and traditions of immigrants);
- Immigrants and the French must be treated equally, without developing the idea that immigrants are treated better than French citizens.

However, a cursory examination of these principles leads us to question the conventional images of Jacobinism as erasing all differences in its construction of a unified and centralized French nation-state. Frequently, and mistakenly, referred to as the right (if not the duty) to 'sameness', the core objective of the French model of integration has been based on the right (if not the duty) to 'be different'. The goal of homogeneity has, in practice, spawned a heterogeneity that is problematic and dysfunctional within the French system. Two historical moments in the evolution of the French model of integration illustrate the core ambivalence of republicanism: the emancipation of the Jews, and the colonial period.

15.1.1   The myth of the ethnic and religious blindness of the French model

The Jews were among the first to be engaged with the republican conception of integration. The emancipation of the Jewish 'community' laid down the fundamental principle of the republican model (as illustrated by Clermont Tonnerre's statement in 1791[1]) – an 'ethnic blind' model with no room for 'community' or any collective identity. Thus, the Jews were the first to encounter both the limitations and ambiguities of this model.

In August 1789 the National Assembly adopted the Declaration of the Rights of Man and Citizens – which is still the cornerstone of the republican model of integration. The Declaration recognized that 'men are born equal and remain free and equal in rights. Social distinctions may be based only on common utility...No one should be disturbed for his opinions, even in religion, provided that their manifestation does not trouble public order as established by law'. The National Assembly, however, did not grant civil rights to French Jews until September 1791. The Assembly's refusal to grant rights to the Jews clearly laid out in the words of the Declaration highlights the ambivalence of the republican model since its birth: men are equal in rights but some men are more equal than others.

The debate about Jewish emancipation raised two questions: Are Jews to be considered as individuals of a different religion or as foreign nationals living in France? Do the requirements of the Jewish religion allow its adherents to fulfill the requirements of citizenship, or do religious restrictions prevent them from full participation? Obviously, these questions find resonance with the current debate about Islam in France. Emancipation was finally granted, first to Sephardic Jews in January 1790 and then to Ashkenazy Jews in September 1791. The Clermont Tonnerre option thus prevailed. Because Jews were granted civil rights as individuals, they had to give up their communal autonomy and to dissolve into the majority. Yet, assimilation was not defined; it was simply assumed that the Jews would adjust in exchange for their civil rights. More to the point, while French Jews were considered equals as individuals, the Jewish community as a collective was nevertheless the target of specific, discriminatory regulations on a collective basis. Emancipation thus inaugurated a 'differential integration' process. The process revealed the tensions between universalism and particularism that undermine the republican model. It generated a question; once a group is emancipated, do its members enter French society as individuals, as a new version of their group, or as a combination of both?

Jews, for example, – unlike Christian French citizens – remained responsible for the debts of the *communautés* to which they (or their ancestors) had belonged before the Revolution. In their petitions and legal briefs, Jewish leaders argued that if Jews were to be considered as French citizens, they should not be considered as 'Jews' before the law. The National Assembly had refused the rights of Jews to retain their communal institutions but obliged them to remain organized as a 'community' to collect money to repay the debts. In addition to this issue of communal debts, there was the issue of the religious taxes. Jews were allocated a sort of corporate identity in matters relating to taxation because, until 1830, religious expenses were funded by a special 'Jewish tax' (which Christians did not have to pay). As the Central Consistory pointed out, 'Frenchmen are Protestant, Catholic or Jewish before God. But they are Frenchmen before the law. The law cannot oblige certain Frenchmen to pay a religious tax'. A third example of this differential treatment was the 'Infamous Decree' issued by Napoleon in 1808 forbidding the Jews of Eastern France to borrow or lend money (the ban remained in effect until 1818). The Vichy regime was therefore not the only time in French history when unequal treatment was applied.

The colonial experience showed similar contradictions, with the distinction between citizens and subjects. In Algeria, for example, a new law provided Muslims with the formal title of citizens (1947), but lacked any substantial components. Three different categories were introduced by French authorities: French citizens,[2] French Jews,[3] and indigenous. It is worth noting that the current rejection of ethnicity, as illustrated by the ongoing debate about the relevance of 'ethnic data' or religious categorization, is often legitimized as a way to balance the negative legacy of the colonial regime. Current opponents to traditional republicanism have to concede that the 'ethnic blindness' paradigm was aimed at fighting the legacy of racial colonialism and identity-based racism. Essentially, in the post-World War II context, the non-recognition of racial or ethnic categories was not illiberal. It was, rather, grounded in a set of democratic principles and institutions sketched out in 1946 and consolidated by the 1958 Constitution.

15.1.2 The myth of migrant integration

The French model of integration was not designed to achieve the integration of immigrants. On the contrary, the objective was to achieve the integration of nationals though a more rigid distinction between French citizens and foreigners. This 'nationalization' of France began during the early decades of the Third Republic.

The Nationality Law of 1889 is often cited as an illustration of the universal principles of the republican ideology. The law gave those born in France automatic citizenship regardless of their parents' birth place. The motives for this new law were economic, demographic and militaristic. France needed immigrants. However, foreigners were still suspected of proving inadequate as citizens. This suspicion subsequently led to the implementation of a 'dual naturalization' process, that is, incorporation of foreigners into citizenship in two stages: New nationals had to wait five years before being awarded the right to vote, and 10 years for the right to eligibility. This two-stage naturalization was finally revoked in 1973 (for the right to vote) and in 1983 (for the right to eligibility).

Furthermore, the nationalization of French citizens was made possible through the institutionalization of discriminatory practices. The objective of the Third Republic was to turn 'peasants into Frenchman', not to turn foreigners into French nationals. Thus, the story (brilliantly told by Eugen Weber) was more complex, and less Jacobin, than sometimes imagined. Approximately 50 propositions relating to immigrants and foreigners were introduced between 1883 and 1914. Many of them produced legally, administratively and ideologically the new concept of 'immigrant', such as the tax on foreigners (to protect the jobs of French workers); a new employment status that obliged immigrants to declare their residence (for security purposes); and the creation of an identity card for immigrants. In addition, immigrants were excluded from access to social benefits, right of association and protection against accidents at work. It was not until 1981 that a new law on the freedom of association for foreign nationals suppressed the limitations imposed by the Third Republic.

Cultural assimilation was also limited, despite the alleged unifying role of the public schools in the Third Republic. It is true that the goal of the national curriculum was to transform little Bretons, Corsicans and Provençals into citizens of the Republic. The requirements of cultural uniformity were less obvious for immigrants because they were seen as temporary workers. As the Rapport de la Commission de la Nationalité stated in 1988, assimilation referred to the public sphere but 'in private, "naturalized citizens" preserved their religious and cultural loyalties'. In fact, assimilation was not systematically pursued. Only a tiny proportion of native Algerians attended French schools during the colonial period. Assimilation was never intended for whole populations and, in any case, it was a highly complex process even for those who did 'assimilate'.

In the aftermath of World War II, numerous initiatives intended to maintain the distinctive cultural traditions of minority groups were undertaken. State agencies in charge of housing, education and access to social benefits based their activities on ethnic quotas. For example, HLM (public housing) authorities were asked to relocate immigrants on the basis of their national origin in particular urban areas. As a result, the percentage of immigrants in these areas increased from 15 percent in 1975 to 24 percent in 1982, and 28 percent in 1990. Concentrations of ethnic groups consequently arose and ethnic differentiation turned into ethnic segregation and discrimination. Public authorities also facilitated the installation of Muslim places of worship in hostels, HLM blocks and state-controlled companies such as Renault. French officials promoted the Islamization of Muslim immigrants – in order to keep repatriation open – but refused to exercise control over it. As a result, the Islamization of Maghrebi immigration turned into the ethnicization of Islam. In the field of education, the 'classes d'initiation' for the teaching of 'Homeland Languages and Cultures' were initiated in 1973. The main objective was not to integrate immigrants but to import foreign labor.

Yet, when the government ordered that labor immigration be halted in 1973–74, the vast majority of the 'guest workers' remained in France. Family reunification started, raising the issue of the so-called 'second generation immigrants'. Although they have not migrated from anywhere, the children of immigrants are still perceived as immigrants. This has led to their exclusion by denying their 'Frenchness' regardless of their civic status. Subsequently, the government made it easier for ethno-cultural groups to mobilize around a succession of issues. Minority associations were supported by the FAS (Fonds d'action sociale), the National Council of Immigrant Populations and other state agencies. Policies based on implicit ethnic categorization contributed, therefore, to the development of an 'ethnic market' where groups compete for resources and public recognition.

The diversity that characterizes France today is not a sign of the failure of the integration 'model' but the result of its implementation. French 'liberal' republicanism contains elements of legal and social discrimination which supersede all forms of equality, ethnic blindness and cultural unity. 'Equality before the law', coupled with civic individualism and ethnic blindness, never prevented France from engaging in a communitarian form of organization. Paradoxically, it is not the presence of communitarianism that is surprising; it is why it is not stronger that is surprising.

15.1.3   The unexpected success of the French model of integration

When viewed through historical lenses, the French model has proved to be unexpectedly successful. There is no denying that previous immigrants suffered from xenophobia and discrimination. No period of the history of immigration to France was characterized by a 'happy welcome'. Each historic wave – from the late nineteenth century to the post-World War II period – raised objections to successive 'new comers'. However, there is strong evidence that the French Republic actually turned immigrants into Frenchmen. Notwithstanding the absence of any integration policy designed for immigrants, school, then the army and – more importantly – the labor market played a key role.

The integration of immigrants did make progress as shown by greater access to employment providing a limited but effective means of integration, especially for second generation native-born children of immigrants who achieved slight upward mobility. In the construction industry they represented 29 percent of employees in 1973 and 21 percent in 1985. Their proportion in the unskilled workforce also decreased significantly over time (49 percent in 1975, 33 percent in 1988) and their proportion in the skilled workforce correspondingly increased (44 percent in 1975, 51 percent in 1988). Another element of social mobility was the increasing participation of immigrants in business start-ups with a growing number of 'artisans' (2 percent in 1975, 4 percent in 1982, and 6 percent in 1990), trades people (3 percent in 1982, 5 percent in 1990), and entrepreneurs (5.4 percent of the foreign population in 1987). All the evidence of upward social mobility tends to prove that immigrants are being incorporated into nearly all levels of French economy.

A second indicator is the high rate of intermarriage: the number of mixed unions has regularly increased in France, reaching 30 percent for men and 40 percent for women in 1990. Exogamy increases with the duration of settlement and concerns a growing number of Maghrebis: 20 percent of men who settled in France after the age of 15 (22 percent for those who came to France before the age of 15) married non-Algerian Frenchwomen; for women, the rates are respectively 9 percent and 12 percent. Considering the number of children of mixed unions (despite the statistical dubiousness due to the evolution of the French code of nationality), the percentage of children with Algerian fathers increased from 12.5 (in 1975) to 19.4 (in 1990). The percentage of children with Algerian mothers also increased from 6.2 to 27.5 during the same period. Another indicator of symbolic integration is the names given to children of mixed Franco-Maghrebi parentage. Streiff-Fenart estimated that 58 percent had identifiably French names and that 18 percent could be classified as Arabs. About a quarter of the names were 'neutral'.

Furthermore, the presence of immigrants in France is also better tolerated than is usually depicted by the media and some political leaders. From 1988 to 2006 the percentage of people who believe that 'immigrants are too numerous in France' decreased while the percentage of people who oppose this statement increased – as illustrated by Table 15.1.

The relatively high percentage of negative perceptions of immigrants in 1995 was due mainly to the impact of the presidential election campaign (with the re-activation of the headscarf issue at school), and terrorist threats made by the Algerian GIA. The percentage also rose in 2005, following the riots, but then declined rapidly. The notion of a 'national preference' (whereby one gives priority to French citizens over immigrants) with regard to access to social benefits was supported by 43 percent of French people in 1991. By 2006 the percentage had decreased to 21 percent.

Table 15.1   Presence of immigrants – tolerance

There are too many immigrants in France (%)						
1988	1995	2002	2003	2005	2006	1988–2006
35	41	25	27	32	25	−10
There are not too many immigrants in France (%)						
1988	1995	2002	2003	2005	2006	1988–2006
29	25	38	38	31	36	+7

Sources: CEVIPOF surveys; TNS-Sofres/Le Monde/RTL opinion polls.

Traditional racism, based on the pseudo-biological differences between races, is declining in France. In 2004 only 15 percent of the French population actually subscribed to the idea that 'there is a hierarchy between races'. Only 24 percent of the French believed that 'some races are less capable than others'. To the question 'Who can be defined as "others"', only 1 percent referred to the notion of race. And to the question 'What does it mean to be racist', only 3 percent cited the rejection of race. Consistent with these trends, tolerance is also gaining ground in France. According to a CNCDH report published in 2004:

- 74 percent of the French population believe that immigration was 'a source of enrichment';
- Discrimination against minority groups was condemned by a large majority: 61 percent agreed, for example, with the statement that 'to deny North African immigrants access to labor market is a very grave offense'; and 67 percent supported the idea that the fight against racism and discrimination should be more effective;
- Religious tolerance is quite widespread: 77 percent believed that Muslim practices should be respected and 44 percent favored the idea that more Imams should be trained in France;
- Only 33 percent believed that Muslims will never integrate into French society.

Indeed, Muslims are more integrated in France than many people tend to believe. There are about 4 million 'potential' Muslims in France (less than 6 percent of the total population). Among them, 66 percent identify themselves as Muslims, 36 percent say they are 'observant believers' and only 20 percent claim to regularly go to Mosque on Fridays. However, they remain a weak political force. Half of them are not French citizens or are under 18 years of age. They subsequently cannot vote. Those who are eligible have a very low propensity to vote.

The RAPFI survey, conducted by the CEVIPOF in 2005, focused on people of North African and Turkish origin. It was the first such study of its type and generated interesting findings. The survey organizers also conducted a shadow study of the general population (a 'mirror sample') and the contrasts were quite stunning:

- 41 percent of the respondents believed that 'immigrants can easily integrate into French society' (compared with 33 percent of the French electorate);
- 49 percent believed that 'in France, everybody can succeed whatever the color of his/her skin' (compared with 43 percent of the French electorate);
- 88 percent believed that secularization was positive, because it was the 'only way for people with different beliefs to live together' (94 percent);
- 84 percent wished to enroll their children in a public secular school, while only 33 percent claimed that 'wearing an Islamic scarf in class should be tolerated'.

Despite the 'hijab issue', which led to the adoption of the 2004 law on *laïcité* (secularism), studies suggest that France seems to be the country where Muslims integrate the best compared with other western countries. Most French Muslims and Muslims living in France indicate that they indeed have a sense of belonging to French society and that they have confidence in its democratic institutions. Next to their religious and ethnic identities, Muslims are at least as likely to claim a strong national identity as members of the general population. A Gallup poll in 2006–07 found that Muslims in Paris tend to identify strongly with France (46 percent) with the same frequency as members of the general public (46 percent).

To summarize, tensions between Islam and the French way of life are often exaggerated – and seeming to be declining. Some commentators have claimed that the 2005 riots were organized by radical Muslim movements, as a prelude to a sort of 'Jihad' in France. Certainly many perpetrators of the violence – as well as many of their victims who lost their cars – were of Muslim extraction. But many of the young rioters were not Muslim, and the unrest was not about religion. The head of the *Renseignements Généraux* (secret police service) denied any explicit Islamic component to the riots as early as 5 November. The absence of any religious dimension was made apparent by the powerlessness of Muslim organizations to re-establish order. The Union of Islamic Organizations in France (UIOF) issued a fatwa, expressing the view that it was 'strictly forbidden for any Muslim to take part in any action that strikes blindly at private or public property or that could threaten the lives of others'. The fatwa had no visible effect for one simple reason: while pockets of radical Islam may exist in some of the areas where the riots took place, its supporters – and therefore those most likely to obey the fatwa – were not the ones who burnt cars.

Table 15.2   Anti-racist legislation in France

Anti Propaganda:	
– Legislation against racist and anti-Semitic propaganda (hate speech) – Legislation against the apology or denial of the Holocaust (negationism) – Restrictions on the freedom of the press	– Law of 1 July, 1972 (**Pleven Law**) completed in June 1977 (limitations to the freedom of the press by modification of the law of July 29, 1881) – Law of 13 July, 1990 (**Gayssot Law**) penalizing hate speech – Law of 9 March, 2004 (extension of the period of prescription to one year) – Law of 21 June, 2004 on racist propaganda via Internet
Anti Extremist Behavior and Discrimination:	
– Legislation against militarization of political parties (militias) – Legislation against the bearing of arms – Legislation restricting freedom of assembly (preservation of public order) – Legislation regulating the modalities of street demonstrations (public order)	– Decrees of 23 October, 1935 (new article 7 Law 1901, prevention of subversive activities by restrictions on street demonstrations, no bearing of arms) – Penal Code (ex: articles 187-1, 187-2 and 416-1 in 1972 on racist and discriminatory behavior) + new Penal Code in 1994 (articles 225 and 432) – Civil Code (article 1131) – Law of 16 November, 2001 and Law of 9 March, 2004 (augmentation of penalties for racist discrimination) – Law of 3 February, 2003 (the notion of 'aggravating circumstances' that enhances penalties)

15.2   Policy consequences and paradoxes

The major paradox of republican integration is the coexistence within French society of a greater tolerance towards immigrants coupled with an increasing level of xenophobia. French authorities have attempted to address this issue by enacting impressive anti-racist and anti-discrimination legislation. Table 15.2 summarizes the main anti-racist initiatives which have been adopted since the 1970s.

In spite of the fundamental nature of the values defended, the provisions that make discrimination illegal in France are relatively new. The Minister of Employment and Solidarity launched a program in 1998 designed to facilitate the acquisition of citizenship, to fight against discrimination and to create a tolerant atmosphere towards newcomers. A Group for the Study of and Fight against Discrimination (GELD) was created in 1999 and a hot line (114) for victims of discrimination was established. The French government has recently introduced a series of anti-discrimination measures – as required by the new EU legislation. In 2000 two directives were adopted at the EU level: The Racial Equality Directive, and the Employment Equality Directive (Directive 2000/78/CE, and Directive 2000/43/CE). One of the French initiatives for the implementation of these directives was the creation of the HALDE (High Authority for the Fight against Discrimination and for the Promotion of Equality). Its mission is to help the victims of discrimination (for example, to lodge a complaint). The anti-discrimination framework also includes the Law of November 2001 on the fight against discrimination and the Law of January 2002 on social modernization (in the fields of housing and employment).

15.2.1   The ambiguities of republican anti-racism

Despite all the legal improvements, the legislation has had only limited effect. Between 1992 and 2000 the implementation of the Gayssot Law concerned only 29 cases. The total number of condemnations has remained quite low (only 74 percent of the cases in 2005, for instance, despite the introduction of new regulations in 2004). For some experts, limitations are mainly due to 'technical' reasons such as the difficulty of identifying the perpetrators of racist offenses (in 2005, only 67 percent of the cases managed to do so), the ability to get round some aspects of the law,[4] the sensitive issue of the burden of proof, the complexity of procedures, the problem of striking a balance between the protection of free speech and the repression of hate speech. Another perspective highlights the limitations of the republican approach to anti-racism, by suggesting that French legislation only deals with the manifestations of racism, while not effectively addressing the roots of exclusion.

In point of fact, the multiplication of new regulations has proved to be ineffective in reducing the number of racist offenses and discouraging the diffusion of racist ideas. Put bluntly, no law has the power to eradicate either racism or anti-Semitism, and to suppress the social malaise that fuels discrimination. The republican denial of the category of 'race' does not solve the problem of the resilience of racial prejudice. According to certain arguments, France should adopt a 'race relations regime' by learning from the British context. They commonly refer to the Race Relations Act of 1965 and 1976 which contributed to the emergence of special group rights. Unfortunately, the implementation of this system of 'harmonizing' race relations did not prevent race riots (such as the civil unrest that took place in Northern England in the summer of 2001) nor did it secure immigrant integration. British authorities are currently accentuating their retreat from multiculturalism based on an ethno-racial conception of identity, in order to promote a new Britishness regardless of race and religion.

Most importantly, anti-racist legislation cannot fight the 'racism of social exclusion' (Wieviorka). Social exclusion works both ways. It feeds discrimination by increasing the visibility of immigrants because of their socio-economic exclusion, *and* it fuels xenophobia because natives perceive immigrants as competitors (in terms of access to the labor market, housing and social benefits). This explains the complex relationship between the excluded, the victims and the perpetrators. Tensions also arise between different minority groups. In 2005 24 percent of anti-Semitic threats and 41 percent of violent anti-Semitic acts were committed by Muslims (broadly defined as 'milieux arabo-musulmans'). Meanwhile, Muslims/North Africans remain the most targeted population.

Immigrants and other 'visible minorities' are discriminated against, although there is no clear connection between xenophobia and immigration. A number of studies and collected survey data provide evidence that xenophobia has little to do with actual levels of immigration, nor is it based on traditional racist ideologies. Rather xenophobia is based on prejudice which is fuelled by dissatisfaction with national governments, low confidence in national political leaders and institutions, and distrust in EU policies. This suggests that anti-racist measures could be effective only if they address the root causes of discrimination (that is, socio-economic exclusion), and also the motivations for xenophobic feelings (social and political distrust). To date, this has not been the case.

15.2.2   Anti-discrimination v. ethnicity

In contrast to anti-racist legislation, the recent anti-discrimination framework is designed to address the root causes of exclusion. A brief assessment of this framework, however, highlights a series of difficulties faced by the French republican model. How can the Republic respond to ethnic discrimination if there are no reliable data about ethnic minorities? Might the introduction of ethnic categorization strengthen the ethnicization of public policies and, subsequently, legitimize ethnic discrimination?

Despite recent legislative improvements the implementation of the anti-discrimination framework raises major concerns. For instance, the difficulty in providing proof of discrimination remains strong. The burden of proof is so stringent that most cases are dismissed. Another problem is related to the complexity of legislation on discrimination, which may be a deterrent to victims of discrimination. According to EU directives Member States must ensure that individuals are protected from any adverse treatment as to the result of a complaint made. In France individuals are protected only from disciplinary action or dismissal by the employer (rather than 'any adverse treatment' as mentioned by the directives). Other limitations can be listed briefly:

- The low level of participation of national minorities in decision-making processes at governmental, national and local levels;
- The limited role of independent specialized bodies (such as NGOs, social partners, associations) at national, regional and local levels;

 – The problem of promoting measures to ensure that all members of targeted groups are aware of the remedies available and how to use them;
 – The total or partial absence of structures for informing the broader public about anti-discrimination legislation.

Limitations to the French system have been underlined by a series of reports, such as the Stasi report on the fight against discrimination, the 2004 report on migrant integration published by the *Cour des Comptes*, and the 2006 Gil Robles report on human rights published by the Council of Europe. They re-ignited the debate over the need to generate reliable data to assist in addressing the current integration or segregation experienced by some minorities. For some the introduction of ethnic data would legitimate discriminatory measures by providing the notions of race or ethnicity with scientific authority. Others suggest that if the fight against discrimination is based on ethnic affiliation it must be possible to identify this affiliation in order to act. Despite certain recent initiatives, such as the RAPFI survey, work on racism still encounters intellectual hostility in France with regard to identifying ethnic categories. But, while choosing not to use ethnic and racial categories in statistics, the French scientific community prevents the accumulation of discrimination data and contributes to euphemizing the social impacts of racism.

   More to the point, particular measures designed to assist 'visible minorities' are an essential step, but they are not enough. Xenophobia is the product of a deep 'democratic disenchantment' fuelled by social distrust and economic pessimism that affect broad segments of French society. Public policies must address broader issues, such as unemployment, the crisis of the middle classes, housing, and the dysfunctions of the educational system. The unrest of 2005 ultimately revealed the deep-rooted malaise of French society. The 'immigrant dimension' of this urban crisis is only the tip of the iceberg.

15.3   Current challenges

Although ethnic identification and social categorization are distinct processes, each is routinely imbricated in the other. Ethnicity can be strengthened or generated as a response to social categorization based on social status, level of education, spatial distribution and level of skills. And the self-image of a stigmatized minority can interact with discrimination and exclusion in a vicious circle of cumulative disadvantages or 'micro-inequities' in the labor market, at school, and in urban neighborhoods.

15.3.1   The disintegration process

The problem of the high rate of unemployment illustrates this process. It is obvious that ethnic differentiation plays a role in the dysfunction of the job market. The failure to find a job makes insertion – and thus integration – more difficult, if not impossible. In 2005 unemployment in the *cités* (social housing) reached 20 percent. In some areas (like Clichy-sous-Bois) it reached 40 percent and affected all the different populations living in these 'difficult suburbs'. Similarly, poverty rates are higher in these areas than the national average (26.5 percent in the *cités*, compared to 6 percent nationally). Young people suffer more than their elders: currently, 50 percent of young non-EU immigrants are unemployed. Immigrants are therefore stigmatized as a large number of them are socially excluded and this exclusion is correlated with their ethnic identification.

French authorities have tried to address urban and social problems in recent years. Between 1977 and 2005 about 15 programs designed to regenerate the most sensitive suburbs have been implemented.[5] For example, in order to limit the 'ghettoization' of French society, a Solidarity and Urban Renewal Act (loi de solidarité et renouvellement urbain) was adopted in 2000 following the unrest that took place in Vaulx-en-Velin (a suburb of Lyon) and in the Minguettes (near Marseille). It required that at least 20 percent of the housing capacity of *communes* (urban districts) be reserved for social housing. But this measure was not effectively implemented. In 2002 subsidies to local associations and social workers in the most sensitive neighborhoods were cut, weakening the social fabric. Furthermore, neighborhood policing (*police de proximité*) was also limited – so the only contact with the police force took place during identification checks. The 2005 riots were the result of long-standing problems that were never properly addressed, such as run-down housing, poor transport links, bad schools, and rampant crime. The French government recently publicized a three-year proposal to deploy 4000 more police and roll out half a billion euros of aid to flashpoint neighborhoods. Stating that 'the very idea of the nation is at stake', in February 2008, President Sarkozy declared a 'war without mercy' on drug dealers and proposed transporting students to schools in different neighborhoods to help social groups to mingle. This type of attitude tends to generate the characterization of immigrants as scapegoats and accentuates their social and geographical exclusion.

Education policy has also failed. The French system is inherently exclusive – with, for instance, the distinction between different categories at university level (Grandes ecoles, universities, etc.). The system is currently undergoing a crisis: 2000 young people left secondary education with no diploma last year. The educational system is not only unable to train young people to get a job, it is also undermined by social violence. Schools are commonly depicted today as 'the lost territories of the Republic'. In recent years the French government established ZEPs (areas of priority education) in the most sensitive areas. The ZEPs today include 15 percent of middle school pupils (*collège*) and 18 percent of high school pupils (*lycée*), not all of whom are immigrants. However, the teachers in these schools are characteristically the least experienced, those with experience having the choice to work elsewhere.

15.3.2   The securitization of integration issues

Beyond the controversy over the production of ethnic data and the introduction of some degree of *positive discrimination*, the reformulation of republicanism in France raises crucial issues, especially in the aftermath of the terrorist attacks that occurred in the US and Europe in recent years. Since 9/11 it is the republican model itself that is threatened by the proliferation of a discourse on security and a related practice of policing. The anti-terrorist legislation (including the *Loi de sécurité quotidienne*, the statutes of March 2003 and March 2004, and the law of January 2006) may favor a regime of exceptions in which 'Others' (notably the Muslim 'enemy inside') will suffer from tougher discrimination. The amalgamation of 'immigrants' (including French citizens of foreign origin) and terrorists is gaining currency and negatively impacts on the perception of Muslims in France. There is strong evidence to suggest that the category of 'Others' is expanding. It includes today all those who threaten – or are perceived to threaten – national unity and societal security. It conflates foreigners, immigrants, and nationals – irrespective of their actual status, as long as they constitute a threat (real or subjective).

Yet migrants and minorities are then asked to become integrated into a 'society' defined by 'values and principles', 'rights and duties', although the content of these 'values, principles, rights and duties' are put into question by the proliferation of exclusionary trends. This is illustrated by the recent *contrat d'insertion* (adopted in 2003 and strengthened by the law of July 2006). Immigrants have to sign this 'integration contract' and to agree to undergo language training and instruction on the 'values of French society' – whatever that means. Today the French government is emphasizing the need for a normative assimilation although the definition of 'national identity' is even more problematic nowadays than before.

Furthermore, the framing of ethno-cultural diversity as a security issue has led to the securitization of integration. There seem to be increasing security concerns about the loyalty of first and second generation immigrants along with the reassertion of national identities under the pressures of security threats. There is strong evidence that there is no 'clash of civilizations'. However, there is an increasing 'clash of perception'. A Gallup poll in 2006–07 found that only 35 percent of Germans, 41 percent of the French, and 45 percent of the British think that Muslims are loyal to the European countries in which they live. This is in sharp contrast to what European Muslims themselves believe; 74 percent of the Muslims in London, 73 percent in Paris, and 72 percent in Berlin think that Muslims are indeed loyal to the western countries they live in.

Most importantly, the multiplication of security measures tends to aggravate the problems it is supposed to solve: more security creates more insecurity, with increased feelings of insecurity among mass populations. Furthermore, the invocation of threats – coupled with the pretension of guaranteeing security – creates high expectations and thus raises questions about the government's capacity to manage public order and social safety. The current failure to address public anxieties then undermines the authority and legitimacy of policy-makers, increases 'democratic disenchantment' and contributes to the radicalization of the relationship between 'native' citizens and 'Others'.

15.4   Conclusion

French republican principles and institutions have proved to be unable to prevent the emergence of new forms of racism, specifically the differential racism of social exclusion. As a result French society is facing an increasing tension between the belief in formal republican principles of equality and ethnic blindness, and the persistence of socio-economic inequalities coupled with ethno-cultural discrimination and racial prejudice. It is the gap between the French model and the constant spatial and social segregation of French citizens of immigrant origin that is currently fueling communitarianism. Laying more stress on a mythical national identity or on abstract notions will not solve the problem of exclusion.

French citizens of 'ethnic' origin do not oppose the idea of integration. They even call for more integration – defined as effective equal opportunities, socio-economic mobility and political participation. Henceforth, they strongly support the French model while they are perceived as threatening core republican values. The riots of 2005, as well as the urban unrest that took place in Villiers-le-Bel in November 2007, gave credence to the portrayal of young people in the *banlieues* (suburbs) as violent delinquents. These events also tend to legitimize the use of police force and the strengthening of the 'law and order' policy. In turn young people in the *banlieues* express their frustration through violence, targeting police stations and other state institutions which they perceive as being in some way related to their exclusion. This violence meets with the state's repressive response. And the vicious circle of violence is then complete.

The current failure to address public anxieties thus contributes to the radicalization of the relationship between native citizens and those who are perceived as 'Others'. The question of socio-economic and civic integration encompasses not only the 'immigration problem' but also issues that are located at the very heart of French society. A dramatic re-evaluation of public policies designed to improve social cohesion would be necessary at this stage to restore public confidence in the French republican credo.

What is at stake is not only the relevance of the French abstract model of integration. Rather, the persistence of ethno-cultural discrimination raises concerns about the ability to address deep-rooted problems such as unemployment, job insecurity, poverty, and unacceptably run-down housing. With regard to French citizens of foreign origin, the current posture is almost nonsensical. Official authorities use ethno-cultural classifications to discriminate against French citizens of non-European origin; yet, they refuse to develop 'ethnic data' that might improve the fight against discrimination. There is a need for greater consistency: either French republicanism should adopt a new multiculturalist perspective (for both the categorization of individuals and the implementation of 'affirmative action' measures), or it should treat inequalities in the name of equality of rights – regardless of the national origin, ethnicity and religion. Thus, a truly universalistic model should avoid any reference to the so-called 'first' or 'second' generation.

Notes

1. 'Everything must be refused to the Jews as a nation and everything granted to the Jews as individuals.'
2. A 1865 decree provided all Europeans who had lived in Algeria for at least three years the opportunity of becoming French, while the 1889 Law on Nationality extended *jus solis* to any European child born in Algeria.
3. French as a result of the Crémieux decree.
4. For instance, article 24.A repressed the denial of the Shoah but not the minimization of the number of victims.
5. Among the major initiatives one can quote the 1977 program for 'Habitat and Social Life', the 1981 program for the 'social development of suburbs' (DSQ), the creation in 1990 of the Ministry for Urban Affairs and Housing (Law Besson), and the Urban Initiative of 1996.

Bibliography

Amiraux, V. and P. Simon (2006) 'There Are No Minorities Here. Cultures of Scholarship and Public Debate on Immigrants and Integration in France', *International Journal of Comparative Sociology*, 47(3–4), 191–215.

Brouard, S. and V. Tiberj (2006) *Des Français comme les autres?* (Paris: Presses de Sciences Po).

Chapman, E. and L. Levine Frader (2004) *Race in France: Interdisciplinary Perspectives on the Politics of Difference* (Berghahn Books).

Chebel d'Appollonia, A. (1998) *Les racismes ordinaires* (Paris: Presses de Sciences Po).

Freedman, J. (2004) 'Secularism as a Barrier to Integration? The French Dilemma', *International Migration*, 42(3), 5–27.

Hargreaves, A.G. (1995) *Immigration, 'Race' and Ethnicity in Contemporary France* (London, NY: Routledge).

Jennings, J. (2000) 'Citizenship, Republicanism and Multiculturalism in Contemporary France', *British Journal of Political Science*, 30, 575–98.

Kertzer, D. and D. Arel (eds) (2002) *Census and Identity: The Politics of Race, Ethnicity and Language in National Censuses* (Cambridge: Cambridge University Press).

Laachir, K. (2007) 'France's Ethnic Minorities and the Question of Exclusion', *Mediterranean Politics*, 12(1), 99–105.

Mason, D. (1991) 'The Concept of Ethnic Minority: Conceptual Dilemmas and Policy Implications', *Innovation*, 4(2), 191–209.

Mucchielli, L. (1999) 'Il n'y a pas de statistique raciste, seulement des interprétations', *Mouvements*, no. 3, March–April.

Munoz-Perez, F. and M. Tribalat (1984) 'Mariages d'étrangers et mariages mixtes en France: évolution depuis la Première Guerre mondiale', *Population*, no. 3, 427–62.

Schnapper, D. (1990) *La France de l'intégration: sociologie de la nation en 1990* (Paris: Gallimard).

Simon, P. (1999) 'Vers des statistiques ethniques?', *Plein Droit*, no. 41–42, April, 3.

Streiff-Fenart, J. (1993) 'The Making of Family Identity among Franco-Algerian Couples', in: A.G. Hargreaves, M.J. Heffernan (1993) *French and Algerian Identities from Colonial Times to Present* (Lewiston and Lampeter: Edwin Mellen), 225–37.

Taguieff, P.A. (1995) *Les Fins de l'antiracisme* (Paris: Michalon).

Ticktin, M. (2005) 'Policing and Humanitarianism in France: Immigration and the Turn to Law as State of Exception', *Interventions*, 7(3), 347–68.

Tribalat, M. (1995) *Faire France* (Paris: La Découverte).

Weil, P. (1991) *La France et ses étrangers: l'aventure d'une politique de l'immigration de 1938 à nos jours* (Paris: Gallimard).

Wieviorka, M. (2000) 'Contextualizing French Multiculturalism and Racism', *Theory, Culture, Society*, 17(1), 157–62.

Index